Spinoza
Essays In Interpretation

Spinoza
Essays In Interpretation

Edited by Eugene Freeman
and Maurice Mandelbaum

 Open Court   LaSalle, Illinois

SPINOZA: ESSAYS IN INTERPRETATION

The essays by G. H. R. Parkinson, Stuart Hampshire, Wallace I. Matson, Douglas Odegard, Robert J. McShea, Willis Doney, Warren Kessler, Lee C. Rice, Ruth Saw, and Errol E. Harris were first published in *The Monist,* Volume 55, Number 4 © 1971, The Open Court Publishing Co., La Salle, Illinois

Library of Congress Cataloging in Publication Data

Freeman, Eugene, 1906-   comp.
    Spinoza: essays in interpretation.

    (Monist library of philosophy)
    Bibliography: p.
    1. Spinoza, Benedictus de, 1632-1677—Addresses, essays, lectures.
I. Mandelbaum, Maurice H., 1908-   joint comp.
B3998.F7   1974   199'.492   72-84079
ISBN 0-87548-079-9
ISBN 0-87548-196-5 (pbk.)

Contents

Preface *by Maurice Mandelbaum*   3

Philosophy of Mind, Ethics, and Politics

G. H. R. Parkinson
Spinoza on the Power and Freedom of Man   7
Stuart Hampshire
Spinoza's Theory of Human Freedom   35
Wallace I. Matson
Spinoza's Theory of Mind   49
Douglas Odegard
The Body Identical with the Human Mind:
A Problem in Spinoza's Philosophy   61
William K. Frankena
Spinoza's "New Morality": Notes on Book IV   85
Robert J. McShea
Spinoza: Human Nature and History   101
William Sacksteder
Spinoza on Democracy   117

Epistemological and Metaphysical Issues

Willis Doney
Spinoza on Philosophical Skepticism   139
E. M. Curley
Descartes, Spinoza and the Ethics of Belief   159
Warren Kessler
A Note on Spinoza's Concept of Attribute   191

Lee C. Rice
Spinoza on Individuation   195
Frederick C. Copleston
Spinoza as Metaphysician   215
Ruth Saw
The Task of Metaphysics for Spinoza   235
Errol E. Harris
Spinoza's Theory of Human Immortality   245

Bibliography (Compiled by E. M. Curley)   263

Index (Arranged by William Sacksteder)   317

Index of Authors   317
Index of Topics   319

Spinoza
Essays In Interpretation

Maurice Mandelbaum
Preface

In introducing an earlier volume in this series, Lewis White Beck remarked, "The reputation of, and the interest in, a philosopher of the past rises and falls from decade to decade. Some will see in this only fads in intellectual history. But there is more to it than that. Philosophy uses its past."[1] One can see such fluctuations in the reputation of Spinoza; for more than a generation scholarly interest in his work has been at a relatively low ebb in the English-speaking countries, as an inspection of the bibliographies compiled by Oko[2] and by Wetlesen,[3] and the present bibliography compiled by Professor Curley, will serve to show. However, as is the case with all of the great philosophers, there has always remained at least an appreciable interest in his thought. What is perhaps more striking in his case than in others is that the focus of interest in his work has so frequently shifted. Such a shift is apparent in the papers which are here published, and it was also apparent among many other papers which, for lack of space, we could not include.

The intense interest which Spinoza's religious thought formerly aroused among both his antagonists and his devoted followers seems now to have all but disappeared. Unless or until the orientation of contemporary religious thought in the West undergoes a radical revision, one cannot expect any echoes of the feelings of those generations during which he had been anathematized, nor of those in which he had been extolled. In order to remind us of the depth of feeling which his name at one time aroused, a single passage from Schleiermacher should be sufficient:

> Offer with me reverently a tribute to the manes of the holy, rejected Spinoza. The high World-Spirit pervaded him; the Infinite

was his beginning and his end; the Universe was his only and
everlasting love. In holy innocence and in deep humility he
beheld himself mirrored in the eternal world, and perceived how
he also was its most worthy mirror. He was full of religion, full of
the Holy Spirit. Wherefore, he stands there alone and unequalled;
master in his art, yet without disciples and without citizenship,
sublime above the profane tribe.[4]

Some hundred years later the focus of interest had shifted from
Spinoza's religious thought to his *system*, considered as a
metaphysical system; for example, problems concerning the
relations of Substance and the modes tended to dominate most of
the major works on Spinoza in that era, and A. E. Taylor saw these
issues, rather than any others (such as Spinoza's naturalism), as
crucial to "Spinozism."[5] In this respect the focus of dominant interest has once again changed, although the essays of Father
Copleston and Professor Saw, as well as Professor Curley's recent
book, serve to remind us that an interest in the nature and difficulties of Spinoza's systematic metaphysics is not likely to disappear.

Judging by the papers which the editors received, the new
focus of interest may be said to lie in Spinoza's philosophy of mind.
However, it is not in terms of traditional formulations of the mind-
body problem that these discussions approach Spinoza's theory; in
fact, unlike earlier discussions, they tend to reject the relevance of
any of the traditional formulations for an understanding of
Spinoza's thought. Instead, their attention is focussed directly on
more specific problems, such as the nature of freedom, and the ontological distinctions and problems which arise in connection with
Spinoza's view of human beings as seen under the attributes of
thought and extension. It is here, perhaps, that the most original
reformulations of Spinoza's meaning are to be found, and these
reformulations offer evidence of the ways in which present
philosophic concerns can helpfully serve to highlight selected
aspects of the past.

Surprisingly enough, when one considers how large a role such
issues play in contemporary Anglo-American philosophy, there was
a comparative dearth of papers on Spinoza's ethical and social
views. We were fortunate to have the papers here included to round
out this important aspect of Spinoza's thought. There was,
however, no such dearth with respect to papers dealing with specific

aspects of Spinoza's theory of knowledge and his metaphysics. As is suggested by the essays which are here published, there was considerable diversity in the methods of interpretation which these papers displayed. In general, however, most of the papers approached their topics as epistemological or metaphysical issues which were of importance in their own right, rather than viewing them primarily in terms of their connections with Spinoza's system as a whole. This fundamentally *un*systematic mode of viewing philosophic problems can probably be said to be highly characteristic of recent Anglo-American philosophy, including our recent historical scholarship. While this is surely not the only legitimate form of such scholarship (and papers of the other type are also here included), it does constitute one legitimate way of making available the philosophic past; that it can do so without leading to a distortion of the thought of a great systematic thinker should be evident in many of these essays.

It is the hope of the editors that the present volume may contribute to eliciting further studies of the various aspects of Spinoza's thought, for there are many other topics, particularly in moral psychology, which contemporary Anglo-American philosophers should find it important to consider and discuss. Perhaps it is not too much to hope that by 1977, the tercentenary of his death, Spinoza studies will once again flourish in the English-speaking world.

The editor of *The Monist*, Professor Eugene Freeman, joins me in thanking all of the contributors to this volume, which grew out of the special issue of *The Monist* devoted to the philosophy of Spinoza (Vol. 55, No. 4, October, 1971). In addition to the papers there published, we are happy to be able to include other papers written especially for this volume by Father Copleston and Professors Curley, Frankena, and Sacksteder. In addition, we are extremely grateful to Professor Curley for preparing a bibliography which brings the previous bibliographic work of Oko and of Wetlesen up to date through December, 1972.

MAURICE MANDELBAUM

THE JOHNS HOPKINS UNIVERSITY

[1] Lewis White Beck, ed., *Kant Studies Today* (LaSalle, Ill.: Open Court Publishing Co., 1969), p. vii.

[2] Adolph S. Oko, ed., *The Spinoza Bibliography* (Boston: G. K. Hall & Co., 1964; published under the auspices of the Columbia University Libraries).

[3] Jon Wetlesen, *A Spinoza Bibliography: Particularly on the period 1940-1967* (Oslo: Universitetsforlaget, 1968).

[4] Friedrich Schleiermacher, *On Religion: Speeches to Its Cultured Despisers* (New York: Harper Torchbooks, 1958), p. 40.

[5] A. E. Taylor, "Some Incoherencies in Spinozism," *Mind*, 46 (1937), 137-158 and 281-301; also, "A Further Word on Spinoza," *Mind*, 55 (1946), 97-112.

Philosophy of Mind, Ethics, and Politics

G. H. R. Parkinson

Spinoza on the Power and Freedom of Man

I

At first sight, the philosophy of Spinoza may seem wholly alien to what is now generally regarded as philosophy in the English-speaking world. For some decades, the dominant trend in that philosophy has been linguistic and antimetaphysical; the philosopher is held to be concerned with the analysis of language, and not with speculative system-building. Spinoza, on the other hand, is very much a system-builder; as to the analysis of language, he says explicitly that this is of no interest to him. 'It is not my intention', he says, 'to explain the meanings of words; it is my intention to explain the nature of things'.[1] However, the paper which follows will attempt to show that Spinoza's philosophy is not wholly without relevance today. It will try to do this by placing one of Spinoza's most important doctrines, his theory of human freedom, within the context of recent discussions.

Before going into detail, it will be worth while to give a brief account of the general framework of the discussion. What has already been said will have warned the reader (if, indeed, he needs any warning) not to expect from Spinoza what would be found in the majority of contemporary discussions of human freedom: that is, detailed analyses of the ordinary usage of terms such as 'can', 'possible', 'cause', 'reason', and so on. What, then, do we get from Spinoza? On the surface, we seem to have a deductive exercise in the working-out of the consequences of a technical and highly personal vocabulary. But this is only on the surface. To see how Spinoza's views are relevant today, one may look briefly at one of the problems which relate to human freedom and which still exercise contemporary philosophers: namely, the problem of the

relations between human freedom and the causal explanations that
are offered by the sciences. Some of the sciences, it is argued, offer
causal explanations of human behavior. These sciences are still a
long way from explaining all human behavior, but such explanation
is in principle possible. That is, although scientists are not yet in a
position to state the cause or causes of each and every human act,
every such act *has* its cause or causes. Now, if all human behaviour
is caused, then no human being can do other than what he does, for
the effect of a given cause follows necessarily from that cause. From
this it follows that no human being is free, if freedom is defined as
the power of a human being, on some occasions at any rate, to do
something other than what he actually did.

This is the problem with which Spinoza's theory of human
freedom is concerned. One way of solving the problem would be to
say that the causal explanations that are typical of the sciences are
not applicable to human actions. This, however, is not Spinoza's
way. He maintains (to paraphrase the title of Professor Ayer's
Auguste Comte Memorial Lecture) that man is a subject for the
sciences, and his concern is to work out the logical consequences of
this. He would add that if some of these consequences conflict with
certain of our everyday ways of thinking, then so much the worse
for our everyday ways of thinking. In fact (as is well known) Spinoza
believes that in one sense of the term 'free', no man is free, but that
in another sense of the term some men are free. It will be the task of
this paper to explore the basis of his belief, and to offer some com-
ments on it.

It is clear that in the argument just stated there are two key
concepts. One is the concept of cause; the other is the concept of
power, particularly as it relates to human beings, and what they
can and cannot do. Our first task must therefore be to examine
what Spinoza means by such terms as 'causa' and 'potentia',
naturally translated as 'cause' and 'power'. The chief concern of
this paper will be Spinoza's concept of power in its relations to
human freedom, and an attempt will be made to relate Spinoza's
views to some remarks made by M. R. Ayers in his book *The
Refutation of Determinism* (London, 1968). However, if Spinoza's
views on freedom are to be discussed with anything approaching
adequacy the notion of cause cannot be wholly neglected, and this
will be discussed first.

II

What, then, does Spinoza mean by the term 'cause'? The question cannot be answered satisfactorily if the discussion is restricted exclusively to Spinoza's words; if we do that, we shall merely revolve in the squirrel-cage of his technical terminology. Instead, what he says must be put in the context of the thought, and in particular the scientific thought, of his age. It has already been suggested that Spinoza maintains that man is a subject for science, and indeed there can be no reasonable doubt that he was much influenced by the science of his times, and particularly by its physics. Now, it is well known that the method of the seventeenth-century physicist was a mathematical one. He rejected the Aristotelian approach to the physical world, according to which things were regarded as striving for a certain end, and explained by reference to their end or 'final cause'. Instead, he regarded things as having just those properties which can figure in mathematical calculations, and so he viewed the physical world as consisting of things which have such and such spatial dimensions and move at such and such speeds. These things were regarded as moving each other by means of impulse, i.e. by pushing one another. In traditional language, the causes which the seventeenth-century scientist sought when trying to explain physical events were 'efficient', not 'final' causes. Since it is customary to regard explanation in terms of impulse as fundamental to explanation in mechanical terms, it may also be said that the physics of Spinoza's time was fundamentally mechanistic.

Relatively little is known about Spinoza's physics, but it is clear that he was in general sympathy with the views that have just been described. He regards as fundamental concepts of physics what he calls 'extension', 'motion' and 'rest'; he clearly approves of the mathematical trend of the new sciences (Eth. I App., G ii.79: '*Unde pro certo . . .*'). He is sharply opposed to the idea of explanation in terms of final causes (Eth. I App.), but is ready to talk in terms of efficient causes (e.g. Eth. I 16 Cor. 1, I 25, II 5). It will be seen later that he also holds that explanation in terms of efficient causes applies, not only to the physical world, but to the mind as well. (See below, II C.)

Whether Spinoza can give an adequate account of the mind and its processes in terms of efficient causes is a matter which must be considered later; at present, it is necessary to take note of an obvious objection—namely, that Spinoza's account of the nature of efficient causation is notoriously inadequate. He regards an effect as following from its cause with logical necessity; in other words, to say that A is the efficient cause of B is to say that B follows logically from A. (See, besides the well-known phrase '*causa seu ratio*', Eth. I 11, G ii.52, the nature of the argument in Eth. I 16 and I 16 Cor. 1.) The unsoundness of such a view has been recognized since Hume, and this may seem to make it unnecessary for anyone to enquire further into Spinoza's views about the causation of human actions. But this would be too easy a method of dismissal. What Spinoza says about human freedom is not linked inseparably with his views about the logical character of the causal relation. It is sufficient for his arguments that cause and effect shall be linked by *some* kind of necessity.

It is now time to consider Spinoza's concept of power. He speaks both of the power of God (e.g. Eth. I 34) and of the power of particular things, such as this or that mind or body (Eth. III 28). This paper is concerned primarily with the power of particular things, and especially of human beings—though it should not be forgotten that, for Spinoza, particular things are 'modes' of God. It will be convenient to begin, not with a discussion of power in general, but with a consideration of a particular sort of power, which is fundamental to Spinoza's account of man. Spinoza asserts that 'Each thing, insofar as it is in itself (*quantum in se est*), endeavours (*conatur*) to persevere in its being' (Eth. III 6). In the next proposition (Eth. III 7) he speaks of this 'endeavour' (*conatus*) as a 'power' (*potentia*), referring to 'the power, or endeavour, by which (each thing) endeavours to persevere in its being'.[2] It is clear that in ordinary usage the terms 'power' and 'endeavour' are not equivalent. We say that a man may endeavour to do things which are beyond his power (e.g. to lift weights which turn out to be too heavy for him, to solve problems which turn out to be too difficult for him); conversely, we say that there are things that are in our power which, at some given time, we do not endeavour to do (e.g. a man may have the strength or power to lift heavy weights, but he is not always endeavouring to lift such weights). Spinoza would doubtless agree; but he would point out that when he seems to equate power and endeavour (i) he is speaking of a certain kind of endeavour—the endeavour to persist in being, and (ii) he is speaking of a thing insofar as it is 'in itself', by which he seems to mean 'insofar as it is unaffected by anything else'.[3] In effect, Spinoza is putting forward a theory about the way in which things interact. He is saying that the universe contains a large number of things, or 'modes', which affect each other; each thing tries to preserve its own being, but what it actually does is not the outcome of this endeavour alone—rather, it is the outcome of the interaction between its endeavour or power and the endeavours or powers of other things which affect it.

A number of questions arise here.

A. What exactly is meant by the 'endeavour (or power) to persevere in one's own being'?

B. How does Spinoza try to prove that there is such an endeavour or power?

C. How is this endeavour or power related by Spinoza to efficient causality?

A. The first of these questions is really two: first, what is meant by 'being' in this context? and second, what is meant by 'endeavour'? An answer to the first of these can most easily be provided by a consideration of Spinoza's physics, and in particular (since human beings are the chief concern of this paper) his account of the physics of the human body. Here it is necessary to refer to 'a few remarks on the nature of bodies' (Eth. II 13 Sch.) which are contained in the axioms, lemmata and postulates which follow Eth. II 13 Sch. For Spinoza, the fundamental units of physics are 'most simple bodies' (*corpora simplicissima*) which differ from one another only in respect of motion and rest, speed and slowness (Lemma 1 and Lemma 7 Sch.).[4] Now, when a number of such bodies are so constrained (*coercentur*) by others that they lie upon each other, or move in such a way that they communicate their motions to each other in a certain determinate ratio,[5] then it may be said that they constitute one body or 'individual', which is distinguished from others by this union of its component bodies (Def. after Ax. 2). Bodies of this sort, whose components are 'most simple bodies', will be called here 'composite bodies of the first order'. Such composite bodies can be the components of composite bodies of a more complex kind, which may be called of the second order; these in turn can form composite bodies of the third order, and so on until we reach a composite body whose components are all the bodies there are (Lemma 7 Sch.). It is not clear from Spinoza's account to what order the human body is to be assigned, though it is clear (Posts. 1 and 2) that it is of an order higher than two.

It can now be seen what kind of 'being' Spinoza would have in mind in saying that the human body endeavours to persevere in its being. He would mean that it endeavours to maintain that union of component parts which makes it one composite body. In short, the 'being', the '*esse*' that the human body, and indeed any composite body endeavours to preserve is a unity of order. In Lemmata 4-7 Spinoza shows how a composite body's nature can be preserved even if its components change considerably: if, for example, they are replaced by others, or if they grow or diminish, or if they change the direction of their movement. In all cases, what is preserved is the '*forma*', the structure of the composite body. However, it would be wrong to suppose that, according to Spinoza's physics, all preservation of being is preservation of form. The 'most simple bodies', too, endeavour to persevere in being, but they are the ultimate units as far as physics is concerned; they are elements of a complex which has form or structure. Since they are differentiated only by motion and rest, speed and slowness, it may be assumed that what each of the 'most simple bodies' endeavours to preserve is the motion and rest, etc., which differentiates it from others.[6]

Obviously, there is more to be said about the 'being' which things endeavour to preserve—nothing has so far been said about the human mind and its 'being'—but this must be deferred for the moment, for it is now time to consider the nature of 'endeavour', as Spinoza understands it. It is clear, to begin with, that Spinoza does not mean by 'endeavour' simply the endeavour of someone who has conscious aims, for the body as well as the mind is said to 'endeavour'. What, then, does he mean by the term? It was noted earlier in this section that Spinoza identifies the terms 'endeavour' and 'power'. In at least some cases (the reason for the caution will be clear shortly) he is also prepared to identify 'essence' and 'power' or 'endeavour'. Thus, in Eth. I 34 the power of God is said to be his essence, and in Eth. I 36 it is said that what expresses the nature or essence of God expresses the power of God. Similarly (Eth. III 7) the endeavour by which each thing tries to persevere in its being is called the 'actual essence' of the thing, and in Eth. IV 53 it is said that to speak of the essence of man is to speak of the power of man. (Cf. Eth. V 9, in which the same is said of the human mind.)[7] Spinoza offers deductive proofs of these propositions, proofs which rest in the last analysis on the ontological argument. (See especially Eth. I 34, with its reference to Eth. I 11.) However, expressed as far as possible in nonmetaphysical terms, his view seems to be that, in some cases at least, what follows from x's nature or essence is in the power of x, and what is not in x's power is what does not follow from x's nature (Eth. I 17 Sch., G ii.61; Eth. II 49 Sch., G ii.136). From this, it is easy to see how Spinoza can identify power and essence.

This is at first sight a puzzling view, whose oddity can be brought out by a passage from Eth. I 17 Sch. (G ii.62). Spinoza says there that 'from the supreme power of God, i.e. his infinite nature. . .all things have necessarily flowed, or always follow, with the same necessity; just as from the nature of the triangle it follows from eternity and to eternity that its three angles equal two right angles'. What is odd here is that one does not normally speak of the *power* of a triangle. Perhaps Spinoza might do so, but it is not certain that he does, or that he need do. He could say that a triangle is an 'entity of reason', and that what he says about power holds only in the case of 'real entities'; the triangle is adduced only as an example of something whose properties belong to it eternally, and is not adduced as an example of power. (Compare his distinction, in Ep. 83, between the definitions of entities of reason and of real things.) This is why it was suggested earlier that Spinoza identifies power and essence in some cases only—namely, in the case of real entities.

But even if it is supposed that when Spinoza equates 'essence' and 'power' he is speaking only of real things, difficulties remain. First, when he says that what follows from x's nature or essence is in the power of x, what exactly is it that is said to follow? In the case of God, Spinoza says that 'all things' (*omnia*) or 'infinite things in infinite ways' (*infinita infinitis modis*) follow. (Eth. I 17 Sch., G. ii.62; cf. Eth. I 16.) Now, if one were describing x's power in the normal sense of the term, one would refer to what x does and will, or would, do; one would not refer to *things* that 'follow from' x.[8]

Spinoza would probably agree. The term 'things' in our translation could be misleading—Spinoza uses the vaguer terms *'omnia'* and *'infinita'*; more important, a comparison of Eth. II 3 Sch. with Eth. I 16, to which it refers, shows that what follow from the divine nature may also be *acts*. If one asks what kind of acts these are, the answer is probably: motion, in the case of the attribute of extension, and the 'infinite idea' (or judgment) of God, in the case of the attribute of thought.

It must now be asked whether, in the ordinary sense of the word 'power', it can be said that *actions* follow from the nature of the thing to which power is ascribed. To say that a car has the power of going at 100 m.p.h. is not to say that a certain action follows from its nature, in the sense that it has ever travelled, or ever will travel, at this speed; it may, for example, always have cautious drivers. To ascribe this power to it is to say what it will do, *if* certain circumstances arise. Spinoza would probably agree where modes (such as a car) are concerned, though not in the case of God. According to Spinoza, the fact that God's power is his essence means that God cannot be conceived except as acting (Eth. II 3 Sch. This, Spinoza adds, is why it is wrong to compare God's power with that of a king). It may now be objected that if to say that a man has such and such powers is to say that certain acts follow from his essence, then this seems to mean that a man, too, cannot be conceived except as acting. The answer seems to be that there is an important difference between man and God. Spinoza does indeed maintain that each man, insofar as he is in himself (*in se*), endeavours to persevere in his own being, which should mean that it follows from a man's nature that he acts in a way which does preserve his own being. Spinoza would reply that a man would do so if he were *in se*, if he were independent, as God is. But in fact a man is affected by things which are external to him, and to that extent he is not *in se*, and his actions do not follow from his nature alone. Rather, they follow from his nature and from that of the things which affect him.[9] So it appears that, in the case of the power of modes, an element of the hypothetical enters. To speak of the power of *x*, where *x* is a mode, is to speak of what *x* will do if not interfered with. What it will do, in this case, is persevere in its own being.

If this is Spinoza's view of the nature of power (and it must be stressed that his account of this concept is not easy to follow) then it can at least be said in favour of the view that it avoids the idea that a power is some kind of occult or hidden entity.[10] This is an idea which Spinoza, who shared the general hostility of seventeenth-century scientists to 'occult qualities', might be expected to avoid. (Cf. Ep. 56, G iv.261.)

B. The second of the questions raised earlier concerned proof: namely, how does Spinoza think that he can show that each thing, insofar as it is in itself, endeavours to persevere in its own being? In Eth. III 6 Spinoza offers a deductive proof, based upon his views about the nature of God and upon a supposedly self-evident proposition (Eth. III 4). The argument is both metaphysical and obscure, and is best relegated to a footnote.[11] More interesting is the fact that Spinoza seems also to offer an empirical argument, to the effect that we are conscious of the endeavour in question. To follow what he says, it is necessary to develop further his views about this endeavour, this *conatus*.

First, a brief reminder must be given about some features of Spinoza's theory of mind-matter relations. So far, this paper has considered the human body and its endeavour, insofar as it is in itself, to persevere in its own being. Spinoza holds that essentially the same account can be given of the human mind. Just as the human body is a composite body, composed, in the last resort, of 'most simple bodies', so the human mind is a composite idea, 'composed of very many ideas' (*ex plurimis ideis composita.* Eth. II 15). For Spinoza, there is no mere parallelism between mind and body; rather, they are one and the same thing, expressed through different attributes. The human mind just *is* the idea of the human body (Eth. II 13); that is, it is the expression in thought-terms of that of which the body is the expression in physical terms. There is no space to comment here on this 'double aspect' theory of the relations between mind and body; all that can be done is to explain its consequences as far as the endeavour to persevere in being is concerned.

Given Spinoza's views about mind-matter relations it is not surprising that he should assert that, like the body, the mind endeavours (insofar as it is in itself) to persevere in its own being (Eth. III 9). He adds (*ibid.*) that the mind is conscious of this endeavour (*hujus sui conatus est conscia*). At this point he introduces (Eth. III 9 Sch.) some new technical terms—or rather, some old terms in a new sense. He calls this endeavour, insofar as it is related to the mind alone, 'will' (*voluntas*); when it is related both to the mind and the body, he calls it 'appetite' (*appetitus*). Appetite, therefore, is the very essence of man. The only difference between appetite and 'desire' (*cupiditas*) is that desire is usually ascribed to men insofar as they are conscious of their appetites, and so may be defined as 'appetite, together with an awareness of it' (*appetitus cum ejusdem conscientia*).

It may seem, then, that Spinoza is saying that we can identify empirically our endeavour, insofar as we are 'in ourselves', to persevere in our being. This might seem unexceptionable; one would certainly say that, in the ordinary sense of the word 'appetite', we are conscious of our appetites, or at any rate of some of them. But there is a difficulty as far as Spinoza is concerned. He holds that the human body, like all physical objects, is affected by an infinity of other things (Eth. I 28); how, then, can we be aware of the endeavour of our body as it is in itself? Suppose, for example, that a man is passionately in love, and is aware of this fact. Such a man has a certain desire, both in the ordinary and in the Spinozist sense. Spinoza would call such a desire a passion—indeed, he would call it a kind of insanity (Eth. IV 44 Sch.; Eth. IV App., par. 19)—and by calling it a passion he means that the man in question is affected by, and indeed mastered by, causes which are external to him. This means that what the man is aware of is not his endeavour, as far as he is "in himself", to persevere in his own being, but rather this endeavour as modified by external influences (cf. Eth. IV 5).[12] Spinoza is far from maintaining that every desire is a passion; on the contrary, he holds that we have the power of doing certain things which can be understood through the laws of our own nature alone (Eth. IV Def. 8, IV 24, III 3). The question here, however, is whether there is a difference which can be detected by introspection between a desire of the latter kind and a desire which is a passion. If there is, Spinoza does not make this difference clear.

So far it appears that Spinoza has been unable to prove, either deductively or by an appeal to introspection, that each thing, insofar as it is in itself, endeavors to persevere in its being. It might now be suggested that Spinoza's theory of *conatus* can be defended if it is regarded as an hypothesis, which is justified insofar as it enables him to explain what human beings do, and to point out the most advantageous course of action for them. To see whether the doctrine of *conatus* can be defended in this way, it is necessary to look further at the kind of hypothesis that would be involved. It would, no doubt, be generally agreed that if an hypothesis is to be scientific, it must be capable of being falsified. Spinoza's theory of *conatus*, on the other hand, does not seem to be falsifiable. The obvious objection to the view that each man, insofar as he is 'in himself', tries to persevere in his own being is the fact that there are such people as suicides and martyrs. Spinoza accounts for suicides by saying (Eth. IV 20 Sch.; cf. Eth. IV 18 Sch., '*tertio*. . .') that such men are 'mastered by external causes'. In himself, i.e. insofar as he is unaffected by external causes, the suicide endeavours to preserve his own being. Spinoza would doubtless give the same account of the martyr, and as this is so, one may wonder what would refute his doctrine. It would appear, then, that the hypothesis is empty, and it is pointless to speak of anything confirming or supporting it—for nothing would be allowed to do anything else.[13]

But it by no means follows that the doctrine of *conatus* is entirely idle.

(i) Spinoza may be pointing to the fact that people are not merely static. The nature of the human being, he may be saying, is to endeavour to act in certain ways. This may seem a tame assertion, but at any rate it is not empty.

(ii) The apparent unfalsifiability of the doctrine of *conatus* may reflect the fact that to some extent it is not a scientific doctrine at all; rather, it is in part a *moral* view, about the way in which human beings ought to act. This point will be developed later (Part III, *ad fin.*).

C. The third question was, how does Spinoza relate what he says about *conatus* to his views about efficient causes? Is *conatus* a cause, and if so, in what sense? The short answer is that *conatus* is a cause, and an efficient cause—though it is an efficient cause of a special kind.

In developing this answer, we begin by taking up a point made earlier (Part II, *ad init.*): namely, that Spinoza holds that explanation in terms of efficient causes applies to the mental as well as to the physical world. Consider the explanation of a human activity:

say, the building of a house. The question 'Why was this house built?' could have as an answer 'So that someone has somewhere to live'. In Aristotelian terms, having somewhere to live is, in this case, the final cause of the activity of building the house (Cf. Eth. IV Pref., G ii.207: someone might say that 'habitation was the final cause of this or that house'). Spinoza, however, argues that to say this is really to say that someone had the appetite for building the house (*appetitus aedificandi domum*), and this appetite is the efficient cause of the activity in question (*ibid*. See also the definition of 'end', Eth. IV Def. 7). It will be remembered that in Spinoza, 'appetite' is a term that refers both to mind and to matter. The building of the house, therefore, is to be explained both in physical and in mental terms: but in each case the causes involved are efficient causes.

It now has to be asked how the appetite is to be related to the activity. It may seem that Spinoza is viewing appetite as a kind of inner thrust, which drives our body in the case of the attribute of extension, and somehow drives our ideas in the case of the attribute of thought—much as the uncoiling of a spring drives the wheels of a watch. In other words, he may seem to regard an appetite or desire as one among a series of causes. In the case of the building of a house, the series might be: the imagination of home comforts causes a man to have the desire to build a house, which causes him to build a house.[14] There are notorious difficulties in such a view, but in fact the view does not seem to be Spinoza's. Here it is necessary to refer to the so-called 'double causal relation' in Spinoza, as stated in Eth. II 9 and II 45.[15] Eth. II 9 says that each single thing is caused by another, and that by another, and so *ad infinitum*; it does not, however, follow from what may be called the 'absolute nature' of God—i.e. from God insofar as he is an absolutely thinking or extended being, or, insofar as he is infinite. However, in Eth. II 45 Spinoza says in effect that each single thing 'necessarily involves the eternal and infinite essence of God'. He explains in the Scholium that 'although each single thing is determined by another to exist in a certain way' (evidently a reference to Eth. II 9) 'yet the force (*vis*) by which each perseveres in existence follows from the eternal necessity of the nature of God'. This is clearly a reference to *conatus*, and it seems that Spinoza is saying that an explanation of some event in terms of endeavour or power is of a different type from one which explains an event in terms of some other event. He is arguing in effect that it is one thing to say (e.g.) that a man moves his hand in a certain way because of a prior movement in another part of his body; it is another thing to say that he moves his hand in a certain way because he wants a house to live in. In the former case, an action follows from a prior action (in Spinoza's terms, one mode affects another); in the latter, an action is seen as following from an endeavour—in the last resort, an endeavour on the part of a thing, insofar as it is 'in itself', to persevere in its own being. In the latter case, one does not explain the action by saying that the endeavour in some way pushes it; rather, one explains it by seeing it in the light of, in the context of the endeavour. This means that one sees it in the context of the essence or nature of the person in question, as someone who will act in such a way as to persevere in his own being, unless interfered with from outside.

As the two types of causality are different, it may seem misleading that Spinoza should refer to both as cases of efficient causation. He might reply, however, that the two types have something in common, and so deserve the same name. In each case, something (an effect) is explained as following from something else (a cause), and in neither case is the cause a final cause. Spinoza might perhaps mark the difference between the two by saying that *conatus* is an *internal* efficient cause; the agent whose acts follow from his *conatus* is thus in a sense self-caused. In this connexion it may be noted that Spinoza says explicitly that an efficient cause need not be external.[16]

At this stage we may refer back to a point made early in Part II. It was suggested there that Spinoza's account of causality and power has to be seen in the light of seventeenth-century physics, and that this physics was 'mechanistic', a mechanistic system being defined as one in which the movement of one body by another is explained in terms of push. The account just given of Spinoza's view of the nature of causality—more exactly, of external efficient causality—is consistent with this suggestion. It should be added that if a mechanistic system were defined as one in which *all* movement has to be explained in terms of push, then Spinoza's physics would not be mechanistic. However, the definition adopted here has referred only to the movement of one body by another.

III

Now that Spinoza's views about causality and power have been expounded, it is possible to approach the main questions of this paper:

(i) What consequences did Spinoza think that these views have for human freedom?

(ii) Are these consequences validly derived by him?

(iii) If validly derived, do they follow from premises some at least of which are false? (If this is so, then the consequences cannot, without further argument, be said to be true.)

The first question will be discussed in the present part of this paper; questions (ii) and (iii) will be discussed in Part IV.

Spinoza argues that it follows from what he has said that a man's actions, whether of mind or of body, 'are necessitated'. It is important to see exactly what this means. Spinoza says that a thing may be called 'necessary' in either of two ways: 'either by virtue of its essence, or by virtue of its cause' (*vel ratione suae essentiae, vel ratione causae*. Eth. I 33 Sch. 1). A thing which is necessary by virtue of its essence is one whose existence 'follows necessarily from its essence or definition' (*ibid*); it may also be defined as that whose nature is such that it would imply a contradiction for it not to exist (*De Intellectus Emendatione*, G ii.19. Cf. Eth., *loc. cit.*, on the term 'impossible'). A thing which is necessary by virtue of its cause is something which 'follows necessarily from a given efficient cause' (Eth. *loc. cit.* Cf. *Cogitata Metaphysica*, I.3.3)—or rather, as the context (*'vel quia nulla . . .'*) shows, from a given *external* cause. A thing which is necessitated by an external cause, or 'determined by something else to exist and operate in a certain and determinate way' is called by Spinoza 'necessary, or rather compelled' (*necessaria, vel potius coacta*. Eth. I Def. 7).[17]

Some comment is called for here. (a) One might perhaps think that Spinoza is here recognising two senses of the word 'necessary', the first being logical necessity and the second causal necessity. However, this cannot be so; for it will be remembered that, according to Spinoza, causal necessity simply *is* logical necessity. A thing which is necessary 'by virtue of its cause' is, therefore, one whose existence follows with logical necessity from the existence of something else. (b) The notion of a 'necessary thing' or 'necessary being' is often found obscure; one is told that propositions, not things, are necessary. It seems clear from the context, however, that when Spinoza calls a thing 'necessary' he means that either (i) the proposition which asserts its existence is such that its truth follows from the definition of the thing, or (ii) the proposition which asserts its existence follows logically from some true proposition about the existence or nature of some other thing. (c) The notion of necessity in Spinoza has so far been explicated in terms of existence. For Spinoza, however, 'necessary' is also a term that can be applied to acts, such as volitions [Eth. I 32. Cf. Eth. I 28: each single thing (*singulare*) is determined to exist and to act (*ad existendum et operandum*)]. It is clear that an act can be necessary either by virtue of the essence of the agent (as in the case of God, Eth. I 17 Cor. 2), or by virtue of some external cause which affects the agent (Eth. I 28).

It now has to be seen how all this applies to human actions. It seems to be Spinoza's view that human actions are necessary in both of the ways described. He regards every human action as having an external cause; for (Eth. I 28) the human being, like everything else which is 'finite and has a determinate existence' is determined to existence and to action by another cause. This means, then, that each act of a human being is 'necessary, or rather compelled'. So much is clear; but it may be wondered how a human act can be necessary in the other sense—for it is surely God alone whose existence follows necessarily from his essence or definition. Here the notion of *conatus* plays an important part. In Part II C of this paper reference was made to two types of causality in Spinoza; one of these (Eth. II 45 and Sch.) is *conatus*, which is referred to when Spinoza says that the force by which each thing perseveres in existence follows from the eternal necessity of the nature of God. This force, then, does not come into existence because of some other finite thing; it exists because God exists and acts. Nor (insofar as it is in itself) is it determined to action by some other thing. In short, insofar as an action follows from *conatus*[18] it is necessary, but it is not determined from outside, i.e. it is not compelled. This is of the utmost importance for Spinoza's theory of freedom.

It seems, then, that a man's actions are necessitated in two ways—through his own *conatus*, and through external causes. This means that a man must act as he does; he cannot act in any other way.[19] It may also be said that, in a standard sense of the term 'power', he has no power to do anything other than what he actually does. Spinoza goes so far as to say that what a man does not do, that he cannot do; or, more generally, that what does not occur, cannot occur. This is because 'whatever we conceive to be in God's power' (i.e. whatever is logically conceivable) 'necessarily exists' (Eth. I 35). Since this view is logically independent of the views discussed so far, it need not be considered here.

We can now move from Spinoza's concept of necessity to his concept of freedom. If 'x is free' is taken to mean 'x can act in some way other than that in which x actually does act', then it follows from what Spinoza has said that no man is free. However, Spinoza defines freedom in another way. He says (Eth. I Def. 7): 'That thing is called "free" which exists from the necessity of its nature alone, and is determined to action by itself alone'.[20] It may seem at first that a man still cannot be called 'free', for only God satisfies the conditions laid down by the definition. Indeed, Spinoza says (Eth. I 17 Cor. 2) that God alone is a free cause. It is here, however, that the importance of the notion of *conatus* appears. It has already been noted that, insofar as an action follows from *conatus*, it is not determined by an external cause. To this must be added the fact that, for Spinoza, a mode (such as a man) is not the source of its own activities. The Spinozist mode must not be confused with the Leibnizian monad. Rather, the *conatus* with which each thing, insofar as it is itself, endeavours to persevere in its own being is really God's *conatus*. This is not something which is outside the mode, as another mode is; the mode is a mode of God, and its *conatus* is God's *conatus*. Hence, insofar as a man's acts follow from *conatus*, he can properly be called 'free'.

To round off this discussion of Spinoza's account of human freedom, it remains to consider the kinds of actions that follow from man's *conatus*. Here it is necessary to introduce the further notions of 'virtue' (*virtus*) and reason. The notion of virtue contains little that is new. Spinoza says that the term refers to human power, which is defined by the essence of man alone, i.e. solely by the *conatus* by which a man endeavours to persevere in his own being (Eth. IV 20; cf. Eth. IV Def. 8). 'Virtue', then, seems to be a special kind of power—the power of man.[21] Now, Spinoza asserts (Eth. IV 24) that to act in accordance with virtue is simply to act, live and preserve one's being (the three, he says, mean the same) as reason guides one (*ex ductu rationis*. Cf. Eth. IV 37 Sch. 1, and also Eth. IV 52 and IV App., par. 3, in which the power of man is equated with reason). In short, the free man lives as reason guides him; in this way he does those things which his own nature, considered in itself alone, demands (Eth. IV 37, Sch. 1).

Before this view is criticised, two problems of interpretation must be discussed. The first concerns Spinoza's famous assertion that men think themselves free 'because they are conscious of their actions, and ignorant of the causes by which they are determined' (Eth. III 2 Sch., G ii.143. Cf. Eth. I App., G ii.78). The question here is whether Spinoza means that men think themselves free (a) because they think that their actions are uncaused, whether internally or externally, or (b) because, being ignorant of the external causes of their actions, they think that their actions are internally determined. In view of Spinoza's definition of freedom, the latter seems more likely; for it is only determination by an external cause which is inconsistent with human freedom.

This leads to the second problem, namely: can Spinoza consistently say that a man is free? The difficulty is this. Spinoza says (Eth. I 28) that every mode is determined from outside, and it is determined both in respect of its existence and of what it does.[22] This being so, how can any human act be free? It is true that Spinoza does not seem to think of any act as determined wholly from outside, for he regards each thing, insofar as it is in itself, as endeavouring to persevere in its own being. What each thing does, then, seems to be the outcome of an interaction between its own *conatus* and external causes. But for an act to be free, it would have to be determined wholly by *conatus*.[23]

How, then, can Spinoza get round this difficulty? One may disregard the idea that determination from outside is merely phenomenal. There is no hint that Spinoza thought this,[24] and if he had done so, this would have had the consequence that every man is really free, which is certainly not his view. It might be the case that Eth. I 28 is stated carelessly, and that Spinoza did not intend it to apply to *all* the acts of a given single thing. If so, however, the oversight would be a glaring one, and one ought to look for another explanation if possible. Perhaps the answer is to be found in Eth. III

Def. 2. Here Spinoza is defining what he calls an 'action', i.e. a
manifestation of the power of man (Eth. IV App., par. 2). He says
that by an action he means something of which we are the adequate
cause, i.e. something which follows from our nature and which can
be understood clearly and distinctly through that nature alone. The
relevance of this to the present problem is as follows. Spinoza may
be saying that we can explain the action of a man through its external causes: to do this would be to view it as a scientist might
do—e.g. in terms of some physical science, such as neuro-
physiology, or in terms that might belong to psychology. But we can
also assess the action in terms of its rationality; we can say, for example, that the man has understood (or failed to understand) the
situation in which he finds himself. It is the same action which is
assessed in each case, but in a different way; and insofar as the act
is rational, it is the act of a free man.

If this interpretation is correct, then what Spinoza is saying is
related to the familiar point that it is one thing to assess a person's
conduct in terms of the reasons for it, and another to assess it in
terms of its causes. If the assessment is made in the latter way, then
(according to Spinoza) there can be no question of an act's being
free; every act is determined externally, and therefore is compelled.
But if a man's acts are assessed in the former way, then it may be
correct to say that they are free: namely, if the reasons for the acts
are good reasons, i.e. if the acts are genuinely rational. It will be
noticed that, for Spinoza, to be free is not something negative, in
the sense that a free act is one which is not determined; rather, to be
free is to be determined, but determined by the laws of one's essential humanity, which are the laws of reason.

This discussion can now be linked to a point made earlier (II B,
ad fin.), concerning the unfalsifiability of Spinoza's views about
conatus. It has now become clear that the 'being' that each man, insofar as he is *in se*, tries to preserve is his rationality, and that insofar as he is rational he is genuinely himself. This is clearly not a
scientific proposition; rather, Spinoza is setting up a standard of
human activity which is moral in nature.

IV

It is now time to try to assess the views that have been expounded. There seems to be nothing formally wrong with Spinoza's

arguments, so that, of the questions formulated at the beginning of
Part III, question (ii) need not detain us. The question, then, is
whether there are any errors in the views from which Spinoza
derives his conclusions. It has been suggested above that these
views are not altogether clear; in particular, it has been suggested
that the doctrine of *conatus* may have a moral aspect, though it
does not seem to be entirely a moral theory. The moral aspect of the
theory will not be discussed here; instead, attention will be concentrated on problems that belong to the philosophy of mind. As
already stated, our chief concern will be with Spinoza's views about
power, and especially the powers of human beings. However, it
would hardly be an adequate account of Spinoza's views on freedom
which contained no reference to recent discussions about the causes
of human actions, and in particular to A. I. Melden's influential
book *Free Action* (London, 1961). Briefly, Melden's view (*op. cit.*,
p. 182) is that 'the ordinary causal model' cannot be applied to
human actions; that 'an action is no mere effect of an internal mental doing in the way in which an explosion is an effect of the introduction of heat in a mixture of hydrogen and oxygen'. Now it is
clear that, whatever the validity of Melden's arguments, for much
of the time he is arguing against theses that Spinoza did not hold.
The view just cited—that a (physical) action is the result of a mental occurence—is such a view; so are the more specific theses that
certain mental acts called 'volitions' produce muscular movements
(Melden, Chap. 5), and that motives cause bodily movements
(Melden, p. 84). Spinoza would have said that matter does not act
on mind, and mind does not act on matter. In his view, to speak of a
human action is to speak of something that can be described both
in physical and in mental terms. Each description is complete as far
as it goes—e.g. in explaining a human action in physiological terms
we need not, and indeed must not, introduce into our account factors which belong to an explanation in mental terms; further,
neither type of description is reducible to the other.[25] It is an obvious and important question, whether one can give a self-
contained account of a human action in physiological terms.
Spinoza warns his readers not to assume dogmatically that this
cannot be done; so far, he says, no one has such a precise knowledge
of the structure of the human body that he can explain all its working (Eth. III 2 Sch., G ii.142). Melden, too, warns against
dogmatism of this kind (*op. cit.*, p. 59). His concern is with a certain

model—the model of the central nervous system as somehow manipulated by an invisible agent. This model he rejects; and Spinoza would reject it too.

A further point may be made here. In attacking the view that volitions are causes, Melden (Chap. 5) attacks the idea that there *are* volitions, in the sense of mental acts whose presence or absence is responsible for the difference between a voluntary and an involuntary act. That there is such a difference is agreed, but Melden's point is that the difference is not to be explained by postulating mysterious causal agents called 'volitions'. Once again, this seems to be a case of an attack which (however damaging to some views) does not seem to affect Spinoza. It has already been argued (cf. II A, *ad fin.*) that Spinoza's *conatus* (of which 'will' is a type: Eth. III 9 Sch.) is not a mysterious urge, some kind of 'occult quality'. Further, Spinoza does not use the idea of *conatus* to explain the difference between the voluntary and the involuntary. For him, everything that a human being does follows, at least in part, from *conatus*—both the actions that we call 'reflex' and those we call 'deliberate'; the blink of an eye, as much as someone's winking at somebody. In each case, someone is trying to preserve his own being. The former—the blink—may be regarded as, for example, the removal of impurities that might damage the eye. The latter is much more complex; it might, perhaps, be seen as following from the desire to attract attention, which in turn is related to a man's endeavour to preserve his own being. However, whether or not Spinoza can give an adequate account of this difference is not at issue here; what is relevant is the fact that he does not try to account for the distinction between the voluntary and the involuntary by the presence or absence of acts of will.

After this discussion of objections that do not seem relevant to Spinoza, it is time to consider some objections that are relevant. These involve the notion of power; the notion of what a thing can and cannot do. It has already been seen that Spinoza holds that a thing must do what it does, and cannot act in any other way. This obviously clashes with the ordinary use of words. For example, one might well say of a certain car, 'This car can do 100 m.p.h.', even though the car is not moving. Now, it would be hard to accept the idea that beliefs of this kind are mere superstitions—relics of the days before the appreciation of the fact that all events have causes.

Nor does Spinoza have to say this. He could consistently say that a car can (in a sense) do 100 m.p.h., even though it cannot do anything other than what it is now doing, namely, standing still. Suppose, for example, that at a given time t the car is in its garage and that the engine is not running. The car does not do 100 m.p.h. at time t, and, in these circumstances, it cannot do 100 m.p.h. at time t. But this does not prevent Spinoza from saying that the car can do 100 m.p.h. at another time, under different conditions, or that it could have done 100 m.p.h. at time t, had the conditions been different. The notion of natural law seems relevant here. Spinoza could consistently assert that when we say that something can do what it is not doing, what we say involves a general statement of law. Such an analysis of the powers of things is considered, but rejected, by M. R. Ayers (*op. cit.*, pp. 75 ff.). The view discussed by Ayers is that the statement that this car can do 100 m.p.h. is to be analysed as follows: Let (some of) the properties of this car be F, then it is not a law that anything F does not do 100 m.p.h. There seems to be a conclusive objection (not mentioned by Dr. Ayers) to this analysis. It is not a law that anything painted red does not do 100 m.p.h., but one would hardly say that it follows that this red car can do 100 m.p.h. If, therefore, an account of possibility in terms of law is to stand up to criticism, the analysis must be reformulated. The following seems to be better: to say that this car can do 100 m.p.h. is to say that it follows from natural laws known to us that any car which has the properties F will, under certain specifiable conditions (e.g. if driven competently, on a good straight road, etc.) do 100 m.p.h.; and this car has the properties F.

But however one formulates the view that the powers of a thing are to be defined in terms of natural laws, Ayers would argue that such a view is inadequate. His objection is that the same issues arise at the level of generality (i.e. at the level of natural law) as arise at the level of the particular (i.e. at the level of the powers of, say, this car), so a move from the particular to the general cannot settle them (*op. cit.*, p. 77). The argument appears to be that to say (e.g.) that it is a law that ravens are black is not just to say that every actual raven has been, and will be black; it is to say that a nonblack raven is *impossible*, i.e. that a raven *cannot be* nonblack. The impossibility to which Ayers refers here is of a nonlogical kind; he is saying in effect that if it is a law that all ravens are black, then the proposition that all ravens are black is necessarily true, though it is not a logically necessary truth. Ayers argues that as this is so, we may not use the notion of natural law to explain the notion of what a thing can do, for problems of "can' and 'cannot' recur at the level of natural laws themselves. Against this, it may be pointed out that the notion of nonlogical necessity is a highly controversial one; but even if one grants, for the sake of argument, that there is a necessity of this kind, it is hard to see why it should be wrong to use the notion of natural law to explain the notion of the powers of a thing. Ayers' contention that the same problems recur does not seem to be justified. The problem of the nature of the necessity of natural laws is not *the same as* the problem of the nature of the powers of a thing, it is merely involved in it. By explaining power in terms of natural law we do not (as Ayers seems to suggest) meet the same old problem; we meet a new problem.

However, there is another, and more important objection to be met. Dr. Ayers would argue that, even if Spinoza can give a satisfactory account of propositions such as 'This car can do 100 m.p.h.'—whether in terms of natural law, or, as Ayers would argue, in some other terms[26]—the analysis provided cannot be applied to human beings. This is because (pp. 102 ff.) the power of a person to perform an action is essentially different from the power of a thing. Now, Spinoza does not appear to draw a distinction between the two; so much seems implied by his view that man is to be treated as a part of nature. It is important, therefore, to see if there is a distinction here.

Ayers' argument involves a distinction (pp. 81-82) between what he calls 'extrinsic' and 'intrinsic' circumstances. For example, to say 'If this car is provided with eight cylinders, it will do 100 m.p.h.' does not support the claim that this car can do 100 m.p.h. For a hypothetical statement to support such a claim, the 'if' clause must not refer to something internal or intrinsic to the subject, affecting its essence. In other words, 'x can do a' does not mean that, in certain intrinsic circumstances, x will do a. Rather, it means that it will do a in certain extrinsic circumstances—e.g. (in the case of the car) if driven skilfully. Ayers admits (p. 85) that there are borderline cases—e.g. is a damp match capable of starting a fire?—but says that this fact does not cast doubt on the validity of the distinction. Let us, at any rate, accept the distinction. Its relevance to the question of the difference between the powers of persons and of things is as follows. The powers of a thing (p. 103) depend, not on extrinsic, but on intrinsic circumstances. A car does not lose its powers if locked in a garage; it does lose them if its engine is removed. If one compares the powers of persons one notes that these, too, may depend on intrinsic circumstances. For example, one may say of a man that he cannot excape if he has been in a cell so long that he has lost the use of his limbs. This case is comparable to that of a car with no engine, or perhaps to one whose engine is rusty with long disuse; however, the powers of a person, unlike those of a thing, may depend very much on extrinsic circumstances. For example, a perfectly healthy man, locked in a cell, is deprived of some of his powers. It would be absurd (p. 104) to take 'The prisoner can escape' as meaning 'In certain circumstances—e.g. if not locked in a cell—he will do so'. In sum, to ascribe a power to a thing is merely to say something about the thing's nature; to say that a man can do a certain action is not only to imply something about the man himself, but is also to imply that the circumstances are favourable to the action.

But does this mean (as is argued by Ayers, p. 106) that it is a mistake to see in the powers of an inanimate object any close logical analogue to the powers of a person? It has already been noted that some 'cannot' statements which refer to human beings are of the same type as 'cannot' statements which refer to objects; to say of a paralysed man that he cannot escape is to use 'cannot' in the same way as when one says that a car without an engine cannot do 100 m.p.h. In other words, to speak of the powers of a man is *sometimes* to speak of intrinsic circumstances; we may give as further examples the statements 'He can play the piano' and 'He can pick locks', both of which can properly be made of a prisoner locked in a cell. Why, then, should it be said (as it certainly would be said) of a locksmith locked in a cell, and without the tools of his trade, that he cannot escape? Surely because he lacks a necessary condition for an actualisation or demonstration of his skill—much as a pianist may say, of a battered cottage piano, 'I can play the piano—but not *that* piano'. Now, it is true to say that a man cannot display a power if a necessary condition of that display is absent; but this is an analytic truth, following from the very meaning of the term 'necessary condition'. It is hard to see how an analytic truth of this kind can show that there is any fundamental difference between the powers of persons and the powers of things.

However, there is still another argument in favour of drawing a distinction between the powers of persons and of things. It may be the case (cf. Ayers, p. 106) that given the opportunity and the capacity to escape, a man still does not escape. But if an object has the power to do x, and if the extrinsic circumstances are right (e.g. a car is on a race-track, and is adequately supplied with fuel) then one expects it to do x; indeed, if in these circumstances it does not do x, one would deny that it had the power. Against this, it may be argued that what has been said is true only of the powers of some things. Suppose, for example, that there is a car which can do 100 m.p.h., but which, if it did so regularly, would have a relatively short working life; consequently, the engine is fitted with a governor which stops the car going at this high speed. It may be argued that one may say of this car that it can do 100 m.p.h. but that it does not, even though the extrinsic circumstances are right. The important question here is whether the governor is to be counted as an extrinsic or an intrinsic circumstance. Ayers' thesis would not be affected by the mere fact that a car which can travel at 100 m.p.h. does not do so. Such a car might, for example, always have cautious drivers, a fact which Ayers would count as an extrinsic circumstance. On the other hand, a built-in governor does not seem to be an extrinsic circumstance; if it is removed, the car is radically altered.

It might be objected that, even if the governor is regarded as an intrinsic circumstance, the counter-instance is not a genuine one; for the car, fitted with its governor, *cannot* go at 100 m.p.h. Yet there seems to be a sense in which it can—it is assumed to have the requisite engine, the requisite gears, etc. The objection might also be answered by saying that it could with equal justice be asserted of the prisoner who (it is alleged) could escape if he wished, that really he cannot escape. The factors that prevent him from escaping—e.g. a fear of what will happen to him if he is recaptured—are such that, given them, he cannot escape.

Our discussion has moved some way from what Spinoza wrote, but it has always been relevant to his theories. The upshot of the inquiry has been that there seems to be nothing in the arguments discussed here to support the conclusion that the powers of persons differ essentially from the powers of things. To this extent, then, Spinoza's view that all human actions are necessitated has not been refuted. This is not to imply that other arguments cannot be brought successfully against such a view; but a consideration of this issue would go beyond the scope of the present paper.

G. H. R. Parkinson

University of Reading

NOTES

[1] *Ethics*, III, Definitions of the Affects, No. 20. Translations from Spinoza are my own. The text used is that of Gebhardt (4 vols.; Heidelberg: Carl Winter 1925); this is referred to as 'G'. References are to volume number and page.

[2] A number of similar passages can be cited. Thus, in Eth. III 54, which refers to III 7, Spinoza speaks of 'the mind's endeavour or power', and in Eth. III 28 he speaks of 'the mind's endeavour, or power of thought' (*conatus, seu potentia in cogitando*) and of 'the body's endeavour, or power of action' (*conatus, seu potentia in agendo*). Cf. Eth. III 8, in which Spinoza speaks alternatively of 'the power by which a thing exists' and 'the endeavour by which a thing exists'.

[3] Cf. Eth. III 6, which states that nothing has 'in itself' anything by which it can be destroyed. Eth. III 4, to which the proof refers, says that 'While we attend only to the thing itself, and not to external causes, we can find nothing in it which could destroy it'. Compare also Spinoza's geometrical version of Descartes' *Principles of Philosophy*, II 14, in which he states that 'Each thing, insofar as it is simple and undivided, and is considered in itself alone, insofar as it is in itself (*quantum in se est*) always perseveres in the same state'. From this he infers (*op. cit.*, II 14 Cor.) that a body which is once in motion will always continue to move, unless it is retarded by external causes.

Strictly, only substance or God is 'in itself' (Eth. I Def. 3); but it is permissible to speak of a particular thing or mode as 'in itself', insofar as its power is the power of God or nature (Eth. IV 4; cf. Eth. I 24 Cor., II 45 Sch.).

[4] Exactly what Spinoza means by 'motion' and 'rest' is not wholly clear, though it seems that motion is not merely change of position, nor rest the same as absence of motion. Rather, 'motion' seems to be a kind of force which a moving body has, and 'rest' seems to be resistance to impact. (See, e.g. Spinoza's geometrical version of Descartes' *Principles*, II 21, 22, and 22 Cors. 1-3.)

[5] On the communication of motion, cf. Ep. 32, G iv, 171-72; *The Correspondence of Spinoza*, trans. A. Wolf (London, 1928), pp. 210-11.

[6] It may be asked whether motion and rest, speed and slowness can differentiate one body from all others. Could not two or more 'most simple bodies' have the same

amounts of motion and rest, speed and slowness? Spinoza might reply that they could, but that physics would not differentiate between such bodies.

⁷ For the view that a thing's endeavour or power is the essence of the thing, and conversely, see also Eth. III 54, IV Def. 8, IV 53. It should be noted that Spinoza is not merely saying that endeavour is *essential* to a thing, so that given a thing there is necessarily given an endeavour of that thing, and conversely (cf. Eth. II Def. 2). Rather, he is saying that 'essence' and 'endeavour' (or 'power') are *identical*.

⁸ One could, of course, say that *x* has *power over* things (cf. *Tractatus Politicus*, 2.9-10, on the phrase *'sub potestate'*). However, one would not mention these things when describing *x*'s powers, though one would mention them if one were describing what *x* owns.

⁹ It should be noted that there is in Spinoza a technical sense of the word 'action', according to which an action is what can be understood from our nature alone (Eth. III Def. 2; cf. IV App., par. 2). But this sense is not what is in mind here.

¹⁰ For objections to this view, cf. M. R. Ayers, *op. cit.*, pp. 61, 74.

¹¹ Spinoza argues that each thing 'expresses' God, that is, the power by which God exists and acts. (By 'expressing God' he seems to mean—cf. Eth. I 25 Cor. and the references cited there—that each thing is in God and cannot be conceived without God). Now, if 'power' means 'endeavour to persevere in one's own being', then one might suppose that Spinoza could stop there; though if he did, it could be objected that his argument rests ultimately on the ontological argument (Eth. I 11), to which Eth. I 34, cited in Eth. III 6, refers. However, Spinoza does not stop at this point, but goes on to say that no thing has in itself that by which it can be destroyed, but rather is opposed to everything that can destroy it (Eth. III 4 and 5). From this he draws the desired conclusion. The relation between this part of the argument and the part that refers to God is not clear, but it is possible that Spinoza is offering what amounts to an alternative proof. If so, the proof seems to fail. In saying that a thing is opposed to everything that can destroy it, Spinoza is really making a logical point, of the following kind. If a thing is not opposed to everything that can destroy it, then something that can destroy it can be *in* that thing; but Spinoza has just shown (Eth. III 4) that a thing can be destroyed only by an external cause. Given the premises, the conclusion follows; but this is to say nothing about what a thing *endeavours*.

¹² Compare Spinoza's account of two types of desire in Eth. IV App., pars. 1-2; the one type consists of passions, the other of 'actions' (on which cf. n. 9 above).

¹³ It might seem open to Spinoza to say that the theory of *conatus* is about the way in which *most* people *usually* behave; in this form, the theory would state that most people most of the time (and perhaps some people all of the time) endeavour to preserve their own being. In other words, it could be seen as a theory about the average or typical human being, and as such it would be falsifiable. But Spinoza would not regard such a theory as his own. He is concerned to make universal statements about human beings, and not statements about what *most* people. do.

¹⁴ This is suggested by Eth. IV Pref., G ii.207: to say that habitation is the final cause of this or that house is to say that 'a man, from the fact that he has imagined the conveniences of domestic life, had the appetite for building a house'.

[15] Cf. H. Höffding, 'Das erste Buch der Ethica', *Chronicon Spinozanum*, ii, 1922, pp. 23, 39. The propositions in question are stated in terms of modes of thought, but may be generalised to cover modes of extension also, since 'the order and connexion of ideas is the same as the order and connexion of things' (Eth. II 7).

[16] Ep. 60, G iv.271; Wolf trans., p. 301. There, Spinoza is referring to God (cf. Eth. I 16 Cor. 1), but it seems that he could say the same of the *conatus* of a mode, such as a human being.

[17] See also Eth. I 32, *ad fin*. The words '*vel coacta*' seem demanded also at the end of the enunciation of this proposition, otherwise Spinoza will be opposing 'free' to 'necessary', which is not his usual practice. Cf. Ep. 56, G iv.259; Wolf trans., p. 287. See also L. Robinson, *Kommentar zu Spinozas Ethik* (Leipzig, 1928), p. 221.

[18] On what 'follows' from a thing's essence—i.e. from its *conatus* or power—cf. II A above.

[19] This would follow from Eth. I 29, which states that 'in nature (*in rerum natura*) there is nothing contingent'. The line of argument developed above is equally Spinozist, but is more concrete.

[20] Or (as implied by Eth. I 17 Cor. 2), that thing is called 'free' which exists and acts by the necessity of its nature alone.

[21] In Eth. IV Def. 8 Spinoza says that by 'virtue' and 'power' he means the same. If this were so, it would be hard to see why he should need the term 'virtue'. It seems more likely that he meant to say that by 'virtue' (which is of course connected with '*vir*', 'man') he means a type of power, namely human power. But the point is not of great importance.

[22] Cf. Eth. IV App., par. 7, which states that man cannot but be a part of nature and follow its 'common order'. (To speak of following the 'common order of nature' is to speak of external necessitation: Eth. II 29 Sch.).

[23] Cf. Spinoza's account of a 'passion' in Eth. III Def. 2; we 'suffer' insofar as something happens in us of which we are only a partial cause. It should be added that for Spinoza, 'passion' indicates impotence, Eth. IV App., par. 2, and so the man who has passions is *ipso facto* not free.

[24] Eth. I 28 is derived deductively from propositions about God, and there is no hint that it applies only to phenomena. It may be noted in passing that Spinoza's modes are not illusions; what would be an illusion would be the supposition that what are really modes of substance are separate and independent objects.

[25] Cf. Melden's rejection, p. 212, of the epiphenomentalist view that 'the status of a person reduces to the vaporous after-effects of physiological processes'.

[26] Cf. Ayers, *op. cit.*, pp. 68 ff., 80 ff.

Stuart Hampshire

Spinoza's Theory of Human Freedom

I

Stimulated by the other contributors to this issue, I return to Spinoza's philosophy of mind and to the account of freedom of mind which he considered compatible with the thesis of determinism.

Spinoza argued for the following propositions:

(1) For any human action or state of mind, a causal explanation could in principle be discovered of why exactly this action or state was performed or occurred.

(2) The explanation usually mentions modifications of things in the subject's environment among the principal causes of the action or state of mind. The action or state of mind is usually, at least in part, the effect of an interaction with external things; and the relation between the external things and the effect is a law-like relation. I add the qualification 'usually', because there are occasions on which a person's activity of thought proceeds independently of external things, in accordance with the universal laws of purely rational thinking.

(3) Human beings have a drive to preserve themselves, and a power of self-assertion, which has a physical and mental aspect, and which constitutes their essence as individuals. The mental aspect of this power is the capacity to think actively and the natural tendency to substitute clear and adequate thought for inadequate thought.

(4) Their actions and states of minds are, at least in part, effects, not only of external things, but also of their appetites, which are not

necessarily conscious, and of their desires, which are conscious appetites.

(5) Their fundamental appetite, from which all their more specific appetites are derived, is to preserve themselves and their own power and liberty in relation to external things.

(6) The power of thought can be expressed at different levels of activity, and at different levels of independence of particular external things. At the highest level of thought and of knowledge, and in the tracing of intrinsic logical connections between thoughts, the subject's activity is completely independent of particular external things in his environment. This activity of mind constitutes the freedom of the subject; for this activity is not to be explained as the effect of particular external things acting upon him.

(7) Different persons have this power of purely active thinking in different degrees, and each sane person has this power to some degree at some time. No one exercises this power for most of the time.

(8) Some men may sometimes be liberated, to a greater or lesser degree, from their passions and become more active and enjoy more freedom of mind. When this happens, an explanation might be given of why this happened; and this explanation would mention the fortunate effect of external things as well as the previous states of the subject, and his inherent powers.

(9) This partial liberation from the passions can be assisted in two principal ways; first, by an intellectual conversion consequent upon following the arguments which Spinoza provides. This is the utility of philosophy. Secondly, by medicine, that is, by an applied understanding of the mechanisms of the body; the powers of the body incorporate the powers of the mind, and mental and physical powers must increase or diminish in unison.

(10) Every man can truthfully say to himself that he *could* enjoy more freedom of mind than he actually now does: he could, if he resolved to turn his thought away, more than he does, from its passionate involvement with particular things around him and towards eternal things, which can be understood in the light of

reason. Reflecting on this possibility of liberation is by itself useful, although mere reflection is not by itself sufficient to liberate a man from his passions; for they depend upon his desires, which in turn depend, at least in part, upon the effect of external things upon him. Liberation from the passions is always partial, and most men will in all probability always be governed more by their passions than by their reason.

The following consequences can perhaps be drawn from this general position:

(1) Philosophical argument and moral exhortation are both useful and may often contribute to the liberation of men. It is not a waste of time to tell men how they ought to think and to live, and what the dictates of reason are, and what the genuine virutes of a free man are. Having these thoughts presented to them will have some effect upon their desires and interests, which determine their conduct.

(2) The moral virtues and defects of particular men are no less the intelligible effects of particular natural causes than the physical strengths and weaknesses of men. Any doctrine of moral responsibility which implies a sustainable distinction between natural and moral qualities is false doctrine.

(3) A truthful treatise on ethics, such as Parts II and IV of the *Ethics*, is to be compared with a treatise on medicine; it tells the reader what powers and strengths of mind a man may have, at best and at worst, and what the range of possibility is; and it describes the weaknesses men commonly have, and how these weaknesses commonly arise; just as a treatise on medicine tells the reader what an ideally healthy condition of the body is, and how various morbid states normally arise. The reader is told about the innate strengths of mind and of the body, and of their natural tendency towards a normal state, and of the external influences which will generally either sustain or undermine these strengths.

(4) On the other hand there is an important difference between the purpose of writing, and the effect of reading, a treatise on ethics

and a treatise on medicine; thoughts are altered by other thoughts, and bodily states and processes by other physical processes. Whatever a man thinks, his thought is *directly* affected by hearing or reading the thoughts of others, and either assenting to, or dissenting from, them. So reading a treatise on ethics, such as Spinoza's, and following its arguments, will have some immediate and direct effect, and be directly beneficial; but reading a treatise on the health of the body will only be indirectly beneficial, through the effect that it has on the subject's thought about the physical operations to be performed. So philosophy has a certain priority, or advantage, over other studies as an instrument for increasing human happiness; it has this advantage, because in reflection, which is the work of philosophy, thought is directly modifying thought. If you succeed in changing a man's conception of what is good for him, and therefore change the direction of his interests, you will directly affect his happiness.

(5) Spinoza plainly denies the following proposition: that to tell some individual what he ought to do (e.g. to be calm and rational and to look for causes) is to imply that there exists nothing which is sufficient to prevent that individual on that occasion from so acting. To prescribe what ought to be done is to say what a rational and free man would do. It is not useless to call attention to the dictates of reason, even if, in the particular circumstances, and because of the particular causal factors in the case, the particular man or men addressed will not follow the dictates of reason. Any attention to the dictates of reason will have some effect, and generally a good one.

II

We come therefore to the traditional and post-Kantian problem of free-will, and to the interpretations of the relevant uses of 'can' and 'could have', which Spinoza's doctrine allows.

First, a general point about 'can', to which Professor Parkinson alludes and which is not to be found explicitly stated in Spinoza. When we say of an individual, or of a class of persons, or of men in general, that they can do Y, or that they have the power or capacity to do X, the context determines what the implied conditions of the possible performance are. A power to do X is always a power to do X under certain conditions, supposed to be held constant in the context; and one cannot know a priori, but only from the context, what these limiting conditions are supposed to be. Unless we know what these supposed conditions are, we cannot determine the truth or falsity of the statement of possibility.

In the *Ethics*, and in the *De Emendatione*, Spinoza is appropriately concerned with the powers of men, and the powers of the mind, *in general*, and when men are functioning under the best possible conditions; and the limits of possibility here are set by the status of men as finite modes, and by their inevitable interactions with external things. He is not writing about the powers that you or I usually possess, or that you or I possess at any particular time. He does sometimes mention powers which all normal thinking men at all times possess; for instance, the power to form common notions and to apprehend immediately the truth of certain fundamental necessary truths. His discussion of the possibilities of improvement open to men, and of what they are capable of and can achieve, remains entirely general; and this is what one would expect in a treatise on ethics. The writer of such a treatise will naturally presuppose the normal conditions of social order as he knows them, and the normal variety of human dispositions, as he knows them, and then consider the gap between what men are capable of achieving under these usually prevailing conditions and what they would be capable of achieving under the best humanly attainable conditions. The absolute upper limit of possibility is fixed by more general philosophical arguments; men are finite modes, and what they can know and understand about the eternal structure of things is therefore limited.

There is a third kind of implied condition which someone writing a treatise on ethics is likely to invoke; the powers that men would possess if they thought correctly about ethics and if they recognised the truth of the writer's conclusions. It is a reasonable assumption that someone who writes about the utility of philosophy, as Spinoza does in the introduction to the *De Emendatione* and elsewhere, must believe that philosophical errors have helped to prevent men from achieving what they are capable of achieving under conditions of philosophical enlightenment. He therefore writes about the powers of men to do things which they do not now do, because of their curable illusions and intellectual confusions. Their powers are limited by purely intellectual errors and by false philosophies of mind. Their actual freedom and happiness are, in this particular respect, less than they *could* be—i.e. less than they would be, if they were converted by argument to a less partial understanding of their own powers and interests. For example, they have the power to control many of their passive emotions, and to substitute active emotions for them, provided that they once realise that the objects of their passive emotions are not the true causes of them, and provided that they set themselves methodically to understand the true causes of their emotions. Men are capable of enjoying much greater happiness than they ordinarily enjoy, and of freeing themselves from much fear and suffering, provided that they train themselves to think clearly in the manner that Spinoza describes.

It may in fact be beyond the power of any given individual reader of Spinoza to think sufficiently clearly, and with sufficient detachment, to liberate himself from his most destructive passions. There may be factors in his history and environment which have destroyed this power of detachment in him. A test of whether he does in fact possess this power will be found in his actual performances, and in the history of his thought, after his reading of Spinoza. An individual reader may even fail to understand, or fail to be convinced by, Spinoza's arguments, and his passions may make him cling to the conventional morality of free-will, divine freedoms and punishment; he may be incapable of enlightenment because of the ruling passions that overwhelm his detached thought. Spinoza cannot know what the effect of his argument will be in any individual case, unless he knows a vast amount about the history, and consequent temperament, of the person concerned. He can only hope that his arguments come to the attention of persons whose power of active, clear thinking has not been destroyed by their passions. Spinoza is certainly not always clear about the implied limiting conditions when he is writing about what the free man can do in the way of controlling and directing his emotions; sometimes he has in mind an ideal social order, and an ideal psycho-physical temperament, and conditions which, though not unattainable in principle, are very improbable; and sometimes he has in mind (particularly in his two political works) a not improbable, improved social order, and not improbable, improved psycho-physical temperaments.

When we consider the possibilities from the point of view of the reader, it is obvious, first, that he is interested at all times in increasing his own powers and liberty in relation to external things; this is the innate drive, or *conatus*, common to all men. Whatever a man's actual powers of mind may be at any time, and whatever the degree of his servitude to the passions and of his confusion of mind, he will wish to strengthen his own power and liberty, even if his attempts to do this are entirely misguided and if they in fact have the opposite effect. There is therefore a sense in which any man always sees open possibilities of action before him. At least he is always striving, or trying, to achieve a greater power and liberty, and a greater happiness, than he actually possesses, even though his conception of what constitutes his power and liberty may be entirely confused and erroneous. What he actually achieves will never be the effect only of his own efforts and activity of mind; it will also be the effect of the influence of external things upon his less than conscious thought and on his feelings. The principal difference between the comparatively free man, the successful Spinozist, and the unenlightened man, slave to his passions, is that the free man has an active understanding of the causes of his passions, and by means of this understanding, and of his scientific and philosophical interests, he is partially liberated from the passions. This is the turning point in Spinoza's theory which allows him, as he believes, to maintain the stance of a prescriptive moralist while still holding to the thesis of determinism. The thesis of determinism is that every case of success and every case of failure in self-liberation is to be explained by some antecedent natural causes, and that, given these antecedent conditions, the outcome could not have been different from what it actually was.

Spinoza's argument turns on his conception of thought and of reflection, developed as a correction to the Cartesian philosophy of mind. When I reflect on the causes of my particular beliefs, desires and sentiments, and ask myself why I have them, my beliefs, desires and sentiments are directly modified by the process of reflection. If the thought of the causes of my belief, or my desire, or my fear, is changed, the belief, or desire, or fear itself is changed. When the subject's conception of the cause is changed, the object of the belief, desire, or fear is usually changed also; for we cannot clearly specify the object of the belief, desire, or emotion without considering what determines us to have this state of mind or attitude, and what would change it. The questions 'Why do you think that?', 'Why do you want that to be true?', 'Why do you fear that?' are not independent of 'What do you think, want, fear?', and the latter questions are not independent of the former. The precise relation between specifying the cause and specifying the object is different in the three cases: Spinoza concentrates attention on the relation of the cause of the thought to the object, or content, of the thought.

Reflection is the normal functioning of the conscious mind. Beliefs and desires, and the sentiments compounded out of them, are constantly being changed, and directed towards different objects, not only by the association of ideas, but also by active reflection. These are the two mechanisms by which thoughts are recombined and modified: they are the two levels of thinking, the one passive and largely unconscious, the other constituting actively directed, fully conscious thinking.

Most of our ordinary beliefs, and particularly perceptual beliefs, are formed without conscious reflection and through the mechanisms of the association of ideas; they are not the outcome of conscious and controlled inference and argument. The beliefs and desires so formed may at any time be amended, and the associative links replaced, by conscious inference and argument, as a man actively reviews his own thought. This activity of conscious reflection on the sources of beliefs and desires justified Spinoza in taking the stance of a prescriptive moralist. He can reasonably call on his readers to examine, or re-examine, the sources of their beliefs, desires and sentiments, and to do this systematically. He proposes a programme of reviewing the interconnections of thought, and this programme is the first precept of the morality that he prescribes. Everyone is capable of this activity of reflection, though to different degrees, and therefore the prescription cannot be useless; not only that, but the programme shows thought as it can be in a rational mind, and makes explicit and clear the distinction between different levels of knowledge, a distinction that is confused and uncertain in most men's minds. The reader is given a clear target at which to aim; and having this target suggested to him will always have some effect upon his thought.

III

The causes of thoughts are other thoughts, and the laws of the concatenation of thoughts are either laws of association or laws of rational necessity. Every passage of thought, or sequence of ideas, is embodied in some physical changes in the body; and every bodily change is represented in thought, although not necessarily, or usually, in conscious thought. A man's desires and emotions are thoughts and they also represent a particular configuration of bodily elements. There are physical causes, within and outside the body, of the configuration of bodily elements, and the thoughts of the objects of desire and sentiments can be explained in accordance with the general laws of thought.

Professor Matson interestingly explains the identity of specific thought and specific bodily change by an analogy: a sequence of type, of inscriptions, can also be a sequence of meanings. I think that the analogy can be brought nearer to Spinoza's intention if the identity resides in the *activity* of writing the inscriptions and the *activity* of thinking the thoughts, which are both activities of a person. As he writes, and in writing, he thinks, and as he thinks, he writes. The sequence of thoughts is to be explained by the laws of thought; the sequence of muscular movements and the marks on paper by physical laws. Perhaps closer still; there is the physical activity of looking at an object (motions of muscles, eyes, and brain) and the activity of determining what it is: again, there is the bodily activity which heard music stimulates (motions in ears and brain et cetera) and the activity of descrying the musical themes. There is a sense in which thinking, as an activity, is inseparable from an activity within the body, and particularly in the brain. But there is no proper sense in which the motions in the body explain the changes of thought, or in which changes in thought explain changes in bodily states and motions. Thoughts cannot be subsumed under laws of motion, and physical motions cannot be subsumed under laws of the concatenation of ideas. My body physically records the features of the natural order, as external things impinge upon it: the collection of ideas, which constitutes my mind, is a reading or representation of this record.

Not all modifications of the body are at the same time modifications of consciousness. In Spinoza's theory of mind reflexive thought corresponds to fully conscious thought. There are many perceptions which are in no sense conscious perceptions. Active thinking is described by Spinoza as if it were a kind of perception, and he discriminates the different levels of thought by the nature of its objects as well as by the active-passive contrast. Common notions, which are Spinoza's version of innate ideas, are the natural materials of active thought. Their physical embodiments are universal features of physical things. Freedom, and liberation from the passions and from muddled thinking, depends on the power of an individual's mind to follow a truly consecutive order of thought, and not to be diverted by every transient stimulus from outside; and there is a corresponding power of the body to maintain itself in a normal state in spite of external disturbances.

Spinoza holds himself to be justified in describing at length the contrast between servitude and freedom of mind, because there is something that each individual can do to make himself less the slave of his passions than he actually is: 'Can do', where the implied condition is 'if he will constantly direct his reason to reflect on the causes of his passions', and if everything else is held constant. He has the power to reflect on the causes of his own beliefs, desires and sentiments; and, by reflecting, and by bringing the less than conscious causes to consciousness, he can change them. He *can* do this, in the sense that he possesses the requisite instruments of thought; but it does not follow that I, who possess these instruments of improvement, *can* use them, in the sense that there is no external cause which will prevent me from using them. Abstracting from the particular external causes that have formed, and are forming, my passions, it is true to say that I have some power, but not unlimited power, to liberate myself from my passions and to convert them into active emotions. But I will discover experimentally, that is, by trying, what limits have actually been set by particular external things and by native endowment on the full exercise of these powers. And there are general laws of psychology to be discovered which would explain by reference to causes my failures to think clearly about the causes of my passions, and which would thereby explain my failure to modify my passions. But each individual may usefully ask himself whether he is using his inborn power of clear and detached reflection to the utmost. From the standpoint of any individual, that is the central moral question.

There are two respects in which Spinoza's doctrine is altogether different from that of the ordinary scientific materialist:

first, Spinoza held that there was a peculiar feature of psychic causality, which sets it apart from physical causality, namely, that a man's thought about the causes of his thoughts modifies the original thoughts: secondly, that the operations of the mind, when employed on its proper business of pure thought, are not to be explained in the common order of nature and by transient causes; the mind is capable of following an entirely rational order of thought, and of being altogether independent of external causes. I cannot think of a scientific determinist who has suggested, or who would accept, either of these two characteristic doctrines of Spinoza. Spinoza is sometimes wrongly represented as defining the freedom of the agent simply as knowledge of the necessity of the causal connections that determines the agent's actions and passions: as if his philosophy of freedom was a form of stoicism. This is a misreading of the *De Emendatione* and of the *Ethics*. He does not identify freedom of mind with knowledge of the necessity of my actual states of mind; this is indeed a necessary condition of freedom, but it is not a sufficient one. Scientific determinism, and the doctrine that the agent's freedom consists in the recognition of the necessary connections which science discovers, are naturally and often combined in a single philosophy. But this is not Spinoza's final position in the *Ethics*, which makes larger claims, and upon two main grounds. First, that the knowledge that a man has *sub specie aeternitatis* of the rational order of things is a quite different kind of knowledge, and is part of a quite different state of mind, from the knowledge that a man may have *sub specie durationis* of the common order of nature: and secondly, a radical turning away, or conversion, from one level of understanding to another is possible for some men at some times, and temporarily. When this transition has been made, and while its effects last, a man is not principally interested in his own particular and temporary situation or in the objects and persons who happen to be in his environment. He enjoys his detachment from these interests and for a time he enjoys also a very clear and comprehensive vision of reality; and this vision has its own internal marks of adequacy and truth, and his mind is at rest in it and is satisfied by it. We all intermittently enjoy this satisfaction when our thought is rational and clear and entirely adequate. But very few men are capable of bringing their own immediate interests and passions under the continuing attention of this detached reason. When they do, they are free men, and they enjoy their power.

I do not claim to understand what Spinoza meant when he wrote of the immortality of the mind in some of its aspects. But it is certain that, unlike scientific determinists of the present day, he did claim that some thought is not to be explained within the framework of events in the common order of nature at all; such higher thought is to be explained by reference to a rational order which is not an order of temporal succession. Some part of one's mind survives the destruction of the body, in virtue of being part of the infinite idea which reflects the permanent structure of the physical universe. This claim is a corollary of the claim that, at the highest level of knowledge, men's ideas coincide with the infinite idea of God. This transcendence of the immediate environment, spatial and temporal, is the way to freedom of mind; and of course this is not a possibility which a scientific determinist recognises.

IV

As I have suggested elsewhere ("A Kind of Materialism," Presidential Address in *Proceedings of the Eastern Division of the American Philosophical Association*, 1970), the present relevance of Spinoza's philosophy of mind, as I understand it, is to be found in the twin doctrines (1) that causal explanation of thought differs from causal explanation of physical states in one respect: that the subject's inquiry into, and knowledge of, the cause always modifies the effect, and (2) that any thought can be made the object of another thought, and through this power of reflection human beings can be, temporarily and to some degree, independent of their environment in their activity. I think that (1) is a truth which is overlooked by most contemporary philosophers of mind. The argument in Part III and Part IV of the *Ethics*, sketching the conversion of the passions into active emotions, makes most of the essential points by implication rather than explicitly; and the scholastic terminology obscures the argument for a contemporary reader. I would restate the argument as follows. (1) The emotions and propositional attitudes are distinguished from each other principally by their actual and notional causes, where the notional cause is the subject's thought about the cause. (2) The subject's thought of the object of the emotion (what he fears, is angry with and about) and of the propositional attitudes includes a thought about the cause or occasion: if his thought of the cause or occasion is substantially changed, his thought of the object will be changed; and if the subject's thought of the object is changed, his dispositions and behaviour are correspondingly changed. (3) The subject of any emotion, or propositional attitude, which has an intentional object, has an authority, though not an overriding one, in determining what his state of mind is and what its object is (e.g. whether he fears and what specifically he fears): if he believes that he fears A, or is envious of B because of C, or that he is discouraged by D, or hopes for E because of F, this belief has to be included in any adequate account of his state of mind, even if the belief is erroneous. If the belief is erroneous, then his state of mind must be a confused and complex one.

It follows that if a man's beliefs about his own states of mind are changed, as a result of systematic reflection on causes and of a better understanding of the psychological laws involved, his emotions and his attitudes change also: and consequently his pleasures and pains, and his conduct: for men are governed by their emotions. That which a man thinks that he loves or hates, and the reason why he loves or hates it, as he thinks, may not coincide with that which, in the light of full self-knowledge, he would say that he loves or hates. But perhaps he does, to some extent and in some way, confusedly want what he thinks that he wants, merely in virtue of the fact that he thinks that he does, and because he therefore sometimes acts as if he does. Spinoza's account of the intellectually unenlightened man is a description of confused and conflicting emotions and desires, of 'fluctuation of mind'. The enlightened man, who has true beliefs about the causes of his own emotions and who knows clearly what he wants and why he wants it, is comparatively singleminded. A perpetual effort to be more detached and reflective is the best that we can do towards attaining some degree of self-knowledge and some degree of autonomy.

His is an interesting, not implausible, account of freedom of mind, as the detachment from causes in the common order of nature, a detachment that lasts while self-critical thinking lasts.

STUART HAMPSHIRE

WADHAM COLLEGE,
OXFORD

Wallace I. Matson

Spinoza's Theory of Mind

Spinoza has told us that knowledge of the union that the mind has with the whole of nature is the true and highest good (*De Intellectus Emendatione*, ed. Van Vloten and Land, p. 6). That union (*Ethics*, II, Prop. XIII) consists in the body's being the object of the idea constituting the mind; or as stated slightly differently (e.g., at II, Prop. XIX),[1] the mind's being the idea itself or the knowledge of the human body. If to interpret this cryptic pronouncement we appeal to the definition of idea as "a conception of the mind which the mind forms because it is a thinking thing," then mind turns out to be a conception which the mind forms of the body. This looks deplorably circular. Let us go at it more obliquely.

I. *The Division of Man*

Man is composed of mind and body (II, Prop. XIII, Cor.). Spinoza defines neither mind nor body. If this does not matter about body, which "exists as we perceive it," it is otherwise with mind, which in philosophy is a theoretical term. The distinction of these components in man is not obvious to perception, nor is it unambiguously marked in ordinary discourse, nor do philosophers who make the distinction agree on how to make it and what is to go on each side.

In considering Spinoza's use of the word mind it is not much help to notice that the *mens* of the *Ethics* is evidently the same as the *ziel* of the *Short Treatise*, for the soul presents at least as many problems of circumscription as the mind does. Perhaps Spinoza's shift of terminology between the two works is explained in the remark after the definition of *Mens* in the *Principles of Cartesian Philosophy* (VL page 118): "I speak here of Mind rather than Soul, for the latter is equivocal and often misused as a name for a bodily thing." But Spinoza would not accept the definition (or rather, theory) there given: "Substance in which thought inheres immediately, is called Mind"—and even if he did, it would not help us.

Before we can try to state Spinoza's theory of mind clearly, we need to know what comprised the denotation of the term for him. A survey of the *Ethics* shows that the mind, in general, acts (II Def. 3) and suffers (III 1); more particularly, it forms conceptions (II Def. 3); perceives (II 11 C) the body and what happens in it (II 12, 13), as well as the nature of many other bodies (II 16 C 1); remembers (II 17 C); knows itself (II 23) and the body (II 19) in a way, but in another way does not (II 23, 24), yet has adequate knowledge of God (II 47); imagines (II 17 S); affirms and negates (II 49 S); and restrains the affects (III 56 S). We are told explicitly that the mind does *not* form images (II 17 S), nor move the body (III 2; nor is the mind moved by the body), nor tremble or laugh (III 59 S).

This list is not consonant with ordinary English usage, nor, I daresay, Latin. We may say of a man that he has an active mind, but we do not construct such sentences as "my mind perceives my body," "my mind knows the nature of yonder tomato," "my mind restrained my lust," nor even, *pace* Descartes, "my mind is now thinking." In fact, a single instance is hard to find in which the word mind occurs straightforwardly as the subject of a transitive verb of action in the active voice. To point this out is not to reproach Spinoza for sins against language, but to show that he does use the word as a term of art whose meaning we must not suppose we know just because we pronounce the vocable every day.

The list is, however, a typical (incomplete) philosophical inventory of "the mind's operations." Perceiving, conceiving, remembering, knowing, imagining, affirming—why do philosophers pick these out to form a special list from which they exclude inspecting, composing, testifying, narrating, laughing, swearing, and digesting? They think of the former as constituting a natural class. What is its defining characteristic? To this question various answers are given, each of which supplies the substance of a "theory of mind": (1) that they are private; (2) that they are the immediate operations of the mind; (3) that they are the varieties of consciousness; (4) that they constitute the domain of the predicate "is certain of." But as for Spinoza, (1) he expressly rejects privacy (II 3); (2) he does not allow for any mediate operations of the mind with which these might be contrasted (III 2); (3) he does not make consciousness a necessary condition for mind (II 12 would otherwise be incredible), nor even a sufficient condition (III 59 S); and (4) he utterly rejects skepticism (III 10 *et passim*).

But the items in the Mind list have a negative characteristic in common: they are evidently not motions nor reducible to motions. They are human activities (or at any rate it is natural and tempting to use this word about them—they are at least happenings, changes of some sort) that do not involve gross, observable movements of the tissues. This is perhaps the real underlying rationale for the division between the mental and the physical that philosophers have drawn even when their official descriptions are in terms of other features. Motionlessness easily accounts for privacy: any outward sign, by which you might detect my thoughts, is necessarily a motion. But I can think without moving. And that, it seems, is all I can do without moving; thought and privacy are coextensive.

Having established this equation, other human activities such as piano-playing, lecturing, and fighting, which do include motions, and which seem to the naive observer to be unities (hence "I lecture," etc.—neither "my mind lectures" nor "my body lectures," much less "my mind and my body join in lecturing"), are philosophically analyzed into two parts, one the bodily motions, the other the motionless/"conscious" accompaniments.

This is the way Spinoza divided up mind and body, as appears from his making motion and understanding the immediate infinite modes of the attributes of extension and thought respectively (KV, Chapter 9)—indeed it is clear from the very distinction of the two attributes themselves. Understanding must here be taken as the name of the class of all items of reality, that can come within our cognizance, that are not particular modes of the infinite mode of motion and rest. Thus it includes feeling and willing, for example, and as we have noticed already, it is not limited to items of consciousness.

II. *The Mind-Body Problem*

Actions of the one class impinge on those of the other in almost everything a man does. But philosophers, including Spinoza, have concentrated their attention on two types of situations: sense perception and willing. To describe these as neutrally as possible: sense perception is when movements of the world exterior to my body induce motions in my body, particularly in the eyes and other sense organs, and concomitantly with these motions there occurs an awareness of some sensation or feeling. Willing is when I decide to do something—this deciding is an identifiable feeling, or if that is not the right word, at least it is an awareness—and shortly afterwards the appropriate muscles move to initiate the action decided upon.

Yet these descriptions are far from neutral—we don't use such words as sensation, feeling, and awareness in these ways, not because philosophy is so strange to us, but because this division is. Be that as it may, the happenings on the physical side are (and already were in Spinoza's day) in broad outline, subjects of uncontroversial knowledge. Spinoza expounds the physiology of sense perception in terms of a change in the body's proportion of motion to rest, brought about by external causes impinging on the sense organs, the change being propagated ultimately to the central nervous system (II 14 and preceding lemmata; KV, Appendix 2). In vision, an image is formed inside the body; but Spinoza warns us emphatically (II 48 S, II 49 S) not to confuse images, which are physical, "formed of bodily motions alone," "at the back of the eye, or, if you please, in the middle of the brain," with ideas, which are thoughts and not pictorial.

Spinoza had no need to discuss the physiology of voluntary action, which, once we get beyond its putative mental precursors, is if anything more straightforward in its physiology.

The Mind-Body Problem, generalized from such commonplace examples, may straightway be put as: How are those human activities that are not motions related to those that are? (For reasons mentioned above, Spinoza would reject the commoner but less perspicuous formulation, How is consciousness related to bodily activity?) But before going ahead to the philosophical theorizing, let us ask what need there is for it. Leaving aside the historically decisive motive, the desire to provide a separable personality to survive death, is there any reason not to be content with physiology? We want an explanation of sense perception. Why is it not enough to do the best we can to describe how the cornea, tympanum, taste buds, nerves and brain all do their work? That would be like the way we explain earthquakes, supernovas, and digestion. Why can we not set out the ascertainable facts, add "—and that is what seeing (smelling, thinking, deciding) is.", then stop? What would be left out?

Some philosophers have held that indeed nothing would be left out, that the physiological explanation is in principle complete. Rejecting the distinction between bodily motions and other human activities, they postulate micro-motions under the skin as the putatively private happenings. There can be no change of any kind that is not at bottom a motion of bodies, they hold. Significantly, they are accused of denying mind. But many will agree that Hobbes, the foremost advocate of this view, in the very act of stating it exposed its inadequacy: "All which qualities called *sensible*, are in the object that causeth them, but so many several motions of the matter, by which it presseth our organs diversely. Neither in us that are pressed, are they anything else, but divers motions; (for motion, produceth nothing but motion.) But their appearance to us is Fancy. . ." (*Leviathan*, Chapter 1.) For the Malmesburyan philosophy (so they say) here is forced into making two correlative distinctions in violation of materialist principles: the first, between motion and its appearance, the second, surreptitiously, between the us who *are* matter in motion and the us to whom the appearance of motion is "Fancy." And any attempt to make the appearance and the deutero-us into motions would generate a vicious regress. So, they conclude, physiology is not enough. Only philosophy can make the Mind-Body relation intelligible.

Spinoza did not deem reductive materialism worthy of discussion. In two passages of *The Improvement of the Understanding* the notion "that there are bodies which, by their composition alone, give rise to intellect" is offered as a specimen of obvious falsity; and he tells us that "when we know the nature of the soul, we cannot im-

agine it as square, though anything may be expressed verbally." In
the *Short Treatise* (Part II, Preface), seeking an appropriate
categorical pigeonhole for the soul by exhaustive division, he says
that soul "cannot be a mode of extension, because, etc."—which is
the *via brevissima* in refutations.

Spinoza has nothing to say about reductive idealism. Now if
not everything is matter, nor mind, the possibility still remains that
the two exhaust reality between them. And if the Mind-Body
Problem is a genuine problem, the dualist solution of Descartes is
perhaps the solution that presents itself with maximal obviousness,
and has the greatest immediate appeal. Thus Spinoza, who generally eschews polemics, devotes two fairly long passages (III 2 S and V
Preface) to its demolition. The attack is focused not on the doctrine
of two substances, from which his own view might be thought to
differ only subtly and minimally, but on the speculations concerning interaction. Thus Descartes has the honor (I use the word
without irony) of being the only philosopher of Spinoza's era to be
discussed by name in the *Ethics*. It suffices against the pineal gland
to set out the hypothesis in deadpan summary. In III 2 the target is
not an exclusively philosophical theory but the monarchical model
of man, which, though perhaps originated by philosophers and
theologians, has passed into the common consciousness. After
denying the possibility of interaction in III 2, Spinoza in the
scholium battles against our habit of conceiving deliberate action
as analogous to command and obedience (or rebellion). He is particularly concerned to abolish this kind of thinking because of the
support it affords to the doctrine of free will. He repeats his anti-
libertarian argument from I Appendix, that we believe we are free
only because we are ignorant of the causes that determine the mind.
Proceeding to observe that we are ignorant likewise of "what the
body, without being determined by the mind, can do. . . from the
laws of nature alone, in so far as nature is considered merely as corporeal," he instances the amazing feats reported of sleepwalkers.
This indecisive empirical argument should be read *ad hominem*, for
on Spinoza's own principles the separation of body from mind for a
method-of-agreement experiment is necessarily out of the question.
The passage is additional evidence that Spinoza did not equate
mind and consciousness.

III. *Mind and Body as Attributes*

From his rejections we can infer that Spinoza recognized two necessary conditions of an adequate theory of mind:

1. It should be nonreductive: mind is not really matter, nor is matter really mind. "The [material] object has nothing of Thought, and is *realiter* different from the Soul." KV, Appendix 2. "Man is composed of mind and body." (II 13 C.)

2. It should reject interaction: "The body cannot determine the mind to thought, neither can the mind determine the body to motion nor rest, nor to anything else, if there be anything else." (III 2.)

These conditions imply psychophysical parallelism, which indeed seems to be the express content of the master proposition II 7, "The order and connection of ideas is the same as the order and connection of things." We may thus be tempted not to take seriously Spinoza's insistence that mind and body are not substances but attributes of one substance, especially when we remember that not only substance but each attribute of substance must be "conceived through itself" (I 10). And after all, Spinoza himself apparently once used the words substance and attribute synonymously (KV, Chapter 7). If we see clearly that thought and extension have "nothing at all in common" (KV, Chapter 2), it seems merely verbal to explain their union by averring that they are united in God—like saying that parallel lines meet at infinity. Anyway, if you are going to insist on this device, why not make the connection of mind and body to be that of being joint effects of the divine causality—in other words, why not be an Occasionalist and have done with it? And language can be found susceptible of interpretation in such a sense.

Nevertheless, these speculations are unprofitable. II 7 S is decisive: "A mode of extension and the idea of that mode are one and the same thing expressed in two different ways," a dictum repeated at III 2 S. Mind and body cannot determine each other simply because nothing can intelligibly be said to interact with itself. And it is misleading, at least, to speak of "psychophysical parallelism" when the alleged parallels are not separable. The other label that one finds in the textbooks, "double aspect theory," presumably derives from the remark just quoted, "one and the same thing expressed in two different ways" (*"una eademque est res, sed duobus modis expressa"*). But this says nothing of two *aspects*, only of two *expressions*. The difference is important. Two aspects require two observers, or at least two observation points; and what might those be? That is how mythological entities proliferate.

But now, what has become of the distinction *realiter* between mind and body? To answer this question we need only to take seriously Spinoza's doctrine of one substance with different attributes. This is no mystery. Suppose the world were the infinite Library of Borges: we could describe it, Spinozistically, as one substance with two attributes, typography and meaning—which would be to say, we could give a complete description of the library in exclusively typographical terms, and another complete description in terms of meaning. Typography and meaning are distinct *realiter*, and it is nonsense to talk of one causing the other; yet a book is not an assemblage of two things, (1) letters and (2) meanings. Rather, the meaning is the idea of the typography.

This analogy is intended to be suggestive rather than exact, since meaning is a relation (involving a mind), hence cannot be "conceived through itself." (But later I shall suggest that perhaps neither can mind.) To take a more prosaic example: a world of individual material objects, with no variations in density. This would be one nature with at least two attributes, volume and mass. Given the volume of any thing, we could determine its mass, and vice versa; changes in the one would correspond exactly to changes in the other (cf. e.g. II 17 C, Demonstration, etc.); yet there would be no interaction between the attributes. It is nonsense, moreover, to speak of the length of mass or the shape of inertia. There would be, in short, a functional but not a causal relation between the attributes. And that is how Spinoza conceives mind and body.

Formally, then, the substance-attribute scheme affords adequate terms in which to conceive the union of mind and body. But we are still far from understanding the particular nature of their relation.

IV. *Mind: The Idea of the Body*

Spinoza says that the mind is an idea (or rather, II 15, a composite of many ideas; but it is convenient to follow Spinoza's usage of the singular number). The object of the idea is the body "and nothing else" (II 13). Some have taken this to express the paradox that my mind perceives only my body—a position that might be called psychophysical solipsism.

This is a misunderstanding. Spinoza repeatedly reminds us that the human mind can be aware of external bodies only through their effects on the perceiver's body (II 14-29, *passim*), and he expresses this notion, as so many philosophers do, in an alarming and pessimistic manner: "The ideas we have of external bodies indicate the constitution of our own body rather than the nature of external bodies" (II 16 C 2); "the idea of each affection of the human body does not involve an adequate knowledge of an external body" (II 25); all our perceptual knowledge, whether of external bodies, our own body, or even of our own mind, is "multilated and confused" (II 29 C). Nevertheless Spinoza allows us, though grudgingly, to perceive "the nature of many bodies" (II 16 C 1).

What is this perception? The tomato works on me, producing an image—an affection of my body, a change in the ratio of motion to rest, a physical happening. The idea of this affection is not some product of the affection, nor yet a miraculous counterpart, but the affection itself under the attribute of thought. It is necessary to emphasize the point: there is no process whereby the affection of the body gives rise to an affection of the mind; there is no mental receiver, bringing in the broadcast from the physical transmitter; still less is there a ghostly observer of interior theatricals. Nor yet are there two parallel processes; there is only the bodily process and the idea of it—roughly, as there are the letters C A T and the meaning they convey; or as when a governor mechanism whirls faster, the configuration changes so that the weights are farther from the center and the moment of inertia increases.

Neither the physical process nor its idea need terminate once the tomato has been recognized. Appropriate bodily organs and members may be caused to salivate and grasp; on the mental side the will may come into play, and from the affirmation "There's a tomato" I may proceed to the volition "I have to have that tomato." But (II Axiom 3; II 49 and Corollary) a volition is only a variety of affirmation, it is an idea. Indeed there are no separate mental faculties at all, there are only species of ideas. Not only is the notion of volition assimilated to that of affirmation, so is that of "affect," or, in later terminologies, passion or emotion. (III, general definition of the affects.)

Spinoza, like Schopenhauer, makes will or appetite to be the very essence of man (III 9 S) and indeed of all things. But he turns Schopenhauer around: will is explained as idea, not vice versa. The difference between the two thinkers on this point. however, may be merely verbal. Spinoza affirms of every thing, man, worm, stick, stone, that it endeavors to persevere in its being (III 6). Its effort to do so is its very essence (III 7); and the essence of every thing is its idea (I Definition 4). But Spinoza ascribes consciousness only to human beings and perhaps the higher brutes (II 22).

Bearing this in mind, we may make some progress in comprehending the intent of the grand assertion that (II 7) "The order and connection of ideas is the same as the order and connection of things." For every thing does endeavor to persist in its being; this effort is its essence or idea; hence it is not astonishing but obvious that there is an idea of every thing, and that these ideas duplicate the order and connection of things. It is not yet so obvious what the idea of a tomato (in this sense) has to do with what I think of as a tomato; and what it means to say that the mind is the idea of the body.

We can now essay answers to these questions. The tomato is not a conscious being, but it does endure and endeavor to maintain itself in existence—by which is meant nothing anthropomorphic but only such facts as that it offers some resistance to knives and forks. This endeavor is a sort of rudimentary affirmation of existence. Some of the consequences flowing from this positive characteristic may involve me, e.g., the tomato may be thrown at me. In that case a particular affection of my body results. I am conscious of this affection, i.e., the idea of it forms part of my mind, and it involves a reference to its remoter cause. Thus "my idea of the tomato" comes into being. It is miserably (and doubly) inadequate, but such as it is, it bears some relation to that adequate idea of the tomato which exists in God.

Here something should be said about the objection brought against Spinoza that he cannot allow for intentionality. A tomato (they say) is what it is, it has no meaning, it points to nothing beyond itself. Similarly with my body, or any other particular mode of extension. Now if "the order and connection of ideas is the same as the order and connection of things," every idea must be as devoid of intention as is its object. But that would be to deny mind.

The reply to this objection is to be found in Spinoza's recognition of the affective modes of thought: joy, sorrow, and all the rest that derive from them. Certainly these are intentional; they derive their origin from the idea *tout court*, just because (so Spinoza holds) there cannot be an affect without an object: that is to say, intentionality is of their essence. (II Axiom 3; discussion in KV, Appendix 2.) It is of the essence of the very idea itself as well, for the endeavor to self-preservation stems from self-love (*ibid.*). So far from not being able to account for intentionality, Spinoza in effect anticipates the definition of mind in terms of that notion.

To emphasize this, however, is to expose Spinoza to another fundamental criticism. He insists that each attribute not only can but must be "conceived through itself" (I 10). But it is hard to comprehend how thought can be conceived without reference to an object of thought, and that object, on Spinoza's own showing, must at least sometimes be an extended thing. This difficulty is (it seems to me) insuperable if intentionality is held to be a universal character of thought. But it may be permissible to doubt whether the absolute equality of the attributes is indispensable to Spinoza's philosophy.

In all this we should bear in mind Spinoza's warning (II 43 S) that by idea he does not mean "something dumb, like a picture on a tablet," but "a mode of thought, that is to say, intelligence itself." (Cf. II 49 S.) We do not contemplate ideas.

Thus to say that the mind is a conception that mind forms of the body, is as harmless a circle as "to be is to be the value of a variable." And "the mind is the idea of the body" says that the mind is (the summation of) the thinking (the affirming and negating) that a person does—"intelligence itself." This formula, so far from being obscure, suffers from the opposite defect of being so obvious as to be seemingly unhelpful. We knew that to begin with, we say. But did we really? Did we conceive of mind as intelligence itself?—or did we go on thinking, at least in our philosophical closets, of the mind as what we are intelligent *with*?

But where is the explanation of consciousness? Where is the solution to the Mind-Body Problem?—There is no Mind-Body Problem, Spinoza has told us. Consciousness has been explained in the only way it can be explained—in terms of the body, but functionally, not causally (*passim*, but see especially V 39).

Now we see why it is so hard to find the right label for Spinoza's theory of mind. If a theory of mind is a survey of thinking, willing, feeling, and the like—the natures of these concepts and their interrelations, our powers and limitations with respect to them—then Spinoza's theory of mind is by general consent one of the greatest contributions ever made to human understanding. It is not a rival of some other theory, hence needs no label.

But if "theory of mind" means psychophysical parallelism, two-way interactionism, double-aspect theory, epiphenomenalism, and all that, then Spinoza has no theory of mind. He leaves everything just as it is—in philosophy a feat as difficult as it is rare.

WALLACE I. MATSON

UNIVERSITY OF CALIFORNIA,
BERKELEY

NOTES

[1] References in the paper beginning simply with a Roman numeral are all to *The Ethics*. A following Arabic numeral refers to a proposition. This is sometimes followed by S, for Scholium, or C, for Corollary. Other abbreviations used in the paper include VL and KV. VL stands for Benedicti de Spinoza Opera Quotquot Reperta Sunt. Recognoverunt J. Van Vloten et J. P. N. Land. Editio Tertia. Hagae Comitum, 1914. KV stands for Korte Verhandeling (i.e., Short Treatise) van God, de Mensch, en deszelfs Welstand.

Douglas Odegard

The Body Identical with the Human Mind: A Problem in Spinoza's Philosophy

The question 'For Spinoza, what body is identical with the human mind?' deserves more attention than it has received. On first view it looks plausible enough simply to answer 'the human body', using the latter expression in its ordinary sense. Yet a second look, prompted by the question 'What then are we to make of the human brain?', can easily create dissatisfaction and send us searching for firmer guidelines in Spinoza's philosophy. I want to unearth such guidelines here. My investigation will be undertaken mainly from the viewpoint of someone familiar with issues of current interest in philosophy of mind. It will therefore be helpful to begin the discussion with a brief attempt to classify his general position on mind and body from a contemporary point of view.

I

For Spinoza, each existing thing, whether substance or mode of substance, is both mental and physical in the sense that it is conceivable either under the attribute of thought or under the attribute of extension: "substance thinking and substance extended are one and the same substance, comprehended now through one attribute, now through the other. So, also, a mode of extension and the idea of that mode are one and the same thing, though expressed in two ways" (II. 7 Sch.).[1] Since a human being is for him a mode of substance, a human being is therefore a single being conceivable either under thought as a mind or under extension as a body: "mind and body are one and the same thing, conceived first under the attribute of thought, secondly, under the attribute of extension" (III. 2 Sch.).

Spinoza thus rejects the Cartesian view that a subject of mental predicates cannot also be a subject of corporeal predicates.[2] The expressions 'mind' and 'body' must have a different meaning, since their use involves conceiving things under different attributes, but they are nevertheless coextensive. In rejecting a dualism of mental and corporeal subjects, he thereby undermines any theory which presupposes such a dualism: e.g., interactionism, epiphenomenalism, the doctrine of pre-established harmony, occasionalism, the view that a man is a composite of two subjects, and the view that a man is a mental subject who owns a corporeal subject.

Spinoza's position excludes the Humean view that a mind is a collection of mental states which, although they do not belong to a subject (either incorporeal or corporeal), are nonetheless in some way unified and associated with a given body.[3] Granted, at times he may seem to make the mind a mere collection of perceptions of various parts of the body, combined perhaps with certain other mental states. But even if he holds such a view, he still makes each collection identical with a body, and 'being identical with' is a stronger relation than 'being associated with'. Moreover, the way he talks about a body strongly suggests that a body is a subject of corporeal predicates (e.g., motion, divisibility, extension), albeit one which "exists in" substance.[4] It is not a mere collection of corporeal states. And since each mind is identical with some body, it is therefore unlikely that Spinoza would refuse to regard a mind as a subject of mental predicates. Of course, he does not think that for *every* feature f, if x is identical with y and x is f, then y must be f. For instance, if mind M is identical with body B, and M's fear of snakes causes M to feel faint, it would not be true to say 'B's fear of snakes causes B to feel faint'. All that would follow is the truth of 'B is identical with a being whose fear of snakes causes it to feel faint'. But the feature of being a subject of predicates seems to be of sufficiently fundamental importance that if $x = y$ and x is a subject of predicates, then y must be a subject of predicates.

G. H. R. Parkinson raises this problem and suggests that, although Spinoza refrains from a Humean "psychological atomism" (since for Spinoza ideas are modes of thinking substance), "the mind is simply a number of ideas, and is not something other than they."[5] Parkinson qualifies the latter remark, however, when he says:

he also holds that there is no mind other than its ideas—for what would 'the mind' be, other than will, intellect, feeling and so on? . . .Spinoza identifies the mind with its ideas—or, more exactly, he says that the mind is one idea, but an idea (E ii. 15) which is complex, being 'compounded out of very many ideas . . .'

A human mind, therefore, is a complex idea, and to say that the mind forms ideas is no different from saying that there are ideas which are constituent parts of a certain complex idea. (p. 103)[6]

Even when qualified, remarks of this sort can give the impression that for Spinoza a mind is nothing but a collection of mental states, such as willing, thinking or feeling, where each is a state of God, or, perhaps, that a mind is a single continuing perception of a given body, with states of willing, thinking and feeling organized together as parts of that single perception, where each state is a state of God. Such an impression is mistaken, I think, to the extent that for Spinoza a mind is something which perceives "its" body, which wills, thinks, feels, desires, and judges, which God can be said to "constitute" (II. 12 Proof), and through the nature of which God is "displayed" (II. 11 Cor.). Thus, it is not the case that God has certain bits of knowledge of certain bodies with human minds merely consisting in these bits of knowledge. God does have such knowledge, but only insofar as he is, or is modified as, the *thinking beings* who are those bodies and who as such must perceive them. To this extent a mind is not simply "a number of ideas" and it is something distinct from willing, thinking, and feeling in the sense that the sentence 'That mind is thinking' does not just mean 'That collection of mental states includes thinking' or 'That awareness of a body includes a thought'. This is not to say that a mind is either a substance or a substratum underlying mental states (see II. 10). Nor is it to say that a mind is something separable from mental states in the sense that it could exist without such states. It is merely to insist on a distinction between the concept 'a mind' and the concepts 'a mental state' and 'a collection of mental states', however such concepts might otherwise be related.

Now, such a view must, and can, allow room for saying that a mind *is* an "idea" which contains other "ideas" as parts, if this means that a mind is a mode of substance conceived under the attribute of thought with other modes, similarly conceived, as parts. Spinoza does use 'idea' in this quite special way (e.g., in II. 9 Proof, II. 12) and it is to be distinguished from a rather plainer use according to which, e.g., an idea is "the mental conception which is formed by the mind as a thinking thing" where "conception seems to express an activity of the mind" (II. Def. 3). Granted, his discourse sometimes puts considerable pressure on this distinction because he feels that a mode conceived under thought is related to the same mode conceived under extension in something like the way an "idea" and its "object," in plainer senses of these expressions, are related. He therefore finds it useful to talk about "God's having an idea of a certain body" instead of talking about "substance modified under both thought and extension" (see II. 11 Cor.). But this is because for him a mode conceived under thought necessarily perceives or knows itself conceived under extension (II. 12 and 13), as well as itself conceived under thought (II. 20), and thus God's knowledge of a mode conceived under extension is in part a matter of his being modified as that mode conceived under thought (see II. 9 Cor., II. 11 Cor., and II. 19 Proof). In calling a mind 'an idea of a body' he therefore has this feature primarily in view. But there is nothing in this view which obliges him to regard a mind as a mere mental state or collection of mental states.[7]

Before moving on, it is worth noting another way in which Parkinson's remark "to say that the mind forms ideas is no different from saying that there are ideas which are constituent parts of a certain complex idea" can be misleading. In one sense of 'idea', I, as a mind, am a complex idea to the extent that I am a mode conceived under thought and contain other modes, similarly conceived, as parts (see II. 15). For example, if one of "my" brain cells, C, is a part of "my" body, then C, conceived under thought, is a part of me. Now, it may be that Spinoza would say that when I am said to "have an idea" in a case where, e.g., I think of my wife, then there is a mode conceived under thought which is a part of me—say C conceived under thought—*and* that *this* mode is thinking of my wife. The ascription of the mental state 'thinking of my wife' to me is thus derivative upon the ascription of it to a part of me in the same way that ascribing an energy discharge to my brain might be derivative upon ascribing it to C. In this sense, *my* forming the thought is a matter of my containing an "idea" which forms the thought, and this could be the sort of thing which Parkinson is suggesting on Spinoza's behalf, with some effect I think. But the remark is misleading if it suggests that *every* ascription of a mental state to a human mind must be derivative in this sense. Just as, e.g., 'occupies *n* cubic feet' and 'is agitated throughout' are non-derivative corporeal state ascriptions, so there must be some mental state ascriptions which are nonderivative—perhaps 'knows the existence of the whole human body' or 'has an intellectual love of God'. To this extent as well, then, the mind resists being reduced to a mere collection of ideas.

Thus, it is inaccurate to say that for Spinoza a mind is nothing more than a collection of ideas or mental states. And it is even misleading to say that a mind is a complex idea without making it clear that this means that a mind is a mode conceived under thought with other modes, similarly conceived, as parts. On the other hand, although a mind is a subject of mental states in the sense of an individual who perceives, thinks, feels sensations, remembers, etc., the concept of a 'subject' is restricted in two important ways in this context. First, a mental subject is a modification of substance and does not have an independent existence; in other words, for any given mental subject, God is that subject, modified in a certain finite way. Second, a mental subject can have other mental subjects as parts. The "idea" of any part of my body, i.e. any part of my body conceived under thought, is itself a mental subject which is a part of me. It has its own mental states, although in some cases they may be ascribed to me in a derivative sense. Given these two restrictions, however, it is useful to portray Spinoza as someone who holds that a mind is a subject of mental states.

Since Spinoza acknowledges both minds and bodies, he avoids versions of materialism which reject the existence of minds and versions of immaterialism which try to do the same with bodies. His claim that each mind is a body is not the reductionist's claim that what we call 'a mind' is really only a body and not a mind at all. And his claim that each body is a mind is distinct from the idealist's claim that what we call 'a body' is nothing but a set of ideas existing in one or more minds—although he does hold that each body is in some sense perceived by a mind, viz. the mind which that body, conceived under thought, is. He also refrains from analyzing the concept 'mind' in bodily (including behavioural) terms and vice versa. The attributes of thought and extension are for him distinct expressions of God's essence and when we conceive things under each attribute, we engage in quite different conceptual activities. Indeed, the two activities are so different that if we mix the two kinds of concepts in a causal statement like 'He's perspiring because he's nervous', we fall into conceptual error (see II. 7 Sch.).

Spinoza is opposed to neutral monism to the extent that he leaves no room for the concept of an "intrinsically neutral stuff" by reference to which our mental and corporeal concepts might be constructed.[8] Something is what it is by virtue of sharing in God's attributes. This means that there is no way of conceiving x except under the attributes of thought or extension or under an alternative attribute. Therefore if x were not conceived as intrinsically mental or as intrinsically corporeal, x would be conceived under some other attribute. And, even waiving the fact that such a conception would be beyond human powers, this means that x would be conceived in a way which is just as separable from the concepts we have under thought and extension as concepts under extension are separable from concepts under thought. Consequently, such a conception would not yield concepts out of which our mental and corporeal concepts could be *constructed*. This would be like saying that one of God's attributes could be conceptually constructed out of some other attribute and for Spinoza that would be absurd.

Spinoza differs from central state materialism—the theory that the mind is contingently identical with the central nervous system—in four ways:[9] (a) He does not try to identify the human mind invariably with the central nervous system, nor, as I shall show below, is he committed to such a view. (b) He does not think that the identity of mind and body is a contingent matter; it is deducible from definitions and axioms which are eternally true. (c) He holds that all bodies, including so-called "inanimate" ones, are conceivable under the attribute of thought and are in that sense mental. (d) He thinks that everything which exists can be explained by reference to a comprehensive set of mentalistic laws as well as by reference to a companion set of physical laws.

In certain respects Spinoza's view is similar to the kind of position adopted by P. F. Strawson in "Persons," according to which a human being, or person, is a subject of both mental and corporeal predicates.[10] Like Spinoza, Strawson dismisses Cartesian and Humean dualism, avoids reductive forms of materialism and immaterialism, excludes neutral monism, claims more than a merely contingent connection between mind and body and refrains from identifying a person with the central nervous system. Unlike Spinoza, of course, Strawson does not think that every corporeal subject can also be correctly conceived as a thinking subject. Nor does he offer a metaphysics which makes a man a modification of an infinite being and introduces an infinity of attributes under which each man can be conceived. A less deeply metaphysical, but more interesting, difference, however, lies in the distinction between the Strawsonian remark 'A man is a single subject of both mental and corporeal predicates' and the Spinozistic remark 'A man is a subject of mental predicates when conceived under thought and a subject of corporeal predicates when conceived under extension'. Both remarks imply that there is just one subject throughout, but the second remark, unlike the first, warns us not to mix our mentalistic and physicalistic talk indiscriminately. Thus, Strawson allows us to say things like 'Your headache was started by the blow on your head' and 'He shivered because he suddenly felt a chill', whereas Spinoza rules them out on the ground that they illegitimately cross attribute boundaries: "Body cannot determine mind to think, neither can mind determine body to motion or rest" (III. 2). The only way such sentences can be true is by being elliptical for 'Your headache was the same as corporeal state C and C was started by the blow on your head' and 'His body shivered because physical event P occurred and P was the same as his suddenly feeling a chill' (see III. 2 Sch.).

In this respect Spinoza is closer to central state materialism than to Strawson, an affinity he expresses in the remark: "a mental decision and a bodily appetite, or determined state, are simultaneous, or rather one and the same thing, which we call decision, when it is regarded under and explained through the attribute of thought, and a conditioned state, when it is regarded under the attribute of extension, and deduced from the laws of motion and rest" (III. 2 Sch.). Indeed, I think Spinoza has a slight *initial* advantage over central state materialism in this respect. For, his rejection of discourse which illegitimately crosses attribute boundaries undermines the objection, often brought against central state materialism, that identifying something like the making of a decision with a bodily event generates the absurd consequence that the making of the decision is located somewhere in the body. Spinoza could accept the absurdity of bodily locating the decision-making and argue that, rather than sanctioning such an absurdity, the way he seeks to identify the decision-making with a bodily event explains why there should be just such an absurdity. He identifies the two events in such a way that they are really a single event conceived under two attributes—under thought as the making of a decision and under extension as a bodily event. Now, in conceiving the event as a bodily located event, we conceive it under extension. And if we try to conceive it *both* as the making of a decision *and* as bodily located, by thinking of it as a piece of decision-making *which is* bodily located, as distinct from a piece of decision-making which is identical with an event which is bodily located, then we illegitimately mix a concept appropriate within the attribute of thought with a concept appropriate within the attribute of extension. This is not to say that Spinoza faces no difficulties in this respect, however. For instance, his opponents could still press him to explain what 'is the same as' can mean in the context 'The decision-making is the same as a bodily event' beyond the unacceptably trivial 'occurs at the same time as'. He presumably would then have to appeal to the unified nature of substance and to the principle that different attributes merely constitute different ways of conceiving the essence of substance. At this point he and central state materialism would again be travelling on quite different metaphysical paths.

Summarizing briefly, then, Spinoza's general position on mind and body resists being placed in any of the categories commonly employed in philosophy of mind today. In certain respects he resembles Strawson. In others he resembles central state materialism. Yet he also differs from both positions and the differences should not be neglected merely for the sake of preserving a simple classificatory scheme. Indeed, since adopting a position on mind and body can involve answering a wide range of associated questions, it should be no surprise to find a philosopher who undertakes as synoptic an investigation as Spinoza falling outside a classificatory scheme which covers only a limited set of alternatives.

II

For Spinoza each human mind—in the sense of each human mental subject and not in the sense of a set of capacities which each human subject has by virtue of being mental—is a mode of substance conceived under the attribute of thought. You and I, conceived as mental beings, are paradigm instances of human minds. Now, in one sense of 'human body' it would be trivially true to say that the body with which the human mind is to be identified when conceived under extension is the human body. In this sense 'human body' just means 'the body with which the human mind is identical when conceived under extension'. But if we give 'human body' a more pedestrian use, such that in its mature stages a human body typically has as parts things like eyes, limbs, a heart and a brain, and typically is featherless and largely hairless, and so on, then the question of whether the body with which the human mind is identical under extension is a human body becomes interesting. Henceforth let us use 'human body' in this pedestrian way.

Spinoza himself seems to think that body B in the equation 'Human mind M = body B' is, at least within our experience, a human body and not just some part of a human body. For example, when he says "The object of the idea constituting the human mind is the body, in other words a certain mode of extension which actually exists" (II. 13), he makes no attempt to qualify his use of 'the body' to make it mean anything except what it would ordinarily be taken to mean in this sort of context, viz. the human body. Moreover, Postulates I-VI, which are introduced after II. 13 and which are intended to illuminate the nature of the "human body," introduce no such qualification. Indeed, Postulate II, which says that the "human body" is composed of "hard" as well as "soft" and "fluid" parts, and Postulate VI, which says that the "human body" can move external bodies in a variety of ways, could reasonably be taken to imply that B in M = B is at least not just the human brain.[11] Again, in the *Short Treatise*, he talks about our body when it was an "unborn child," i.e. an embryo or foetus, in a way which suggests that it is a human body and not just a part of the human body (II. Pref. note, sec. 10).[12] And in IV. 39 Sch., while discussing the radical changes which both the mind and the body can undergo, he refers to the circulatory system of the "human body," and talks about the body's becoming a corpse, in a manner which suggests that B in M = B is a human body. In III. 2 Sch., he refers to the mind's being in "a state of torpor" when the body is "at rest in sleep" and thereby suggests that the body is a human body at rest and not just some part of the human body. In the same Scholium he talks about "the actions performed by somnambulists while asleep" in a way which suggests both that the actions involve movements of the body identical with the given mind and that the actions involve movements of a human body and not just one of its parts, which again implies that B in M = B is a human body. And his remark that men often find it difficult to control their tongues implies that in many cases at least "a man's body" contains a tongue as a part and hence is a human body.

Although the passages I have mentioned do indicate that Spinoza likely thinks that B in M = B is a human body, there is still room for wondering whether his general philosophical system *entitles* him to hold such a view. There is no particularly firm commitment in the given passages and if his general system did yield a reason for thinking otherwise, then either the passages or our interpretation of them could easily be altered to accommodate the change. To help remove this source of doubt, I therefore want to introduce two Propositions which for Spinoza might, either individually or jointly, provide a criterion for determining B in the equation M = B and which do support the view that B is usually a human body. The two Propositions are:

(a) "Whatsoever comes to pass in the object of the idea, which constitutes the human mind, must be perceived by the human mind, or there will necessarily be an idea in the human mind of the said occurrence. That is, if the object of the idea constituting the human mind be a body, nothing can take place in that body without being perceived by the mind." (II. 12)

(b) "The human mind does not perceive any external body as actually existing, except through the ideas of the modifications of its own body." (II. 26)

Let us discuss each Proposition in turn.

(a) II. 12 implies that if M = B, i.e. if B is the "object" of the "idea" which constitutes M, then M perceives whatever "comes to pass" in B. And since there is no evident reason for Spinoza not to accept the converse of this implied conditional as well, II. 12 strongly suggests that M = B if and only if M perceives whatever comes to pass in B, thereby yielding a criterion for determining B in M = B.

Now, on first view such a criterion seems to face a difficulty in having to make 'perceives' broad enough to accommodate the "perceptions" of individuals who are "asleep" and yet not dreaming (e.g., when they are sleep-walking; see III. 2 Sch.), while keeping 'perceives' narrow enough to rule out the possibility of an individual's perceiving all the events in a large number of bodies, including bodies which Spinoza would want to regard as external to that individual. Parkinson suggests two ways in which Spinoza might try to explain the relevant concept of 'perception':[13] (i) In "perceiving all that happens in his body" a man does not have an idea of *every* event occurring in his body—say everything which happens at a cellular level. For, ideas of cells are of an "infra-human grade" and hence form no part of the human mind. It is simply "that a man's thoughts are the correlate to the functioning of his organism as a whole (and in this sense all that happens in his body is 'perceived')." (ii) Ideas of events in the body *are* contained in the mind but in many cases they do not involve the mind "noticing" anything, in much the same way that Leibniz's "petites perceptions" do not involve the percipient's noticing their objects.

Although the negative force of (i) and (ii) is clear—viz. either the mind does not contain an idea of everything which happens in the body or the mind does not notice everything occurring in the body—the affirmative content of each proposal is problematic. In the case of (i) it is difficult to see what positive meaning the claim 'A man's thoughts are the correlate to the functioning of his organism as a whole' can have and therefore what sense it gives to the claim 'A man perceives all that happens in his body'. In the case of (ii), the analogy with Leibniz's doctrine of "petites perceptions" is unfortunate, since for Leibniz such perceptions represent the way in which a finite monad mirrors the *whole universe*, whereas the concept of perception appropriate here must be one according to which a mind's perceptions are restricted to the body with which it is identical.

Perception in the context of II. 12 is a matter of acquiring knowledge of the given body, specifically knowledge of "whatsoever comes to pass" in the body.[14] It is something which the mind identical with that body must have and, I have suggested as a natural extension of Spinoza's view, if a mind M perceives everything oc-

curring in body B, then M and B are identical. Spinoza arrives at
this position through holding that God's knowledge of whatever
takes place in the "object" of an "idea" is in God not insofar as he is
an infinite being but insofar as he is modified as that idea (as well
as insofar as he is modified as other ideas causally related to that
idea).[15] Now, it seems to me that Spinoza can hold the view that
God's knowledge of "whatsoever comes to pass" in body B is (in
part) a matter of his being modified as the idea of B, i.e. as the
mind which is identical with B, without concluding that God must
thereby come to know everything in B to such an extent that he
thereby comes to know everything occurring in every part of B,
however small. Spinoza is obliged by II. 9 Cor. to hold that if *b* is a
part of B and *m* is the mind identical with *b*, then God knows
"whatsoever comes to pass" in *b* (partly) by virtue of being
modified as *m*. Spinoza is also obliged by II. 15 to hold that *m* is a
part of M. But from these two views it does not follow that God
must come to know whatsoever comes to pass in *b* by virtue of being
modified as M. Consequently, we can, I think, understand the force
of 'The human mind must perceive whatsoever comes to pass in the
body' in II. 12 in such a way that, *within certain limits*, the mind
must perceive everything which happens in the body identical with
it. To this extent Parkinson's proposal (i) is closer to Spinoza than
proposal (ii). But as yet nothing has been said to indicate the
nature of the appropriate perception or the limits within which it
must operate.

A clue to understanding the relevant form of perception is
given by Spinoza in the *Short Treatise* when he characterizes the
soul's awareness of a change in itself as a "sensation" (II. Pref. note
sec. 13). At the moment, e.g., I feel a chill in my right foot, feel my
stomach moving slightly and feel the back of my neck getting ap-
preciably warmer, and I do so without touching my foot, stomach,
or neck. In a sense, then, I can be said to have "sensations" of
coldness, motion and warmth in different parts of the body normally called 'my body'. I can also, in this nontactual way, feel my whole
body undergoing some sort of energy change as it moves from the
desk to the door. This is a type of perception which other human
minds do not share, indeed could not share without in some sense
coming to share the body itself. And this is the type of perception, I
think, which Spinoza has in mind in the context of II. 12. Since (1)

others cannot nontactually feel what I nontactually feel, (2) nontactual feeling typically encompasses the whole body within its "perceptual field," and (3) an embodied mind cannot normally be conscious without nontactually feeling its own body and events in it, nontactual feeling constitutes an important access to what is happening within a given body, an access which is so important that a complete knowledge of what is going on in a particular body would be impossible without it. Thus, if God is to know what is happening in a given body insofar as he is modified as the mind identical with that body, then it is plausible to say that God must nontactually feel, and in this way perceive, what is happening in that body. I suggest, then, that "perception" in the context of II. 12 consists in the nontactual feeling of what is happening in one's body.

If this account is correct, then perception in II. 12 *is* limited in terms of its possible objects. For one thing, a mind cannot nontactually feel everything occurring in every part of its body, since, e.g., cellular activity is beyond this mode of perception (although the behaviour of one's cells may be identical with something which one nontactually feels). Indeed, there are certain bodily events which may even be theoretically beyond any mode of human perception—say events describable in genetic terms—and these would be outside the range of nontactual feeling. Secondly, one does not nontactually feel things like colour changes, the production of sounds, and changes in tastes or smells—though again what one nontactually feels may be identical with an event of this sort. Consequently, II. 12 cannot include such events among the relevant happenings in the body without broadening the scope of 'perceive' to include visual, olfactory, auditory and gustatory forms of perception, and I suspect Spinoza is not interested in doing this, since such forms of perception do not provide a special access to one's own body.[16] What Spinoza is saying in II. 12, then, is that a mind must perceive whatever occurs in the body which is capable of being perceived via nontactual feeling.[17]

Now, it is true that many of the things which we nontactually feel are not noticed by us. Normally we are too intent on other things to pay much attention to the changes we feel occurring in our bodies. To this extent Parkinson's proposal (ii) is correct and the comparison with Leibniz accurate. It also seems true that in certain

unusual cases, a man can be anaesthetized in such a way that he
cannot nontactually feel certain parts of his body and the things
happening in those parts, even though such events are the sorts of
events which normally fall within the scope of nontactual feeling. In
cases of this sort Spinoza might have to appeal to a rather more
radical form of "unconscious" perception and then the comparison
with Leibniz would become stronger. On the other hand, he might
simply say that in this case, although the "idea" of the given bodily
part itself feels what is going on in that part, and although that
"idea" is a part of the human mind, the human mind does not itself
feel what is happening in the bodily part.[18] In that event his explanation would come closer to Parkinson's proposal (i). At any
rate, however Spinoza might adjust his view to accommodate cases
of this sort, it seems clear that for him a mind must nontactually
feel, or at least in some sense of 'be able', be able to feel nontactually, the various things which occur in the body identical with it and
which are capable of being perceived via nontactual feeling. And, I
suggest as a reasonable extension of this view, if a mind M can nontactually feel the appropriate events in body B, then B is the body
identical with M. Consequently, one criterion for identifying B in M
= B is 'M = B if and only if M is able to feel nontactually the events
occurring in B'.

I think some confirmation for this interpretation is provided by
Spinoza's view of the primary emotions of pleasure and pain. If
'emotion' is used to pick out a state under the attribute of thought,
then an emotion is an idea of a modification of the body, "whereby
the active power of the said body is increased or diminished" (III.
Def. 3). For Spinoza, each thing, conceived under either thought or
extension, "endeavours to persist in its own being" (III. 6) and has a
certain "active power" to so persist. If that active power is increased, the individual passes to a greater perfection and this
change under thought is called 'pleasure'. The opposite change is
called 'pain'. Thus, pleasure is an idea of a change for the better in
the body and pain an idea of a change for the worse; and having
such an idea itself constitutes a corresponding change in the mind
(see II. 11 Sch.).

For Spinoza, then, M = B only if M's pleasure consists in M's
"having an idea of" an increase in B's active power. And I think
that M's having an idea of an increase in B's active power must be

understood in such a way that it at least involves M's nontactually feeling B's states. For, it is only in this way that M can acquire a suitably intimate knowledge of an increase in B's power to persist—a sense of "bodily well-being" as it were. Also, it is only in this way that M's knowledge of the increase in a body's active power can involve the concern which is necessary in order to make it an emotional state. Indeed, there might even be room within such a theory for developing a concept of "bodily located" pleasure by construing M's feeling pleasure with respect to a certain part of his body as M's nontactually feeling an increase in the active power of that particular part. Similarly, feeling a bodily located pain would be a matter of nontactually feeling a decrease in the active power of the appropriate bodily part. At any rate, however the theory is elaborated, we can use it to construct a criterion for determining B in M = B which will serve as a companion to the one introduced above, viz. 'M = B if and only if M's pleasure involves M's nontactually feeling an increase in B's active power and M's pain involves M's nontactually feeling a decrease in B's active power'.

(b) II. 26 suggests the criterion 'M = B if and only if M's perception of an actually existing external body is achieved "through" the ideas of the parts of B'. The notion of perceiving a body "through" certain ideas is a causal notion. II. 26 is derived from "The order and connection of ideas is the same as the order and connection of things" (II. 7) and the order mentioned in II. 7 is a causal order. What Spinoza is claiming, then, is that (1) just as certain bodily events are causally determined by the state of certain parts of the body in which the events occur, so the mental events identical with those bodily events are causally determined by the ideas of those bodily parts, and (2) human perceptions of actually existing external bodies are mental events of this sort.

The problem now arises of how we can make use of such a criterion. In order to use it, we must be able to pick out the ideas which are causally responsible for our perception of actually existing external bodies. But it is of no help to say 'Such ideas are the ones identical with the bodily parts which causally determine the bodily events identical with our perceptions'. For the problem here is to discover just which bodily events are identical with our perceptions. What we must do instead is introduce an assumption which will enable us to bridge the gap between Spinoza's way of regarding the causation of perception and the more usual interactionist's way of looking at it. The assumption is that whenever an interactionist thinks that a given perception is causally dependent upon a certain bodily part and within the framework of interactionism he has not made a mistake, then, although for Spinoza he has made a metaphysical mistake precisely because he is an interactionist, he has his nonmetaphysical facts right. Thus, what he describes as a case of a perception's depending upon the state of such and such a bodily part is in reality a case of the perception's depending upon the idea of the given part. The assumption is, then, that if the *only* reason for rejecting the claim 'Perception P depends upon bodily part *b*' is that it implies mental-corpeal interaction, then we thereby have a reason for saying 'P depends upon the idea of *b* (i.e. *b* conceived under thought)'. Given this, then the proposed criterion in effect says: 'M = B if and only if it is correct within the framework of interactionism to think that M's perceptions of ac- tually existing external bodies causally depend upon parts of B'—or, more briefly, 'M = B if and only if M's perceptions of ac- tually existing external bodies *ostensibly* causally depend upon parts of B'.

Spinoza's Proof for the Corollary of II. 26 draws on the point. that the mind perceives an actually existing external body insofar as the external body has an effect on the mind's body and the resulting changes in the mind's body eventually yield an event which conceived under thought is the perception. In terms of the proposed criterion this is to say that the perception ostensibly depends upon the states of those parts of the body which are affected, either directly or indirectly, by the action of the external body on the body. He elaborates on this process a bit in Postulate V and the Proof to II. 17 Cor. Postulate V says:

> When the fluid part of the human body is determined by an exter- nal body to impinge often on another soft part, it changes the sur- face of the latter, and, as it were, leaves the impression thereupon of the external body which impels it.[19]

In the Proof he repeats the Postulate and then goes on to explain what is involved in the mind's taking an external body to be present when it is not. It is a matter of the mind's "taking cognizance" of the refraction of fluid parts from surfaces of soft parts which have retained an impression originally produced by the action of an external body. Thus, the parts of the body through which the mind ostensibly perceives actually existing external bodies include soft and fluid parts of the body, and these are plausibly associated with the central nervous system. Consequently, if we were to use the criterion proposed here for determining the identity of B in M = B, we should pick out at least a central nervous system. The question now is 'Does the criterion justify our picking out anything more than this?' The first criterion clearly indicates that B in M = B is the whole human body and not just a part, since normally M can nontactually feel what goes on in a whole human body and not just a part. But does the second criterion allow us to go this far?

As it stands, the second criterion does not rule out such a conclusion. It says 'M = B if and only if M's perception of actual external bodies ostensibly depends upon parts of B'. Now, although the fluid and soft parts which Spinoza has in mind in II. Post. 5 and II. 17 Cor. may just be parts of the central nervous system, nevertheless since the central nervous system is a part of the human body, the fluid and soft parts are also parts of a human body. Consequently, as it stands the criterion *can* indicate that B in M=B is a human body. Moreover, it is not certain that for Spinoza the perception of an actual external body does ostensibly depend solely on the nature of neural processes. Granted, he does seem to focus on neural processes in II. 17 Cor., but this is precisely because he there wants to indicate the conditions of our seeming to perceive external bodies when there really aren't any, conditions which are in part, but only in part, the same as conditions governing our perception of actual external bodies. And, I suggest, the latter conditions differ from the former not only in including the existence of external bodies but also in including the action of external bodies on the mind's body through bodily parts like the sense organs. In that case the second criterion also clearly dictates that B in M = B is a human body.

III

Before considering what I think is a serious objection to the view that for Spinoza, B in M=B is a human body, I want to answer very briefly five questions about the second criterion and one question about the two criteria taken together.

(1) "Since external bodies have an ostensible causal role to play in the production of perceptions, how can an appeal to the ostensible causal conditions of perception serve to distinguish external bodies from the mind's body?" The second criterion does not appeal just to the ostensible causal conditions of perception. Rather, it refers to bodily parts through which a mind has perceptions of a certain kind, where these bodily parts persist through a number of experiences. Unlike external bodies, their causal connection with perception is of an enduring nature.

(2) "Components of a perceptual medium (e.g., light particles) have a more enduring ostensible link with perception; therefore why doesn't the second criterion make such components part of B in M= B?" The causal factors which the second criterion picks out must be parts of a body, and not just members of a collection of bodies.

(3) "As it stands the second criterion introduces ostensible causal conditions of our perception of *external* bodies; therefore doesn't it presuppose the ability to pick out which bodies are external and which are not?" This is a cogent objection and it indicates a need to alter the criterion. Such an alteration can be achieved, however, by replacing 'our perception of external bodies' by something like 'our visual, auditory, tactile, olfactory and gustatory perceptions of actually existing bodies', provided that (e.g.) 'visual perception' is used in such a way that having a visual perception doesn't *conceptually* involve being a body with eyes.

(4) "Spinoza's remarks about "images" suggest that he would accept the practical possibility of someone having perceptions which are ostensibly produced by brain probing; in such a case would the probe be a part of the body according to the second criterion?" The criterion is working with ostensible causal determinants of our perceptions of *actually existing* bodies, whereas in the brain probe case the mind's experiences would not fall into this category—even if a description of what is experienced happens to be quite similar to a description of an external body in the mind's immediate environment (cf. having a dream which happens to coincide with real events occurring in the bedroom while one is asleep).

(5) "Does the second criterion leave room for the possibility of someone's perceptions ostensibly depending on the state of parts of

someone else's body—e.g., A's visual perceptions ostensibly depending on whether B's eyes are open?" If Spinoza wanted to preserve such a possibility, then he could adjust the second criterion accordingly by making it read 'M = B if and only if M's perceptions of the appropriate sort ostensibly depend *by and large* on the state of B's parts'. The criterion would then only rule out the possibility of the *bulk* of someone's perceptions being ostensibly dependent on someone else's bodily parts and this seems fair enough. I somehow think that Spinoza would feel that this is being too generous to the question, however. In a case where M's visual perceptions ostensibly depend on whether someone else's eyes are open and healthy, Spinoza would at least insist, I think, that M's visual perceptions must also ostensibly depend upon the state of M's own eyes. Otherwise it might simply be that M is having certain visual experiences which at most happen to coincide with the way certain external bodies are, experiences which are ostensibly causally connected to someone else's eyes. Also, the perspective of M's visual and tactile perceptions, if they are genuine perceptions of existing bodies, must be ostensibly determined by the positioning of M's bodily parts and not by someone else's. For example, if I tactually feel from perspective P1 and see from perspective P2, and if P1 and P2 are radically different (i.e. they are not just from different locations within the space occupied by a single body), then either my tactual or my visual perceptions are not of actually existing bodies. And if P1 falls within the set of perspectives determined by my body, then whereas I feel actually existing bodies I cannot be seeing any. Thus, although Spinoza might tolerate the possibility of someone's perceptions being to some extent ostensibly dependent upon someone else's bodily parts, his tolerance would probably be severely restricted.

(6) "Are the two proposed criteria for identifying B in M = B consistent?" An imaginary case which might lead us to think not is one in which M sees from a perspective determined by a pair of eyes E1 but M cannot nontactually feel E1. Instead he nontactually feels a different pair of eyes E2—e.g., he feels their lids open, feels them move, feels some soreness in them—and the perspective determined by E2 is radically different from that of E1. Thus, E1 and E2 are parts of different bodies B1 and B2. And say that M's visual, auditory and olfactory perceptions are all ostensibly dependent

upon parts of B1. Say also that the other objects of M's nontactual feeling are events in B2. By the first criterion M = B2, but by the second criterion it might seem that M = B1.

Spinoza can avoid this consequence, I think, by arguing that since M nontactually feels B1 and things happening in B1, M's *tactual* perceptions of actual bodies must ostensibly depend upon parts of B1. For example, I cannot nontactually feel the interior and exterior of a certain finger unless I can touch things ostensibly by using that finger. Indeed, he might even make the same point about gustatory perceptions, since they seem closely tied to tactile perception. Given this, he can then argue that M's visual, auditory and olfactory perceptions of actually existing bodies are not really ostensibly dependent upon B1, since the visual, auditory and olfactory experiences in the imaginary case are not perceptions of actual bodies. Therefore the second criterion does not make M = B1.

As I have indicated, the two criteria do support the view that B in M = B is normally a human body and not just a part of a human body. The first criterion clearly offers such support. The second criterion at least accommodates the view and, if developed in a certain way, will provide positive support. We should be careful, however, to avoid concluding on Spinoza's behalf that B in M = B is *necessarily* a human body. For example, it seems possible for a mind M to feel nontactually a certain brain and its parts, and for M's perceptions of actual bodies to be ostensibly dependent on the brain's parts, in a situation where the brain is not a part of a human body. The brain would itself be equipped with various sensors and would be connected to some sort of life support system. M might even be able to manipulate the brain in certain ways and use it to produce visual or auditory signs which are intelligible to others. In that case the two criteria would decree that B in M = B is a brain and not a human body.[20]

If it is possible for a mind to be identical with a brain in such a situation, however, then someone might raise the following objection against Spinoza's making the mind identical with anything more than a brain in *any* situation, including situations of a kind familiar to us:

> In any situation in which we are inclined to think that B in M = B is a human body (H), it is theoretically possible to detach the brain (b1) contained in H in such a way that the detached brain

(b2) will produce intelligible signs, will ostensibly solve intellectual puzzles and communicate its solutions, will ostensibly move
about with a purpose, will ostensibly claim to be M, and so on.
Consequently, it is reasonable to think that M would *be* b2. But
since b2 = b1 and b1 ≠ H, therefore M ≠ H. Therefore even
before any such cerebral detachment B = b1 and B ≠ H. Thus, in
no case is B in M = B a human body.

Spinoza can meet such an objection by denying that the mind
identical with b2 is M. The criterion of the identity of a mind
through time, which he suggests in the *Short Treatise*, II. Pref. Note
and in II. 39 Sch., allows him to reject such an identity. His
criterion simply says that, just as the preservation of a certain
proportion of motion and rest is necessary and sufficient for a
body's continuity, so the preservation of an idea of that proportion
is necessary and sufficient for a mind's continuity. And there is
nothing in the given imaginary case which entails that M and the
mind identical with b2 are or have ideas of the same proportion. All
we have is a situation in which the mind identical with b2 is
strikingly similar to M in certain respects, and this can be explained just as effectively by saying either that the mind identical
with b1 has undergone a radical change in certain of its features, or
that the mind identical with b2 has just been newly created. Now,
there is a species of this situation about which Spinoza *could* say
that the mind identical with b2 is M. This is a situation in which H
becomes b2, say by gradually shrinking and changing its shape,
while somehow keeping its proportion of motion and rest intact.
But then the imaginary case would no longer afford a reason for
thinking that M ≠ H, since b2 now = H. Granted, it would still be
the case that b2 = b1 and b1 ≠ H, but identity does not have to be
transitive when one of the identities in question has to do with
simultaneous identity (in this case 'b1 ≠ H') and the others have to
do with identity through time (viz. 'b1 = b2' and 'b2 = H'). Thus,
the imaginary case would no longer support the claim that B in M
= B is never a human body.

In conclusion, then, Spinoza's general philosophical system
does allow him to think that the body identical with a human mind
is, within our experience, normally a human body. Two important
Propositions within his system underwrite such a view and I can
find nothing which either opposes the view or opposes the use of the

two Propositions for this purpose. This does not mean, of course, that I have considered every question which one might raise in connection with Spinoza's conception of the "human body." For example, I have said nothing about the problem of reconciling his antidualism with the Proposition "The human mind cannot be absolutely destroyed with the body, but there remains of it something which is eternal" (V. 23). Nor have I considered what function the mind's being an idea of the body plays in the mind's acquisition of adequate knowledge. I have restricted myself just to those questions whose answers have a direct bearing on whether Spinoza can justifiably hold that the body identical with the human mind is a human body. The remaining questions must await investigation elsewhere.

DOUGLAS ODEGARD

UNIVERSITY OF GUELPH

NOTES

[1] This is, *Ethics*, Book II, Proposition 7, Scholium. Translations are those of R. H. M. Elwes.

[2] In this respect Spinoza may be called a 'monist' and Descartes a 'dualist'. If 'monist' and 'dualist' are used to mark a different contrast, however, then the same result need not occur. See Jonathan Bennett, "A Note on Descartes and Spinoza," *Philosophical Review*, **74** (1965), 379-80.

[3] Whether Hume himself actually holds this view is of no importance here. This question turns, I suppose, on whether he allows for the existence of *anything* beyond impressions, ideas, beliefs, judgments, habits, etc., and therefore whether he regards the class of bodies as a distinct category. It also turns on the extent to which he is consistent in his treatment of the "self" and related topics. On the latter question see James Noxon, "Senses of Identity in Hume's *Treatise*," *Dialogue*, **8** (1969-70), 367-84.

[4] For example, consider his remarks in the Axioms, Lemmata and Postulates following II. 13.

[5] *Spinoza's Theory of Knowledge* (Oxford: Oxford University Press, 1954), p. 102.

[6] See also pp. 104-105, where he says "Spinoza regards the mind as a complex idea, or set of ideas" and "There is no substratum self which has various mental states, but any human mind is simply a number of ideas organized in a certain way."

[7] H. H. Joachim, in *A Study of the Ethics of Spinoza* (Oxford: Oxford University Press, 1901), pp. 138-44, claims that Spinoza's view of the mind as a complex of "ideas" seems to destroy the unity and continuity of our thinking and that Spinoza tries, unsuccessfully, to repair the damage with his doctrine of "ideas of ideas." Joachim thinks the problem is important because Spinoza's conception of a free human being requires us to view man as potentially an active self. If I am right, then Spinoza's views in Book II do not undermine what he goes on to develop in Books IV and V, and the unity and continuity of a mind is no more problematic than the unity and continuity of a body. See also the *Short Treatise* II, pref. note, secs. 7-15 (quoted in translation by Joachim in a footnote on pp. 128-29).

[8] For a position which is very close to a pure neutral monism, see Bertrand Russell, *The Analysis of Mind* (London: George Allen & Unwin, Ltd., 1921).

[9] The most thoroughgoing statement of central state materialism is to be found in D. M. Armstrong, *A Materialist Theory of the Mind* (London: Routledge and Kegan Paul, 1968).

[10] See *Individuals* (London: Methuen, 1959), Chap. 3.

[11] For his explanation of 'hard', 'soft' and 'fluid', see II. Lemm. 3, Ax. 3.

[12] Both Joachim, *op. cit.* pp. 128-29, and Leon Roth, *Spinoza* (Boston: Little Brown, 1929), p. 94, draw attention to the theory of personal and bodily identity suggested by Spinoza in this context.

[13] See *op. cit.*, p. 111.

[14] Note that, strictly speaking, the view that the mind *is* a body is not introduced until II. 13. In II. 12 it functions only as an hypothesis.

[15] See II. 9 Cor., II. 11 Cor. Note that knowledge in this context concerns actually existing things and not common properties or eternal truths; for relevant distinctions, see II. 29 Cor. and Sch., II. 39, II. 44 Cor. 1 and 2, and II. 46.

[16] For instance, the loss of visual, olfactory, gustatory and auditory capacities would presumably not be impossible for Spinoza, but the loss of the ability to have nontactual feelings would be theoretically impossible.

[17] Thus, in II. 16 he implies that the nontactual feeling of a change in one's own body is involved even in a case of perceiving the existence of an external body.

[18] In this connection, note that in II. 24 he says "The human mind does not involve an adequate knowledge of the parts composing the human body."

[19] The inclusion of "as it were" should not be taken lightly here. In II. 17 Sch. he calls the impressions on the soft parts "images of things," but quickly adds "though they do not recall the figure of things."

[20] A similar imaginary case might be possible in which B is a parrot-shaped, and therefore nonhuman, body.

William K. Frankena

Spinoza's "New Morality": Notes on Book IV

I

When Spinoza died he left to the world a consciously new ethics, one that might today be hailed as a "new morality" and was different from the morality more or less current then in ways that can be only roughly indicated here. First, he took as its central terms or concepts "good" and "virtue," and their cognates, not deontic ones like "ought," "right," "wrong," "duty" or "obligation." In this respect he might be said to have been propounding an ethics of virtue, such as Miss Anscombe and some new moralists have recently favored, rather than an ethics of duty. The word "ought" does appear centrally in one Proposition (V, 16), but in a rather puzzling way.[1] The notion of a "right" also appears but only in a scholium on political philosophy (IV, 37, Schol. 2). There are also occasional uses of expressions like "bound," "unlawful," and "to be sought," but they are not central. For the rest, when he does not use "good," "virtue," and their cognates, Spinoza prefers to say such things as these:

"According to the guidance of reason, we shall. . ."
"By the dictates of reason. . ."
"Men who are governed by reason will. . ."
"A free man never acts deceitfully. . .".[2]

Second, while he gave several somewhat different definitions or apparent definitions of "good" and "evil," these were only partly based on prevailing usage (even though, as we shall see, he sometimes switches from "By good, I understand. . ." to "We call a thing good which. . ."), and his definition of "virtue" would hardly have been an ordinary one.[3] Third, Spinoza uses his central ethical terms to state rather different ethical views from the usual ones. It is true that his chief ethical proposition would have been generally accepted:

> The highest good of the mind is the knowledge of God, and the highest virtue of the mind is to know God (IV, 28).

But the following statements would hardly have been common:

> Pity in a man who lives according to the guidance of reason is an evil (IV, 50).

> The affects of hope and fear cannot be good of themselves.

> Humility and repentance are not virtues (IV, 53-54).

> That every one is bound to seek his own profit is the foundation of virtue and piety.[4]

Actually, it must be admitted that Spinoza's ethics was no more absolutely new than is our so-called new morality of today, since his way of thinking to a considerable extent represents a return to those of the Greeks. Nevertheless, it was relatively new for his time, even radically so in some ways, and this is enough for our purposes.

It is also true that Spinoza advocated this new ethics in a somewhat limited sense, and not in the unrestricted way in which the new morality is presently preached. For he held that humility and repentance, perhaps also pity, may still have to be commended to "the multitude" who are "impotent in mind" and unable to live according to the guidance of reason.[5] He did, however, present his ethics as the ethics for men of reason to live by.

Now, it is not my purpose to expound this newish ethics of Spinoza, to compare it with current views or establish its "relevance," or to discuss his definitions of particular ethical terms or his proofs of particular ethical theorems. My intention is rather to try to say something about two questions:

(1) What led Spinoza to this reconstitution of ethics, and was his movement of thought reasonable?

(2) Was the "ethics" he came out with, whether new or old, a "morality"?

It seems to me interesting and instructive to think about Spinoza in this way. Hopefully this will appear in what follows.

I should say here that I take Spinoza's ethics to consist, not merely of the theorems he deduces in Book IV (plus the Scholia and Prop. 25, V), but of these *together with* the definitions used in deducing them.

II

On the first question, it seems clear that Spinoza thought that, given the extremely rationalistic and intellectualistic metaphysics, epistemology, and psychology (hereafter referred to as MEP) he developed from the principles of Cartesian philosophy, it was necessary to—i.e., it would be irrational not to—reconstruct ethics along his lines, and especially to redefine "good" and "virtue" as he did. That is, he believed that, given the new principles of the nonethical or theoretical part of philosophy, which he regarded as either self-evident or demonstrable after the manner of Euclidean geometry, one must, if reasonable, come to a new practical philosophy or ethics, namely the one he offers us—a new philosophy of life, whether it is a morality or not.

The way in which the movement of Spinoza's thought is represented in the *Ethics* is this. Except for prefaces and scholia, his MEP is presented in Books I-III in the form of a Euclidean system of axioms, postulates, definitions, and theorems. Then at the beginning of Book IV, he adds only one axiom, which is entirely nonethical, and some definitions, including three of ethical terms, viz., of "good," "evil," and "virtue," and goes on to develop more theorems, some of them ethical. Thus his ethics proper consists formally of certain definitions and theorems, virtually all of them grouped in Book IV; and it is integrated into his larger system, which contains no ethical axioms, and derived from it, wholly by way of definitions in which ethical terms are defined by reference to nonethical ones already present.

It will not do at this point to object, as some in more recent times would, that one simply cannot deduce ethical conclusions from MEP premises alone. For Spinoza does not pretend to do this; he seeks to derive his ethical theorems from his MEP premises only with the help of his definitions, and such derivations are quite according to geometrical hoyle. Even the anti-Cartesian, R. M. Hare, recognizes this when he says, ". . .there must be nothing said in the conclusion which is not said implicitly or explicitly in the premises, *except what can be added solely on the strength of definitions of terms.*"[6] Incidentally, it will also not do to attack Spinoza by arguing that, since his MEP is deterministic in an extremely rationalistic way, no ethics, not even his own, can be compatible with, let alone derivable from, it. For, again, if the terms "good," "virtue," etc., are definable as Spinoza defines them, and mean what he understands them to mean, then statements in which they are used are not incompatible with his determinism.

We have seen that Spinoza does not include any ethical propositions among his axioms or postulates. A rationalist and Euclidean might do this, as the examples of Henry More and Samuel Clarke show, but to do so is to treat ethics as fundamentally autonomous. This, however, is not Spinoza's view; for him ethics is not autonomous but is to be derived from one's MEP, else it is just "superstition," which it is anyway if one's MEP is just superstition, as that of traditional theology was in Spinoza's eyes. For him, ethics can be established as rational if and only if it can be grounded on an MEP that is itself rational in the Cartesian sense, and he thought this meant that its substantive principles must be exhibited as theorems following from his MEP via definitions of the central ethical terms. An intuitionist might and would do things different-ly, but Spinoza was no intuitionist in ethics even if he was one in MEP.[7]

Obviously, then, a great deal rests on the definitions of "good" and "virtue" introduced at the start of Book IV, and we must ask about their status. It is clear that for Spinoza they are not and cannot be mere deductions from any MEP; definitions are not things of the sort that can be deduced as theorems. How then are they to be conceived? (a) They might be thought of and used merely as a kind of shorthand arbitrarily adopted to eliminate the need of repeating the longer expressions they are substituted for. It seems clear that Spinoza is not conceiving of them in just this way, even though he typically introduces them with the words, "By . . .I un-derstand. . .". He is not really thinking of his definitions as ar-bitrary, but as in some way reasonable. Else his subsequent theorems could hardly have the interest he supposes them to have.

(b) Today it would be fashionable to assume that, if Spinoza's definitions are to be taken seriously, they must be construed as descriptive elucidations of our actual uses of the terms "good" and "virtue." And I have already observed that Spinoza sometimes switches from "I understand" to "We understand." But this may be only an editorial "we," and, in any case, it is doubtful that Spinoza regarded his definitions in this way, though he probably did hold them to have some footing in ordinary use. He very likely thought that ordinary meanings are too infected with "superstition" to be satisfactory instruments either of philosophical theory or of the practical reflections of men of reason.

(c) On the second of these ways of construing them, Spinoza's definitions would be autonomous with respect to his MEP. So are they on a third view, viz., that they are somehow self-evident, the gift of some *Begriffs-*or-*Wesensanschauung*, some kind of intuition of essences that is itself independent of or even prior to any MEP. While Spinoza is not a Platonic realist, he does suggest some such intuition of meanings by his talk of adequate, clear and distinct, or self-evident ideas. Even if we have such intuitions, it is a bit hard to see how one tells which essences our words "good" and "virtue" should be taken to stand for, but one might argue that, lo, the two essences are there and must figure in our reasoning at a certain point, e.g., at the start of Book IV, whatever words we use to designate them. It may, in fact, be that Spinoza was thinking along these lines. Then his ethics would have a certain autonomy in relation to his MEP, something like that posited by the intuitionists and other antinaturalists, even though it would rest on definitions such as intuitionists deny the possibility of. For, I take it, even if the vision of essences showed us that ethical essences are among those viewed in MEP, still this insight would be an independent one and might have revealed a different situation in the realm of essences. I am supposing and proposing here, however, that this is not Spinoza's view, or at least not what actually happened in his mind as he went about thinking out his position—and that his general program cannot be thrown out simply because it involves such a view. It does not seem plausible to hold that Spinoza regarded his ethics as autonomous in this way either.

Two other views of Spinoza's ethical definitions are possible. (d) One is that they are not really definitions but disguised axioms, disguised normative or substantive positions, or "persuasive definitions" in C. L. Stevenson's terms. Then they might be essentially arbitrary and autonomous embodiments of attitudes or commitments, or they might be held to represent more rational affirmations of practical postures made somehow in the light of the Spinozistic MEP. (e) The other is that they are "descriptive" definitions in S. C. Pepper's sense. In this sense a definition is responsible to the facts, not so much to the facts about ordinary use of the term in question, as to the facts in the appropriate field of inquiry. "A descriptive definition," Pepper says, "stipulates that a symbol shall be defined by a set of symbols which truly describe a field of facts. . . .Such a definition is characterized by truth to fact."[8] It is defended and justified by exhibiting the facts obtaining in the field of inquiry within which it is to function. For a Spinozist this would mean that it is to be justified by the facts established by MEP, even if it cannot strictly be deduced from them. Now, whether they are to be thought of as persuasive definitions of the second kind or as descriptive ones, I suggest that Spinoza's definitions of ethical terms represent posits about the use of these terms in practical discourse taken to be rational because of the preceding MEP, even though they are not self-evident and do not follow deductively from that MEP. I also submit that, if that MEP is true and we know this, then those definitions are rational to adopt.

Let us suppose, then, that Spinoza would claim that his definitions of "good" and "virtue" are simply the most sensible ones to put in, given what has been established in MEP, if one is going to use those words or their equivalents in other languages. The question then arises, why should we retain and use such words at all? Why not kick the habit and express ourselves practically only by speaking of "power," being "free" or "in conformity with reason," or "contributing to the preservation of our being," etc.? A Spinozist might take this hard line. Why did the master not do so? At a similar point in his discussion Pepper writes:

> . . .the terms 'value,' 'good,' 'bad,' and their equivalents . . .could now be dispensed with and nothing of empirical consequence would be lost, though many rich literary connotations would vanish, . . .there is no need to use the terms 'good' and 'value,' and . . .confusions vanish as soon as these terms are eliminated.

> For without them, we are referred directly to the facts. . . . Then why not do without these terms? Because they are convenient. And because it is safer to keep them equated with the various selective systems than floating loose where ingenious men [like Moore] may note their freedom from attachment and proceed to hypostatize facts for them to refer to.[9]

Spinoza might have given a similar reply to our question. He might also have thought that one cannot have an "ethics" unless one affirms propositions using terms like "good" and "virtue" or their equivalents. An opponent might contend that Spinoza retains such terms and defines them as he does, because he is surreptitiously keeping in mind the "commendatory" connotation of these words and thinking that power, etc., are the things to commend, given his MEP. I am inclined to believe myself that there is some truth in this, but Spinoza might reply that he is writing for men of reason, with whom commendation is out of place. But then it would seem that he must grant that ethical terms can be dispensed with, except in addressing "the multitude" or those among them who may yet, perhaps partly because they are so addressed, "become free men, and enjoy the life of the blessed" (IV, p. 54, Schol.).

However this may be, let us interpret Spinoza as thinking that his definitions capture the ways in which it is most rational to use ethical terms like "good" and "virtue," assuming the truth of his MEP. Even then he might have conceived of them in either of two ways:

(a) as being somehow obvious against that background, independently and in advance of any perception of the theorems that would follow from his MEP with the use of those definitions (or of those that would not),

(b) or as being the fruit of a reflection that included looking ahead to see what theorems would or would not follow in an effort to arrive at the deductive system, theoretical and practical, that would be most clear and distinct when taken as a whole.

Now, Spinoza did, of course, think that he had come out with a system as solid as he held Euclidean geometry to be, and stateable in the same form. Just how he pictured his own reflections, whether in the first or in the second way, is not very clear. I suspect, however, that while his geometrical manner of exposition suggests that he conceived of his ethical definitions in the first way, they were actually to some extent a crystallization of a reflection of the second and not merely of the first kind. If this is so, then the acceptability of the definitions and that of the theorems of Book IV go together—and are jointly dependent on the MEP established earlier. And then, once again, the ethics of that book is not simply a logical deduction from that MEP, though it is offered as the ethics men of reason will adopt when they accept the MEP in question.

Some today would maintain that this ethics must be rejected just because it (definitions-*cum*-theorems) is different from our prevailing morality (meanings plus normative judgments). However, it is at least fair to ask if it may not be that, when one rejects one view of man and world and accepts another, as Spinoza did, it becomes rational to revise one's ethics—even if this is not logically necessary. Henry Sidgwick thought not.

> . . .ethical propositions, relating as they do to matter fundamentally different from that with which physical science or psychology [or metaphysics] deals, cannot be inconsistent with any physical or psychological [or metaphysical] conclusions. They can only be shown to involve error by being shown to contradict each other. . . .[10]

Many recent antinaturalists and autonomists have followed him—and Hume?—in this, e.g., G. E. Moore, the emotivists, and Hare. But is an ethics rational to adopt only if it is either self-evident or logically entailed by a rational physics, psychology, or metaphysics?

There is an obvious sense in which new factual knowledge, whether scientific or metaphysical, may dictate revisions in one's ethics. If one learns that one is a father, or that there is a God, that people can sometimes be revived after their hearts stop beating, or that mercury dumped into rivers may kill fish or poison humans who eat them, then one may have to revise one's views about what it is right to do in certain situations. In this sense, "new occasions teach new duties." But such changes do not or need not involve any change in one's fundamental normative premises or in the meanings of one's ethical terms. In the first case, for instance, one's conclusion that one has certain new duties depends on one's old premise that fathers have such duties. What I am asking in raising the above question is whether "time makes ancient good uncouth" in the sense that new factual knowledge may dictate revisions in a rational man's basic normative premises or definitions of ethical terms.

Antinaturalists can admit that, if a certain MEP is known to be true, then a certain ethics may be considered rational to adopt, provided that it is not inferred that it is *logically* necessary to revise one's basic norms or values (e.g., make a new "decision of principle") when or if one discovers a new MEP, though most of them would not in fact concede this because they tend to equate "If p is true, then q is rational" with "q is logically derivable from p by the usual canons of inference." They would in any case insist, however, that it is never rational to conclude from one's new MEP that one should redefine one's ethical terms or revise one's uses of them.

Now one can, of course, reasonably insist on this if one is an intuitionist in metaethics as Sidgwick and Moore were. But, if we give up intuitionism, as most antinaturalists have, is it then so clear that our definitions and uses of ethical (or nonethical) terms and sentences are or can or should be as independent as all that of our beliefs and knowledge about ourselves and our universe? It is plausible to reply that our definitions and linguistic uses, especially in ethical and practical discourse, cannot be dictated simply by our factual beliefs and knowledge because they are and must be responsive to our conations, needs, purposes, or commitments. Even if this is granted, however, one can still hold that, given certain purposes, etc., certain definitions and linguistic uses are rational and others not, just as one can argue that, given a desire for a firm bookcase, the use of nails is rational and the use of scotch tape is not. Besides, what our conations are is itself a function of our beliefs and knowledge about ourselves and the world.

To my mind, at any rate, it seems at least plausible to hold, as Spinoza must have, that if our conative nature is such as his MEP asserts it to be, then we should (it is irrational not to) define "good," etc., as he defines them and accept the ethics he lays out for us. The fashionable simplistic use of the open question argument certainly does not show that this is not so.

At the same time, as I have indicated elsewhere,[11] I tend to remain with the antinaturalists and others in thinking that ethical utterances of a certain sort (i.e., affirmative, categorical, indicative sentences) are typically and noncontingently used at least in part to commend, approve, prescribe, etc., and not just to describe or to assert facts. Moreover, I doubt that this can be true of them if their whole meaning is supposed to be captured in MEP terms, as Spinoza thinks or seems to think, especially if these MEP terms ("power," etc.) do not have built-in normative connotations, as some nowadays say the term "God" has.

I should like to conclude this discussion of my first question by throwing out the suggestion that a Spinozist could be an emotivist of sorts—and admit what I have just said—if he were to regard ethical judgments as "expressions" of the fundamental *conatus* or "endeavor after self-preservation" that is "the very essence of man" (IV, pp. 21-22), rather than as "assertions" of fact or of factual belief. He might or might not then adopt Spinoza's definitions of "good" and "virtue," but, if he did, he would have to offer them as a species of "persuasive definition" made reasonable by the Spinozistic MEP.[12]

III

We come thus to my second question: Is the "ethics" Spinoza regards as rational in the light of his MEP a "morality"? Did he have a morality, a moral action guide? Not all life or action guides are moral ones or moralities, e.g., law, etiquette, custom, and rules of religious observance, prudential action, scientific procedure, or club or organizational membership; and it is not simply to be assumed that what Spinoza lays before us in Book IV is a moral code or morality, just because it tells us what to do, uses words like "good" and "virtue" (for these do have nonmoral uses), or takes the place in the lives of men of reason that morality occupies in those of others. It may be a nonmoral practical system or life-style, a nonmorality, which is not to say that it is an immorality or in any way immoral. It may even be "beyond morality" as the ethics of love is sometimes claimed to be. One might also ask, of course, whether it is an "ethics," as Spinoza calls it. But "ethics" is a somewhat technical term with a wider meaning than "morality"; ethical egoism, for example, is usually regarded as an ethics by philosophers but it is much less natural to call it a morality. At any rate, I am concerned here to ask whether Spinoza's practical guide is a "morality," not whether it is an "ethics."

Actually Spinoza seems to try to avoid using words like "moral" and "morality" to characterize what he is talking about; it is especially striking that in Scholium 1 to P37, IV, he distinguishes and defines *Religionem, Pietatem,* and *Honestatem* as different phases of the life of reason, but does not mention morality by that name.[13] One gets the impression that he tends, when thinking of morality, to think of it, along with civil law and traditional religion, as the code of life of and proper to "those who are ignorant" and "do not live as reason dictates."

Another way of asking our second question is to ask whether "good" and "virtue," as Spinoza defines them, are moral terms or concepts. That "good" is not always a moral idea was cogently pointed out by Moore,[14] even though he regarded it as highly relevant to morality, holding that the morally right action is always that which brings about as great a balance of good over evil as possible in the world as a whole. Indeed, one has only to look at Spinoza's official definition of "good" to see that it is a nonmoral term:

> By good, I understand that which we certainly know is useful to us [Def. 1, IV]. . . . We call a thing good which contributes to the preservation of our being. . . [P8, IV].

What about the concept of "virtue"? It is often mentioned that the ancient words "arete" and "virtus" did not have a moral meaning in our sense, and it seems to me this is true of "virtue" in Spinoza's sense. Indeed, he defines it in terms of a kind of power, as the Greeks and Romans were inclined to do, as is illustrated by Meno's suggestion that *arete* is desiring the good or the beautiful and being able to procure and possess it.[15]

> By virtue and power, I understand the same thing; that is to say. . . , virtue. . . is the essence itself or nature of man insofar as it has the power of effecting certain things which can be understood through the laws of its nature alone [Def. 8, IV].

More briefly, virtue for Spinoza is "acting according to the laws of our nature" (P24, IV). He also deduces these propositions about virtue:

> . . . the foundation of virtue is that endeavor itself to preserve our own being. . . [Schol. P18, IV]. No virtue can be conceived prior to this (the endeavor, namely, after self-preservation) [P22, IV]. The endeavor after self-preservation is the primary and only foundation of virtue. For prior to this principle no other can be

conceived. . . and without it. . . no virtue can be conceived
[Cor.P22, IV]. To act absolutely in conformity with virtue is, in
us, nothing but acting, living, and preserving our being. . . as
reason directs, from the ground of seeking our own profit [P24,
IV].

As I read him, Spinoza is here subscribing to ethical egoism. It is
true that he derives rather "altruistic" theorems farther along, but
he can do so only because of the factual premises he uses in addition
to his definitions and theorems about the nature of virtue. With
different additional premises (i.e., a different MEP) he would have
to accept less altruistic consequences.[16] In my opinion, however, as I
have already intimated, ethical egoism just is not a morality in our
ordinary meaning of this term, even if it is an ethics, and should not
be regarded as one even if one accepts Spinoza's MEP. As P. F.
Strawson has said, ". . .the existence of a system of moral demands
(at least as we now understand this concept) requires some degree
of general readiness to recognize claims made upon one even when
this recognition cannot plausibly be said to be in one's own interest."[17] But a straight-out recognition of such claims is precisely
what Spinoza's scheme disallows. It is true that there is a debate
among philosophers about the definition of morality and about
whether ethical egoism is a morality or not,[18] a debate we cannot try
to resolve here—but it does seem to me that Spinoza is in effect giving up moral talk except for the multitude who do not live by the
dictates of reason as he sees them (which may be all of us some of
the time).

It is sometimes contended at this juncture that an action guide
is a moral one if and only if it is held or taken to be overriding or
supreme, or to have priority over all desires and considerations that
may conflict with it.[19] This view has the advantage, if it is one, of
ruling out the question, "Why should I be moral?" that has been so
difficult to answer otherwise. By the same token, however, it has
the disadvantage of making that question silly, which it does not
seem to be.[20] It also has the consequence that, if an agent or writer
regards a certain action guide as overriding or takes it as such in his
life, then that action guide is a morality—his morality—however
new it may be, whatever its content may be, and whatever may be
the grounds, if any, on which he adopts or would defend it. But this
is hard to believe, for then, for instance, if a person or society takes
aesthetic considerations to be paramount, aesthetic principles will

ipso facto become his or its moral code. It seems clear, however, that we would call that agent or society nonmoral; whether we would also call him or it immoral or not is another question the answer to which depends on our own moral code. Like Strawson, I believe that an action guide is not and should not be regarded as a morality unless it recognizes nonaesthetic and nonegoistic considerations straight out as justifying reasons for doing one thing rather than another at least sometimes, even when one does not enjoy doing it or want to do it and knows it is contrary to his interest or self-preservation.[21] Here by nonegoistic considerations I mean considerations about what one's actions do to other people or sentient beings as such. Egoism may recognize such considerations in a sense, but only indirectly, as in Spinoza's proof of P37, IV, and in his remarks about the treatment of animals in Scholium 1 to that Proposition.

Spinoza's rational psychology includes a denial that such nonegoistic considerations even can—except out of "superstition and womanish tenderness"?—be reasons for action. If such psychological egoism is indeed true, then, though ethical egoism does not follow logically (as Sidgwick and many others have pointed out), it is hardly rational to be anything but an ethical egoist, even if ethical egoism does involve difficulties when it is extended to "those who are ignorant," as Spinoza implicitly recognizes. Then, however, it is also rational to conclude that we should give up morality and replace it with prudence. It still may be, of course, that given the Spinozistic MEP it *is* rational to give up morality with its nonegoistic clause, and adopt Spinoza's "ethics" instead. The substantive question whether one should (in a nonmoral sense) live according to a morality or according to some nonmoral life guide is not closed by defining morality in a way that takes a nonegoistic clause as necessary but not necessarily as sufficient, and it may be that metaphysics, epistemology, and psychology are relevant to and rationally decisive in answering this question.

Actually, Spinoza might well hold that the man who sees the truth of his MEP *will* kick the moral habit in my sense and live by his (Spinoza's) principles—kick it at least for himself if not for society. This is suggested by his "factual" way of speaking when he says that the free man never acts deceitfully, etc. Of course, some will retort that Spinoza is simply converting "free" and "men of reason" into loaded, commendatory, normative terms,[22] but it is not obvious that men who are rational and free in his sense (enlightened and guided by his MEP) will have any use for such terms except in relation to the unenlightened. Even if they do use the words "free" and "rational" as commendatory, it does not follow, of course, that these words will be moral ones, for commendation is not necessarily moral.

In any event, it does seem to me that anyone who defines morality along the lines suggested here, as many do (and many do not), *and* who seeks to hold that men should be moral, can do so rationally only if he postulates or can show that Spinoza's MEP is mistaken in some important respect. Whether Spinoza's ethics is a morality or not, it or something similar should be taken as a rational guide to life *if* that MEP is true, even though it may be rightly insisted that it does not follow *simpliciter* from that MEP. In this way the answer to the final normative question (nonmoral) does depend for its rationality on metaphysics, epistemology, and psychology.

IV

Four conclusions emerge more or less fully from these reflections. (1) If we take Spinoza's "new" ethics to include the definitions as well as the theorems of Book IV, as we must, then he must have thought of it, not strictly as following deductively from his MEP, but still as uniquely rational given that MEP. (2) It or something very like it *is* uniquely rational, given that MEP. (3) But, while it is then authoritative as a guide in life, it is not a form of morality, old or new. (4) Morality is not a rational kind of guide, if Spinoza's MEP is true, except perhaps for the many who are ignorant.

Whether or not Spinoza's MEP is true, I have not tried to determine here, though I do not believe that it is. Nor have I discussed the interesting question whether the fact that morality is irrational if his MEP is true is a good reason for rejecting that MEP, as Kant, James, and others have thought.

Williaм K. Frankena

University of Michigan

NOTES

[1] The Latin word is "debet." It also appears peripherally, e.g., in Schol. P18, IV. Here and throughout I use the W. H. White translation.

[2] See P66, 69, 72, etc., IV.

[3] The definitions are discussed later in the essay, pp. 88 ff.

[4] These passages are not all exact quotations.

[5] See Schol. P54, IV.

[6] R. M. Hare, *The Language of Morals* (London: Oxford University Press, 1952), p. 33. (R. M. Hare's italics)

[7] Except for the kind of intuition involved in his third kind of knowledge, which presumably includes the content of Book IV.

[8] S.C. Pepper, *The Sources of Value* (Berkeley and Los Angeles: University of California Press, 1958), pp. 280 f. Cf. R.B. Perry, *Realms of Value* (Cambridge: Harvard University Press, 1954), p. 13.

[9] *Sources of Value,* pp. 689 f.

[10] Henry Sidgwick, *The Methods of Ethics,* 7th ed. (London: Macmillan and Co., Ltd., 1930), p. 213. Cf. also L.A. Reid, *Creative Morality* (London: George Allen and Unwin, 1937), Chap. 11.

[11] See William K. Frankena, "On Saying the Ethical Thing," *Proceedings and Addenda of the American Philosophical Association,* **39** (1966), 21-42. Cf. also William K. Frankena, *Ethics* (New York: Prentice-Hall, 1963), pp. 83 f., 90; and "Ought and Is Once More," *Man and World,* **2** (1969), 515-533.

[12] P8, IV, does have a somewhat emotivist flavor!

[13] C. Appuhn does however translate *Pietatem* as *Moralité,* in *Spinoza Ethique* (Paris: Librairie Garnier Frères, n.d.), II, p. 75.

[14] George E. Moore, *Philosophical Studies* (New York: Humanities Press, 1951), pp. 323-328.

[15] Plato, *Meno,* 77B. On ancient and modern conceptions of virtue, cf., e.g., G. H. von Wright, *Varieties of Goodness* (New York: Humanities Press, 1963), pp. 137 ff.

[16] This is apparent in Schol. P36, IV.

[17] "Social Morality and Individual Ideal," reprinted in Ian T. Ramsey, *Christian Ethics and Contemporary Philosophy* (New York: Macmillan, 1966), p. 292.

[18] See, e.g., G. Wallace and A. D. M. Walker, eds., *The Definition of Morality* (London: Methuen and Co., Ltd., 1970); Joseph Margolis, *Values and Conduct* (New York: Oxford University Press, 1971), pp. 6-9, 120 f., 182 f.; my *Ethics,* p. 17 f.

[19] For example, Margolis, *Values and Conduct.* Cf. R. M. Hare, *Freedom and Reason* (London: Oxford University Press, 1963), p. 169.

[20] Cf. R. F. Atkinson, *Conduct* (London: Macmillan and Co., Ltd., 1969), p. 94. It also makes silly all talk about action guides that are "beyond morality."

[21] See William K. Frankena, "Recent Conceptions of Morality," in *Morality and the Language of Conduct,* ed. by H. Castañeda and G. Nakhnikian (Detroit: Wayne

State University Press, 1963); "The Concept of Morality," in two versions reprinted in Wallace and Walker, eds., *Definition of Morality*, and K. Pahel and M. Schiller, eds., *Readings in Contemporary Ethical Theory* (Englewood Cliffs, N. J.: Prentice-Hall, Inc., 1970).

[22] See Hare, *Language of Morals*, p. 42.

Robert J. McShea

Spinoza: Human Nature and History[1]

"Human nature" and "history" have come to be terms used to distinguish two radically different ways in which some major political thinkers have approached their subject. "Human nature," or "individualist," theorists, notably Cicero, Hobbes, Locke, and most of those who wrote in English, began by considering the uniformities, necessities, potentialities, and goals of human nature, and went on to discuss the suitability to that nature of different political and social institutions. Others, notably Polybius, Machiavelli, Burke, the Hegelians, and most Continental writers, began with the study of history and of the laws of society and deduced from these the various characters of men; we are to understand men in terms of their social circumstances. A similar distinction is a commonplace among philosophic writers, but I wish, as much as possible, to discuss this matter in the terms used by political theorists. The question raised here is whether we shall regard Spinoza as using the "human nature" or the "history" approach in his political thinking.

A metaphysical form of the problem arises in the *Ethics*. Many readers find there an almost intolerable degree of tension between the principle of the unity of Substance, on the one hand, and on the other of the ideal unity of soul of the individual man seeking to live by the laws of his own being. How can the ideal of human autonomy be maintained in the midst of, as a part of, so overwhelmingly integrated an intellectual and extended universe? Spinoza believes he has maintained the integrity of these two entities, at least, of which one is completely a part of the other; I will not dispute him. The point I wish to make is that Spinoza's basic work, the *Ethics*, is primarily a treatise on human nature; from a theory of human nature he derives an ethics; ethics are a guide to human action; human action should be based, not on the nature of all things, but on the nature of man himself.

Given that Spinoza's metaphysics and ethics are systemically prior to his political thought, he would seem to have had two possible ways of carrying out that thought. He might have maintained that the state and society are "natural" and thus interposed a third entity between human nature and Substance. In this case he would have analyzed the autonomous laws of society, the state, and history, in subjection to which men would find their natural ends. Alternatively, he could have written a stoical treatise emphasizing the uniformity and autonomy of human nature and discussed, with the brevity that the subject deserves, the special problems presented by the fact that man is a social animal. I shall argue that Spinoza actually takes both courses and, what is more, does so without falling into incoherence. Before I do so, however, I would like to illustrate the problem to be solved out of the thought of two men, Hobbes and Burke, who held clearly opposite opinions on this matter.

1. For Hobbes, the study of politics begins with the study of the nature of representative individual man. Society, the useful interaction of such individuals, cannot come into existence until some measure of security is guaranteed by a political sovereign, and sovereignty is an artifact, a machine for keeping the peace. The state is prior to society and human nature is prior to the state. If you would understand why there is a state, how it must be constituted, and what our obligations toward it are, you must study the nature of man and deduce therefrom that single theory of politics which conforms to it. Hobbes understands human nature as the same in all men, as unchanging through history and culture as is the nature of hydrogen atoms. He is no more interested in history or in the study of actual politics than is Euclid, Galileo, or any mathematician or chess player. At all times the same basic political problems confront us and at all times the same solutions apply. Human nature is a universal constant configuration; there is but one political formula under which men may safely and usefully interact. The failure of any particular political mechanism is to be ex-

plained either by the fact that it is not designed intelligently to process its human material or by the failure of men to understand their relationship to the machine.

The compelling quality of Hobbes's argument derives from the simplicity and clarity of his definition of human nature. At the physical level, men are objects in motion. At the organic level, they seek self-preservation; they do so tropistically, "as a stone falls." At the animal level, they learn from experience and acquire prudence. As humans they have the ability to reason from definitions. From this minimum notion of human nature follows what Hobbes himself set forth as a minimum political theory. He can be summed up most briefly as the ideal political philosopher for a purely *Gesellschaft* society. Refuters of Hobbes should be arguing whether such societies are possible, or whether and to what extent they exist. Hobbesians are left with the task of refining and completing his system and applying it to practical problems.

2. Burke sees society itself as the entity to be understood, although by "society" he means something more complex than Hobbes's market-place society, and by "understanding" something closer to "intuitive grasp" than to Hobbes's ideal of that total clarity and certainty which we achieve in geometry. Men are to be understood in terms of the society in which they live and in terms of their function in that society. The principal object of our political and social understanding is the total culture; all is to be understood in terms of that.

Burke does not deny the existence of a basic and universal human nature; he says that prior to or apart from their shaping by some particular society, all men share a common nature. He goes on to add, however, that all men who are really men are encountered in some particular society and that therefore we can have no knowledge at all of what primary human nature is.[2] Of course men cannot be socialized into living on pure sand, or into taking the shape of a cloud, but their nature is very plastic, and so we are more interested in the forms that can be given it by society than in its own characteristics. Even if we did have knowledge of the primary nature of man, we would gain little advantage; we could no more deduce the marvelously complex functionality of society and the state from that nature than we could deduce a Greek urn from a lump of clay. A society is more complex than is an urn; it is a system, and not a system such as is a locomotive or a flower bed which we may rearrange in different ways to suit our fancy, but a system as is a tree or any evolved ecological system with which we ignorantly tamper, to its peril and our own.

Perhaps the underlying insight of this functionalist (or empirical, or historical) tradition is that knowledge of society and politics is, given the number of independent variables, much like knowledge of how to ice-skate or how to be a good husband. It is a kind of wisdom, the intensely motivated, but intellectually unsystematized accumulation of innumerable small insights and kinesthetic experiences, too many and too subtle for precise analysis, yet adding up to what can hardly in a practical sense be called anything but knowledge. The dramatic victory, in the past three hundred years, of systematic investigation over commonsense or intuition, a victory in which all of us have a culturally induced pride, has put commonsense or wisdom in a poor light. Yet, we continue to make our major decisions, personal and political, on the basis of just this form of knowledge, and not because we are uneducated or willful, but because there is no other way to make them. The result of *this* is that we talk in one way and act in another, and the result of *that* is that our talk is but tenuously related to action and our action is based, therefore, on less wisdom than that of which we are capable.

The Hobbesian and Burkean approaches, and their variations, might seem between them to exhaust the possibilities, yet both of them have serious internal difficulties. Hobbes's model of human nature is commonly thought to be too radically reductionist; it is essentially the same as the "economic man" of classical economics, and from it follows political advice which only rarely seems pertinent to actual (and therefore ambiguous) political situations. Theorists before and after Hobbes who have used a richer or more multidimensional model of human nature have achieved results which are highly satisfactory—to those few who accept their models. Further, even if we accept the validity of deductive systems based on clear and certain ideas, the number and generality of such ideas as are available to us seems insufficient for an adequate science of society or politics. To this day, no social science basing itself on the "human nature" approach has produced a generally teachable ("public," in Dewey's sense) body of concepts, techniques, or value judgments which can approach the powers of discrimination possessed by many sane, interested, and experienced persons. If the gaining of knowledge about society and politics is like learning to ice-skate, is the acquisition of an art rather than the learning of a science, then Burkean functionalism is a sound approach.

Burke's approach has its own difficulties. It seems to apply well to stable and relatively static societies which happen also to furnish sufficient satisfactions for its members. Few societies can be so described, and no society has ever had sufficient control over its own structure to bring about such conditions deliberately. If a society did have that degree of conscious control over itself, it would no longer be a Burkean society. The greatest drawback to this approach, however, is its inability to give us political advice. Burke himself, proudly culture bound, could tell us to cherish what we have. Contemporary functionalists, torn between principled admiration for every part of every culture and the scepticism which is the inevitable product of cultural comparison, cannot say that much.

To sum up: the historical approach seems to satisfy our demand for understanding, but in the absence of clear commands from God or History, gives us no clues, beyond the now discredited norms of our culture, by which to regulate our behavior. Once we have dropped human nature from our calculations, we cannot later bring it in for the convenient manufacture of political norms. The human nature approach has a clear advantage in this: if there is a knowable human nature, then a universal ethical system, objective in relation to that nature, is possible. If such an ethical system is possible, then principled political action, directed toward a real general human good, is also possible.

How did Spinoza deal with this question? He does not discuss it as a theoretical problem, but he does discuss social, political, and psychological matters and we should be able to determine his approach by studying his procedure in such discussions. I must plead limitations of space for not taking into account the full complexity of his thought and even for not indicating where I have not.

1. The first and principal impression that Spinoza conveys is that he begins, as an individualist, from the study of human nature.

In the opening paragraphs of the *Improvement of the Understanding,* he tells us why and how we should attempt to transcend the commands of our culture. We achieve happiness not by adjustment to or through society (although both means are often strategically necessary) but by taking independent steps to realize the potentialities of a human nature which is common to all of us. The society we are to abandon in spirit is not merely Dutch or European society, as though there were something peculiarly wrong with them, but any society in which we happen to live. Spinoza addresses himself to all men in all circumstances and times. As the essay continues, his emphasis shifts from individual to political emendation. The way to improve society and government is by improving ourselves, by helping to improve others, by helping to improve the institutions by which others can be improved. It is the change in the individual which makes possible the desirable changes in society. The failures of society are the sum of the accumulated failures or inadequacies of its members. The "experience" referred to in the opening sentence is not the historical experience of a society but the internal history of a single person. The "real good" that is sought is neither transcendent of individual human interests (Substance has no preferences) nor the subjective values of each person; it is a good with respect to a universal and uniform human nature. The statement that we should "have an exact knowledge of our nature which we desire to perfect,"[3] uncompromisingly declares that there is a human nature, that it can be known, and that it can be fulfilled or defeated.

In the *Ethics,* the human nature and ethical theories are joined:

> In what follows, then, I shall mean by "good" that which we certainly know to be a means of approaching more nearly to the type of human nature, which we have set before ourselves; by "bad" that which we certainly know to be a hindrance to us in approaching the said type.[4]

In the *Theological-Political Treatise,* Chapter IV, we learn that the achievement of individual good has nothing essentially to do with culture or circumstance: "our primary aim must be to make our understanding as perfect as possible; for it is in its perfection that our supreme good must lie."[5] In the same chapter it is said that

> Everything, therefore, which follows from the necessity of human nature, *i.e.,* from nature itself conceived in the determinative

form of human nature, follows, albeit necessarily, from human power.[6]

On the same page, and with direct reference to the distinction I have made between metaphysical and methodological questions, Spinoza says:

> We ought to define and explain things through their proximate causes, since general considerations about necessity and causal connection can give us very little help in forming and arranging our thoughts about particular things.

In the same work, at Chapter XVI, he says that "the universal power of nature as a whole is simply the power of all individual things combined,"[7] and at Chapter XVII that

> surely it is not peoples but individuals that nature creates, and individuals are only divided into peoples by diversity of language, laws, and customs; and the two last, *i.e.*, laws and customs, are the only factors which can give a people a particular temperament, a particular nature, and lastly particular beliefs.[8]

It might be considered that in the last part of the above quotation Spinoza has wavered somewhat from a pure individualism, but he later, in Chapter XX, returns to that position when he says that

> a man's judgment can be influenced in many ways, some of them hardly credible. . . yet in spite of all that political skill has been able to achieve in this field it has never been completely successful.[9]

Men will always have individual judgments arising out of the inner necessities of their nature; human nature cannot be made completely plastic to the shaping of any particular culture.

In his *Political Treatise*, Spinoza announces his intention "to deduce from the real nature of man," his political knowledge and recommendations.[10] He goes on to say that a man "can be called free only in so far as he has the power to exist and act in accordance with the laws of human nature."[11] This may seem hedged somewhat later where he admits that individual freedom is impossible except in society, but in the same paragraph in which this admission is made, he returns to his original position by saying that

> if it is because men in the state of nature can hardly be possessed of their own right that the Schoolmen wish to call man a social animal, I have nothing to say against them.[12]

That is, if the Schoolmen want to join Aristotle in saying that man

is a "political animal" that by its *nature* can achieve fulfillment
only as a member of a community, then Spinoza *will* have
something to say against them. On the same page, he puts
Rousseau's thought that a man may be "forced to be free" in his
own terms. A man "must carry out every command laid upon him
by the common decision; or. . . be compelled to do so by right." A
man cannot literally be forced to be free, but he can be forced to
cease obstructing the attempt of other men to be free, and to accept
the conditions under which he himself might become free.

Surely there is enough evidence to establish Spinoza as an un-
mitigated individualist.

2. There is not. The early pages of the *Improvement of the
Understanding* make much of the fact that most men, almost all
men, are completely subject to the values and conventions of their
society, and many phrases in the political treatises indicate that
Spinoza believed that it is a good thing that they are so subject.

The free man does well to rise above his culture; the slave does
well to rise to its level. In the *Ethics*, Spinoza shows not only that
men are subject to the overwhelming power of convention and
culture, but that such subjection is necessary, given the laws of
human psychology.[13] People must live in some society, and the
nature of the society in which they live makes them different from
each other.[14] If Spinoza has shifted to the biological analogy, we
should expect him to say that "every state must necessarily
preserve its own form, and cannot change it without risking complete destruction,"[15] and,

> a people. . . will not be able to uproot the accepted foundation of
> their whole state, and to change its entire construction, without
> great danger of destroying it completely.[16]

As noted, Spinoza intended to deduce his political thought from the
nature of men,[17] but it should be mentioned that the sentence in
which he says this continues with the thought that he will deduce
"nothing save the principles and institutions which accord best
with practice." His thought is that practice has already produced
every form of government which can be devised to secure human
concord, and that history, not the philosophers, has produced these
forms.[18] Later, he states that a certain political conclusion could be
demonstrated

by surveying every civilized state and examining the causes of its preservation and downfall. But to do this would be extremely tedious for the reader.[19]

In other words, if it were not for the tediousness of the task, some, if not all political conclusions could best be reached by appeal to the lessons of history. The history of civilized states teaches us a great deal about social causation, social laws; it is not a source of information for those thinkers who begin with human nature as their object of study.

A good deal of the imaginative appeal of historical-functional approaches lies in the observed disparity between the ignorance and stupidity of individual men and the relative rationality and effectiveness of their social institutions. Spinoza reinforces this impression: "men are led more by blind desire than by reason," and so become pawns of social forces.

> Experience teaches us only too well that it is no more in our power to have a sound mind than to have a sound body.[20]

Man is but a tiny part of the eternal order of nature, and "it is by the necessity of this order alone that all individual things are determined to exist and to act in a definite way."[21] How are we to reconcile this with his statement, on the same page, that a man is free when he can, "to speak generally, live as his own nature and judgement dictate"? Rather crushingly for the individualist position he says:

> hence human right or freedom is a nonentity as long as it is an individual possession determined by individual power; it exists in imagination rather than in fact.[22]

The freedom which characterizes the true individual can only be had in civil society:

> the right peculiar to human beings can scarcely be conceived save where men hold rights as a body, and. . . the more men there be that unite in this way, the more right they collectively possess.[23]

The corollary to this is on the same page: individuals have right and freedom only in society, yet "each of them has the less right the more the rest exceed him in power." In society, "nobody has a right to do anything but what he does by the common decree or consent,"[24] which seems to conflict with his later statement about man: "the more free he is, the more completely he obeys himself."[25]

On the same page occurs the famous "but we must always remember that we are in the power of God like clay in the power of the potter." It is an image from the language of functionalism; men are passive receptors of alien forms.

Spinoza tells us that the right of the sovereign is determined by its power, and its power is the power "of a people which is guided as if by one mind."[26] Elsewhere in the same text we have learned that the most absolute (powerful) state is the best state. It follows that it is best that the people be guided by one mind as much as possible. A subject has "no right to decide what is fair or unfair, moral or immoral;"[27] "citizens are not born, but made,"[28] i.e., made by the society; and

> as the vices of subjects, and their excessive lawlessness and perversity must be attributed to the faults of the commonwealth, so conversely their virtues and steadfast observance of the laws must be chiefly credited to its excellence.[29]

Machiavelli is quoted with approval: "a state, like a human body, is subject to daily accretions which occasionally require treatment,"[30] the very organic analogy which individualists may not use. The cyclical theory, closely associated with the historical approach appears:

> in time of peace men lay aside their fear; savages and barbarians gradually become civilized or cultured, and culture in turn gives rise to softness and laziness.[31]

Finally: "the constitution is the soul of the state,"[32] a remark which we would expect to find in Aristotle, Burke, or Hegel.

3. There is a third class of statements which seems to harmonize the two approaches:

> I call a man completely free in so far as he is guided by reason, for then he is determined to action by causes which can be adequately understood through his own nature alone.[33]

That is, if any men are guided by reason, and if not all men are guided by reason, then men differ in the extent to which they are free, and so individualism, or the human nature approach, is appropriate to the understanding of the actions of some men more than it is for others. A distinction can be made:

we should see what notions are common to all men, and what
notions are only clear and distinct to those who are unshackled by
prejudice.[34]

No man can be completely free to the extent that he can act solely
out of the necessities of his own nature, but degrees of such freedom
are possible.[35] We may characterize free men with adequate ideas
as active, and unfree men without such ideas as passive.[36] Toward
the end of Part IV of the *Ethics*, the difference between the two
kinds of men has become the difference between the slave and the
free man.[37] Of these two kinds of men, those who are free and
rational "necessarily agree in nature,"[38] whereas those who are
slaves, subjects of their passions and ignorance, cannot be in harmony with each other.[39] Unfortunately, "it rarely happens that men
live in obedience to reason."[40] It is a good thing for a man to achieve
autonomy; like other good things, it is as difficult as it is rare.

On the basis of this tangle of quotations, each one somewhat
ambiguous out of context, I suggest that Spinoza's method of studying the social sciences be understood in the following way: Man is a
creature who lives in a double universe. As a member of one universe, he may be considered as an animal whose actions, mental
processes, and desires can be completely explained in terms of
heredity, environment (including the internal environment), and
its individual experience. This "passivity" of animals means that
everything there is to be known about them can be had by resort to
"history."

All men are partly, and most men are all but completely, like
animals in this respect, and therefore the historical or functional
method of studying men actually works. At this level, the major
difference between men and animals is that men's environment is
principally other men and the complex of words, attitudes, and objects which we call culture. Therefore, in order to understand this or
that man, we study his culture and the history of that culture. The
information so produced can be true, important, and in many cases
complete.[41]

Yet, although men can survive as animals, they cannot fulfill
their essence as can an animal immersed in its particular environment. "Man thinks."[42] It is true that man's essence as a thinking
being cannot be perfectly realized. A man cannot become a disem-

bodied intellect, an eternal, omnipotent, and omniscient being. It may appear to us that some few lucky animals may succeed in fulfilling their essence; the best that a few lucky men can do is to see what it would be to act out of the necessities of their own nature only. Even if men could achieve total rationality, they would yet be confined to the system of the Attribute of Thought. That is, their thoughts would be determined by the structure of thought itself, and so they would be in total agreement with each other and with it on every subject. Spinoza's ideal of individualism includes freedom, but not free will; his ideal autonomous men shed their personal egos and merge into the general type of mankind.

Spinoza's primary aim in the *Ethics* is to take the individual out of the realm of history and culture. Once this is done, or begun, the individual must return to society, understand it, and help it to become rational so that his own development may be less in danger and so that others may have the way opened to a similar freedom of their own. The parallel to Plato's thought is striking.

For Spinoza, as a political and social thinker the ultimate approach is individualism; the ultimate unit is the single human type. True, a man would lose his individuality completely at the ideal point where he understands all and his mind merges with the Attribute of Thought, but his mind does not join that Attribute as a cell might join a larger body to which it will be subordinate, but as a circle merges with the class of circles, not subordinated to it, but equal to and identical with the whole class.

The original question, of course, was not about truth but about method, and not ultimate method but a method useful here and now. Spinoza's here-and-now method varies with the level of the material studied. The study of the mind of the ideal man is identical with the study of truth itself, that is to say, with the study of that final unified science which would take the form of a universal deductive "geometrical" system. At the other extreme, the study of "natural" man would be the study of a solitary and debased creature which, unlike other animals, would be almost totally incompetent to deal with its environment and with other natural men. Between these ideal extremes are the men we observe: the highly socialized man, an uncritical cell of his culture, whose actions and thoughts are best understood by understanding the laws of society and politics; the philosophic man, one who is struggling with only moderate success to free himself from the net of circumstance, culture, and passion, who is trying to live in the cool world of the intellect, and who is additionally involved in the reconstruction of his own society and in his role as an exemplar. The prime method for studying this philosophic man is the individualist method, the human nature approach. As we understand an artist in terms of what he is trying to do and what can be done, rather than as a reflection of current trends or his historical circumstances, so we understand philosophic man in terms of the human nature he is trying to achieve.

The contemporary application of Spinoza's distinction is interesting, even if speculative. It is that the present trend toward studying society and politics in functionalist terms is justified, for the "passivity" of the overwhelming majority of men, during most of their lives, makes them suitable subjects for this approach: they are, in Spinoza's word, "slaves." On the other hand, the dogmatic tendency that results from the success of this method, the tendency to judge all persons as "nothing but" the product of their society, the tendency to assume that all thought and evaluation is ideological, culture bound, as relative to the position of the thinker in his society—this is rejected as false.

ROBERT J. MCSHEA

DEPARTMENT OF POLITICAL SCIENCE
BOSTON UNIVERSITY

NOTES

[1] This essay is intended as a footnote to R. D. Cumming's *Human Nature and History*, a book which is currently changing the way in which students of political theory view their subject.

[2] This thought is not necessarily merely a definition. The idea that man has evolved into a creature which survives only as a member of some culture can have empirical support.

[3] TdIE, p. 10. References to *The Improvement of the Understanding* (TdIE), *Ethics* (E), and *Correspondence*, are from *Works of Spinoza*, Vol. II, trans. R. H. M. Elwes (New York: Dover Publications, 1951). References to *Tractatus Theologico-Politicus* (TTP) and *Tractatus Politicus* (TP) are from *Spinoza: The Political Works*, trans. A. G. Wernham (Oxford, 1958).

[4] E-IV-Pref., p. 189. See also TdIE, p. 6, and contrast with Hobbes's *Leviathan*, Chap. 6.

[5] TTP-IV, p. 71.

[6] TTP-IV, p. 67.

[7] TTP-XVI, p. 125.

[8] TTP-XVII, p. 181.

[9] TTP-XX, p. 227.

[10] TP, I-4, p. 263.

[11] TP, II-7, p. 271. See also TP-II-8, p. 273.

[12] TP, II-15, p. 277. See also E-IV-35, p. 210.

[13] E-III-30, p. 150. See also E-III-Def. 27, p. 179: "According as each man has been educated, he feels repentance for a given action or glories therein."

[14] TTP-III, p. 57.

[15] TTP-XVIII, p. 203.

[16] TP-VII-26, pp. 357-59.

[17] TP-I-4, p. 263.

[18] *Ibid*. See also TTP-XVII, p. 149; TP-VIII-5, p. 371.

[19] TP-VII-30, p. 361.

[20] TP-II-6, p. 269.

[21] TP-II-8, p. 273.

[22] TP-II-15, p. 277.

[23] *Ibid*.

[24] TP-II-19, p. 279.

[25] TP-II-22, p. 281.

[26] TP-III-2, p. 285.

[27] TP-III-5, p. 287.

[28] TP-V-2, p. 309.

[29] TP-V-5, p. 311.

[30] TP-X-1, p. 429. See also *Correspondence*, Ltr. xv, pp. 291-92.

[31] TP-X-4, p. 433.

[32] TP-X-9, p. 437.

[33] TP-II-11, p. 275.

[34] E-II-40, p. 111.

[35] E-IV-2, 4, pp. 192-94.

[36] E-II-Def., p. 129, and elsewhere.

[37] E-IV-46, p. 232.

[38] E-IV-35, p. 209.

³⁹ E-IV-31, p. 207.

⁴⁰ E-IV-35, p. 210.

⁴¹ Two notes on this: Despite all the patterns they discover, the world of the historians is essentially arbitrary; knowledge of it is only possible through experience.

Each animal has a nature, the nature of the species to which it belongs, and it attempts to preserve that nature. Yet that nature is the product of the interaction of organisms with environments over a long period of time. It follows that animals can only fulfill their natures in a particular environment. As a rational creature, man can become a citizen of the universe.

⁴² E-II-Axiom II, p. 83.

William Sacksteder

Spinoza on Democracy

I. *Problem and Textual Difficulties*

Democracy has seemed the best, the most natural, or the inevitable form of government to surprisingly few systematic political philosophers. Among those few is Spinoza. However, his analysis has been consistently neglected. There are reasons for this oversight. His political speculations are imbedded in a philosophic context which is forbidding for popular purposes and studded with doctrines uncongenial to modern inclinations. To a superficial view, his political doctrines themselves are easily rejected. Many find altogether too tough-minded the doctrine that right is equivalent to power or the initial resemblances to the reputedly totalitarian philosophy of Hobbes. Others find altogether too tender-minded notions such as natural law and the efficacy of reason. Yet at least one writer of note hailed Spinoza, rather than other more likely seeming candidates, as the prophet of liberalism.[1] And even the subtitles of his political works, as well as many of the devices and conclusions of his treatises suggest ideals to which we pay lip service today. I propose here to present a statement of Spinoza's conception of democracy which shows its connections with other phases of the philosophy in which it occurs and with an intricate set of political principles whereby democracy is called the best form of government. I shall defend the viewpoint only insofar as an effort at clear statement is defense. But I hope to suggest that facile refutations are mistaken and that there may be justice in a reconsideration. Perhaps even cause for admiration may emerge.

However, such an effort at exposition is complicated by certain textual difficulties. For the *Tractatus Politicus*, which is Spinoza's principal political work, was left incomplete at his death, having been broken off after only two pages had been written of a projected series of chapters on democracy. None of the other works treat specifically of the various forms of government or dominion. Insofar as I inquire after his conception of democracy, therefore, I am committed to extrapolation, rather than simple restatement, and shall need to invoke special interpretative devices.

First, and most readily applicable, are the few pages of the incomplete chapter and the incidental remarks on democracy scattered among Spinoza's writings. Second, democracy is one of three basic forms of dominion, of which the other two do receive detailed study. Consequently, insofar as these bear schematic interdependence with each other, democracy's characteristics may be inferred by projecting those of the other two according to a scale construed from democracy's relations to aristocracy and monarchy. Third, the abbreviated discussion of political matters in the *Tractatus Theologico-Politicus* is asserted to be applicable most immediately to democracy, since democracy is the definitive form. That it is basic in this sense is indicated by remarks such as that democracy is "the most natural form of dominion" or "dominion in its best condition." Hence in an abbreviated discussion there is a democratic bias to general political principles, and democracy itself emerges as dominion in the unqualified sense. To this extent, we may translate the properties of Spinoza's generic accounts of the state into characterization of the democratic form in which they exist absolutely. And similarly, to the extent that democracy is the best form of government, we may translate all criteria which are proper to political evaluation into characterization of the form in which they are most completely fulfilled.

Thus the concept of democracy is not a matter of incidental mention for Spinoza. Instead, it has a preeminent ubiquity and excellence, so that discussion of it involves the principles governing his whole philosophy. Therefore I shall begin my investigation with a brief account of the basic principles of that philosophy, citing their special relevance to political theory. Then I shall summarize principles general to political theory and questions concerning the state, concluding with the specifics of the concept of democracy itself.

II. *Politics in its Context*

The complexity and systematic texture of Spinoza's philosophy is notorious. But I need to cite the intricacies of that whole here only sufficiently to show two ruling considerations. First the definition of the part depends on its differentiation from other parts within the whole. Hence I must indicate Spinoza's careful discrimination of the range of his political doctrines, in order to show implicit qualifications on all that is said and to understand omissions which seem glaring when politics is otherwise located. Second, since the part shares characteristics prevailing in the whole, and is in crucial senses determined by the whole, I must notice nonpolitical doctrines which are applicable here or which appear as principles governing political analysis.[2]

The whole within which all political phenomena occur is nature itself. Although there are peculiarities which permit isolation of the specifically political, everything that occurs in the political realm occurs as well in accordance with the laws of nature. To say this is no different from the assertion what whatever is is in God, and it is in this sense that the entire treatment of nature as a whole—or of God, in Book I of the *Ethics*—is involved in, but not sufficient for, any characterization of politics. In that book the groundwork is laid for any analysis of individual things, for these exist according to coherent and universal laws. Hence specific metaphysical doctrines are utilized in politics. For example, the dependence of individual things on God for existence and continuance in existence may be translated, according to the relations of the whole of nature to individual things, into the political principle that right is coextensive with power. Likewise the doctrine that from the divine nature infinite things follow in infinite ways foreshadows the fundamental contingency of political particulars, even within a determinate universe.

Political phenomena are more specifically within *human* nature and dependent upon it. Political structures are built by individual human beings. Hence any presumptions and their consequences which condition individual existence whether general or human enter into political structures. Individual things are finite, enter into causal chains, and involve determinate existence. Man is

composed of a body and the mind which is its idea, being under
each of these attributes a union (according to a certain form) of a
number of individual parts. Also, under each attribute the order of
causes is parallel, and adequacies of organization mutually correspond. The human body is dependent upon external bodies, being
both affected by them and a cause affecting them. The mind is subject to a corresponding association of ideas. With respect to its
knowledge the human mind has inadequate cognizance of itself, of
its body, of external bodies, and of the duration of all individual
things, insofar as it proceeds according to the order of external
stimulation. And, on the other hand, it achieves adequate
knowledge when it conceives through the essence of God. These
doctrines also apply to the limitations of our political awareness, as
they show the path to possible social accomplishment.

So considered human nature is subject to a large variety of
emotions, which are affections of the body together with the mind's
idea thereof. These are actions insofar as we are their adequate
cause, and they are passions insofar as they are conceivable only
through the nature of an external object. The primary emotions are
desire, which is the endeavor whereby each thing seeks to persevere
in its own being, and joy and sorrow, which are respectively the
passions by which the mind passes to a greater or lesser perfection.
From the political standpoint, the exhaustive catalogue and
analysis of these and their derivatives which occur in Book III of the
Ethics provide fundamental patterns of human behavior on which
political expectations must be based. Since the guidance of reason
cannot be presumed, governmental structures must make allow-
ance for human desires as different as that whereby we are similarly moved by that which we imagine to effect a thing like
ourselves, and that whereby we attempt to prevent another's
possession of that in which we imagine he delights. Moreover, to the
extent that political jurisdiction is absent or inadequate, it is in
terms of his own emotions that each person judges good and evil
and pursues or avoids what he supposes to be either. In consequence, realistic political analysis will consider human beings so
conditioned, and it must gauge its precautions and expectations accordingly.

On the basis of Human Nature so understood, Spinoza builds
an elaborate ethical analysis in which it is possible to determine the

causes of human impotence and instability, the prescriptions of reason for their remedy, the power of the intellect to control the emotions, and the conditions and consequences of achievement of freedom of mind or blessedness. Here it is demonstrated that man suffers insofar as he is part of nature; that he necessarily desires what seems to him good; that virtue consists in acting according to the laws of our own nature, and is founded on the endeavor to preserve our own being; that community with like natures is among external things the most useful to man; and that true blessedness is found in that kind of knowledge which consists in the intellectual love of God.

Political theory is to be subsumed under one aspect of this moral analysis, but in another sense it must be radically differentiated therefrom. It is in terms of this dependence plus compartmentalization that an oblique sketch of the bases for political analysis is presented in a Scholium in Book IV of the *Ethics*. Book IV is devoted to human bondage to the passions. It also includes recommendations from reason for its remedy. Reference to community relationships falls under this last rubric, but the remedies of the communal order fall short of true human liberty and the highest moral state, both of which are considered according to a subsequent shift to the more complete moral context of Book V.

Politics is subsumable under ethics, first, in the sense that entrance into the political condition is a moral recommendation. It is part of the moral life to achieve community with other men, and political institutions are both the precondition and the manifestation of that accomplishment. Consequently it is in accordance with reason that men should enter into a social condition. External things are good, that is they are certainly useful, insofar as they agree with our own nature; and men agree in nature to the extent that they live in accordance with reason, whereas they differ in nature insofar as they are subject to passions. Moreover, that power of action in which our virtue consists is augmented by communion with likes and by peace and security of mind, both of which are purposes of the civil condition conducive to the ethical life.

Politics is subsumable under ethics, secondly, in the sense that all political phenomena possess a moral aspect, whether good or bad. The same given facts of human nature, which form the basis for the later ethical elaboration and which are subjected to ethical criteria, are presumed and utilized for political analysis. For example, the fact that an emotion is restrained or removed by an opposed and greater emotion, which is cited for analysis of human nature in an ethical mode, indicates also an important means for political control. In this sense, certain demonstrable human tendencies which moral achievement at its greatest heights seeks to control or minimize become crucial means in relation to the less complete moral achievements of politics. For example, the emotions of hope, fear, humility, and repentance always involve some element of passivity, and they might be surmounted by the fullest moral development. Yet, since men do not all live according to reason, these emotions may be more beneficial than not in controlling human ills and they may even serve as stepping-stones useful in pursuing more active states. It is such second-best adjustments which become dominant in the political mode.

But on the other hand, politics is to be distinguished from ethics, since the aims which it pursues are more restricted than those of ethics and also subordinate to them. In addition the means which it uses are only incidentally means to the moral states of rational control and blessedness. Ethics is concerned with analysis of man's highest intellectual and moral attainments, whereas politics is founded on the recognition that most men follow their desires as much or more than they follow the dictates of reason, while only a few achieve the highest moral development. We may distort political uses in either of two ways: we might mistakenly expect that political devices will make men good in higher ways, whereas by hope and fear they are merely compelled to those actions which the moral man does for other reasons; and we suppose mistakenly that human excellence consists in that minimum which is politically achievable. Although communal achievements are minimal, they are nonetheless moral, inasmuch as they provide material conditions conducive to the moral life and they are ingredient to its fullest acquisition. But they only control the acts of men, and they are accomplished by setting up institutional conditions permitting peace and security regardless of the moral state of the person subjected to them.

The political sphere is paralleled by the religious. Religion similarly has regard to obedience, to the achievements of as much as possible by lesser means among men incapable of ethical virtuosity or of sufficient understanding. But there is furthermore a complex interrelation between political and religious concerns. The outward ceremonies of religion, like the actions of justice and charity, are matters of public welfare rather than blessedness, hence they gain legal force from political authority. But by contrast with ceremonies, inward religion and piety can not be subjected to political authority. Whether they are regarded as divine laws (according to the popular understanding) or as eternal truths (according to the philosophic), they are directed instead to the highest good, which is intellectual perfection or the knowledge and love of God.

A political theory so isolated and determined will have certain peculiarities. It will not analyze, nor provide means for seeking, man's highest ends; yet it will provide means toward human goodness and it may be judged in moral terms. It will not differentiate the peculiarities of social phenomena in a given historical epoch; yet it will delimit the nature involved in any human association and it will show conditions inherent in human nature and in the circumstances of any time and place. In such terms analysis must discuss governmental forms according to the rights they allocate as well as according to their excellence respecting general human conditions. Their utility and stability irrespective of any particular problems which might be brought under them is what is in question. By being restricted in this way to general conditions, theory may achieve a mode of certainty applicable to all possible cases despite our incomplete knowledge of the peculiarities of given cases which might arise. Resultant doctrines must conform to human experience and practice, though they will not depend upon these for their validity, but rather on deduction from conditions general to human nature. Both the meanings and the limitations of the political analysis will be lost, if that analysis is not understood to be defined by the remainder of the system sketched above. Likewise, the cogency of many of its arguments will be lost, if they are not understood both as deriving principles from a more fundamental analysis and as constituting a unique subject matter.

III. *General Political Principles*

When general relationships between nature and man are translated into right (*iura*), natural right becomes the very laws (*leges*) or rules of nature in accordance with which everything takes place.[3] Hence natural right is the same as the power (*potentia*) of nature as a whole. Since the beginning and continuing in existence of any individual natural thing cannot be inferred from its essence, the thing exists and operates by the power of God, which is to say it accords with rules of nature and in consequence its natural right is coextensive with its power to exist and to operate. Whatever a man does in accordance with the laws of his nature, he does by the supreme right of nature.

In accordance with the laws of our nature considered alone the dictates of reason may preserve our power of existing and operating, that is our freedom. Yet it is not in everyone's power to strive after that preservation by use of reason. Human nature is so constituted that men live according to blind desire and appetites arising from the passions as well as according to the dictates of reason. From the standpoint of the universal right of nature no distinction between desires arising from reason and those arising from other causes can be made. Both are equally embodiments of the force of nature, and both are followed in accordance with the laws of nature or by natural right. Consequently everything that is done is in accordance with the laws of universal nature whether it follows from reason or from desire. It is done by natural right, which forbids nothing which is desired and possible.

A man is said to be dependent on his own rights (*sui iuris*) insofar as he can live after his own mind, and he is dependent on another's rights (*alterius iuris*) insofar as he is in the other's power, being bound either bodily or by hope and fear. But one man alone is scarcely able to support life or cultivate his mind. Yet by nature all men are liable to passions based on hatred, they are parted and opposed to each other, and they fear each other. Therefore, so long as right is determined by the power of each individual, and each is dependent on his own rights, the rights of each are so insecure that they are practically nonexistent. That is, individual men under natural right alone are powerless. Conversely, to the extent that men come together and unite their strength, they increase their powers, and consequently their right. Merely natural rights proper to a man are thus made secure and supplemented when many men have created common rights by which they may protect themselves and live according to the common judgment of all. In such a condition, the right of each is both limited and augmented by the power of the remainder, that is, by the common right.

That right which is determined by the power of the multitude and which can compel each to do what is ordered by the common consent is called dominion (*imperium*). And dominion is held absolutely by an agent to whom charge of public affairs has been given by common consent, be that agent a council of the common multitude (democracy), a council of a chosen few (aristocracy), or a single man (monarchy). It is only in relation to such an established dominion that wrongdoing (*peccatum*), or action that is forbidden by right, is possible. By contrast under the ordinance of natural law alone, everything which can be done is done by natural right, and wrong is possible only in the sense (improperly called "wrong") that one may violate the dictates of reason, and bring about one's own downfall. Likewise justice (*iustitia*) and injustice, which are respectively dispositions to render or not to render to each what is determined by the common right to belong to him, are conceivable only under dominion, that is, where there are common rights.

In this way there arises dominion which may be called "civil" with respect to its condition, and a "state" (*civitas*) so far as it forms a whole body. More detailed political analysis may thus be conducted in terms of traits generic to the civil condition, the first of which is the supreme right of the state or of the supreme authorities (*summa potestates*).

Just as the rights of the individual are coextensive with his power, so the rights of dominion held by the supreme authorities correspond to power: they are simply the rights of nature as further limited by the power of a unified multitude. In turn, the right of any citizen or subject is diminished to the extent that the state exceeds him in power. He acts and possesses only as he can according to the general decree of the state. Moreover, for the supreme authorities to give to another the right and power to live in any way he wishes, or to interpret for himself the decrees and rights of the state, is to divide the state. To give these rights to each citizen (or in effect to return them) is to destroy the state. Therefore such an abandonment cannot be conceived as occurring according to the ordinance of the state, but only through reversion to a merely natural state. In consequence, each citizen is dependent not on his own right, but on that of the state whose commands he is thus bound to execute.

That such a submission is not contrary to the dictates of reason will be seen by recognizing that reason would contradict nature if it dictated dependence solely on one's own rights in a natural state among men subject to passions. Instead reason teaches us to seek peace, which in turn depends on maintaining the state's general rights. Reason also suggests an endeavor to prevent general fear and suffering, to which ends the civil condition is dedicated. Finally, according to reason's own law of choosing the lesser of two evils, one should elect the general benefit derived from the state in preference to whatever harm and even repugnance to reason might be involved in a particular decree.

It is also the case that the power (and consequently the right) of the state is severely limited in certain respects. First, as is true for the individual man, that state is most powerful and independent which is founded and guided by reason. For the right of the state is limited by the power of the multitude, and its unity of mind is inconceivable apart from the pursuit of the interests of all in accordance with sound reason. Secondly, since the subjects are bound by hope and fear, the right of the state can extend neither to such things as no one can be induced to do by these means, nor to that which is abhorrent to human nature. Thirdly, just as the right of the state is created by the common power of the multitude, so it is abrogated by such things as cause indignation common to the majority. Finally, against the world at large the rights of one state are limited by those of other states, after the manner of individuals in their natural condition.

The right of the supreme authorities, limited in this way, consists chiefly in being "the mind, as it were, of the dominion," by which all ought to be guided. Their functions, consequently, consist in deciding what is good and evil, equitable or not, and what is to be done and omitted. Accordingly, the supreme authorities have the right to legislate, to interpret laws, to judge particular cases by them, and to handle foreign affairs. And conversely, the private citizen who attempts (whatever his intention) to fulfill these offices is a pretender to the dominion. The state so conceived can do wrong only in one sense which is metaphorical, since wrong properly refers only to violation of civil laws. It can bring about its own ruin, which amounts to acting against the dictates of reason. In this sense, for example, the state is bound to preserve the causes of fear and reverence and to avoid actions that convert fear into indignation and actions which breed hostility rather than the civil condition. Violations of this sort can not be vindicated by civil rights, but only by a return to the right of nature alone. Even the decision whether it is for the general welfare for the contract or laws of the original transfer of rights to be broken lies with the holder of dominion. Yet the violation of these fundamental laws, if it weakens the state by arousing indignation, to that extent dissolves the state and is vindicated by the law of war.

Such a state is most powerful and most dependent on its own right when it is founded and guided by reason. Thus it follows the best plan of living and assures to the utmost its own preservation. Since the purpose of a civil condition is peace and security of life, that dominion is best under which men live in unity (*concordia*) and rights are not violated. Peace must here be understood not merely as the absence of war, but as a state of virtue springing from strength of mind. The life of men in such a condition is not merely animal. Rather it is defined chiefly by reason, by true virtue and by the life of the mind. But a dominion serving this end is one established by a free multitude, rather than by the rights of war. For the multitude is guided more by hope aimed at cultivation of life and at one's own ends than by fear or by escape from death at the price of freedom. Thus, though the dominion created by a free multitude, and that gained by right of war do not differ essentially in the rights which are established, yet both their ends and the means of their preservation are sharply opposed.

IV. *Monarchy and Aristocracy*

The general problem concerning specific forms of government, democracy among them, is to select those fundamental rights—constitutional rights, we should say—which will lead to the preservation of the existing form. If the internal causes of dissolution of the state are removed by some constitution, then it is only disrupted by external fortune, and in this sense it is made as everlasting as possible. The discussion of each form may be limited therefore to those foundations which are best in that their violation arouses the indignation of the multitude whereas accordance with them produces peace and security. Such are in each case the foundations which can be instituted by a free people, and from which will follow peace and pursuit of the public interest. Such institutions are so framed that men will preserve public right in preference to private advantage, whether they act in accordance with reason or follow their passions. Such fundamental laws are instituted in accordance with general human nature, and by them the safety of the state is entrusted to the fidelity and constancy of no one person.

The problem of a monarchy founded on these principles is to preserve the liberty of the multitude by contriving that the power of the king will be both limited by the power of the multitude and preserved by its defense. In this way, consulting the common welfare preserves the monarch's independence, and he remains safe while his people remain peaceful. To this end, it is necessary to form a general council, having subordinate administrative and judiciary bodies, the function of which is to relate the decision of the monarch to the whole of the state. This council can make known to him the condition of the dominion, it can advise concerning the common welfare, and it can supply continuity of rule at his death. Such a state remains a monarchy inasmuch as decision lies with the king, yet it is the king's highest right, because most consonant with his independence, to choose the opinion of the greater part of the council; and not everything the king wills is law, though all law is the will of the king. In a free monarchy, only those rights which a group cannot hold—ending of controversy and dispatch of decision—are transferred to the king. These rules for excellence in monarchy all oppose the complete transfer of right to him. Such absolute rule is impossible in practice, and it would in any case diminish both the king's independence and the well-being of the citizens. Rather, the foundations of the dominion themselves are binding on the king, though they are to be regarded as his own eternal decrees. Any resistance to the king is by the rules of war, rather than by the laws of the state. With this fundamental constitutional organization, remaining regulations proper to monarchy are designed to prevent corruption and to attain balanced representation, equality, and stimuli to peace. It is also desirable to avoid a noncitizen military organization and to achieve an armed and informed body of citizens.

The problem in founding an aristocracy is to see that it rests on the sole will and power of the council of patricians when it acts as a whole. This is possible when the peculiar dangers of this form of government are avoided. First, it is peculiarly liable to factionalism, a difficulty which must be remedied by the careful maintaining of a proportion of patricians to masses such that it is impossible to form power constellations around a few of the latter. But second, since any form is in its best condition insofar as its rule is complete, and since in practice dominion is limited to the extent that there is a cause of fear in the multitude, a series of provisions is necessary in order to eliminate such causes of fear. In an aristocracy, dominion is held by certain chosen men formed into a supreme council, which passes all laws and chooses its own members and ministers. Unlike a monarch, this council's every will should be law, for unity of mind among so many will be possible only on rational decisions. This council is supplemented by a smaller council of syndics, who guard the fundamental laws, by a senate, which has charge of executive matters, and by a court devoted to decision of private disputes. As in monarchy, subordinate provisions are made to prevent corruption and military dominance, to preserve equality (here only among the patricians), to secure pursuit of the general welfare, and to provide stimuli to peace. A variant (and better) form is that aristocracy which is formed by confederation of many cities. In this case, greater care for the multitude and greater liberty are maintained by the effects of local government on partrician ambitions, while the strength of each of the various cities is limited by that of its partners.

V. *Democracy*

In the few pages of the incomplete chapter on democracy, Spinoza defines it as that form of government in which the right to a vote in the supreme council is contingent on fulfilment of certain conditions laid down by law, rather than on election by other members as in an aristocracy. He states that the variety which it is appropriate to discuss (i.e., the best) is that in which this right is granted by law to all who are native, independent, and respectable.[4]

The problem of founding such a dominion is the opposite of that in a monarchy. Since in the latter, decision was provided by the unitary decree of the king, the difficulty in a good monarchy was to see that the decision so provided conformed appropriately to conditions set by the will of a multitude as unified as possible. Thus in general councilors were needed as sensory organs which could provide a monarch with the awareness of general conditions necessary for wise decision. In a democracy, conversely, since the supreme authority corresponds almost exactly with the multitude, the difficulty of approximating decision to the desires of the multitude is solved, but the opposite difficulty arises. Democratic decision, that is decision by all the people acting as a whole, will be rational and agreeable to the multitude, but it will be enormously difficult to achieve such unified decision. There will also be danger of factionalism wherein the multitude splits into several unified but sharply opposed camps. There is a corollary problem of securing expeditious execution. And it will be difficult to preserve fundamental rights to the extent that any decision does not represent complete unity. All of these dangers are shared with aristocracy to some extent. Consequently hints concerning the devices for meeting them may be extrapolated from recommendations for aristocratic institutions.

Aristocracy stands midway between monarchy and democracy. It shares the tendencies and difficulties of both, and hence it illustrates the institutions appropriate for avoiding the dangers of each. In an aristocracy proportionate magnitude in the council solves the monarchical problem of correlating decisions to needs of the state as a whole, and prevents the formation of factions around a few outstanding men. In a democracy, such magnitude is carried to its extreme, though, doubtless, as in federal aristocracy, formal meetings of the whole council become impractical. In a large council, such unity of decision as is achieved cannot help but be in the general interest, and the influence of a few outstanding men will be limited by sheer numbers. But in aristocracy there are also converse problems which call for a series of governmental bodies subordinate to the supreme council. Since these are needed precisely because of the size and unwieldiness of the body possessing ultimate decision, it may be presumed that their analogues will be even more desirable in a democracy. In an aristocracy a lifetime council of syndics is appointed with a severe guardianship over the fundamental laws, and in particular over the tendency for dominion to pass into fewer and fewer hands; a senate is needed to promulgate and execute the council's orders, with subordinate consuls forming a continuous executive; and lower courts are needed to decide issues between private persons. Moreover, the very existence of these groups generates a new constitutional need to insure their responsibility to the supreme council. Such responsibility is maintained (except in the case of the syndics) by rotation of office, and by increasing their size and interdependence. The tendencies requiring these devices are intensified in a democracy, and it may therefore be presumed that some such bodies would also be necessary for a democratic constitution.[5]

Since democracy differs from aristocracy in the size and composition of the supreme council, and since the difference would increase the need for subordinate bodies, it may be presumed that the problems generated by such bodies, their mutual relations and their subordination to the supreme council, would become even more acute in a democracy. Consequently, an institution similar to the council of syndics, whose primary responsibility is preservation of the constitutional structure, would become peculiarly important in a democracy. Moreover, there is a persistent tendency for democracy to degenerate into aristocracy and thence into monarchy by concentrating power in the hands of fewer men. Consequently some preventive mechanism must be built into the fundamental rights if the state is to be internally sound and liable only to external destruction. The alternative to periodic dictatorship is the council of syndics which embodies something analogous to the "sword of the dictator" in a civil rather than a natural person, and thereby constitutes a source of fear only to the wicked, rather than to good and evil alike, as does a dictator. The function of this body would thus be to preserve the form of the dominion, which in democracy would involve principally guarding the suffrage and preserving equality among citizens. It must also prevent the citizens themselves from breaking the fundamental laws and secure responsibility of subordinate groups to the full ruling body.

My remarks thus far have shown defining characteristics of democracy insofar as Spinoza either shows it to differ in kind from the other forms or implies institutions it might require in virtue of its similarities to certain other forms. Yet, even in so proceeding, I have utilized the fact that democracy relates to the other forms of government on a continuous scale on which it forms one extreme with respect to various qualities, aristocracy being in the middle and monarchy at the opposite extreme. To the extent that such a scheme holds, we may infer certain characteristics of democracy, after the manner of geometrical determination of a direction by projecting a line determined by two given points. I now turn to the traits of democracy resultant on its culminating position in this sequence of forms.

Spinoza's own dependence on such a schematism may be seen most clearly in a passage in which he specifies the differences between monarchy and aristocracy. The latter possesses great advantage over the former in that, having a council rather than an individual as supreme authority, it possesses power more adequate to the support of a dominion without a system of councilors; it is not subject to death but is continuous; it never holds its dominion on sufferance, as does the king when youthful, ill, or senile; and it possesses a stability and constancy whereby its every will should be law, unlike a king, whose every will need not be law, even though every law should derive from his will. Since in the number of the supreme authority, the characteristic generating these differences, democracy surpasses aristocracy, democracy may be presumed to be at the extreme opposite to monarchy in all these respects.

Moreover, for these and other like reasons, an aristocratic federation of many cities is preferable to an aristocracy in one city, the principal additions being the close link of local authorities to the people and the greater dependence on devices of mutual consultation, discussion and persuasion as preliminary to making decisions. In a democracy, both proximity and consultation would be intensified, since sensitivity to popular opinion would be a precondition of personal power, and discussion and debate would be a precondition of any unity of decision.

Spinoza sums up the passage comparing aristocracy and monarchy by asserting that these are so many ways of saying that an aristocracy approaches more nearly the absolute, for a state is more absolute according to the adequacy and continuity of power held by its supreme authorities. However, in an aristocracy, these are limited by fear of the multitude and by the possibility of reversion of dominion into their hands. This is to say, therefore, that however absolute in principle, aristocracy is in practice limited by the watchfulness of the multitude, if only according to a "tacit understanding." Moreover, the characteristics whereby federal aristocracy differs from aristocracy also make for greater approach to absolute dominion by increasing the consultation and harmonization of the needs of the many, and so eliminating possible causes for their indignation. Notice that Spinoza's use of the word 'absolute' seems paradoxical to modern ears. Its meaning, echoed in our own verbal associations, is the absence of limitation on rule, the power to rule on one's own right. But the ultimate threat to rule, for him, lies in the aroused indignation of the nonrulers. Hence—contrary to modern connotations—the monarch, who is most apt to arbitrary action in ignorance of the multitude's state of mind, is *least* absolute. His rule is most qualified by the threat of indignation. Conversely, the rule of a democracy is *most* absolute, because it is not qualified by a multitude outside such decision making, and because there will be rule by unified decision only when the many are of one mind.

The specific characteristics considered by these comparisons are summarized by recognizing that the rule by the larger number approaches the absolute, since the qualification imposed by fear of the multitude is progressively removed. It follows that a rule which is to be strictly absolute must be free of any fear of a multitude external to and limiting of the rulers. But this could only be the rule which is held by the entire people, and so would be nothing other than democracy itself. Democracy, thus, even more than aristocracy, involves adequacy of power to the support of the dominion, continuity of rule without either reversion or diminution, and complete legislative sufficiency.

To say, however, that the democratic state is absolute is to say that it *is* a state more fully than other forms, and that the general characteristics of the state itself fit the democratic state with least qualification. It is in this sense that in the *Tractatus Theologico-Politicus*, where Spinoza gives a general account of the state in order to relate it to religious ceremony rather than a full treatment of various forms of dominion, he claims that his explanations fit democracy immediately and other states only obliquely. It is in this sense, further, that my exposition of democratic principles returns to those passages in which a generic account of the state is given. Thus we may see the traits of democracy in terms of those qualifications necessary for discussion of all forms, and we may find the sense in which democracy is the "most natural" form of government.

Dominion itself is defined as care for the affairs of the state which is entrusted by the common consent. It is consequently a power which is in all cases limited by the power of the multitude. Dominion may be held by one man, or by a council, but always with the implicit qualification of its dependence on the common consent or its limitation by the power of the multitude. In such cases it is conditioned by the continual possibility of its dissolution or its reversion to the state of nature. Indeed, the very possibility of a state depends on the existence of willingness to obey, and to the very extent that there is persistent disobedience, the state is dissolved. In a democracy, however, all of these qualifications are minimized, since the common consent *is* the supreme authority, rather than a condition of it at one step removed. Obedience disappears in that there is no external authority, and conformity is exacted only with respect to that which has been agreed upon by all. Democracy is thus the opposite of the state of nature, rather than its equivalent as it appears to those critics who see in it anarchic tendencies. Democracy is not that condition in which each follows his own will irrespective of others, but rather that in which all will the same thing, or that in which dominion wields its power as a whole.

Moreover, it is absurd to think that any right would be given up except the expectation of a greater advantage. Thus a free people will transfer their rights completely only to a democratic dominion, that is, to one in which they maintain a voice. Those rights achieved by enslavement are the powers whereby a state lays the groundwork for its own ruin. A democracy is a society in which all men collectively maintain the highest right against all insofar as possible. In any other society, precautions are taken against the supreme authorities, or appeal to the natural state is a threatening possibility.

Finally, a state exists to the extent that there is a unity represented by the existence of general rights. But one right is limited by another, and therefore that unity is achieved precisely to the extent that the rights of all individuals have been transferred to all collectively. Such transfer, again, is possible without reservation only in a democracy.

But not only is a state most completely a state insofar as it approaches the absolute, but it is also to that extent a state in its best condition. Since democracy is dominion in an unqualified sense, it is also the best state. We may therefore further our investigation of its nature by stating the criteria entering into the evaluation of states, and by indicating their higher achievement by democracy.

The state, like the individual, is most powerful and most independent (*sui iuris*) when it is guided by reason. Since the best order of living, which yields utmost preservation, is that which accords with reason, that is done best which is done independently. Furthermore, the quality of any dominion's condition may be seen in the extent to which the ends of the civil condition, peace and security of life, are attained by a free multitude.

First, that a democracy is most guided by reason is seen from the fact that in proportion to the number deliberating, unity of mind becomes less achievable except on those things which are in accordance with reason. Instead, dispersal and disagreement will follow from pursuing objects of the passions. Therefore, the rights and policies instituted and recommended by a democratic unity will accord with the dictates of reason. In addition, the fundamental rights of democracy themselves will be most in accordance with reason, for the very entrance into the civil condition is itself a dictate of reason. Civil life is most completely entered into under this form, and the ends for which reason makes this recommendation are most fully achieved.

These achievements lead, in a democracy, to the best possible condition of the state, for it will be most independent and most likely to survive: most independent, because it will not have within it groups excluded from participation, whose potential indignation is an implicit threat limiting the power and hence the independence of the state as a whole; most likely to survive, because the potential causes of dissolution involved in failure to achieve unity of mind will be prevented, since there will be no one whose consent is excluded, hence disunity will be avoided. These remarks have reference to the internal independence and preservation of the dominion. As for external threats, except those dependent on fortune alone, which have no bearing on the value of the fundamental laws, the conditions of preservation and independence are the same, and they accord with the unity instituted by the fundamental rights.

Democracy will be the best form of dominion, secondly, because it will achieve most completely the ends—peace and security—for which the state is instituted. By peace is meant a virtue springing from a certain strength of mind (*fortitudine animi*) whereby men live in unity a life defined above all by excellence of mind. It will be most achieved in that dominion which is instituted by a free multitude and which is led rather by hope than fear, so that the people follow their own purposes instead of those of conquerors. But I have already shown that unity of mind is most to be achieved in a democracy. Even those rights which in other forms are given to a king or select council by a free multitude are given with a tacit qualification, and so they establish a certain source of fear whereby the liberty of the many is diminished.

Security of life is achieved when the rights of the dominion are kept unbroken. Since this is the virtue of a dominion, and neither contempt for the law nor obedience are to be attributed to the vice or virtue of the citizens, but rather to the condition of the dominion, security will depend on the careful foundation of the dominion. But that dominion in which obedience is most likely to be achieved is democratic, for only here is there obedience by all to that which each has had a voice in instituting, and only here is the right of the state attained absolutely in the sense that causes of sedition and fear of civil war are avoided.

Thus for Spinoza democracy is the best form of dominion. The term is not only a useful propagandistic device or an unavoidable cultural inheritance. Rather it emerges in a careful political analysis isolated within an elaborate metaphysical and epistemological system and utilizing a detailed analysis of human nature, its bondage and liberty. Democracy is found to fulfil the institution of dominion most completely. It is not merely one form of dominion. It is that form which embodies the full nature of dominion itself, and it is more likely to achieve the ultimate purposes of any dominion. Conversely, that analysis does not justify the institutions of any particular time and place. In its terms the claim of any given government to be democratic designates a severe standard, according to which its relative achievement may be subjected to specific criticism.

In our own age, when all parties to any political controversy claim the value adhering to democracy, we are under continuous obligation to consider carefully what is meant by the notion and what is involved in commitment to it. Study of a neglected but powerful doctrine of democracy may suggest useful models. It is possible that the highest degree of lucidity may be attained by avoiding theories noted for historical influence or whose usages and principles have become platitudinous symbols. We may benefit instead from an exercise in close reasoning deliberately isolated from practical engagement. Spinoza's notions concerning democracy did not enter the mainstreams of either intellectual influence or creative action; and his prevailing mood is one of reflective but strong-minded rumination from a distance. Hence an effort at reconstructing his version of our most intense political ideal may serve us well.

Furthermore there is always the disarmingly simple possibility that a traditional doctrine so reconsidered may turn out to be true and to have continuing significance for the needs and political controversies of our own times.

WILLIAM SACKSTEDER

UNIVERSITY OF COLORADO

NOTES

[1] Morris R. Cohen, "Spinoza: the Prophet of Liberalism," in *The Faith of a Liberal* (New York: Holt & Co., 1946).

[2] This section follows the order of the *Ethics*, and is principally based thereon, except for the final paragraphs, which derive largely from the *Tractatus Theologico-Politicus*, particularly Chaps. IV and XIX.

[3] This section follows the order of *Tractatus Politicus*, Chaps. II-V, and is principally based thereon.

[4] The previous section, and the present paragraph follow the sequence of *Tractatus Politicus*, Chaps. VI-XI. At the point matched by my exposition here, the treatise is left unfinished. Hence my further discussion of democracy must select and interpolate, making use of materials from passages already cited.

[5] My exposition has avoided historical and institutional references, but I cannot forebear noting here that the institutions suggested by these safeguards bear a striking resemblance to various bodies and doctrines in the American constitutional scheme, particularly the constitutional role of the Supreme Court, the large legislative body, the subordination (more complete in Spinoza's recommendations) of Executive to Senatorial powers, the separation of powers, and the system of checks and balances. The very arguments employed are quite close to those of the

Federalist Papers. The analogues in Spinoza's thought to early American theory and practice are much greater than those to be found in such standard forerunners as Locke. I do not argue an influence hitherto unnoticed. I suspect that the true common ancestor of both is Hobbes. His toughness survives in Spinoza's thought which was extraordinarily influenced by him. The same crisp quality, after being lost in the subsequent milder British tradition, is salvaged under practical exigencies by the founding fathers.

Epistemological and
Metaphysical Issues

Willis Doney

Spinoza on Philosophical Skepticism

In the *Ethics,* Spinoza is not expressly concerned with skepticism and the possibility envisaged by Descartes that clear and distinct ideas or conceptions may not be true. There is reason for this, as he was of the opinion that, if as in the *Ethics* we proceed in our thinking in the right order, doubt will not arise.[1] In his earlier works, however, he is concerned with skepticism and, in particular, with the questioning of clear and distinct ideas. In the Prolegomenon in Part One of *Descartes' Principles* (G I, 145-49), he sets forth what he takes to be Descartes' attempt to allay doubts about clear and distinct perceptions. He finds there that Descartes does not succeed in answering an objection to his procedure, and he proposes an alternative way of escape from doubt. This alternative is also stated in the *Improvement of the Understanding* in the section on doubt or *idea dubia* (G II, 29-30); and considerable light is cast upon it by his discussion in this section of the nature of doubt. Distinguishing genuine doubt (*vera dubitatio in mente*) and merely verbal doubt, i.e. professions of doubt when "the soul does not doubt," he explains what leads to genuine doubt and how such doubt is to be removed. In my paper, I shall explicate the view stated in these passages and raise questions about the relations of this view to other views of Spinoza's. I shall also be concerned with a short and cryptic passage earlier in the *Improvement of the Understanding* in which he deals with professions of doubt that, farther on, he deems merely verbal (G II, 18). In a final section, I shall assemble the views about skeptical doubt stated in the various places and give a summary statement of Spinoza's attitude toward philosophical skepticism.

I

Interpretation of Descartes. In the Prolegomenon, Spinoza presents his alternative way of resolving skeptical doubts about clear and distinct perceptions after criticizing Descartes' procedure in the *Meditations* and in Part One of the *Principles*. Since his own view is stated in the context of the Cartesian philosophy, I shall begin with his account of Descartes' procedure. The question that I want to raise is why he thinks that this procedure is faulty. The account is divided into three parts. First, he raises the question why Descartes is led to doubt everything. He distinguishes and considers separately Descartes' reasons for doubting what is "received by way of the senses" and reasons for doubting "the most general matters" and also mathematical truths, that is, what is "perceived solely by the intellect." Discussing the latter, he takes Descartes' principal reason for doubt to be the supposition that "there is a God who can do everything. . . and had perhaps made him to be deceived in the very matters which seemed clearest to him" (G I, 143). Here and farther on in his account, he implies that for Descartes the most threatening and seemingly inescapable reasons for doubting clear and distinct perceptions are based on ignorance of one's origin.

This is, I believe, a correct interpretation of Descartes. In *Meditation* I, Descartes considers various possibilities concerning his origin: that he is the creature of a deceiving God, that he has come about by fate or chance or a succession of causes, and also that he is the victim of an evil genius. Maintaining that, if any of these possibilities has been realized, his faculties would not be reliable, he implies that, so long as he lacks knowledge of his origin and does not know that he is not a creature of a deceiving God, etc., there is cause for doubt. For Descartes, then, ignorance of one's origin is a sufficient condition of doubt. But it is also a necessary condition, for he maintains that, once he attains knowledge of his origin, i.e. of a nondeceiving God, he can prove that clear and distinct perceptions are necessarily true and *a fortiori* that there can be no reason for doubting them.[2] In his discussion of skepticism in the Prolegomenon and also in the section on *idea dubia*, Spinoza tacitly accepts this assumption of Descartes'; namely, that ignorance of one's origin is a necessary as well as a sufficient condition of doubt—or, as Spinoza specifies in the *Improvement of the*

Understanding, of genuine doubt—about clear and distinct perceptions.[3]

In the second part of his account, he describes Descartes' use of the *cogito* to establish a basis of knowledge, the formulation of a rule of truth, and the conclusion that he is a thinking thing. These doctrines are stated very briefly. They are presented *more geometrico* in the body of the work, and Spinoza's concern here is not with the doctrines themselves but with how they fit into Descartes' program of raising and then resolving skeptical doubts. The final section of the Prolegomenon is about Descartes' liberation from his initial doubts. Spinoza points out that Descartes attempts to remove doubt about clear and distinct perceptions by proving the existence of a nondeceiving God. He also indicates that this attempt has not gone unchallenged and that the following objection has been raised:

> Since the existence of God is not known to us through itself, we apparently can never be certain of anything; and we can never know that God exists. For from uncertain premises (since we have said that all things are uncertain so long as we are ignorant of our origin) nothing certain can be concluded (G I, 146).

In the objections and replies appended to the *Meditations*, criticism along these lines was made on at least two occasions.[4] One feature of the objection that Spinoza formulates is to be noted: he implies that, if the existence of God were self-evident, this objection would not arise. Reporting Descartes' reply to the objection, Spinoza refers to passages in which Descartes is concerned about the certainty of conclusions of demonstrations: *Principles* I, 13; "Second Replies," thirdly; and the latter part of *Meditation* V. On the basis of these passages, he construes Descartes' reply as follows:

> Although we do not yet know whether the author of our origin has created us to be deceived even in things which appear most evident, still we cannot, on this account, doubt things which we clearly and distinctly understand either in themselves or through a process of reasoning in which we are actually engaged. We can only doubt things which we have demonstrated heretofore, and which recur to our memory although we no longer contemplate, and have probably forgotten, the reasons from which we deduced them. So even if the fact that God exists could not be known through itself but only through something else, still we could arrive at a definite knowledge of God's existence by accurately

studying premises from which we conclude His existence (G I,
146-47).

Like many commentators, Spinoza reads the passages cited in such
a way that, in these passages, Descartes sets a limit to the scope of
his ostensibly universal doubt. On this interpretation, although
conclusions reached in the past are subject to doubt, present clear
and distinct perceptions—whether of axioms or demonstrations—are exempt. Since, according to Descartes, an argument
for God's existence can be grasped within the compass of a present
clear and distinct perception, the conclusion that God exists can
be established with certainty, and doubt about one's origin is
removed.

I shall not be concerned with the accuracy of this interpretation
of Descartes except to say that, for reasons given elsewhere, I think
it is untenable.[5] In the Prolegomenon, Spinoza does not say why he
thinks that Descartes' reply so interpreted is unsatisfactory, but his
reasons can be safely surmised. In the *Meditations*, Descartes
appears to be raising a radical doubt about everything (with the
possible exception of the *cogito*) that seems to be most evident, and
this doubt appears to be directed, not just toward past clear and
distinct perceptions, but toward any clear and distinct perception.
In an important passage at the beginning of *Meditation* III,
Descartes describes his state with respect to propositions that seem
most evident.[6] When, he says, he attends to them, he is entirely per-
suaded of their truth; yet, when he is not attending to them and
thinks of the possibility of a deceiving God, he is forced to
acknowledge the possibility of error. Although he claims that this
reason for doubt is "metaphysical," he concludes that, "without
knowing this [the existence of a nondeceiving God] I seem unable
to be quite certain of anything else."[7]

This appears to be a straightforward expression of doubt—i.e.
of "metaphysical" or skeptical doubt—about everything clearly
and distinctly perceived. Though, according to Descartes, this
doubt cannot be raised about a proposition *while* it is clearly and
distinctly perceived, it can be raised afterwards; and it must be
acknowledged that, though the proposition seemed at the time to be
so certain that it could not be doubted, there was nonetheless the
possibility of error. On Spinoza's interpretation, however, it seems
that, in his attempt to validate clear and distinct perceptions,

Descartes arbitrarily and unjustifiably restricts the range of skeptical doubt to conclusions reached in the past. It is not clear why past clear and distinct perceptions should be subject to doubt and present perceptions not. And if, as one commentator suggests, Descartes "imperceptibly transferred the doubt from clearness and distinctness to memory," a skeptic can press his question as to whether clear and distinct perceptions themselves may not be false.[8] On Spinoza's interpretation, Descartes has no answer to this important question, and his attempt to emerge from doubt cannot be judged to be successful.

II

Nature of Doubt. Immediately following his account of Descartes' reply to the objection raised, Spinoza goes on to say, "Since this reply may not satisfy everyone, I will give another" (G I, 147). This reply is the same as the procedure proposed in the section on *idea dubia* in the *Improvement of the Understanding*; and, since it presupposes Spinoza's theory of doubt, I shall consider that theory first. Distinguishing genuine doubt from professions of doubt that are in his opinion merely verbal, Spinoza takes it to be an essential feature of genuine doubt that it "is never produced in the mind by the thing doubted" but arises "due to another idea. . ." (G II, 29). By this he means that, in the case of genuine doubt, some idea other than the idea of the object doubted causes doubt; and he implies that a person who is genuinely in doubt has a cause or reason for his doubt and that this characteristic distinguishes genuine expressions of doubt from merely verbal professions of doubt. In this section of the *Improvement of the Understanding*, he is concerned exclusively with genuine doubt, i.e. with expressions of doubt based on a cause or reason; and when he adverts to philosophical skepticism concerning clear and distinct ideas, he has in mind skeptics who support their professions of doubt with reasons. In an earlier section of the *Improvement of the Understanding,* he deals with skeptics whose professions of doubt are in his opinion merely verbal; that is, in terms of the distinction made here, with skeptics who do not have a reason to back up their professions of doubt. His arguments there differ markedly from the refutation of skepticism proposed in this section; and it is clearly Spinoza's strategy in attacking skepticism to divide in order to conquer. Against skeptics who undertake to support their position with reasons, he argues in one way, and he has other arguments in store for those who simply say "I know nothing."

Spinoza makes two points about genuine doubt that are relevant to his discussion of skepticism. (1) But for the idea causing doubt, the idea of the object doubted would be accepted without question. This point is illustrated in the following way: "Supposing that a man has never reflected, or been taught by experience or by any other means, that our senses sometimes deceive us, he will never doubt whether the sun is larger or smaller than it appears" (G II, 30). This statement is in keeping with Spinoza's rejection of Descartes' theory of judgment, which distinguishes having an idea (an act of intellect) and assent to that idea (an act of will).[9] According to Spinoza, to have or conceive an idea is *eo ipso* to accept that idea—provided that there is no cause or reason for doubting or rejecting it.[10] In more recent terminology, it is not as if a person could "entertain a proposition" independently of taking some "propositional attitude," such as assent or doubt, toward that proposition. In the case of clear and distinct ideas, this is clearly Spinoza's view: if someone has a clear and distinct idea of a triangle having angles equal to two right angles, no wedge can be entered between his conceiving this and judging that it is so. But this is also his view regarding "ideas of imagination," though here there is no question of actively conceiving or judging. In the case of the rustic who has not reflected about perceptual illusions, his perception of the sun is constituted by a single idea. Spinoza maintains that, in this case, there would not be doubt or indeed certainty either, but mere awareness (*sensatio*). He implies, however, that though the rustic does not reflect and actively judge that the sun is of the size that it appears to be, he nonetheless passively takes it for granted that this is so.[11]

(2) "Doubt," Spinoza says, "will arise through another idea, not clear and distinct enough for us to be able to draw any certain conclusion with regard to the matter under consideration; that is, the idea which causes us to doubt is not clear and distinct" (G II, 29-30). This point is also illustrated by the example of perceiving the sun. If someone lacks knowledge of the operation of his senses yet is aware that his senses have sometimes deceived him, he may come to doubt that the sun is of the size that it appears to be on the

ground that his senses may deceive him. But, if he acquires a clear and distinct perception of the operation of his senses, his doubt will disappear. He will no longer doubt that the sun is of the size that it appears to be, for he will realize that it is not. The point that Spinoza makes here seems to be well taken. If someone claims that *p* is doubtful because it is possible that *q*, he implies that he does not know that *q* and also that he does not know that *not-q*. In the case of the skeptic who argues that he may be the creature of a deceiving God, it follows that, if he knew that he was the creature of a deceiving God, he would not be in doubt as to whether his clear and distinct perceptions are true—he would know that they are not. If, on the other hand, he knew that he was not the creature of a deceiving God, again he would not be in doubt, i.e. genuine doubt, for he would lack a reason for doubting that his clear and distinct ideas are true.

III

Spinoza's Alternative. There is, however, the problem of how a skeptic can come to know that he is not the creature of a deceiving God. In the Prolegomenon, Spinoza proposes the following alternative to the answer he ascribes to Descartes. He argues at first that the conclusion of the *cogito* is secure against the skeptic's doubt:

> We saw above, when we were discussing the certitude and evidence of our existence, that we could infer it from the fact that, wherever we turned our minds we found no reason for doubt which did not in itself convince us of our own existence, whether we contemplated our own nature, or supposed the author of our nature to be a skilled deceiver, or, finally, called in from beyond ourselves any reason whatsoever for doubt. . . (G I, 147).

The principle that Spinoza seems to invoke here is that, in order to be deceived or be mistaken, one must exist; and the question can be raised why he thinks that this principle is immune from doubt. Since the answer to this question is related to what he says farther on, I shall leave it for the moment and consider his proposal for resolving a skeptic's doubt about clear and distinct perceptions in general.

According to Spinoza, the skeptic who gives as his reason for doubt the possibility that he is the creature of a deceiving God must be in doubt about, and hence lack a clear and distinct idea of, his origin. This deficiency, he argues, can be remedied. Just as someone who is in doubt about his origin and questions his clear and distinct perceptions can come to have a clear and distinct idea of a triangle and perceive that the angles of a triangle are equal to two right angles, so too someone who is in doubt about his origin and questions his clear and distinct perceptions can come to have a clear and distinct idea of his origin and perceive that he is not the creature of a deceiving God. When the skeptic acquires a clear and distinct idea of a triangle, he can come to doubt that its angles are equal to two right angles by attending to the idea that he has formed of a possibly deceiving God. But when he acquires a clear and distinct idea of his origin, he cannot come to doubt that he is not a creature of a deceiving God by reflecting on the idea he has formed that he might be the creature of a deceiving God; for that obscure idea has been replaced by a distinct idea of his origin, and there is no cause or reason for doubt.

Spinoza was aware of one objection that might be raised against this way of allaying skeptical doubt, and he guards himself against another. (1) In the Prolegomenon he considers the following objection:

> We can be certain of nothing before we have a clear and distinct idea of God. But we cannot have a clear and distinct idea of God so long as we do not know whether the author of our nature deceives us. Therefore, we can be certain of nothing so long as we do not know whether the author of our nature deceives us. . . (G I, 149).

Granting the objector's first premise, he rejects the second, maintaining that we can have clear and distinct ideas even though we do not as yet know whether or not the author of our nature deceives us. Giving this reply, Spinoza is in a sense simply reminding the skeptic of the question that he raises, namely, whether his clear and distinct ideas are true. Since, in asking this question, he presupposes that he has clear and distinct ideas, he cannot consistently raise this objection. A skeptic can reformulate his question and ask whether the propositions that seem to him to be self-evident are really self-evident and whether the arguments that seem to him to be valid are really valid. But this move accomplishes nothing since Spinoza can reformulate his reply and say that, once we acquire a clear and distinct idea of our origin, there is no reason for doubting that propositions that seem to be self-evident are really self-evident, nor doubting that the arguments that appear to be valid are really valid. It is worth noting that, in giving a reason for his doubt, a skeptic implies that the reason he gives seems at any rate to be a good reason and that he can distinguish what seems to be a good reason from what does not. Since he is committed to the view that there is a way of distinguishing apparently valid arguments from others, he cannot consistently argue that, in view of controversies and disputes, this distinction cannot be made.

(2) It can also be objected that, when someone attains a clear and distinct perception of his origin and perceives that he is not the victim of a deceiving God, he cannot claim to know that this is so without begging the question at issue; that is, without assuming that at least one clear and distinct perception—the clear and distinct perception leading him to this conclusion—is true. From Spinoza's theory of doubt, it is clear how he would answer this objection. If someone argues that his clear and distinct perception that he is not a creature of a deceiving God may be false on the ground that it is possible that he is the creature of a deceiving God, his argument violates a condition of genuine doubt. Letting p stand for the proposition that I am the creature of a deceiving God, the skeptic's argument is of the form: *not-p* is doubtful because it is possible that p. The object of doubt and the reason for doubt both contain (though in different senses or ways) the same proposition, namely, p. According to Spinoza, there would not be two ideas; and his condition that the content of the idea causing doubt must differ from the content of the idea doubted is not satisfied.

In non-Spinozistic terms, the skeptic's reason for doubt can be said to turn out to be no reason at all. Again letting p stand for the proposition "I am the creature of a deceiving God," someone who has a clear and distinct idea of his origin concludes not just that *not-p* but that p is impossible; for, as Spinoza maintains in Proposition XLIV of Part Two of the *Ethics*, "it is not of the nature of reason to consider things as contingent but as necessary" (G II, 125-126). Given the very plausible principle that the denial of a proposition cannot serve as a reason for doubting that proposition, it follows that the denial of the proposition "p is impossible" cannot be a reason for doubting that this proposition is true. And it is

precisely this principle that is violated when the skeptic questions
Spinoza's conclusion that *p* is impossible and gives as his reason
that he may after all be the creature of a deceiving God, viz. that *p*
is possible.

On my interpretation of Spinoza, it is important to note just
how someone possessing a clear and distinct idea of his origin "rejects" the skeptic's reason for doubt. He does not reject this reason
on the ground that, possessing a clear and distinct idea of his origin,
he cannot entertain the possibility suggested by the skeptic that he
is a creature of a deceiving God (though indeed Spinoza thinks that,
while someone is clearly and distinctly conceiving his origin, this is
so). If this were his ground for rejecting the skeptic's reason, the
skeptic could justifiably retort that an incapacity to think that *p* is
possible does not show that *p* is impossible. Nor does someone
possessing a clear and distinct idea of his origin reject the skeptic's
reason on the ground that he has demonstrated that his clear and
distinct idea of his origin is true and that the skeptic's reason for
doubt, i.e. that *p* is possible, is false. This claim would clearly involve *petitio principii,* and Spinoza would be open to the objection
raised against Descartes' procedure. Rather, Spinoza thinks that
the skeptic's "reason" can be rejected on the ground that his claim
that *p* is possible is not a *reason* for doubting that *p* is impossible.
The burden of proof is placed on the skeptic; and, armed with the
principle that the denial of a proposition does not constitute a
reason for doubting the proposition, he thinks that he is in a position to fend off any skeptical assault.

In an important respect, Spinoza's defence of clear and distinct
ideas is like his defence of the conclusion of the *cogito.* In both
cases, he finds that the "reasons" that the skeptic offers are defec-
tive as reasons. In the case of clear and distinct perceptions, the
skeptic violates the principle that the denial of a proposition does
not constitute a reason for doubting the proposition; while, in the
case of the *cogito,* he violates the principle that, if *p* entails or in
some way implies *q,* "It is possible that *p*" cannot serve as reason
for doubting *q.* Thus, regarding the *cogito,* he says:

> We saw. . . that we could infer our existence from the fact that
> wherever we turned our minds we found no reason for doubt
> which did not in itself convince us of our own existence, whether
> we contemplated our own nature, or supposed the author of our
> nature to be a skilled deceiver, or, finally, called in from beyond
> ourselves any reason whatsoever for doubt. . . (G I, 147).

Since any "reason" that a skeptic gives for doubting his existence entails that he exists, he cannot find a reason for doubting that he exists.

IV

Relation to Other Views. On my interpretation, Spinoza is committed to the views (1) that, unless a person has a clear and distinct idea of his origin, he can come to doubt his clear and distinct ideas and (2) that, once this doubt has been raised, there is a way in which it can be removed. There seems, however, to be evidence against Spinoza's holding either of these views.

(1) In Proposition XLIII in Part Two of the *Ethics*, it is contended that "someone who has a true idea knows at the same time that he has a true idea, nor can he doubt the truth of the matter" (G II, 123-125), and it seems to follow from this proposition that clear and distinct ideas cannot be doubted. Joachim maintains that, for Spinoza, "doubt, i.e. genuine uncertainty of mind, can only be felt *about*, or *in respect to*, an object of imaginational experience—i.e. something the doubter either perceives by sense, or 'pictures' by producing or reproducing a sensible image."[12] To show that, on Spinoza's view, "*strictly speaking*, it is impossible to doubt 'whether God is or is not an Arch-Deceiver' or, again, 'whether the internal angles of the triangle are together equal to, or greater or less than, the sum of two right angles'," he argues in the following way:

> The First Cause or Origin of all things (and nothing else, and nothing less, than this can, *strictly speaking*, be called "God") is not a sensible or imaginable thing or person, but an intelligible reality, the uniquely singular (yet universal) Individual. To think of it, is to form a clear and distinct conception of a definable nature or essence. And to know it, is to affirm with absolute truth and certainty whatever follows inevitably from the essence thus conceived. The First Cause, or "God," is whatever it must be conceived and demonstrated to be; and "about" it, therefore, no genuine doubt is possible, and nothing can be merely supposed or erroneously believed.[13]

When Joachim claims that "*strictly speaking*" we can neither suppose that God is a deceiver nor be in doubt whether He is or not, it is not clear what meaning is to be attached to the qualification "strictly speaking." If he means that, when we clearly and distinct-

ly perceive our origin and perceive that deception cannot be
predicated of God, we cannot suppose that God is a deceiver nor be
in doubt as to whether He is or not, his account of Spinoza's view is
perfectly correct. But he seems to mean something other than, or
more than, this; for he proceeds to criticize Spinoza for not taking
into account "the 'rational doubts'. . . which every philosopher or
man of science is liable to experience from time to time. . ."[14]
Among these "rational doubts," I believe he includes skeptical
doubts that a philosopher may raise regarding the reliability of his
faculties; and he strongly suggests in this passage, if he does not say
outright, that, according to Spinoza's theory of doubt, such
doubts—or, at any rate, genuine doubts of this sort—cannot be
raised.

It is difficult to reconcile Joachim's interpretation with
Spinoza's statements in the section on *idea dubia*. He does say
there that "we cannot cast doubt on our true ideas by the supposition that there may be a deceitful God who leads us astray even in
what is most evident. . ." (G II, 30). But he immediately qualifies
this by saying: "except while we have no clear and distinct idea of
God. . ." And he goes on to explain:

> Reflection on our idea of the origin of all things teaches us that
> God is not a deceiver in the same way as reflection on the nature
> of the triangle teaches us that its three angles are equal to two
> right ones. As soon as our knowledge of God is like our knowledge
> of the triangle, all doubt is dispelled.[15]

Spinoza clearly implies here that, unless or until we have a clear
and distinct idea of the first principle of all things, we can entertain
the hypothesis of a deceiving God and, entertaining this hypothesis,
can doubt that our clear and distinct ideas are true.

Although it is true that, on Spinoza's view, we cannot doubt,
say, a present clear and distinct idea of a triangle having angles
equal to two right angles, there are two ways in which the proposition that the angles of a triangle are equal to two right angles can be
doubted. As Joachim points out, "no finite thinker is ever in fact
aware of all, or often aware of more than a few, of the necessary implications of the 'essences' he conceives";[16] and it may be that,
although we have a clear and distinct idea of a triangle, we are not
aware of this "implication" and are in doubt as to whether it can be
proved that the angles of a triangle are equal to two right angles.

There is another way in which doubt about clear and distinct ideas can be raised. Though no one clear and distinct idea is singled out for attention, doubt can be raised about clear and distinct ideas collectively. In this case the "object" of doubt would presumably not be a clear and distinct idea; for from Spinoza's contention that truth is its own standard, I believe it follows that there cannot be a clear and distinct idea of what a clear and distinct idea as such or in general is. But, employing this obscure and confused or "universal" idea, someone who lacks a clear and distinct idea of his origin can doubt that the clear and distinct ideas represented by this idea are true.

(2) There is another passage which seems to tell against my interpretation. In the *Improvement of the Understanding*, Spinoza raises the following objection to his procedure:

> If our reasoning be sound, we must take as a starting point a true idea. Now, to be certain that our starting point is really a true idea, we need a proof. The first course of reasoning must be supported by a second, the second by a third, and so on to infinity (G II, 17).

To this objection, he replies:

> If by some happy chance anyone had adopted this method in his investigations of Nature—that is, if he had acquired new ideas in the proper order, according to the standard of the original true idea—, he would never have doubted of the truth of his knowledge, inasmuch as truth, as we have shown, makes itself manifest, and all things would flow, as it were, spontaneously towards him (G II, 17).

Replying in this way, Spinoza seems to concede that no proof can be given that the clear and distinct idea serving as the starting point of his investigation is true, and he implies that no proof is necessary.

On the basis of this concession, it is tempting to attribute to Spinoza the view that, if a general doubt is raised about the truth of all clear and distinct ideas, there is no way in which such a doubt can be removed. In his account of Spinoza's theory of knowledge, Hampshire draws this conclusion. According to Hampshire, Spinoza argues that, "unless we accept the self-evidence of a proposition as not only a necessary, but also a sufficient, condition of its truth, we must be led into total skepticism by way of an infinite regress. . ."[17] Commenting on the aphorism that truth is the criterion of itself, he adds that, "if it is once allowed that a proposition which is self-evident and logically necessary may not be true, any argument to remove this skeptical doubt must presuppose what it is trying to prove, and so be circular."[18] Although it is not clear whether, in the last sentence, Hampshire is stating or supporting Spinoza's position, it is clear that, on his interpretation, doubt as to whether the self-evidence of a proposition is a sufficient condition of its truth is irresoluble. As Hampshire interprets Spinoza, such a doubt must lead to "total skepticism."

Although the passage quoted from the *Improvement of the Understanding* is not unambiguous, it does not seem to support Hampshire's interpretation. When Spinoza asserts that, "if anyone had acquired new ideas in the proper order, according to the standard of the original true idea, he would never have doubted of the truth of his knowledge. . . ," he seems to mean by "original true idea" a clear and distinct idea of one's origin—that is, on Spinoza's view, of the principle of all things or of absolutely infinite substance or "God or Nature." Interpreted in this way, his contention is that, if someone proceeds from *this* idea in an orderly fashion, doubt cannot arise. It does not follow that doubt about clear and distinct ideas cannot arise if one proceeds from some other idea, say, of the principles of geometry. Moreover, conceding that the starting point of his investigation cannot be proved to be true, he does not commit himself to the view that a doubt about clear and distinct ideas cannot be removed. It cannot of course be removed by demonstrating that a clear and distinct idea of one's origin is true nor *a fortiori* by demonstrating that all clear and distinct ideas are true. But it can be removed by acquiring a clear and distinct idea of one's origin and coming to realize that no reason can be given for doubting that clear and distinct ideas are true.

V

Verbal Doubt. In the section of the *Improvement of the Understanding* in which he raises and replies to the objection concerning an infinite regress, Spinoza considers the possibility that someone aware of his first principle and the propositions deduced in accordance with it should nonetheless profess doubt. According to the view that I have attributed to him, skeptics of this sort have no cause or reason for doubt, they are not really in doubt, and their professions of doubt are merely verbal. In the section on *idea dubia,* he says that the treatment and cure of these skeptics belongs to an inquiry concerning obstinacy and its cure and not to a treatise on method (G II, 29), and in the earlier section, he says that either they "Speak *contra conscientiam,* or we must confess that there are men in complete mental blindness, either innate or due to misconceptions, i.e. to some external influence" (G II, 18). In the earlier section, however, he does not simply deride and dismiss these skeptics: he indicates what arguments can be used against skeptics who persist in professing total doubt and who simply say, "I know nothing." In this highly compressed paragraph, three arguments are suggested. They are not stated fully or in detail, probably because Spinoza thought that they were not germane to a discussion of method. As I read this paragraph, the arguments are exceedingly ingenious and interesting; and they provide additional evidence that, contrary to the impression of one commentator, Spinoza was indeed concerned about philosophical skepticism.[19]

(1) Spinoza's first point is that skeptics of this variety "are not conscious of themselves; if they affirm or doubt something, they do not know that that they are affirming or doubting, for they say they know nothing. . . ." (G II, 18). He considers here a possible extension of doubt beyond any of the doubts envisaged by Descartes, namely, doubt about one's existence and present state. Against skeptics professing total doubt, his point is that, if someone asserts that he knows nothing, he cannot consistently claim to know that he is making this assertion. The following *reductio* argument is suggested. Suppose that someone who utters the words "I know nothing" is making a true assertion. If his assertion is true, he cannot know that he is making this assertion. On the assumption that a person cannot make an assertion without knowing that he is making the assertion, it follows that he is not making an assertion and *a fortiori* that he is not making a true assertion. Hence, someone uttering the words "I know nothing" cannot be making a true assertion; and it can be argued that, if the words "I know nothing" cannot be used to make a true assertion, someone uttering these words is merely uttering words—he is not asserting that he knows nothing, nor is he expressing doubt.

(2) After making this first point, Spinoza turns to difficulties confronting a skeptic when he is asked whether he knows that he knows nothing. Although he does not say why a skeptic cannot

answer this question affirmatively, it is clear enough why an affirmative answer is ruled out. If a skeptic were to assert that he knows
that he knows nothing, his assertion would entail a contradiction.
For, granted that "S knows that *p*" entails that S knows something,
"I know that I know nothing" entails that I know something; and,
given that "S knows that *p*" entails *p*, "I know that I know nothing"
entails that I know nothing. The objection is obvious, and Spinoza
takes the skeptics' position to be that they do not know that they
know nothing. He then points out that they do not "positively
assert" even this "for fear of admitting that they exist while they
know nothing" (G II, 18). The argument that Spinoza appears to
have in mind is this. If a skeptic "positively asserts" that he does
not know that he knows nothing, he implies that what he is asserting is true. Given the principle that, if an assertion ostensibly
about one's own mental state is true, it must be known to be true, it
would follow that, if what he is asserting is true, he does indeed
know something, namely, that he is in a state of not knowing that
he knows nothing and *a fortiori* that he exists. To avoid this un-
welcome implication, the skeptic should "remain silent for fear of
haply supposing something that smacks of the truth" (G II, 18).

Finally, (3) Spinoza points out a discrepancy between the
skeptics' professions of doubt and their nonphilosophical behavior.
In personal and social life, they behave as if they exist: they seek
their own advantage, and they affirm and deny various things
sometimes on oath. Their behavior indicates that, on many
matters, they are not in doubt. Yet they profess to be in doubt
about everything. There appears to be, in non-Spinozistic terms, a
conflict of criteria. Pointing out this discrepancy, Spinoza does not,
as has been suggested, simply deny that skeptics are, or really are,
in doubt on the basis of their everyday behavior.[20] His point is more
subtle. When a skeptic professes total doubt, it is clear that he
thinks the statement that he is making cannot be confirmed or dis-
confirmed by his behavior in society or in everyday life. On the contrary, he thinks that he is making a theoretical or philosophical
point. The question that Spinoza raises is whether he can be doing
what he thinks he is doing. If he is in fact making a theoretical
statement, there must be some way in which his statement can be
supported or defended. But, by his own admission, there is no way
in which this can be done, for he claims "not to know whether an

argument is or is not sound" (G II, 18), and he implies that no one can know this. Making this claim, he debars himself from theoretical discussion; and, since, when he professes doubt he is clearly not making a statement in any way connected with his ordinary behavior and since he cannot be taken to be making a theoretical claim, it follows that he is making no claim at all. There is, in other words, no function that his utterance can serve, and his words are idle.

VI

Summary. Against the skeptic who professes absolutely universal doubt and (if he is consistent) does not back up his profession of doubt with reasons, Spinoza concludes (1) that, when he utters the words "I know nothing," he cannot be making a true assertion; (2) that he cannot consistently assert either that he knows that he knows nothing or that he does not know that he knows nothing; and (3) that his utterance "I know nothing" can serve no purpose and his words are idle. His admonition is that such a skeptic remain silent. If, on the other hand, a skeptic enters the arena of philosophical discussion and gives a "reason" for saying that even clear and distinct ideas may be false, his reason can be shown to be no reason at all. Since, on Spinoza's view, ignorance of one's origin is a necessary condition of doubting clear and distinct perceptions, the only really serious "reasons" that a skeptic can produce are based on the lack of a clear and distinct idea of his origin. This deficiency can (without circularity) be removed; and, when someone has a clear and distinct idea of his origin, he is in a position to reject any reason that a skeptic can propose for doubting clear and distinct ideas.

ẂILLIS DONEY

DARTMOUTH COLLEGE

NOTES

[1] *Improvement of the Understanding*, G II, 17. I have used short titles, *Improvement of the Understanding* and *Descartes' Principles*, in referring to Spinoza's *Tractatus de Intellectus Emendatione* and *Renati des Cartes Principiorum Philosophiae*,

Pars I & II. "G" stands for the Gebhardt edition: *Spinoza Opera*, edited by Carl Gebhardt (Heidelberg: Carl Winters, 1925). Quotations in English are from Frank A. Hayes's translation of *Descartes' Principles* in *Earlier Philosophical Writings* (Indianapolis: The Bobbs-Merrill Company, 1963), R. H. M. Elwes's translation of the *Improvement of the Understanding* (New York and London: M. Walter Dunne, 1901), the White-Stirling translation of the *Ethics* (Oxford: Oxford University Press, 1930), and A. Wolf's translation of Spinoza's correspondence (London: Frank Cass & Co., 1966). I have emended the translations where necessary.

[2] *Meditation* V, AT VII, 70. "AT" stands for *Oeuvres de Descartes*, ed. by Charles Adam and Paul Tannery (Paris: Léopold Cerf, 1897-1913).

[3] About skeptical arguments from conflicting judgments, Spinoza expresses the following opinion: "From the fact that divine and human sciences are full of disputes and controversies it cannot be inferred that all the things which are treated therein are uncertain. . ." (Letter LVI to Boxel, G IV, 260). In this letter, he refers disparagingly to Sextus Empiricus and other skeptics who "say that it is not true that the whole is greater than its part . . .and have the same view of the other axioms."

[4] In the Second and Fourth Sets of Objections, AT VII, 124-125 and AT VII, 214.

[5] "Descartes' Conception of Perfect Knowledge," *Journal of the History of Philosophy*, **8**, No. 4 (October 1970).

[6] AT VII, 35-36.

[7] AT VII, 36.

[8] A. K. Stout, "The Basis of Knowledge in Descartes," reprinted in *Descartes: A Collection of Critical Essays*, ed. W. Doney (Garden City, N. Y.: Doubleday & Company, 1967), p. 183.

[9] As in *Meditation* IV, AT VII, 56-58.

[10] *Ethics*, Part Two, Proposition XLIX (G II, 130-36). In the Scholium to this Proposition, Spinoza expresses his view that "an idea, in so far as it is an idea, involves affirmation or negation."

[11] Cf. his example of a boy imagining a winged horse in the Scholium to Proposition XLIX, *Ethics*, Part Two (G II, 134).

[12] Harold H. Joachim, *Spinoza's Tractatus de Intellectus Emendatione: A Commentary* (Oxford: The Clarendon Press, 1940), p. 189.

[13] *Loc. cit.*, p. 190.

[14] *Loc. cit.*, p. 191.

[15] I have used here Joseph Katz' translation of the explanatory clause, *Spinoza: On the Improvement of the Understanding* (Indianapolis: Bobbs-Merrill Company, 1958).

[16] Joachim, *op. cit.*, p. 189, n. 3.

[17] Stuart Hampshire, *Spinoza* (Harmondsworth, Middlesex: Penguin Books, 1951), p. 105.

[18] *Loc. cit.*, p. 105.

[19] H. G. Hubbeling makes the following remarks about Spinoza's treatment of skepticism: "Spinoza has not really struggled with doubt as for example Descartes did. . . . [His]rejection of Scepticism is harsh and by no means does justice to the often sincere and deep-going struggles of the Sceptics. Spinoza reasons: if the Sceptics deny that they exist, they presuppose this existence in everyday life so that their thoughts are not worth while." *Spinoza's Methodology* (Assen: Van Gorcum, 1967), p. 35.

[20] *Vide* Hubbeling, *op. cit.*, p. 35.

E. M. Curley

Descartes, Spinoza and the Ethics of Belief*

"When Newman was a child," writes Strachey, with characteristic malice, "he 'wished he could believe the Arabian Nights were true.' When he came to be a man, his wish seems to have been granted."[1] The contempt implied here for what Strachey plainly regards as Cardinal Newman's willful credulity is only a comparatively recent expression of a view about what we may properly believe which, since the time of Descartes, has become increasingly widespread in philosophy.

We tend to associate the notion of an "ethics of belief" with W. K. Clifford and his dictum that "it is wrong always, everywhere, and for anyone, to believe anything upon insufficient evidence."[2] But the man who coined the term "agnosticism" knew what he was about when he traced his intellectual ancestry back to the *Discourse on Method* with its golden rule for finding the truth:

> . . . give unqualified assent to no propositions but those the truth of which is so clear and distinct that they cannot be doubted.

> The enunciation of this great first commandment of science consecrated Doubt. It removed Doubt from the seat of penance among the grievous sins to which it had long been condemned, and enthroned it in that high place among the primary duties, which is assigned to it by the scientific conscience of these latter days.[3]

Descartes was the first philosopher of the modern period "to obey this commandment deliberately . . . as a matter of religious duty,"

* I am very much indebted to Peter Sheehan, Reginald Naulty and John Kilcullen for their helpful discussions of this topic with me.

and for this accomplishment alone, Huxley suggests, he deserves to be regarded as the founder of modern philosophy.

Of course, those who hold views similar to Huxley's and Clifford's do not always speak in the exuberant categorical imperatives and prohibitions of Victorian moralism. Hume seems to be offering a counsel of prudence when he tells us that "a wise man . . . proportions his belief to the evidence."[4] It is arguable that Descartes too is addressing his injunction to doubt everything that can be doubted, not to all men, at all times, but only to those who are seeking the truth, once in their life.[5] And even Huxley will sometimes attempt to justify his religious duty of intellectual asceticism with delightfully pragmatic appeals to "the success which follows upon" application of the Agnostic principle.[6] Still whatever differences of tone or doctrine may divide these men from one another, or from their own selves in different moods, their common hostility towards beliefs which "go beyond the evidence" gives them a sufficient family resemblance to warrant our grouping them together, and dubbing them, perhaps, the cautious believers.

Now there are a variety of objections one might make against the philosophy of cautious belief. Some philosophers have argued that we should adopt a more venturesome, enterprising attitude in our believing. So H. H. Price, arguing for a policy of accepting testimony unless there are specific reasons for doubting it, writes that a person "cannot value knowledge very highly, if he does not even attempt to get it when there is a risk that his attempt will fail."[7] And if it should be objected that we cannot achieve *knowledge* by believing on insufficient evidence, Price may reply that "the end we seek" is not knowledge, in the strict sense, but the acquisition of "as many correct beliefs as possible on as many subjects as possible."[8] I rather doubt that this is so,[9] but the view has appealed to other people besides Price. William James, for example.

James has also contended, in his famous essay on "The Will to Believe,"[10] that there are certain situations in which we have to believe on insufficient evidence. Where the option between believing and disbelieving is a live one (one where both alternatives strike us as having some likelihood), a momentous one (one, roughly, where the choice between alternative beliefs is important to us), and a forced one (where attempting to withhold judgment is tantamount to making a choice), and where the choice cannot be made on intellectual grounds, we not only lawfully may, we *must* let our "passional nature" make the choice.

It is not altogether clear what sort of 'must' this is. As George Nakhnikian suggests,[11] given that the option is a forced one, where some commitment is inescapable, given that intellectual grounds are insufficient to determine which commitment is made, and given that James' "passional nature" is construed so broadly as to include all nonintellectual determinants of belief, James' thesis seems analytic. The "must" looks like a logical one. But though James' thesis may be logically necessary, it is not evident that he himself regarded it as logically necessary. It is true that he speaks of our passional nature as an "inevitable" determinant of our choice, at least in certain situations (p. 101). But since the requirements that the option be a live and momentous one play no role in Nakhnikian's explanation of the logical necessity, it is puzzling that James should have included them.[12]

In any case, Nakhnikian himself argues for two stronger theses: (1) that wherever the option is a live and momentous one, not decidable on intellectual grounds, our passional nature may lawfully decide it, even though the option is not forced, and (2) that there are or can be situations in which we ought to believe propositions against which (almost) conclusive evidence is available (p. 277). The first thesis he regards as self-evident, the second he argues for by appealing to the following example. It may be that conclusive (or almost conclusive) evidence is available for the proposition that my wife has, on one occasion, been unfaithful to me. And it may also be that I am so constituted that, if I came to believe this, it would lead to the breakup of an otherwise happy marriage and much misery for our children. It would be a heartless and unreasonable man, Nakhnikian contends, who would say that nevertheless I ought to believe that my wife has been unfaithful to me, no matter how strong the evidence is that she has (p. 257).

This example reminds us that, quite apart from any problems which may be peculiar to the ethics of belief, *if* there is an ethics of belief at all, then it must share in certain problems which pervade all moral philosophy. It may be, as Jonathan Bennett has recently argued,[13] that there are no defensible moral principles of the form: "It would always be wrong to. . ., whatever the consequences of not doing so." If so, then Clifford's austere dictum that it is always wrong to believe on insufficient evidence is not defensible.

Unfortunately the same sort of considerations which appear to rule out principles of the form: "It would always be wrong to . . . whatever the consequences" also seem to rule out principles of the form: "It would always be right (i.e. permissible) to . . . whatever the consequences." And if that is so, then presumably Nakhnikian's 'self-evident' thesis, "It would always be right to believe what our passional nature prompts us to believe, provided the option is living and momentous and cannot be decided on intellectual grounds," will not be defensible either. It should be possible to construct a counterexample to it just as plausible as Nakhnikian's counterexample to Clifford's moral law of belief. Suppose my wife to be in fact innocent of infidelity, but compromised by damaging, though hardly conclusive, evidence of infidelity. I, suspicious and sadistic, desire not the breakup of a happy marriage, but a plausible ground for abusing her and destroying the love our children have for her. The option is both living and momentous. Still, would it not be a heartless and unreasonable man who would say that I act rightly (permissibly) by following the promptings of my passional nature and believing in her guilt?

Principles of the form "It would always be wrong (or right) to . . . whatever the consequences"—and attacks on them—raise difficult problems in moral philosophy which we fortunately need not pursue. Venturesome believers are no more obliged than cautious ones to state their principles in absolute form. They may well wish, on reflection, to say something more like: "It is permissible, where the option is a live one, to believe on insufficient evidence, unless there are very powerful reasons for not doing so." This is still, I think, a moral principle, and one sufficiently like those which venturesome believers have actually held to be grouped with it.

If there is an ethics of belief at all, then it must share the problems which pervade all branches of ethics. But is there such a subject? Spinoza, if I understand him rightly, thought not. For one presumption which seems to be common both to the cautious and to the venturesome believers is the view that belief is a kind of voluntary action, which may sensibly be the object of commands, prohibitions, permissions and policies. And Spinoza, as I understand him, denies that belief is a kind of voluntary action. If that view is right, it seems to follow that there can be no ethics of belief and that the whole controversy between the cautious and the venturesome believers rests on a mistake.

If Spinoza is right, the apparent consequences are, indeed, quite considerable. That his claim has implications for the philosophy of religion and the traditional problem of the relation between faith and reason is obvious. That it also has implications for epistemology is perhaps not as obvious as it should be. But classical skepticism—the skepticism of Lucian and Sextus Empiricus, whose revival in the Renaissance was so important for the subsequent development of modern philosophy—is not just a thesis about the weakness of the evidence we have for what we believe. It is also a thesis about what, in view of the weakness of the evidence, we ought to believe. "Be sober and doubt all things." "Nothing must be determined."[14]

Again, what we think about the nature of belief may affect what we think about the political problem of toleration. If we hold that belief is not a voluntary action, then, on the face of it, heterodox opinions are not a proper subject for legislation. Perhaps the reverse is not true. I think one might hold that belief is a voluntary action, but is still not a proper subject for legislation because belief in itself is never sufficiently 'other-regarding' to be legislated against. We may not punish beliefs, though we may punish the actions they lead to. But whether or not that is a viable position, I suspect that a Spinozistic view of belief—not often articulated, and rarely argued for—may lie behind the willingness many people have had to tolerate opinions other than their own.[15]

Is Spinoza right in his view of the nature of belief? Fundamentally, yes, I think. In what follows I propose to see what can be said for that view. But because Spinoza's own statement of his position is developed as an attack on the opposing view of Descartes, we must start with a look at the Cartesian texts he is criticising.

I. *Descartes*

In the Third Meditation, before setting out to consider whether or not there is a God, Descartes divides his thoughts into three classes: some, he says, are *like* images or pictures of things, as when he thinks of a man, or a chimaera, or the sky, or God—only these are properly called ideas; others have different 'forms', as when he wills, fears, affirms or denies. These other thoughts, Descartes holds, always involve an idea of something as the subject of the thought, but they add something to it. They may be divided into volitions, or affections, and judgments.[16]

Volitions and ideas, Descartes goes on to say, cannot properly be called either true or false. Whether I imagine a she-goat or a chimaera, it is nonetheless true that I imagine the one thing rather than the other. And whether what I desire is evil or even nonexistent, it is nonetheless true that I desire it. It is only 'thoughts' of the third sort, judgments, that can properly be called true or false. And there the chief error which I need to avoid lies in judging that the ideas which are in me are like the things outside which they are ideas of.

Now as Kenny has pointed out, the argument Descartes uses here is a very odd one.[17] It seems to invite the objection that, whether or not what I judge is true or false, it is nonetheless true that I judge it. But Descartes' point is, on the face of it, a valid one. If what I judge is true, then I not only judge, I judge truly. But we do not assess acts of willing or thinking of an object as either true or false.

The distinctions drawn in the Third Meditation are deployed in the Fourth, where Descartes' aim is to prove that God is not a deceiver. He has already shown, he thinks, that he has been created by a supremely perfect being, and that the desire to deceive his creature is incompatible with the nature of such a being. So it is puzzling to Descartes that he should ever err. The doubts raised in the First Meditation cannot be completely put to rest until he has discovered how it can happen that the creature of such a being has false beliefs. Accordingly, it is an important part of his program to show that his intellectual mistakes are his fault, not God's.

So Descartes argues that error depends on two faculties which he finds that he has: the faculty of knowing, or the intellect, and the faculty of choosing, or the will. For error is properly predicable only of judgments, and judgment is a compound of two elements. It involves an idea, which is the subject of the judgment, and which is due to the intellect, and a volition, a decision to make an affirmation or negation concerning that idea.[18]

Error, according to Descartes, results from the fact that, whereas the human intellect is finite, the human will is not. By this he says he means that there are countless things of which we have no idea, though we can conceive an intellect (God's) which is not limited in this way. But we are aware of nothing, Descartes holds, which can be the object of any other will (even God's), which cannot be the object of ours.[19] It is in virtue of the infinitude of the human will that man knows that he has been created in the image of God. But because we do not restrain our will to judging only those things which we understand, we fall into error.

Such is Descartes' official explanation of error. Nevertheless, the situation is plainly more complicated than this summary suggests, and a closer examination shows that Descartes is not entirely consistent. It is necessary for us to have some idea in order for there to be something for us to make a judgment about.[20] So we cannot, strictly speaking, affirm or deny what we do not understand at all. The statement that "we err because we do not restrain our will to judging only those things we understand" must mean "we err because we do not restrain our will to judging only those things we understand clearly and distinctly."

Moreover, there are evidently further limits on the will which Descartes himself acknowledges, though he maintains that they do not derogate from our freedom. When I do understand something clearly and distinctly, then I am in a state in which I cannot but believe it. So, for example, when in the Second Meditation Descartes understood clearly that he existed, he was not able not to judge that what he understood so clearly was true (*non potui quidem non judicare illud quod tam clare intelligebam verum esse*). He was nonetheless free in so judging. For Descartes deliberately[21] defines freedom in such a way that it will be consistent both with the will's being determined by the intellect and with its being determined by God. Freedom in judging does not consist in our being able to either affirm or deny, but in our being so moved to affirming or denying that we are aware of no external force which determines us.[22] When we perceive something clearly and distinctly we are drawn irresistibly but freely to believe it. *Ex magna luce in intellectu magna consequuta est propensio in voluntate.*

But where the perception of the intellect is not clear and distinct, then the will is always more or less indifferent to what is proposed to it and therefore able to choose either. There may be a great inclination to believe one thing rather than another, or there may be no inclination at all. In the latter case, indifference is at its height and presumably it is very easy for me to either affirm or deny (though Descartes says, rather significantly, that this state of complete indifference is the lowest degree of liberty). In the former case, however probable the reasons may be which draw me in one direction, the mere knowledge that they are only probable reasons, not certain and indubitable ones, suffices to draw my assent in the other direction.[23] So the Cartesian account of judgment attributes to the mind a rather considerable ability to believe or disbelieve or suspend judgment at will.

Given this account of the nature of belief, Descartes propounds what looks like as cautious an ethics of belief as could ever be proposed. If we abstain from judging whenever we do not perceive something clearly and distinctly, we act rightly and are not deceived. But if we make an affirmation or denial when our perception is not clear and distinct, we misuse our free will. Even if we chance to judge truly, we are culpable. And since we cannot do otherwise than assent to what we perceive clearly and distinctly, Descartes in effect enjoins us to abstain from judgment wherever we can. "Be sober and doubt what you can."

It should be noted that there does not seem to be any sign, in the mature Descartes, of the doctrine of a qualified assent which has been so popular among the British empiricists. When a Hume recommends that we proportion our belief to the evidence, or a Locke says that we ought not to entertain any proposition "with greater assurance than the proofs it is built upon will warrant,"[24] he is plainly supposing that there are degrees of belief, and that the right course of action, where the evidence for a proposition is not conclusive, is to give it only a limited degree of assent. But this option, with its characteristically British appeal to common sense, is not, on the whole,[25] one that Descartes considers. Like Newman, he treats assent as an all or nothing action; though unlike Newman, he takes a very strict view about the circumstances in which this action should be performed.[26]

Of course, Descartes' ethics of belief is not in fact as rigorous as it sometimes seems. As a reader of the *Discourse on Method* might expect, Descartes distinguishes between the requirements of con-

templation and those of daily life, recognizes that we may often
have to act on hypotheses for which we do not even have probable
evidence, and recommends that we then act as resolutely as if we
were certain.[27] And he is quite prepared, under the prompting of
Arnauld, to make a further exception in favor of the articles of
religious faith.[28] So in fact he allows the things which have been of
the greatest interest to people like Newman and James.

But whatever Descartes' limitations may be as a precursor of
Huxley, it is essential that the theory of judgment in the Fourth
Meditation not be dismissed as merely an *ad hoc* device for dealing
with his peculiar, epistemological version of the problem of evil. It
has considerable importance for Descartes' method as well. The
ability to doubt whatever is not clearly conceived is a presupposition of his use of doubt as a methodological tool. It is because
Descartes has suspended judgment about even the most probable of
his former opinions that he claims to be building on a solid foundation.[29] And it is equally vital that there be some propositions
which resist his attempts to suspend judgment or think the contrary. If his 'antecedent skepticism' is to be a means to knowledge,
and not, as Hume warned, a final resting place, there must be some
propositions which he finds that he cannot but believe.[30]

II. *Spinoza*

When we turn from the Fourth Meditation to Spinoza's judgment on it at the end of Part II of the *Ethics*, we find that there are
two main themes in his criticism: first, that the faculties of the will
and the intellect which play such an important role in Descartes'
theory are fictions (IIP48S), and second, that to the extent that we
may speak about the will and the intellect at all, they are identical
(IIP49C). But the proofs Spinoza offers for these counterclaims do
not, I think, help very much to explain why Spinoza makes them, or
what their exact bearing on the controversy is.

The first seems to be argued for on general deterministic
grounds. In IIP48 Spinoza maintains that there is no absolute or
free will in the mind, but that the mind is determined to willing this
or that by a cause which is itself determined, and so on to infinity.
The argument for this, essentially, is that the mind is finite and has
a 'determinate existence', i.e. exists in a particular way. Everything

which is finite and has a determinate existence is determined to exist and act in the way it does by something which also is finite and has a determinate existence (IP28). So the mind cannot be a free cause in willing this or that. In the same way, Spinoza says, we can show that there is no absolute faculty of the intellect, but that these faculties are either quite fictitious, or else nothing but 'metaphysical entities' or universals which we are in the habit of forming from particulars. The will and the intellect are related to particular volitions and 'intellections' as 'stoneness' is to particular stones. But Spinoza's view of universals is that they are not real entities.[31] So the will and the intellect, considered as something distinct from particular volitions and intellections, are not real.

Presented thus abstractly the argument is hardly compelling. Still, I think it does make a valid point, which we might put in the following way:[32] Suppose we conceive of the will, as Descartes seems to, as a capacity for making affirmations and denials. This capacity is common to all particular volitions, it is manifested equally in each particular affirmation or denial. As a consequence it cannot *explain* any affirmation or denial. It is no explanation of my affirming *p* to say that I have a capacity for affirmation and denial, since my having that capacity is quite consistent with my denying *p*. Anything which is put forward to explain my affirmation must, if it is satisfactory, be specific enough to make it intelligible that I make *this* affirmation rather than some contrary one.

But however correct this may be, it does not get us very far. The really crucial point is Spinoza's second one, that the will and the intellect are identical, or rather, that there is in the mind no volition, no affirmation or negation, beyond that which an idea involves insofar as it is an idea (IIP49). And unfortunately the proof we are given of this proposition is quite inadequate.

Spinoza's 'demonstration' is divided into two parts. First, he argues that an affirmation can neither be nor be conceived without an idea. We are asked to consider the particular volition by which the mind affirms that the three angles of a triangle are equal to two right angles. This affirmation can neither be nor be conceived without the idea of a triangle, says Spinoza, citing IIA3:

> Modes of thinking, such as love, desire, or whatever is signified by the term *affects of the mind*, do not exist unless there is in the same individual an idea of the thing loved, desired, etc. But an idea can exist even though no other mode of thinking exists.

But then the thesis in favor of which this axiom is adduced is not controversial. It is just good Cartesian doctrine.

Second, he argues, the idea of a triangle must involve this affirmation about the triangle, viz., that its three angles are equal to two right angles, so that the idea can neither be nor be conceived without the affirmation. This step in the 'proof', which *is* controversial, is not justified by the citation of anything that has gone before. With it asserted, however, Spinoza can go on to say that since the idea can neither be nor be conceived without the affirmation, the affirmation pertains to the essence of the idea (by IID2). And since this affirmation has been chosen at random, he takes himself to have shown that no particular volition (i.e. affirmation or negation) is anything more than an idea. That will and intellect are one and the same is an easily demonstrated corollary, for it has already been shown that the will is nothing more than the particular volitions of the mind.

Now this is most unpromising. Where we are looking for an argument, we get only an assertion. Moreover, it is natural to object that the assertion gets whatever plausibility it has from the fact that the affirmation which Spinoza alleges to have been chosen at random is really a very special case. It is a necessary property of (Euclidean) triangles that their three angles are equal to two right angles. So we might be willing to agree that an idea of a triangle which did not in some sense 'involve' its having that angle sum would not be an idea of a triangle at all, though no doubt we would want this notion of 'involving' explained.[33] But what of contingent properties? Can I not have an idea of a triangle without that idea's involving, in any sense, that triangle's having the particular area it does?

If this is a natural objection, then I suppose it is equally natural to reply, on Spinoza's behalf, that the distinction assumed here between necessary and contingent properties is an invalid one, whose invalidity Spinoza claims to have shown in Part I (IP33S1). But I think it may be more profitable not to venture into that thicket, and to try a different approach instead.

Let us take for our text the following remark from the Scholium which concludes Part II:

> Those who think that ideas consist in images which are formed in us by contact with [external] bodies are convinced that those ideas of things [which can make no trace in our brain or] of

> which we can form no similar image are not ideas, but only fic-
> tions which we invent by a free decision of the will; they look on
> ideas, therefore, as like silent pictures on a tablet, and preoc-
> cupied by this prejudice, they do not see that an idea, insofar as it
> is an idea, involves an affirmation or negation [Gebhardt II, 132;
> Elwes II, 122].

This is a very interesting passage. The beginning is reminiscent of
the opening of the Sixth Meditation, or of Descartes' reply to
Hobbes' objection that we can have no idea of God.[34] The distinction between ideas and images is vital to Descartes' program, for he
wants to maintain that we can have ideas of a great many things
which we cannot imagine—not just God, but thousand-sided
polygons as well. That there is such a distinction is certainly good
Cartesian doctrine. But the conclusion of the passage is manifestly
anti-Cartesian: to trace the doctrine that ideas per se involve no affirmation to a confusion of ideas with images is to suggest that there
is an important incoherence in Descartes' notion of an idea.[35]

Now it seems to me that Spinoza is right to find Descartes' conception of ideas incoherent and right also to connect this with a confusion of ideas and images. First of all, there is a purely logical
point. Cartesian ideas are supposed to be, in themselves, neither
true nor false. They are supposed not to involve, in themselves, any
element of affirmation or negation. But they are also supposed to be
the objects of affirmation or denial, and it is natural to feel that the
object of an affirmation or denial must be a proposition. Paraphras-
ing Alan Gewirth[36] we might ask: if it is simply by an act of affirming or denying an idea that a judgment comes into being, must
not the idea have previously been a proposition? If the idea were the
sort of thought which would be expressed linguistically by a term,
the addition of an act of affirmation or denial to it could not result
in a judgment. And certainly in the Fourth Meditation, where
Descartes is most concerned with the analysis of judgment, the examples of ideas that he considers are always ideas *that something is
the case*—that I, insofar as I am a thinking thing, exist, or that the
thinking nature by which I am what I am is distinct from the cor-
poral nature which also seems to pertain to me (*AT* VII, 59; *HR* I,
176). He finds that he cannot but affirm the first, though he is indifferent to the second. Still, in each case *what* we affirm or deny or
'suspend judgment' about must, it seems, be a proposition, if the
theory is to be intelligible.

Secondly, there also seem to be general systematic reasons for regarding Cartesian ideas as propositional. One of the key features of ideas in Descartes' philosophy is their role as 'representative' entities. It is in virtue of this role that they are said, not to be images, but to be *like* images. Consider the two ideas I have of the sun:

> . . . one which apparently takes its origin from the senses . . . by which it appears to me to be extremely small, the other taken from astronomical reasoning . . . by which it seems to me several times larger than the earth [*AT* VII, 39; *HR* I, 161].

There should be no serious temptation to think of this second idea as *being* an image of the sun; but it is *like* an image of the sun in that it represents the sun as having a certain characteristic. And to say that it does this is to say that it is implicitly propositional. It is an idea *that something is the case*.

This much seems to have been seen, albeit confusedly, by the anonymous correspondent whose letter of May 19, 1641 was communicated to Descartes by Mersenne (*AT* III, 375-377). Obviously troubled by Decartes' use of the term 'idea', he writes that most philosophers usually signify by it a simple concept "like the image which (as they say) remains in the phantasy, which is also called a phantasm." He recognizes that Descartes does not mean by "idea" an image, but he is still puzzled. When he considers the example of the two ideas of the sun, he finds that he has, through vision, an idea of the sun consisting of a very bright but not very large circle. This idea is expressed by a simple name ("the sun"), for "names signify only simple concepts." After reasoning he infers that the sun is many times larger than it appears to be to the eye, and then either he forms a different idea, a circle which is equal in its dimensions to the sun, but is still an image, or, without any idea beyond his original visual one, he says (thinks) that the sun is much larger than it seems. The correspondent assumes that for Descartes having an idea is having a thought of this last sort, a thought which he goes on to call a complex concept and which would be expressed by a proposition, not by a name.

Now this, I suggest, is right in its general direction, even if wrong in certain details. It is right in its contention that the idea one has of the sun through astronomical reasoning is implicitly propositional, but wrong in holding that this is not equally true of the visual idea of the sun. For Descartes says even of the idea of the sun which apparently comes from the senses that "through it the sun appears to me to be quite small." To have that sort of idea is also to be in a state in which it seems to me that something is the case.[37]

It is wrong also in confusing the distinction between terms and propositions with the distinction between the simple and complex. The difference between "the sun" and "the sun is large" is not simply a difference between the simple and the complex, any more than a sentence is simply a string of terms. In the sentence something is said of the sun, so that we have a linguistic expression which is true or false, which would not be so if we had only a complex expression like "the large sun."

Or at any rate, it would not necessarily be so. It might be argued that a complex expression like "the large sun" should be parsed as equivalent to a noun phrase ("the sun") plus relative clause ("which is very large"), and that, though the resultant expression might, from a grammatical point of view, not constitute a complete sentence, still it would, from a logical point of view, involve an assertion which would be either true or false. "The sun, which is large, . . ." makes a truth-claim, even if the rules of grammar require a further truth-claim to be made.

This holds, I think, only for what the grammarians call nonrestrictive relative clauses, where the relative clause is not essential to identifying the subject of predication ("the planet Earth, which is third from the sun, completes its orbit in approximately 365 1/4 days"), not for restrictive relative clauses ("the planet which is third from the sun completes its orbit in approximately 365 1/4 days"). And the need to make this qualification shows that the distinction between simple and complex concepts is a red herring. Only those complex expressions which are, or are equivalent to, nonrestrictive relative clauses involve an assertion.[38]

His correspondent's confusion of the simple/complex concept distinction with the term/proposition distinction colors Descartes' reply. "Your friend," he writes to Mersenne in July, 1641,

> has not grasped my meaning at all, when to indicate the distinction between ideas which are in the phantasy and those which are in the mind, he says that the former are expressed by terms and the latter by propositions. For whether they are expressed by terms or propositions, it is not that which makes them belong to the mind or to the imagination. *Each kind of idea can be expressed in either way*. It is rather the manner of conceiving them

that makes the difference. Whatever we conceive without an image is an idea of the pure mind, and whatever we conceive with an image is an idea of the imagination [*AT* III, 395; *Philosophical Letters,* 106-107; my italics].

So the difference between the sensory or imaginative and the rational ideas of the sun, insofar as it is not a difference in content, i.e. a difference in the characteristics which the two ideas represent the sun as having, depends on whether or not the idea is accompanied by (or causally connected with) an image in the brain.[39] Both are thoughts which might be expressed in a form of words which involves at least a tentative affirmation: "It seems to me that. . . ." And so Descartes will quite cheerfully allow that both may be expressed by a proposition.

But he also maintains that both may be expressed by a term. This seems to be because he shares the tendency of his correspondent to confuse the simple/complex concept distinction with the term/proposition distinction. For when Mersenne puts to him again the question 'Whether our ideas are expressed by a simple term?', he replies that he does not understand it. "Words are human inventions and we can always use one or several to explain the same thing" (*AT* III, 417; *Philosophical Letters,* 108). But the fact that one and the same thought may be expressed with more or fewer words is irrelevant to the question whether ideas involve an element of assertion.

We are now, I hope, in a position to see why Spinoza thought Descartes was confusing ideas with images when he claimed that ideas as such do not involve any affirmation or denial. In at least one important use of the term "idea",[40] an idea is supposed to be a representative entity which can be affirmed or denied. Now an image or a picture can represent an object as having certain characteristics simply by being a good likeness of the object. When we spiritualize our representative entity and deprive it of all the characteristics of material objects, it is hard to know what to make of this notion of a resemblance between the idea and its object. We can do something with the notion if we regard the idea as the sort of thought which might be expressed by a proposition. But if we do that, then we can no longer say that the idea in itself involves neither an affirmation nor a denial and is neither true nor false.[41]

Nevertheless, once we conceive of ideas as being true or false in their own right and as involving, in themselves, an element of assertion, there does not seem to be any need for a further act of the will to produce a judgment. If we suppose that there is, are we not taking the substantial expressions "the will" and "the intellect" too seriously and treating them as distinct agents rather than distinct functions of one agent? If my intellect affirms that the sun is very large, am *I* not already judging that it is? Is it really necessary for my will to add its concurring 'opinion'? Suppose these two judges disagree. Shall I intervene to cast the deciding vote? If so, what faculty will I be exercising when I do? And if no further act of the will is needed to produce a judgment, is not Spinoza right to say that "there is in the mind no volition, or affirmation and negation, except that which an idea involves, insofar as it is an idea" (IIP49)?

As I indicated earlier, I think Spinoza is fundamentally right. But I don't suppose that he can be shown to be right quite so easily as the rhetorical questions of the preceding paragraph may suggest. One of the things which lends plausibility to the Cartesian analysis of judgment is the phenomenon of suspended judgment. We might put the Cartesian case as follows. Normally at least, the only sort of affirmation which an idea involves as an act of the intellect is a more or less tentative one. Though having an idea (insofar as this is an occurrence relevant to the analysis of judgment) is always having an idea that something is so, it is also always appropriate to paraphrase this by saying that when we have an idea that *p*, then it seems to us that *p*. And it is quite possible for it to seem to us that *p* without our judging that *p*. We can withhold our judgment, all the while allowing that the weight of evidence favors *p*. Indeed, we can even judge not-*p* and yet allow that the evidence favors *p*. This is simply a fact of experience which it would be folly to deny.[42]

Spinoza, of course, considers this objection, though not quite in the form in which I have presented it. And he makes two useful suggestions about it. First, he does not deny the existence of the phenomenon, but argues that it is misdescribed as an act (or nonact) of the will:

> When we say that someone suspends judgment, we are saying only that he sees that he does not perceive the thing adequately. Suspension of judgment, therefore, is really a perception, and not free will . . . Conceive a boy imagining a winged horse and not perceiving anything else. Since this imagination involves the existence of the horse [by IIP17C] and the boy does not perceive anything which contradicts the existence of the horse, he will

necessarily contemplate the horse as present, and will not be able to doubt its existence . . . I deny that a man affirms nothing insofar as he perceives. For what is it to perceive a winged horse except to affirm of the horse that it has wings? If the mind were to perceive nothing except a winged horse, it would contemplate it as present to itself, it would have no cause for doubting the horse's existence, and no faculty of dissenting, unless the imagination of the winged horse should be joined to an idea which denies the existence of the horse or the mind perceives that the idea of a winged horse which it has is inadequate. And then either it will necessarily deny the existence of the horse, or it will necessarily doubt its existence [Gebhardt II, 134; Elwes II, 125].

Spinoza's argument here is partly based on his peculiar theory of the imagination, which I do not propose to go into now, and partly based on the confusion between complex concepts and propositions, which I criticized earlier in this paper. But it has appealed to a variety of phenomenologists of belief quite independently of the arguments Spinoza uses, and I think rightly so.[43]

We might put Spinoza's point in the following way. Doubt is inherently a second-order activity. I cannot doubt whether *p* unless I already have some existing tendency to believe that *p*, unless it already seems to me in some measure that *p*. I cannot 'suspend judgment' unless there is in some sense a judgment to suspend. But equally, I cannot doubt whether *p* unless I already have some existing tendency to believe *not-p*, unless it already seems to me in some measure that *p* is false. These conflicting tendencies are necessary conditions for doubt, and insofar as I am aware of them and find them to be of approximately equal strength, they are sufficient. Suspending judgment—insofar as it is something mental, not the abstention from a public pronouncement—is not an action I take as a consequence of finding the arguments pro and con are pretty evenly balanced. It is simply the state itself of finding them to be so.

I put this claim forward not as a piece of introspective psychology, nor as a piece of armchair linguistics, but as a sample of what we now like to call conceptual analysis.[44] I take it that it can be decisively confirmed or refuted only by a detailed and tedious examination of the way in which expressions like "belief", "doubt" and "suspense of judgment" and their linguistic equivalents in other languages are used, particularly by philosophers for whom the subject of belief is important. Without undertaking such an examination here, I can make some suggestions as to how it might proceed and the conclusions which might result.

If you look at the way the notion of a suspense of judgment is used by a classical skeptic like Sextus Empiricus, you may be surprised by what you find. You might expect that he would be as much a voluntarist about belief as Descartes appears to be. But though Sextus sometimes talks as though suspense of judgment were an act, as when he compares the Skeptic's suspension to the painter Apelles' act of throwing his sponge at the canvas (*Outlines of Pyrrhonism*, Bk. I, Sec. 12), he usually represents it as a state of mind which results either from the activity of inquiry or from a consciously adopted policy of seeking out grounds for doubting what we would otherwise naturally be inclined to believe (Secs. 4, 13, 22 and, with some reservations, 20 and 33). It is a state of being indifferent, not an action we take because we are indifferent or in spite of not being indifferent. And it might be argued that there is an implicit recognition of this in Descartes, so that even he is not quite the voluntarist he represents himself as being. This, perhaps, is why he insists on having reasonable grounds for doubting his former beliefs and why he urges his readers to reflect carefully and frequently on those grounds, treating the First Meditation as a kind of spiritual exercise.[45] We cannot just decide not to believe something we find highly probable, but we can bring it about that we no longer find it probable by attending to arguments which cut against the belief or against the grounds on which we hold it.

If this is right, and if Descartes' apparent voluntarism about belief is an indication of conceptual confusion, it is natural to ask how the confusion comes about. And this is the point at which we may find the second of Spinoza's suggestions useful. In the Scholium at the end of Part II of the *Ethics*, Spinoza warns us to avoid two common confusions about ideas. One is the tendency to confuse ideas with images, which we have already touched on. The other is the tendency to confuse ideas with the words by which they are expressed. "Those who confound words with an idea, or with the affirmation which an idea involves, think that they can will [i.e. affirm or deny] contrary to what they perceive, when, by mere words, they affirm or deny something contrary to what they perceive."[46]

Like most of Spinoza's suggestions, this one needs a good deal of filling out before it is of any use. Consider the theory of judgment recently put forward by Peter Geach in *Mental Acts*.[47] There Geach develops the notion of judging as an (irreducibly) analogical extension of the concept of saying, and contends that the analogies are systematic rather than casual. The whole linguistic scheme which we use in talking about judgments is an extension of the linguistic scheme we use in talking about utterances. Predicates like ". . . is true" are "properly and primarily applicable to statements in language, rather than to thoughts or judgments . . ." (p. 98).

Now this seems to me to be confirmed by reflection on the vocabulary traditionally used by philosophers who have had theories of the nature of belief. Certainly one of the most striking features of that vocabulary is the extent to which the terms used to denote the act of judging are borrowed from our discourse about statements in language. We affirm, deny, assent, consent, acquiesce, etc.

But as Geach has also stressed, "the important thing about analogical extensions of a concept is that we should know . . . how far to carry the analogy" (p. 101). Judging, or 'saying-in-one's-heart', though *like* saying, is still not the same thing as saying. Nor is it the same thing as saying subvocally. Geach argues, for example, that judgments, unlike utterances, have no more than "a loose connection with physical time" (pp. 104-106). And the argument is persuasive, if not compelling.

I suggest that Spinoza has located another important disanalogy between saying and judging. It makes perfectly good sense to speak of someone as saying what he does not perceive to be true. The occasions we have for this criticism of others' utterances are all too frequent. But it is nonsense to speak of someone as saying-in-his-heart or judging what he does not perceive to be true. Unless he perceives it to be true, he cannot properly be said to believe it.

One final consideration. Most writers on this topic who have thought that belief can be a voluntary action have allowed that there are some constraints on belief. Descartes, as we have seen, holds that when we perceive something clearly and distinctly, we cannot but believe it. Just what Descartes means by clarity and distinctness is a much disputed question, whose solution is not greatly aided by the definitions he offers, but one interpretation which comes naturally to mind in contexts like this is that a clear and distinct idea is one for which we have conclusive reasons, one which is rendered absolutely certain by the evidence we have.[48]

Locke allows rather less scope to the will. Assent is involuntary not only where we have intuitive or demonstrative knowledge (IV, 2, 1 and 5; IV, 13; IV, 14), but also where experience and testimony give rise to a "clear and strong" probability (IV, 16, 6-9; IV, 17, 16; IV, 20, 12-16). It is only where the arguments establish but a weak probability, or there is some reason to suspect a fallacy in them, or reason to expect that equally good evidence to the contrary may be produced, that assent is voluntary.[49]

The picture these writers suggest, then, is of belief as a kind of action which may be impossible in some circumstances, very difficult in others, and presumably, rather easy in still others, depending on the state of the evidence. I cannot now believe that the *Arabian Nights* are true. But perhaps if only I tried harder, or if only the stories weren't quite so improbable, I could do it. I propose, then, that we test this view by conducting the following 'thought-experiment'. Consider some proposition for which you have literally no evidence at all one way or the other. It may not be as easy as you might suppose to think of an example which strictly satisfies that condition, but I am in this situation with respect to the proposition "it rained three hours ago on Jupiter." Now, paying careful attention to what is happening in your mind, believe it. Or, if you prefer, disbelieve it. Or do both, in turn. Did anything happen? Unless your experience is very unlike mine, I suspect not. Indeed, I fear that if my salvation depended on my either believing or disbelieving this particular proposition, I should be damned.

III. *The Ethics of Belief*

I have argued that Spinoza is fundamentally right, that belief is not a voluntary action, not something that we decide to do, but something that happens to us, that coming to believe is something much more like falling in love than like raising one's arm. Does it in fact follow that the whole controversy between cautious and venturesome believers rests on a mistake? And doesn't the very practice of using moral language about belief—of ascribing to people duties or rights to believe or not to believe and appraising their beliefs as reasonable or unreasonable—doesn't the existence of this 'language game' constitute some kind of argument against Spinoza? Why should we do this unless we suppose that, when someone believes something, he could have believed something else instead? And can such a very general misconception be explained away simply by pointing to our tendency to confuse saying-in-one's-heart with saying?[50]

Now I think we must concede that there is merit in this objection. There is, as Hampshire remarks, "a whole range of idioms that assimilate belief to action."[51] We not only blame people for believing things too readily, and say that they ought to or ought not to or may believe certain things, we also say things like "I refuse to believe that" or "I prefer to believe this," and so on. The evidence of linguistic usage does not all point in one direction. Most of us, I suppose, would find it odd, to say the least, to be asked what our motive for or intention in believing something is. We do not excuse people's beliefs in the ways in which we characteristically excuse their actions, as being unintentional, inadvertent, accidental or performed under duress. And I find more than a faint whiff of the absurd in the suggestion that we should. Still, I am not sure that my linguistic intuitions would be shared by all native speakers of English. It has been suggested to me that the negative result of the thought-experiment proposed at the end of the preceding section might be explained by the absence, in that case, of any plausible motive for believing. The view would be that, though we can believe without evidence or even what we take to be evidence, we cannot believe without some motive. I find it a bit difficult to take this suggestion seriously. Those who can should ask themselves whether the lack of a motive might not be remedied by offering a reward? Would this alter the result?

Nevertheless, the practice of appraising beliefs in moral or quasi-moral terms is too widespread to be attributed to any simple mistake. Seeing what it does rest on is a complicated business. In closing this essay I should like to suggest very briefly what I think the rationale for the practice is.

That some of the moral dicta advanced about belief rest on a confusion cannot be denied. Huxley writes:

> Agnosticism is not properly described as a "negative" creed, nor indeed as a creed of any kind, except insofar as it expresses absolute faith in the validity of a principle, which is as much ethical as intellectual . . . that it is wrong for a man to say that he is certain of the objective truth of any proposition unless he can

produce evidence which logically justifies that certainty . . . that
which Agnostics deny and repudiate as immoral, is the contrary
doctrine, that there are propositions which men ought to believe,
without logically satisfactory evidence; and that reprobation
ought to attach to the profession of disbelief in such inadequately
supported propositions.[52]

Clearly something has gone wrong here. "You ought not to *say* you
are certain of *p* when you do not have adequate evidence for it" is
not contrary to "You ought to *believe p* even though you do not
have adequate evidence for it." Huxley could not slide in such a
short space from a thesis about the profession of belief to one about
belief and back again to one about the profession of belief, unless he
were fairly seriously confused.

The profession of belief is only one of the varieties of action in
which beliefs are typically expressed. Often when people use moral
language in connection with belief, it seems that they are concerned
not so much with belief as with the actions in which belief issues.
Locke writes of "the odd opinions and *extravagant actions*
enthusiasm has run men into." When he speaks of "not *entertaining* any proposition with greater assurance than the proofs it is
built upon will warrant,"[53] perhaps what he really means is that we
ought not to *act* on uncertain beliefs in a way which would be appropriate only to beliefs we are certain about. There are some actions whose consequences may be so harmful if the beliefs they are
founded on are mistaken that we normally should require very good
evidence indeed for the beliefs before we act on them.

Clifford's shipowner is a case in point. He sends to sea an un-
seaworthy ship, laden with emigrant families seeking a better life in
a new country. And he suppresses his doubts about the adequacy of
his ship for its task by a series of more or less elaborate self-
deceptions. He reflects that the ship has weathered many a long
voyage before, reminds himself that there is a benevolent God who
is unlikely to let so many innocents suffer, and so on. His ultimate
belief in the safety of the vessel is firm and comfortable, and when
she sinks with no survivors, he collects his insurance money with an
easy conscience. "What shall we say of him?" asks Clifford.

Surely this, that he was verily guilty of the death of those men. It
is admitted that he did sincerely believe in the soundness of his
ship; but the sincerity of his conviction can in no wise help him,
because *he had no right to believe on such evidence as was before*

him. He had acquired his belief not by honestly earning it in patient investigation, but by stifling his doubts. And although in the end he may have felt so sure about it that he could not think otherwise, yet inasmuch as he had knowingly and willingly worked himself into that frame of mind, he must be held responsible for it [p. 178].

This is interesting in a number of respects. First, Clifford's argument clearly does not rest on any naively voluntaristic conception of belief. He treats belief not as an act which we may or may not perform, but as a state which we may or may not induce in ourselves indirectly through our performance or nonperformance of a variety of other activities: reflection on the evidence already at hand, searching for new evidence, focussing our attention on some considerations rather than others, etc. Commenting on the case a bit further on, he remarks that "it has been judged wrong to believe on insufficient evidence, *or to nourish belief by suppressing doubts and avoiding investigation*."[54] It is no accident that this section of his essay is entitled "The Duty of Inquiry."

But though the shipowner may in this indirect way be responsible for his belief, it is not clear that he is culpable because he has that belief acquired in that way. We may want to object that what is culpable is not the belief, but acting on a belief which has not been fairly examined, in circumstances where the possible consequences of acting on the belief—and in particular, the possible consequences for other people—are so momentous. Clifford considers an objection like this and allows it some merit, but remarks that "it is not possible so to sever belief from the action it suggests as to condemn the one without condemning the other" (p. 181).

This, however, is not to the point, as we can show by altering the case in various ways to highlight its relevant features. Suppose we have another man who holds the same belief in the ship's seaworthiness, arrived at by a similar process of rationalization, who nevertheless does not occupy a similar position of responsibility for sending it to sea. To give him a motive for the rationalization, we can make him a prospective passenger, eager to leave a hostile and alien country, but too poor to afford the fares of a more reputable line. To insure that his belief affects only himself, let us imagine him to be a man with no family, enveloped in no network of affections, disabled from communicating his belief and its 'reasons' to his fellow prospective passengers by some linguistic barrier.

What shall we say of him? Surely not that he was "guilty of the death of those men." He believed the ship seaworthy. He acted on this belief. But in his case *acting on the belief* was not *sending the ship to sea*, and his belief, however ill-founded, injured no one but himself. We might find him pitiable, but hardly culpable.

Or consider a case more like those that interest James. Let us go back to our shipowner, but alter both the situation in which he acts and his motives. This time we have as passengers a band not of emigrants, but of refugees, fleeing religious persecution. The situation is desperate. There is no time for a careful examination of the seaworthiness of this ship. Nor does there seem to be time to seek another, more obviously sturdy ship in another port. The shipowner, sympathetic to their plight, persuades himself, by a similar process of stifling his doubts, that his ship will survive the voyage. He is captain as well as owner, so in his case sending the ship to sea involves going with it. Would it not be a heartless and unreasonable man who would hold him culpable either for sending the ship to sea or for believing in its seaworthiness on such grounds as he had? But if beliefs arrived at by rationalization were always wrong, he ought to be blamed for the belief at least.

What these examples suggest, I think, is that belief "on insufficient evidence" has moral significance principally where the belief is more or less directly connected with some action fraught with potentially serious consequences for others. Where the belief has this practical import, what counts as sufficient evidence is very much a function of the particular features of the situation. What we are concerned with fundamentally is the action. We may excuse an action whose consequences were harmful, if we think that it was prompted by a sincere belief that those consequences were very unlikely or less likely than the equally harmful probable consequences of alternative actions. Or we may not, if we think that the grounds for belief were not scrutinized with the care required in those circumstances. But whether or not we treat the belief as an excuse, our concern as moral critics is primarily with the action it suggests. Insofar as we are concerned with the antecedents of the action, we want to know whether the belief resulted from a failure to reflect and inquire and we want to know what motivated that failure.

If this line of reasoning were generally applicable then our practice of assessing belief in moral terms might be dismissed as involving a failure to distinguish just what it is that is culpable in situations where we act on our beliefs. But not all appraisal of belief is of this sort. Sometimes, for example, we are held to have an obligation to believe certain religious doctrines which have no direct bearing on our conduct towards others. It is true that disbelief in the doctrines may involve others, if it is propagated in such a way as to affect their faith, thereby jeopardizing their salvation. But this kind of consideration must here be irrelevant. Their salvation could not be jeopardized unless moral significance were already attached to the state of belief in itself, without regard to its consequences for others. It is true also that people who have thought belief important in this way may not always have treated belief as a voluntary human action. Many may have regarded it as a gift of God. But if there has been any substantial number of people who have not so regarded belief, their view of the matter does require some explanation.

The only explanation which suggests itself to me is this. Though belief is not a voluntary action, we must allow that it is often connected with activities of reflection and inquiry which are or can be voluntary. It is not obvious that the distinction between acts we perform and states we produce in ourselves by an action has the moral significance it would have in order to justify our dismissing the whole subject of the ethics of belief on the ground that belief is not a voluntary action. It may be that an indirect influence of the will on belief is sufficient, not only to explain, but also to justify, the moral appraisal of belief.

I am not sure that any careful moralist of belief has ever really required more than this. Certainly James did not:

> A man cannot believe at will abruptly . . . But *gradually* our will can lead us to the same results by a very simple method: *we need only in cold blood act as if the thing in question were real and it will infallibly end by growing into such a connection with our life that it will become real.* It will become so knit with habit and emotion that our interests in it will be those which characterize belief.[55]

The mechanism envisaged here for producing belief is a very different one from those we have previously mentioned. Acting as if we believed, or as James sometimes puts it, "adopting a believing attitude," is quite a distinct process from inquiry and reflection. It might be argued that it must be supplemented by some reflection at least if a genuine belief is to result. But so long as we can produce belief in ourselves by our actions, or preserve it by our inactions, this seems sufficient to warrant the use of moral language in connection with belief.

I conclude, then, that Spinoza's view of the nature of belief is not really an obstacle to the project of developing an ethics of belief. But for reasons which should by now be clear, I find it difficult to see that there are any absolute principles which can validly govern our acquisition and maintenance of our beliefs.

E. M. CURLEY

THE AUSTRALIAN NATIONAL UNIVERSITY

NOTES

[1] Lytton Strachey, *Eminent Victorians* (London: Collins, 1959), p. 47.

[2] W. K. Clifford, *Lectures and Essays*, ed. by L. Stephen and F. Pollock (London: Macmillan, 1879), Vol. II., p. 186.

[3] T. H. Huxley, *Collected Essays* (London: Macmillan, 1893), Vol. I, pp. 169-170.

[4] David Hume, "Of Miracles," in *An Enquiry Concerning Human Understanding*, ed. by C. W. Hendel (New York: Liberal Arts Press, 1955), p. 118.

[5] Cf. Descartes, *The Principles of Philosophy*, I, 1, in *Oeuvres de Descartes*, ed. by Charles Adam and Paul Tannery (Paris: Léopold Cerf, 1897-1913), Vol. VIII, p. 8. *Oeuvres de Descartes* will hereinafter be cited as *AT*.

[6] *Collected Essays*, Vol. V, p. 310.

[7] H. H. Price, *Belief* (London: Allen and Unwin, 1969), Lecture 5, p. 129. Price holds that none of us has adequate evidence for believing that testimony is usually correct.

[8] *Ibid.*, p. 128. That "know" is frequently not used in this strict sense is argued, entertainingly and to my mind convincingly, by Bernard Williams in his article "Deciding to Believe," in *Language, Belief and Metaphysics*, ed. by H. Kiefer and M. Munitz (Albany: State University of New York Press, 1970), p. 106.

[9] It seems that if this were our end, we might achieve it best by not taking the time to consider evidence at all, but simply assenting to whatever propositions occur to us, as quickly as possible, trusting to chance that we will acquire more true beliefs in this way. Justin Gosling has suggested to me that if we restrict our attention to very specific, negative propositions ("this pen does not weigh 247.321 grams" etc.), this belief-strategy might well be the optimum one.

[10] William James, "The Will to Believe," in *Essays in Pragmatism*, ed. by A. Castell (New York: Hafner, 1964).

[11] George Nakhnikian, *An Introduction to Philosophy* (New York: Alfred A. Knopf, 1967), p. 275.

[12] I should not want to press this very far. James is neither careful nor consistent in stating just what thesis he is defending. In one place he writes, "wherever there is no forced option, the dispassionately judicial intellect, with no pet hypothesis . . . ought to be our ideal" (p. 102). Elsewhere, "we have the right to believe at our own risk any hypothesis that is live enough to tempt our will" (p. 107).

[13] Jonathan Bennett, " 'Whatever the Consequences'," *Analysis,* **26** (1966), 83-102.

[14] The first motto is from Lucian's dialogue, "Hermotimus" the second from Sextus' "Outlines of Pyrrhonism," I, 18. See *Hellenistic Philosophy,* ed. by H. Shapiro and E. M. Curley (New York: Modern Library, 1965), pp. 240, 199. But it is not clear that Sextus is committed to a voluntaristic account of belief.

[15] Cf. Spinoza's *Theological-Political Treatise,* Chap. 20, and Locke's *A Letter Concerning Toleration,* in *Works* (London, 1824), Vol. V, pp. 39-40.

[16] Descartes, *AT* VII, 37; *Philosophical Works,* ed. by Elizabeth S. Haldane and G. R. Ross (New York: Dover, 1955), Vol. I, p. 159. *Philosophical Works* will hereinafter be cited as *HR.*

[17] Anthony Kenny, *Descartes* (New York: Random House, 1968), p. 117.

[18] *AT* VII, 56-62; *HR* I, 174-179.

[19] Cf. *Principles of Philosophy,* I, 35; *AT* VIII, 18.

[20] Cf. the letter to Hyperaspistes, *AT* III, 432; *Descartes, Philosophical Letters,* ed. by Anthony Kenny (Oxford: Clarendon Press, 1970), p. 118.

[21] Cf. the Second Replies, 5, *AT* VII, 148-149, *HR* II, 44. The position Descartes maintains here does involve his taking sides in theological controversy—it is very close to one of the theses for which Jansen's *Augustinus* was soon to be condemned—and it cannot be said that Descartes keeps consistently to it. Cf. the letter to Mesland(?), February 9, 1645(?) (*AT* IV, 173-175; *Philosophical Letters,* pp. 159-160), which contradicts the Fourth Meditation as well as the (apparently) earlier letter of May 2, 1644 (*AT* IV, 111-120; *Philosophical Letters,* pp. 146-152). There is an excellent discussion in Boyce Gibson's *The Philosophy of Descartes* (New York: Russell and Russell, 1967, reissue), pp. 331-339, culminating in the conclusion that the teaching of the Fourth Meditation represents Descartes' "truest and most characteristic position."

[22] *HR* II, 175. *AT* VII, 57: *Tantum in eo consistit, quod idem vel facere vel non facere (hoc est affirmare vel negare, prosequi vel fugere) possimus, vel potius in eo tantum, quod ad id quod nobis ab intellectu proponitur affirmandum vel negandum, sive prosequendum vel fugiendum, ita feramur, ut a nulla vi externa nos ad id determinari sentiamus.* The French version is less suggestive of passivity: *nous agissons en telle sort que nous ne sentons point qu' aucune force extérieure nous y contraigne.*

[23] *HR* I, 176; *AT* VII, 59: *sufficit ad assensionem meam in contrarium impellandam.* Again the French version is less suggestive of passivity: *suffit pour me donner occasion de juger le contraire.*

[24] *Essay Concerning Human Understanding,* IV, 19, 1, "Of Enthusiasm."

[25] An exception must be made in the case of the *Regulae*. In Rule XII, Descartes writes that whatever we 'compose' by conjecture does not deceive us, provided we judge that it is only probable and never affirm that it is true, but that it also does not make us more learned (*AT* X, 424; *HR* I, 45). But the *Regulae* is an early and immature work which seems to differ from Descartes' later works in a number of important respects and to contain a great many internal contradictions as well. For example, elsewhere in Rule XII Descartes treats judgment as a faculty of the intellect (*AT* X, 420; *HR* I, 42; but cf. Rule III, *AT*, 370; *HR* I, 8). There is a very thorough, if highly speculative discussion of the problems presented by the *Regulae* in Jean-Paul Weber's, *La constitution du texte des Regulae* (Paris: Sedes, 1964). We might note that there is some disagreement between Descartes' translators about the rendering of *AT* X, 424, 11.15-18. I have followed LeRoy (Descartes, *Oeuvres et Lettres*, ed. by A. Bridoux [Paris: Gallimard, 1953], p. 85), rather than Haldane and Ross. The Haldane and Ross version may be a more natural reading of the Latin, but it is also more difficult to reconcile with the opening of Rule II.

[26] See *A Grammar of Assent* (Garden City: Doubleday & Co., Image Books, 1955), Chap. 6. There is a helpful discussion of Newman's claim that there are no degrees of assent in Price, *Belief*, pp. 130-156. Cf. also p. 207.

[27] *AT* VII, 149, *HR* II, 44. Cf. the *Discourse on Method*, Part III, second maxim.

[28] Cf. *AT* VII, 215-217, 247-248; *HR* II, 93-95, 116. In the Second Replies Descartes distinguishes between the matter or thing to which we assent and the formal reason which moves the will to assent. The matter is obscure, the formal reason possesses a clarity and evidence greater than that of any natural light. This 'formal reason' is said to be a certain internal light, granted to us supernaturally by God. (Cf. the letter to Hyperaspistes, *AT* III, 425-426; *Philosophical Letters*, p. 113, and the letter to Clerselier, January 12, 1646, *AT* IX, 208, *HR* II, 129). I think this latter line of thought might have involved him in some difficulties. For example in discussing the position of infidels, Descartes implies that the supernatural light of grace can be resisted, which is puzzling, since its evidence is supposed to be greater than that of the natural light of reason which cannot be resisted. For an admirably balanced discussion of the relation between faith and reason in Descartes, see Gibson, *Philosophy of Descartes*, pp. 287-292.

[29] Cf. the letter to Picot, Bridoux, p. 562; *HR* I, 208.

[30] We may note in passing that in the *Regulae*, where Descartes does not seem to have arrived at the theory of judgment presented in the *Meditations*, there also does not seem to be any sign of the methodic doubt.

[31] *Treatise on the Improvement of the Intellect*, Section 99, *Opera*, ed. by C. Gebhardt, Vol. II, p. 36; *Chief Works*, ed. by R. H. M. Elwes (New York: Dover, 1951), Vol. II, pp. 36-37.

[32] Cf. Spinoza's earlier, more explicit formulation in the *Short Treatise*, Part II, Chap. 16, Gebhardt, I, 82-83; *Spinoza's Short Treatise on God, Man and his Wellbeing*, ed. & trans. by A. Wolf (New York: Russell and Russell, 1963), pp. 106-108. Cf. also IIP49S, Gebhardt II, 135, 11.1-12.

[33] Spinoza's choice of this example may reflect his reading of the First Replies (*AT* VII, 117-118; *HR* II, 20), where Descartes says that "If I think of a triangle . . . then

certainly whatever I see to be contained in the idea of the triangle, e.g. that its three angles are equal to two right angles, I shall affirm truly of the triangle." Cf. also the Fifth Meditation, *AT* VII, 64; *HR* I, 180.

34 *AT* VII, 72-73, *HR* I, 185-186; *AT* VII, 179-181, *HR* II, 66-68.

35 I did not see that when I discussed this passage in *Spinoza's Metaphysics* (Cambridge, Mass.: Harvard University Press, 1969), p. 122, and what follows is intended partly as a corrective of what is said there about Descartes' use of the term "idea". For further discussion of this very complicated topic, see Kenny, *Descartes*, Chap. 5, and Harry Frankfurt, *Demons, Dreamers and Madmen* (Indianapolis: Bobbs-Merrill, 1970), Chap. 12.

36 Alan Gewirth, "Clearness and Distinctness in Descartes," in *Descartes, a Collection of Critical Essays* ed. by Willis Doney (London: Macmillan & Co. 1968), p. 263.

37 Cf. Kenny, *Descartes*, pp. 69-75.

38 I might just suggest parenthetically that the possibility of analysing complex expressions in these two ways may explain Descartes' apparent inconsistency on the question whether a triangle inscribed in a square has a true and immutable essence. Cf. *AT* VII, 117-118; *HR* II, 20-21; and Kenny, *Descartes*, p. 154. Again, Spinoza's remark in IIP49S that 'perceiving' a winged horse is the same as affirming of a horse that it has wings (Gebhardt II, 134; Elwes I, 125) seems plausible only insofar as we think of complex expressions as equivalent to nonrestrictive relative clauses. But as I hope to show, his argument does not depend on that mistake.

39 I take it that for Descartes an image, strictly speaking, is a purely physical entity in the brain and that the phantasy or imagination is a part of the brain. This image may or may not be connected with external physical objects via the sense organs. Where it is so connected, we would probably find it more natural to speak of the accompanying idea as a sensory rather than an imaginative one, but Descartes, in this period at least, seems to have in mind both sorts when he speaks of ideas pertaining to the imagination. Cf. *AT* VII, 181; *HR* II, 67-68, *AT* X, 414-416; *HR* I, 38-39; *AT* VII, 160-161; *HR* II, 52.

40 As Kenny argues, Descartes' use of "idea" is very varied: "When Descartes announces the presence of an idea . . . he may be intending to signal anything from a remote capacity to a particular actual experience. Sometimes he speaks of ideas in general in terms appropriate to the description of capacities, as when he connects them with the ability to use words. At other times he speaks of them in terms appropriate to episodes, as when he says that ideas are 'operations of the intellect' . . . at other times it is not so much an act of the mind as the object or *content* of such act" (*Descartes*, pp. 98-99). It is the second and third uses which I have been concentrating on, and which are, I believe, the uses most relevant to Descartes' theory of judgment.

41 It is no wonder then that shortly after saying this about ideas in the Third Meditation, Descartes has to introduce his doctrine that ideas can be said to be 'materially true or false'. *AT* VII, 43-44, 232-235; *HR* I, 164, II, 105-107. See also Kenny, *Descartes*, pp. 118-121, and Frankfurt, *Demons, Dreamers and Madmen*, pp. 128-131.

[42] This appeal to experience is particularly prominent in the Fifth Replies, *AT* VII, 376-378; *HR* II, 224-225.

[43] See, e.g., Walter Bagehot, "On the Emotion of Conviction," in his *Literary Studies* (London: Longmans, Green & Co., 1891), Vol. II, and William James, *The Principles of Psychology* (New York: Dover, 1950), Vol. II, Chap. 21.

[44] So I agree with Bernard Williams when he says (in "Deciding to Believe," in *Language, Belief and Metaphysics*) that "it is not a contingent fact that I cannot bring it about, just like that, that I believe something, as it is a contingent fact that I cannot bring it about, just like that, that I'm blushing" (pp. 107-108).

[45] See, for example, *AT* VII, 162, 171-172, 348-350 (*HR* II, 54, 60-61, 205-206). The need for reasonable grounds of doubt has been emphasized recently by Frankfurt, but he appears to be more sympathetic than I would be to the voluntaristic analysis of judgment in the Fourth Meditation. See *Demons, Dreamers and Madmen*, Chaps. 2 and 15 particularly.

[46] Gebhardt II, 132; Elwes II, 122. But Elwes seems to have been nodding when he translated this passage.

[47] Peter Geach, *Mental Acts* (London: Routledge & Kegan Paul, 1957). See particularly Chaps. 17-23. Cf. Plato's *Sophist*, 263e.

[48] Cf. Frankfurt: "A proposition is clearly perceived when the perceiver recognizes that his evidential basis for it excludes all reasonable grounds for doubting it" (*Demons, Dreamers and Madmen*, p. 137). This cannot be the whole story about clarity and distinctness, since there are propositions which are known not by inference from other propositions, but per se (as Frankfurt, of course, recognizes). Of them we might say that clear perception consists in an awareness, resulting from careful consideration of the proposition itself, that there are no reasonable grounds for doubting it. Frankfurt seems to hold something like this (pp. 134-135) and Malebranche also appears to have understood Descartes in this way. See *De la recherche de la verité*, I, 2, 2. If we interpret clarity and distinctness along these lines and accept the thesis of this paper about the nature of belief, then there is no puzzle as to why Descartes should think that in cases of clear and distinct perception, the intellect necessarily determines the will. Cf. Willis Doney, "Descartes' Conception of Perfect Knowledge," *Journal of the History of Philosophy*, 8 (1970), pp. 399-400.

[49] See particularly IV, 20, 15. I realize that I have also cited Locke as someone who agrees with Spinoza, on the strength of this remark in the *Letter Concerning Toleration*: "To believe this or that to be true does not depend on our will." But on this topic inconsistency seems to be the rule rather than the exception. Hume provides another example, as Price has pointed out, *Belief*. Price himself seems to have modified his position considerably between his earlier article on "Belief and Will" (*Proceedings of the Aristotelian Society*, Supp. **28** [1954], reprinted in *Philosophy of Mind*, ed. by Stuart Hampshire [New York: Harper and Row, 1966] and in *Belief*).

[50] Cf. R. M. Chisholm, "Lewis' Ethics of Belief" in *The Philosophy of C. I. Lewis*, ed. by P. A. Schilpp (La Salle, Ill.: Open Court Publishing Co., 1968), pp. 223-227. I paraphrase Chisholm rather freely here.

⁵¹ See Stuart Hampshire, *Thought and Action* (London: Chatto and Windus, 1959), pp. 155-160. Hampshire, however, rejects the conception of belief as a voluntary action: "If I was told that I could satisfy my desire to believe by turning my attention away from the contrary evidence, I would not call my ensuing state, brought into existence by these means, belief. It seems that I cannot present my own belief in something as an achievement because, by so presenting it, I would disqualify it as belief" (Cf. Williams, "Deciding to Believe," in *Language, Belief and Metaphysics*, p. 108). I suspect that someone who thinks belief is a voluntary action might regard this as question-begging. He might also say the same about some of my claims. The charge of begging the question is easier to make than to sustain, but I think it's fair to say that remarks like Hampshire's display, rather than justify, our intuitions.

⁵² *Collected Essays*, Vol. V, p. 310.

⁵³ *Essay*, IV, 19, Secs. 8 and 1 respectively. (Italics mine.)

⁵⁴ *Lectures and Essays*, p. 182. Perhaps it would be more charitable to Locke to interpret him in this way too, as Leibniz seems to have done. Cf. the *Nouveaux Essais*, IV, 20, 16.

⁵⁵ *Principles of Psychology*, Vol. II, p. 321.

Warren Kessler

A Note on Spinoza's Concept of Attribute

One of the central issues of Spinoza scholarship focuses on the status of the attributes. The issue has divided scholars into two groups, which I shall call the objectivists and the subjectivists. Objectivists maintain that the attributes in fact constitute the essence of Substance and that our ideas of these attributes comprise an adequate knowledge of that essence. Subjectivists hold that the attributes are merely inventions of the human intellect which we ascribe to Substance as if they constitute its essence, although our ideas of the attributes do not conform to the actual nature of Substance. The issue is quite complex, and the long history of its discussion has seen the development of a host of arguments for each side. It is not my purpose here to review the entire debate, in part because such a review would be beyond the scope of an article and in part because a very insightful sketch of the most basic arguments has already been produced. Professor Haserot has provided us with a battery of forceful reasons for preferring the objectivist interpretation.[1] In this note I shall merely discuss two heretofore unmentioned arguments from the *Short Treatise* which corroborate the evidence assembled by the objectivists and which seem to constitute decisive evidence against the subjectivist interpretation.

The issue arises because of several ambiguities in the definition of 'attribute' in the *Ethics*:[2] "By attribute, I understand that which the intellect perceives of substance as (as if) constituting its essence. (*Per attributum intelligo id, quod intellectus de substantia percipit, tanquam ejusdem essentïam constituens.*)" (E, I, Def. 4) The central ambiguity arises from the meaning of the Latin word '*tanquam*', which may be translated as either 'as' or 'as if', suggesting the objectivist and subjectivist views respectively. I shall focus on that phrase in the definition which indicates that the attributes are "that which the intellect *perceives* of substance." (My italics.) Professor Wolfson, a subjectivist, asserts: "If the expression 'which the intellect perceives' is laid stress upon, it would seem that the attributes are only *in intellectu*. Attributes would thus be only a subjective mode of thinking expressing a relation to a perceiving subject and having no real existence in the essence."[3] He adds that, in Spinoza's context, "to be perceived by the mind means to be *invented* by the mind. . . ."[4] The arguments in the *Short Treatise* reveal, however, that the idea of the attributes cannot be an invention of the intellect and that the perception of the attributes must have as its source the objective status of the attributes themselves.

The thrust of these arguments is suggested in a distinction drawn by Spinoza in the *Ethics*. In his explanation of the definition of an 'idea', Spinoza carefully distinguishes between conceptions and perceptions:

> I say conception rather than perception because the name perception seems to indicate that the mind is passive in relation to its object. But conception seems to express the action of the mind. (E, II, Def. 3)

This explanation recognizes a connotation of passivity implicit in the term 'perception'. If we take Spinoza's definitions seriously, we must assume that he chose the term '*percipit*' carefully in defining '*attributum*' and that he had in mind the distinction he would make in Part II of the *Ethics*. The plausibility of such an assumption is strongly reinforced by the arguments in the *Short Treatise*.

The first argument purports to show that neither the existence nor the essence of anything depends upon us. Here Spinoza considers three kinds of ideas of things: ideas of impossible things, ideas of things which may or may not exist, and the idea of a necessary being. He notes that impossible things have essences consisting of incompatible traits; hence, both their existence and essence are impossible. Things which may or may not exist have eternal essences; and Spinoza infers, for reasons which are not wholly clear, that the ideas of such things must "have outside me a subjectum."[5] Both the existence and essence of the necessary being are, of course, necessary. Thus, Spinoza concludes:

> I therefore see now that the truth, essence, or existence of anything never depends on me: for as was shown with reference to the second kind of ideas, they are what they are independently of me, whether as regards their essence alone, or as regards both essence and existence. I find this to be true also, indeed much more so, of this third unique idea: not only does it not depend on me, but on the contrary, he alone must be the subjectum of that which I affirm of him. Consequently, if he did not exist, I should not be able to assert anything at all about him; although this can be done in the case of other things, even when they do not exist.[6]

Spinoza adds a virtually explicit rejection of the subjectivist interpretation: "From what has been said so far it is clearly manifest that the idea of infinite attributes in the perfect being is no fiction. . . ."[7] The relevant point here is that all essences, like all things, are either necessary or impossible, according to Spinoza.[8] What the essence of a thing is is therefore independent of us. Specifically, the essence of Substance, which Spinoza identifies here with the infinite attributes, is independent of us, because Substance is a necessary being.

But Spinoza does not rest on the assertion that Substance is a necessary being to justify his view that the essence of Substance is independent of us. Spinoza asks where we get the idea of infinitely many perfect attributes in Substance:

> And whence comes this idea of perfection? This *something* cannot be the outcome of these two [attributes]:[9] for two can only yield two, and not an infinity. Whence then? From myself, never; else I must be able to give what I did not possess. Whence, then, but from the infinite attributes themselves which tell us *that* they are, without however telling us, at the same time, *what* they are: for only of two do we know what they are.[10]

Here Spinoza accounts for the fact that we cannot invent the idea of an infinite multiplicity of attributes, because we do not possess within us a basis for forming such an idea. The idea of an infinite multiplicity of attributes must therefore have a cause or foundation in reality outside the intellect, namely, the infinite attributes themselves. This argument was not originated by Spinoza. however. It is virtually certain that he borrowed the idea from Descartes, who uses a comparable argument to prove that God must be the cause of our idea of Him.[11]

It would be rash to suppose that the recognition of these two arguments will or should be the last word in the subjectivist-objectivist controversy. Objectivists are obliged, for example, to respond to the subjectivist charge that an objective multiplicity of attributes would be inconsistent with the simplicity of Substance, and they must draw out the implications of their interpretation for other Spinozistic doctrines. But it is fair to say that Spinoza's use of these arguments and his explicit acknowledgement of the passivity of perception establish a strong presumption in favor of the objectivist account. It would certainly seem from these passages that Spinoza is committed to the objective status of the attributes whether or not this commitment is consistent with his other views.

WARREN KESSLER

FRESNO STATE COLLEGE

NOTES

¹ Francis F. Haserot, "Spinoza's Definition of Attribute," *Philosophical Review*, **62** (1953).

² See Haserot for a thorough exposition of these ambiguities.

³ Harry A. Wolfson, *The Philosophy of Spinoza* (Cambridge, Mass.: Harvard University Press, 1934), p. 146.

⁴ *Ibid.*

⁵ *Short Treatise*, I, Ch. 1, p. 18, 1. 22. English quotations from the *Short Treatise* are taken from *Spinoza's Short Treatise on God, Man, & His Well-Being*, trans. and ed. A. Wolf (London, 1910).

⁶ *Short Treatise*, I, Ch. 1, p. 18, 1. 29ff.

⁷ *Short Treatise*, I, Ch. 1, p. 18, 1. 29ff.

⁸ See E, I, 29 and E, I, 33, n. 1.

⁹ Spinoza asserts that we are not able to know the nature of more than two attributes, Thought and Extension. Cf. Letter LXIV in *The Correspondences of Spinoza*, trans. and ed. A. Wolf (London, 1928).

¹⁰ *Short Treatise*, I, Ch. 1, p. 19, 1. 24ff.

¹¹ Rene Descartes, *The Philosophical Works of Descartes*, trans. E. Haldane and G. R. T. Ross (New York, 1931 and 1934), Vol. I, p. 161ff. Spinoza paraphrases Descartes' argument in his *Principles of the Philosophy of Rene Descartes*, I, Proposition VI and Scholium in *Earlier Philosophical Writings*, trans. Frank A. Hayes (Indianapolis, 1963), pp. 32-33.

Lee C. Rice

Spinoza on Individuation

Introductory Note

In this paper I wish to examine in detail the arguments which Spinoza uses in a very brief section of the *Ethics*,[1] the lemmas following Proposition 13 of Part II. My aim in this analysis will be twofold: (1) to attempt a preliminary sketch of the nature of a physical system in Spinoza's view, and (2) to clarify what Spinoza means by speaking of certain items as "individuals." At least a partial fulfillment of the first aim is a necessary condition for the second, since most of what Spinoza has to say about individuation in the *Ethics* and elsewhere is expressed in terms of individual bodies. His own solution (or dissolution) of the mind-body problem entails that there will be correlative statements true at the ideational level; but, unfortunately, he usually leaves such correlations to his reader. I use the term "ideational" (and its cognates) herein in preference to "mental" to avoid any dualistic connotation. Ideational and extensional levels for Spinoza refer to a dualism of denoting complexes, but not to a dualism of objects denoted by these.

The second and principal aim has been expressed, like the title of this paper, in a way which consciously avoids initial discussion of the "problem of personal identity." This latter problem, indeed, does not seem to have presented itself with the urgency which it had for the British empiricists. This is not to claim that some solution to it is not implicit in Spinoza's own analysis; for, without a positive solution, the entire aim of the *Ethics* would be placed in check. For the achievement of human blessedness, which the *Ethics* purports to describe, knowledge of one's own nature and place in the universe are necessary: Miss Saw's claim in a recent article[2] that Spinoza must assume the unity of the human individual without question is to that extent justified. Her further claim that his own principles make this assumption not only unjustified but unjustifiable is one of an entire family of criticisms levelled at Spinoza's methodology from a common standpoint. These criticisms, I shall hope to show, result from a serious misinterpretation of Spinoza's claims as well as his general methodology; and, to this extent, the present paper will be somewhat polemical in tone.

Couching the problem of individuation in terms of that of personal identity, as Hume does in the famous Sixth Section of Part IV of Book I of the *Treatise*, also seems to me philosophically perverse: at the very least it carries commitments which should undergo prior analysis. What it suggests is that the problem lies in what constitutes the nature of a person, rather than in what constitutes the identity of something which (perhaps only incidentally) happens to be a person. Hume seems to be aware of this himself when he moves the problem to that of the identity of the church which is rebuilt from wholly different materials. Sameness of churches and sameness of persons may not, of course, be examples of the same kind of sameness; but, pending any linguistic distinction between the two examples, the philosopher has no right to assume that the examples are in fact diverse. Historically, it is easy to see why the problem of personal identity does arise in this form: it results from an attempt to preserve the Cartesian methodology in its essential structure, having once repudiated the substance of Descartes' claims about the nature of the "mental."

Rather than to force the problem in its now-classical form onto Spinoza, therefore, I shall follow the order of his own exposition on the nature of individuation. Given his solution to this problem, I think that it can be shown that he does have something to say about personal identity by way of corollary. Further, what does emerge appears to me as a quite reasonable solution to the problem, and one which is perhaps not very far afield from the general intent of Hume's answer, at least as Hume is interpreted by one of his own commentators.[3] In an earlier article, I have attempted to show that, at the epistemological level, the two philosophers are not so far apart as first appearances would lead one to believe.[4]

I. *Individuation and Bodies*

Part II of the *Ethics* concerns itself with the nature of the human mind; and, more specifically, with the nature of the union of mind and body as Spinoza conceives this in opposition to Descartes. The intent of Spinoza's exposition, however, is not a wholly polemical one, since it is the nature of this unity which will enable him to move, in Part III, to his general analysis of emotions (or affections). Following E2P13, however, Spinoza introduces a series of seven lemmas and five axioms on the nature of bodies. His justification for that is that no one will be able to understand the nature of the mind in its unity with the body (*Mentem humanam unitam esse Corpori*) unless he first have adequate knowledge of the nature of the body itself (*nisi prius nostri Corporis naturam adaequate cognoscat*).[5] The *Ethics* does not claim to be a treatise on either psychology or physics, and Spinoza treats problems arising in connexion with these sciences only insofar as their resolution is a necessary prerequisite to his analysis of morality; so we should not expect to find a complete treatment of even those problems which are raised here. Nor can we, unfortunately, expect to find a systematic treatment of the nature of physical systems in general anywhere in Spinoza's writings; since he informs Von Tschirnhaus in 1676 that he has still at that late date been unable to put his thoughts about matter in proper order.[6] The term "adequate" here can only refer to the adequacy of the lemmas with respect to the moral speculation which follows in the *Ethics*. This is, of course, not the technical sense in which Spinoza customarily employs the term "adequate"; but there are a good number of examples of his returning to the ordinary usage of a term in the *Ethics* even after he has given the term a precise meaning by explicit definition.

The section under consideration may be conveniently regarded as falling into three subdivisions. The first and second axioms, together with the intervening first three lemmas, are concerned with the simplest bodies (*corpora simplicissima*). The following definition, third axiom, and fifth through seventh lemmas deal with bodies composed of similar parts. With the scholium to the seventh lemma and through the six postulates which follow it Spinoza deals with composite bodies consisting of dissimilar parts.

The first axiom states that every body is either at motion or at

rest,[7] and the second that each body is moved at times more slowly
and at other times more quickly.[8] Joachim has reckoned the first as
a continuance of the Aristotelian distinction between *kinesis* and
heremía,[9] but he is clearly in error here. For Aristotle rest (*heremía*)
is merely the absence of motion which occurs when a body reaches
its natural place. Wolfson is correct in noting that Spinoza here
follows Descartes in making motion the contrary, rather than the
contradictory, of rest.[10] This does not entail that for Spinoza there
is some neutral or third state between motion and rest; though such
a claim would entail this for Aristotle. For Spinoza motion and rest
are equally acts (or forms), and their union is exhaustive of all corporeal action. A body neither moving nor at rest would be per-
forming no act; and, since action and existence are coextensive for
Spinoza,[11] such a body could not exist. It seems natural to follow
Hampshire's suggestion[12] to translate the now unfamiliar phrase
"motion-and-rest" as "energy." Then Spinoza's physics rests upon
two principal claims: (1) that the extended world is a mechanical
system whose total quantum of energy is a constant, and (2) that all
changes among the bodies of the system can be adequately
represented solely as transmissions of energy within the system.

This interpretation of the first axiom makes it analytic, and
this is as one would expect; since Spinoza tells us a few lines later[13]
that it is self-evident (*per se notam*) that bodies are distinguished
one from another by their motion and rest—i.e., by the total quantum of energy which they contain. The second axiom, however, is
not analytic in any interesting sense: the temporal specifications
("...*iam*...*iam*...") clearly indicate that what is given here is an
empirical (though all-pervasive) truth. From this it clearly follows
that Spinozistic physics was not to have been the purely a priori
enterprise that some of the commentators have made it out to be.
This consideration also permits us to absolve Spinoza from a dilem-
ma urged upon him by Miss Saw.[14] In dealing with the second axiom at the beginning of E2, "Man thinks," she urges that, if the axiom is analytic then it is not legitimately introduced at this point
(since Spinoza has not defined "man"), and if it is empirical then
"...we are engaged in quite a different enterprise from the one in-
itially presented to us."[15] Like the second axiom considered above,
the axiom "Man thinks" is empirical for Spinoza; but this, far from
vitiating Spinoza's enterprise, merely indicates that Miss Saw has
misrepresented it from the outset.

The first two lemmas deal with the distinction and agreement among bodies: they are distinguished one from another by virtue of motion and rest (*ratione motus et quietis*: by their respective quanta of energy), and they agree in that all "involve the concept of one and the same attribute" (. . .*unius ejusdem attributi conceptum involvunt*). Motion and rest are univocal terms for Spinoza, and thus their differentiation across different bodies is a quantitative one, not a qualitative (or analogous) one.

In the third lemma Spinoza takes up the causal laws of motion, and attempts to explicate these in terms of series of moved movers; but, in direct opposition to Aristotle, he concludes that such a series must proceed to infinity. It is easy to see why such a series cannot terminate, as it did for Aristotle, with an unmoved mover. Spinoza limits the causality of God in a given attribute to a causality immanent to that attribute; and, in the context of this lemma, this amounts to the claim that the cause of motion and rest must be expressible within the attribute of extension.[16] Spinoza's language does not make his point clear, however; since he speaks in the lemma of one body which *has been determined* (*determinatum fuit*) by another, and thus to infinity. If the series is extended to infinity through time rather than simultaneously, then there would be no substantial disagreement here with Aristotle. Such an interpretation would not be consistent with Spinoza's request in the scholium to the seventh lemma, with which we are shortly to deal, that we conceive of an infinite number of bodies constituting the whole of nature as one individual: for, on the temporal reading of the third lemma, no such infinite collection would ever be present at a given time. I conclude, then, that the infinite series of moved movers which Spinoza employs to account for motion is cotemporaneous. Spinoza thus asks us to conceive of an actually infinite collection of bodies; and, though I see no difficulty in this, I am aware that philosophers have been wont to raise a host of objections to it. The objections of which I am aware are usually slogans, and of these the greater number (e.g., "a sum is greater than any of its parts") are false in any event; so I shall assume that, at the very least, Spinoza is not talking nonsense here.

The third lemma asserts that a moved body continues to move until it is determined to rest by another body, and continues at rest until it is determined by another body. Wolfson rightly notes that this is what was later to become Newton's First Law of Motion, which had in fact been anticipated by Descartes in the *Principia Philosophiae* (II, 37).[17] Even in Spinoza's exposition of Descartes the substance, if not the wording, of the law is the same;[18] but there is a serious difference which escapes Wolfson. In PPC as in Descartes, the proof of the law follows from a consideration of God as principal cause of motion (i.e., as a mover outside the *res extensa*); whereas, in the proof of the lemma in E2, proof of the law follows from a consideration of motion and rest within extended substance. The ground here has clearly shifted from Cartesian dualism to Spinozistic monism. It is upon this new and revolutionary ground that Spinoza erects his theory of individuation.

II. *Simple and Complex Bodies*

At the termination of the second axiom following Lemma 3, Spinoza explains that he has been dealing up to this point only with the most simple bodies, and that attention is now to be given to composite bodies. The problem of the nature of the *corpora simplicissima* is perennial among the commentators. Hicks takes an atomistic interpretation, likening them to Leibnizian monads;[19] and such an interpretation is not uncommon. The central difficulty with this reading is that Spinoza explicitly denies the existence of atoms. Since the nature of corporeal substance for him consists wholly in extension, and since extension is divisible (though never divided in any ontological sense), there can be no units which are indivisible: this is the substance of the argument given by Spinoza in PPC.[20] One may object to this that PPC does not represent Spinoza's position, but rather Descartes'; but there is ample evidence of the solidarity of the two philosophers on this point. The objections which Spinoza raises against the conclusions drawn by Boyle in his experiments with nitre hinges on just this issue. Boyle accounted for the differences between nitre and its distillate in terms of a separation of two distinct kinds of particles in the latter. Spinoza answers, through Oldenburg, that such differences may be accounted for by postulating that the particles in the distillate are merely more volatile: note that his explanation is made in terms of motion and rest within an otherwise homogeneous body.[21] But he also assumes the existence of pores in the particles of nitre,[22] in order to account for their combination in a less volatile compound; and he remarks that Descartes does not speak of such particles as being visible.[23] The existence of pores within invisible particles does not augur well for an atomistic interpretation, at least not if the basic "atoms" are supposed to be simple and indivisible. Boyle retorts to this that the existence of the pores and the very subtle matter is without proof, and that he wishes to limit himself to what is visible.[24] Boyle seems to think that Spinoza is assuming the existence of atoms to justify his own interpretation of the experiments. This is, if I am right, not the case, but Spinoza reads Boyle as making the same point: he answers that the existence of a vacuum is not possible, his assumption here being that atoms are not possible without a vacuum.[25] The proof which he gives for this assertion is that nothing has no properties, which is the same proof offered in PPC2P3. I conclude, therefore, that Spinoza follows Descartes in rejecting atomism.

What then are the *corpora simplicissima* if not atoms? It seems to me that Spinoza merely intends this term to refer to bodies with a sufficiently small quantity of motion and rest to be distinguishable from composite bodies. This means that the *corpora simplicissima* are quite divisible, and it also makes the distinction between complex and simple bodies one which is relative to the purposes at hand: what counts as a simple body might not so count in every conceivable situation. If this sounds as though I am fashioning Spinoza in a pragmatic image, we should recall his own insistence that *order* (ordo) is a product of imagination in the first place;[26] and simplicity is certainly an ordering relation.

In a most thorough and penetrating analysis of Spinoza's concept of a physical system, Alexandre Matheron concludes that the *corpora simplicissima* are those individuals which are defined solely through their external relationships ("*des individus qui se définissent entièrement par leur rapport externe à autrui*"):[27] they are thus "pure events" ("*événements purs*"),[28] whose entire activity and essence is limited to their inertial force.[29] This need not contradict my own reading of Spinoza, provided that "pure event" and "external relationship" be taken as somewhat metaphorical, and not in some Whiteheadian sense which characterizes, so to speak, a being with an inside and no outside (or vice versa). I have already noted that for Spinoza agency and being are synonymous terms, so that pure passivity amounts to nonexistence. Inertial force, in brief, is real force; and a being which possesses it is quite active in its own order.

With the definition following the two axioms after Lemma 3, Spinoza takes up the problem of composite bodies. From what has been said, it is clear that any given number of simple bodies which are brought together are so united through the motion of other external bodies. It is also the case that, disregarding the external forces operative in this union, the bodies united will interact among themselves. If this interaction is such that it results in a fixed and determinate relation among the simpler bodies, then the resultant complex is an individual; and it is this fixed relation of motion and rest (or interchange of energy) among its parts which individuates it.[30] It is the relation among its parts, and not the parts themselves, upon which Spinoza fixes in order to characterize an individual. I can clarify this point by pointing out a corollary which we shall pursue later: an individual may be counted as "the same individual" if the relations among its diverse parts are constant, *even if* no one of those parts is "the same part" in any relevant sense.

Spinoza next turns to the problem of change as it effects individuating relations. There may be a continual separation and replacement of parts within a complex structure such as the human body. Should some of the parts then be lost, individuation remains constant (i.e., we have the "same individual" as before) provided that their interactive effect within the whole is supplied from another source.[31] The new source cited by Spinoza is, as one would expect, a new part; but, even if no new part were added to the whole, provided that the interaction among the remaining parts was modified in certain specifiable ways, individuation would still remain constant. The fifth lemma concludes that, whether the parts are increased in number or diminished, constancy of the relationship still remains possible. Note that the only way in which such a preservation of these relations can take place, given that the quantity of the related members varies through time, is that their relationships are purely quantitative. Individuation is thus accomplished solely through the constant presence of a fixed quantum of motion and rest.

The remaining lemmas take up the problem of an alteration of motion and rest when the parts themselves remain constant within the individual. This provides little additional explanation; since, if the change of motion among the constituent bodies is a change in direction, there will in fact be no change whatever in the relations among the parts considered in themselves. Spinoza remarks that this is self-evident:[32] what he fails to note is that its self-evidence depends on his own assumption that direction is a wholly conventional determinant of bodies. The same remark should apply to any change of direction of the entire composite body in a given spatial framework; since, if each part of the individual retains its fixed relation to other parts, again the individuation remains constant by definition. This seems to be what Spinoza intends.[33]

The upshot of all of this is that the greater complexity of organization on the part of a given individual implies the greater ability to undergo change without loss of identity. Here Spinoza makes an important generalization, which is worth citing in its entirety:

> So far we have considered an individual composed only of bodies distinguised one from another with respect to motion and rest, speed and slowness, that is, bodies of simplest nature. If, however, we should now consider another individual composed of several individuals of different natures, we shall find that the number of ways in which it can be affected, without loss of its nature, will be greatly increased. (E2, Lemma 8, Scholium)

Talk about individuals "of different natures" can be misleading, since Spinoza has already insisted that all differences among bodies reduce to differences in their motion and rest; but it is not difficult to see what he has in mind. The composites which we have considered until now have been composed of bodies which, from our point of view, are relatively simple. If, however, these composite bodies become united into a still greater composite, we have, in addition to the simple bodies, two layers of superimposed relations, if I may be permitted this analogy. The resultant individual is determined or individuated by a constant relation among its parts, each of which is in turn individuated by other fixed and internal relations among its own proper parts (in this case, the simple bodies). We can construct still higher orders of individuals, and the higher we ascend, the more determined are the constant relations among the proper parts by internal relations among parts of parts: the higher the composite, the more is it immune to loss of identity through external forces. If we carry this construction of series of individuals out to infinity, we reach the *facies totius universi*, which changes in an infinite number of ways without loss of its identity.[34] This is to raise several new problems which are best avoided here; since our goal is a more proximate individual in the hierarchy—the human body.

It is important to emphasize this notion of orders of individuation corresponding to orders of composition. Every individual is part of an individual of still higher complexity; but it does not thereby sacrifice its own status as an individual, since its very inclusion in the larger whole presupposes the continuation of those very internal relations which determine its own individuation. To neglect this fact is to leave no room for finite individuals in Spinoza's system, and such a reading renders the whole aim of the *Ethics* incomprehensible as a system of moral philosophy. Yet, as we shall see, it is just this neglect which is at the heart of many earlier, and not a few contemporary criticisms of Spinoza.

III. *An Analogy and its Lessons*

The *Ethics*, as has been noted, presents Spinoza's remarks on the nature of individuation almost as an aside. Spinoza makes no attempt to integrate the axioms and lemmas presented after E2P13 into the general context of his discussion of mind, beyond saying that, in order to understand the nature of the human mind, some knowledge of the nature of the body is necessary. It will have become obvious to the reader that I have been scrupulously avoiding talk about personal identity or individuation at the level of consciousness. Spinoza would call this problem, I suppose, that of "mental individuation." Were I to approach it in a direct manner here, I should have to first take a firm stand on how Spinoza's mind-body "parallelism" is to be interpreted; and, for reasons of space, I shall avoid taking any such stand. It does seem to me what Spinoza has to say about individuation of bodies makes reasonable sense on its own ground, without recourse to the mind-body problem; though I shall have a few remarks to make about consciousness in closing.

What is wanted is a more concrete presentation of the status of the individual than Spinoza has given in the *Ethics*; and, though the *Ethics* has little more to offer here than what we have already examined, Spinoza does provide Oldenburg with just such an example. Oldenburg has requested some explanation of the relations holding among the various parts in nature, and Spinoza asks him to consider a small worm living in the blood. The worm is endowed with sight sufficient to discern the particles in the blood, as well as reason sufficient to understand the nature of the interactions which take place among these particles. Such a worm would live in the blood in much the same manner as man inhabits the universe, and so would regard each particle as a whole rather than as a part (*et unamquamque sanguinis particulam ut totum, non vero ut partem consideraret*).[35] His knowledge of the laws governing the interactions would not enable him to see in what manner these laws were consequences of still more general laws governing the nature of the blood. Similarly, we might consider the blood in isolation from all other individuals, and thus viewed as a whole. Spinoza draws two immediate consequences from his example. First, if we consider the entire universe, there is preserved in it the same quantity of energy (motion and rest) throughout. Secondly, since the nature of the universe cannot be limited or determined from without, by other bodies external to it, as is the blood, it follows that the parts of the universe are solely determined by the nature of the whole; and, while these parts can continually undergo changes in their respective levels of energy, the universe can undergo no such change.[36]

The consequences are those familiar already from the *Ethics*: it is the example itself which is of immediate interest. Note that Spinoza's point is not that the worm *errs* in viewing the particles as individuals: the error lies rather in accounting for their individuation (which is given) in terms of isolation from the whole: the individuals are not substances in the traditional meaning of that term, nor do they possess some species of Cartesian inseity. To be an individual is to be a center of action connected in various ways with a network of other individuals. It would be frivolous to claim that this causal connexion with others in a larger whole erases or absorbs individuals; since, on Spinoza's own example, being an individual in one's own right is a necessary condition for being so connected. A second point to note is that Spinoza's example commits him to two rather different kinds of determination or causal sequence. First, the individual particles which make up the blood are

all determined in their actions by other particles—we can say by
other individuals of the same order, for want of a distinct term from
Spinoza. Secondly, however, Spinoza speaks of the particles being
determined to act by the "universal nature of the blood" ("*ab un-
iversali natura sanguinis moderantur*").[37] There are thus two orders
of causal talk in Spinoza. The first we might call "parallel causal
determination": it is expressed by a set of nomological statements
governing the causal interactions among a set of given objects (particles of the blood in this case). The second, which we can call
"perpendicular," is expressed by a set of statements about the
nature of a given whole; and Spinoza seems to view propositions
about the nature of the individuals which make up the whole as
deductive consequences of this set.

    We need not enter into the specific consequences, in his inter-
pretation of scientific methodology, which the claim that there are
two distinct kinds of causal statement produces. What must be
noted, however, is that the nature of individuation presented in the
Ethics functions entirely at the parallel level. This is the point of
the postulates which follow the corollary to the seventh lemma,
which are concerned with the nature of the human body as an individual. The fourth of these asserts that the human body is continually determined and regenerated by a multitude of external
bodies.[38] The claim then is not that the individuals are wholly constituted to be what they are by their position in a larger whole.
Spinoza is not thinking of the infinite whole which is nature when
he talks about what preserves an individual; and, if the indication
in the *Ethics* does not make this point sufficiently clear, Spinoza
reminds Oldenburg that the human body is held together as an individual by the sole weight (we should say "pressure") of air.[39] In
brief, I am an individual, and I preserve my individual identity,
because I maintain a fixed relation with other individuals of the
same relative complexity as me. This fixed relation is, of course, a
causal one; and in fact causal relations are the only real relations for
Spinoza in the last analysis.

    I should not wish to claim that the theory as it stands is a
perfectly clear one. The notion of a fixed relation requires far more
clarification than Spinoza is willing to offer, to mention just one
questionable point. Several criticisms and interpretations of the
theory, however, fall quite wide of the mark. Consider, for instance,

Rivaud's assertion that the essence of individual things is made up entirely of the conditions in which they exist.[40] Rivaud is by no means an unsympathetic commentator of Spinoza, but he is surely overemphasizing the passive side of causal interaction here. It is certainly true, to return to Spinoza's example, that any given particle of blood is in causal interaction with other particles and is moved by these; but passivity is only part of the story—that same particle is also in the same active relation to other particles as they are to it. Part of what makes me the individual man that I am, and part of what preserves this identity, is the fact that I am affected in a diversity of ways by other individuals; but part of what constitutes the nature of those individuals is that they are similarly affected by me.

Joachim provided perhaps the least ambiguous statement of the claim that there is no room for individuals in Spinozism because there is but one substance. Individuals, or modes, are thus absorbed; and to speak of an individual is to speak from a radically subjective viewpoint.

> A single "extended" thing—a particular body, e.g.,—is finite and dependent; a fragment torn from its context, in which alone it has being and significance. Neither in its existence nor in its nature has it any independence. It owes its existence to an indefinite chain of causes. . .[41]

One gathers that what is sought by Joachim and others who pursue this line of criticism is a means of individuating which is context-free. Less ambiguously, what constitutes an individual cannot be a set of relations to other individuals. More ambiguously, what makes me an individual is something which I possess in my own right, and which is not derivative. The last formulation verges, like so many metaphysical pronouncements, on the poetical; but no more than a brief consideration of its possible implementation should suffice to show that it is radically wrong-headed. For, considering a particular human being, attempt to characterize or individuate him without recourse to relations: "the father of x", "a brother of y", "a student of z", "born in w", etc. To attempt to reduce these relations to attributes or monadic predicates via some Leibnizian or even Aristotelian hocus-pocus at the syntactical level only produces a vicious logical circle whereby nothing can be characterized except by reference to something else which cannot be characterized except by reference to something else which cannot be characterized except by reference to it. Spinoza's individuals are centers of real action—they are causally efficacious: were it not for a philosophical tradition of which Joachim is but one representative, Spinoza's point that what an individual is is determined by what it does would be accounted almost a truism.

Miss Saw's more recent criticisms rest upon much the same basis as Joachim's, but are often a bit more confused. Consider her point that "Spinoza has no account whatever to give of the 'I' who does anything at all."[42] According to Miss Saw, Leibniz's monads supply something which Spinoza's account could not provide: beings who actively do something. "Motion and rest" or "energy" may be terms which require considerable clarification, but they do provide at least the beginning of a means of talking about something being done; and, if I am right, it makes good sense to individuate "doings" (or "doers") in terms of what is done. Miss Saw summarizes her criticism in the following manner:

> Thirdly and lastly, Spinoza's human individual is not an agent. Nobody can deny that Spinoza absolutely rejects the notion of free will, but if there is no *free* will, then there is no meaning to 'will.'[43]

The first of these two claims is, I have argued, simply false: not only does Spinoza view human individuals as agents, but he presents good reasons for his doing so. The second claim is, as it stands, not only irrelevant but also a logical howler. I could just as well argue that, if there are no purple apples, then there is no meaning to "apple". This is not to say that the question of freedom is not relevant to the nature of the human individual; but it is to note that we had better have some idea of what we mean by an individual before we set out to ascertain, for any particular example, whether it is free or not. Perhaps what is behind Miss Saw's point is the claim that what constitutes the human individual has to be something distinctly human (in this case freedom). This claim has, however, two senses. In one sense it says only that what makes an individual *human* must be distinctly human, and this appears to be a truism of sorts. In the other sense, it may mean that what makes a human *individual* must be distinctly human; and Spinoza would flatly reject it. The second claim is in some ways analogous to a claim popularly made today by philosophers within the ordinary language tradition: that, in some sense of "act", acts are only ascribable to human individuals, while machines are instruments of human action and animals are acted upon. Ordinary language dressing notwithstanding, Spinoza could easily recognize this as an element of the Cartesianism which he took such pains to reject. Here Spinoza stands firmly on the same ground occupied by Hume. When we say of a man that he is the same individual whom we encountered earlier, we mean much the same thing as when we say of a church that it is the same church that we encountered earlier. Individuation, and criteria of reidentification, are not due to special and mysterious properties possessed by all and only men; and personal identity is a problem of identity to the same extent that architectural identity is.

There is one additional point made by Miss Saw which, though it fails as a criticism, underlines an important consequence of Spinoza's view of identity and individuation:

> Now if the change from the last moment of life to the first moment of death is so decisive. . . , then I cannot help thinking that earlier changes, less violent it is true, must also be described in terms of loss of identity.[44]

The point appears to be that, if individuation is accomplished through a certain constancy in the relations among parts, and thus identity is defined as a preservation of this constancy, then such identity cannot be preserved through duration; since the changes which occur between birth and death differ in degree, but not in kind, from those of death and birth. But Spinoza has a direct answer for this:

> Here I observe only that I understand the body to die when its parts are so disposed to acquire a different proportion of motion and rest one to another. But I dare not deny that the human body, because of the circulation of the blood and other things by which it is believed to live and preserve its identity, may nevertheless be changed into another nature wholly different. No argument forces me to claim that the body never dies unless it becomes a corpse.[45]

In the remainder of the scholium Spinoza speaks of a Spanish poet who was seized with an illness after which he was totally oblivious of his past life. With perfect propriety, we should say in this case that the poet was not the "same person" after the disease as before it. But Spinoza's point is not Locke's: it is not loss of memory which causes loss of identity, but rather loss of identity which causes loss of memory, as Spinoza makes quite clear in couching his discussion in terms of a disease and the proportion of motion and rest in the body. With as much propriety we often speak of a person as "not being the same person" after events of far less destructive (or even constructive) force. The obvious corollary to all of this is that identity is a matter of degree, and there is nothing here to cast a shadow on Spinoza's analysis: talk about preservation of a constant balance of motion and rest among the parts which make up an individual is talk about a relation or balance which is more or less constant. Criteria for the identity of churches may well differ from criteria for the identity of persons (or of cats); but the difference is one of degree, and is determined by the conventions which we establish. I should not have to add that this does not make personal identity a purely conventional matter in some wider sense of that misused term. The criteria for identity are established by convention across duration, but whether those criteria apply in a particular case is by no means a matter of convention.

Spinoza's use of memory in discussing the Spanish poet provides a foothold, however tenuous, by which one may extend what I have said about corporeal identity and individuation to the ideational level. I am more or less inclined to follow Curley's recent suggestion that Spinoza's term *"idea"* is best translated by "proposition" rather than by the English "idea".[46] This makes Spinoza's "parallelism" into the apparently noncontroversial claim that, for every state of affairs, there is a (true) proposition expressing it. The immediate consequence of accepting Curley's reading, however, is that self-consciousness (the *idea ideae*) becomes problematic. How is it that some individuals are conscious and some are not? This is a problem clearly beyond the resources of this paper, but it is not certain that Spinoza would even consider it relevant to the problem of individuation and identity as that problem is usually posed. Whatever we may choose to mean by the identity of a particular "mind" through time, it is quite clear that this kind of talk is rather hazy in a sense in which talk about identity of persons is not. One might even wish to take a somewhat Strawsonian turn and claim that our criteria of identification and reidentification are wholly geared to bodies in space (Spinoza's *res extensae*). Any talk of mental identity would be, on this account, derivative; and Spinoza's example of the Spanish poet would lead one to expect that he would not be unsympathetic to this claim.

IV. *Concluding Note*

I have argued that Spinoza's account of individuation in terms of the active relations holding among the parts of a given individual is a relatively plausible one. I have also attempted to divorce this claim somewhat from the general categories of Spinozism, since I do not believe that accepting it commits one to accept other more general or metaphysical claims made by Spinoza in explicating it. Two of its consequences have been that there is no special problem about personal identity and that identity through time is a matter of degree. Both of these also seem plausible to me, and also appear to be in accord with ordinary linguistic usage; though I should not regard the latter as being a decisive point in their favour.

Some philosophers, Miss Saw among them I should conjecture, would argue that, though Spinoza's analysis of individuation is quite adequate to account for our talk about bodies, it is by no means adequate to account for our talk about persons. More specifically still, it may be claimed that my knowledge of my own identity as a person involves wholly different factors. This would not constitute a counterargument to Spinoza if all that were meant was that I come to know my own identity in a manner different from that by which I come to know that of a dog or church or other person; since there is clearly no contradiction in saying that, though we mean the same by identity in each case, we come to ascertain its presence by varied means. The claim might, however, mean that what we mean by identity for persons is specifically different from what we mean by, say, tree-identity or church-identity. Just as clearly, however, this claim receives no support from the fact, if it is a fact, that we come to know our own identity in ways different from those by which we learn of the identity of other things.

What could one do then by way of arguing for this kind of identity in opposition to Spinoza? Since I confess that I do not really know what sort of identity is at issue here, I cannot even begin to answer this question. Pointing to the fact, if there is such a fact, that we employ wholly different linguistic conventions for discuss-

ing personal identity than we do for discussing identity in general
might lend some initial plausibility to the claim. There is a general
caveat which Spinoza would enter, however, to just this approach:

> I am aware that in ordinary usage these terms have different
> meanings. It is not, however, my intention to explicate the
> meanings of words, but rather to explicate the nature of things;
> and to point out these things using words whose ordinary meaning
> is not completely inconsistent with the meaning which I wish
> them to have.[47]

If we characterize Spinoza's metaphysics in twentieth-century
terms, we are thus compelled to note that it is revisionary and not
descriptive (in Strawson's sense). It follows that Spinoza would
regard ordinary language approaches to any of these problems as
being at best nugatory. If the problem of personal identity is interpreted as a question about the ordinary usage of identity-
statements for persons, then my analysis of Spinoza's theory of individuation will not have shed any light upon the problem; for, far
from having presented a theory which could resolve such a problem,
Spinoza would not even have been interested in raising it in the first
place.

LEE C. RICE

MARQUETTE UNIVERSITY

NOTES

[1] I am employing the standardized English references to the works of Spinoza.
"E2P13" is to be read, for example, as "*Ethics*, Part 2, Proposition 13." Other abbreviations are as follows: "Sch" for "Scholium," "Def" for "Definition," "Ax" for
"Axiom," "Cor" for "Corollary," "Ep." for "Epistola," and "PPC" for the "*Prin-
cipiae Philosophiae Cartesianae.*" All translations from the Latin text are my own.
Page and volume references, where given, are to the Van Vloten and Land edition of
the *Opera Omnia* (4 vols.; The Hague: Martinus Nijhoff, 1914); this edition varies
only in minor points from the critical but less convenient Heidelberg Academy Edition.

[2] Ruth L. Saw, "Personal Identity in Spinoza," *Inquiry*, 12 (1969), 1-14.

[3] N. K. Smith, *The Philosophy of David Hume* (London: Macmillan, 1941), cf. especially pp. 497-505.

[4] L. Rice, "The Continuity of *Mens* in Spinoza," *The New Scholasticism*, **43** (1969), 75-103.

[5] E2P13Sch.

[6] Ep. 83 (III, 243).

[7] E2Ax1: *Omnia corpora vel moventur vel quiescunt.*

[8] E2Ax2: *Unumquodcumque corpus iam tardius iam celerius movetur.*

[9] H. H. Joachim, *A Study of the Ethics of Spinoza* (Oxford: Clarendon Press, 1901), p. 84.

[10] H. A. Wolfson, *The Philosophy of Spinoza* (New York: Meridian, 1958), II, pp. 66-67.

[11] H. F. Hallett, "On a Reputed Equivoque in the Philosophy of Spinoza," *Review of Metaphysics*, **3** (1949), 189-212.

[12] S. Hampshire, *Spinoza* (Baltimore: Penguin, 1962), pp. 71-72.

[13] E2, Lemma 1, demonstration.

[14] R. L. Saw, *op. cit.*, 5-6.

[15] *Ibid.*

[16] E2P6: *Cujuscunque attributi modi Deum, quatenus tantum sub illo attributo, cujus modi sunt, et non quatenus sub ullo alio consideratur, pro causa habent.*

[17] H. A. Wolfson, *op cit.*, I, p. 68.

[18] Cf. PPC2P5Dem.

[19] G. D. Hicks, "The 'Modes' of Spinoza and the 'Monads' of Leibniz," *Proceedings of the Aristotelian Society*, **18** (1918), 329-62.

[20] PPC2P5Dem.

[21] Ep. 6 (III, 13-15).

[22] *Ibid.* (III, 17).

[23] *Ibid.* (III, 18).

[24] Ep. 11 (III, 35).

[25] Ep. 13 (III, 46).

[26] Cf. EI, Appendix.

[27] A. Matheron, *Individu et communauté chez Spinoza* (Paris: Minuit, 1969), p. 27.

[28] *Ibid.*

[29] *Ibid.*, pp. 28-29.

[30] E2, Lemma 3, Def: . . . *illa corpora invicem unita dicemus, et omnia simul unum corpus, sive Individuum componere, quod a reliquis per hanc corporum unionem distinguitur.*

[31] E2, Lemma 4, Dem.

[32] E2, Lemma 6.

[33] E2, Lemma 7.

[34] E2, Lemma 7, cor.

[35] Ep. 32 (III, 120).

[36] Ep. 32 (III, 121).

[37] Ep. 32 (III, 120).

[38] E2, Postulate IV (I, 89).

[39] Ep. 75 (III, 229).

[40] A. Rivaud, *Les notions d'essence et d' existence dans la philosophie de Spinoza* (Paris: Alcan, 1906), p. 120.

[41] H. H. Joachim, *op. cit.*, p. 23.

[42] R. L. Saw, *op. cit.*, 10.

[43] *Ibid.*

[44] *Ibid.*, 8.

[45] E4P39Sch.

[46] E. M. Curley, *Spinoza's Metaphysics: An Essay in Interpretation* (Cambridge: Harvard University Press, 1969), p. 121.

[47] E3Def20.

Frederick C. Copleston

Spinoza as Metaphysician

I

There are obviously many branches of study which could not be described as metaphysics without contravention of ordinary linguistic usage. Nor is this restriction a matter of arbitrary choice. Reasons for it can be adduced. It is thus an exaggeration to say that there is no agreement at all about use of the word 'metaphysics'. At the same time it is also obvious that different views have been and still are expressed about the nature, method and value of metaphysics. Indeed, William of Ockham asserted that to ask what is *the* subject matter of metaphysics is like asking who is the king of all Christendom.[1] Both questions, that is to say, make a false presupposition. If however a philosopher undertakes to tell us what Being 'really' is or to exhibit the nature of Reality, we are probably all prepared to describe him as a metaphysician, provided at any rate that he tries to prove the truth of what he says by philosophical argument or reasoning which does not depend on premises which are claimed to have been revealed by God.

Whatever therefore may be our opinion about what metaphysics ought or ought not to be, we can hardly deny that Spinoza counts as a metaphysician. He does not try to do the scientist's work for him. He is concerned with the nature of ultimate reality and with the metaphysical structure of the universe. And he certainly does not take his premises from revelation or theology. In his view Scripture and theology have the aim of promoting piety and obedience. In other words, they are concerned with fostering certain religious attitudes and with conduct. To try to find speculative truths in the Old Testament, as some medieval Jewish philosophers tried to do, is a mistake. It is philosophy which is con-

cerned with the attainment of objective truth; and philosophy is
based on self-evidently true premises.[2] Spinoza does not suggest
that Scripture contradicts reason, even if he believes that
theologians' interpretations of Scripture may do so. What he insists
on is that it is not a source of speculative truth. It "does not teach
philosophy, but simply obedience."[3] Philosophy therefore cannot
rely on revelation or theology: it recognises no other criterion than
the natural understanding.[4]

It is tempting to depict Spinoza as anticipating the theory of
'stories' proposed by Professor R. B. Braithwaite in his celebrated
lecture "An Empiricist's View of the Nature of Religious Belief."[5]
But Spinoza does not deny, for example, that the Scriptural doctrine that there is but one God can be described as true or as
possessing truth-value. He insists however that it pertains to
philosophy to decide what 'God' means, to exhibit, that is to say,
the nature of the divine reality. And in doing this the philosopher
does not take Scriptural doctrine as a premise but works quite independently.

It must be admitted that if we look at the definitions given at
the beginning of the *Ethics*, the wording certainly suggests that
they express simply the ways in which Spinoza chooses to understand certain terms. For he says explicitly that by cause of itself,
substance, attribute, mode, God and eternity "I understand" this
or that. While however it is obviously open to us to claim, if we
wish, that the definitions are in fact nothing but stipulative
definitions, it by no means follows that Spinoza himself understands them in this way. On the contrary, he regards his
definitions as expressing clear and distinct ideas and therefore as
true.[6] And he regards the logical deduction of propositions from
definitions which express clear and distinct ideas and from self-
evident axioms as a method which, considered in itself, cannot lead
to erroneous conclusions. Further, as "the order and connection of
ideas is the same as the order and connection of things,"[7] logical
deduction of conclusions from the appropriate sets of definitions
and axioms provides us with knowledge of reality. Spinoza does not
claim that the existence of modes, in the sense of particular finite
things, can be deduced a priori from the concepts of attributes or of
infinite modes. On the contrary, he asserts more than once that this
cannot be done. His universe is indeed deterministic throughout.

And the usual statement that he 'assimilated' the causal relation to that of logical implication is justified. Though however he speaks of things as 'following' from the nature of God, he explicitly denies that the existence of particular finite modes can be deduced a priori.[8] At the same time Spinoza is convinced that logical deduction from the appropriate set of premises leads to conclusions which are valid not only in the order of ideas but also in regard to the order of Nature. Even if particular modes cannot be deduced a priori, the metaphysical structure of reality can be deduced. We then have certain metaphysical knowledge. And it is this knowledge of reality which philosophy looks for.

II

If one says that for Spinoza philosophy is concerned with demonstrable truths and that the philosopher is seeking for certain knowledge of Reality (of *Deus seu Natura*), the statement may be challenged. Surely, it may be said, we have only to look at the opening paragraphs of the treatise on *The Improvement of the Understanding* to see that for Spinoza philosophy is the means of attaining man's true good or the supreme human perfection, which can be found only in love of the eternal and infinite. The quasi-mathematical structure of the *Ethics* gives a very misleading impression of Spinoza's basic motivation. Philosophy is for him a way of life or the framework for a way of life. This is shown by the title of his most famous work. It is primarily an ethical treatise.

It is indeed quite true that Spinoza looks on philosophy as an instrument whereby man can perfect himself and attain blessedness or what St. Augustine and the medieval thinkers described as *beatitudo*. We have recalled that in the *Tractatus Theologico-Politicus* Spinoza emphasizes the relation between theology and religious attitudes and moral conduct and contrasts it with philosophy, which is concerned with speculative and demonstrable truth. Though however it is understandable that Spinoza does not wish to cause unnecessary offence either to his Jewish coreligionists or to Christian theologians and that he attributes a positive function to Scriptural doctrine, it seems clear that in point of fact he substitutes philosophy for theology as a way of life for those who are capable of what he regards as genuine philosophical reflection. In the Middle Ages people did not or-

dinarily look to philosophy, in the sense in which it was distinguished from theology, as providing a way of life. They looked to the
Christian faith for this purpose or, if they were Jews, to the Old
Testament and to Jewish tradition. Some Jewish thinkers had indeed tried to find speculative truths expressed in Scripture in ex-
oteric forms; but Spinoza, as we have noted, rejected this
procedure. With him philosophy takes the place of theology as
purveyor of a way of life and as enabling man to perfect himself, in
the case, that is to say, of those who are capable of grasping adequate ideas. We can say therefore that in his concept of the role of
philosophy in human life Spinoza has more affinity with the Greek
philosophers than with the medieval theologians who conceived
beatitudo as a supernatural end or goal, the attainment of which
presupposed Christian faith and divine grace.[9]

Recognition however of the facts that Spinoza is motivated by
desire for the eternal and infinite and that philosophy is for him a
way of life or provides the framework for a way of life is by no means
incompatible with the claim that in his view philosophy is concerned with the attainment of truth and that this truth is attained
through adequate understanding of the order of Nature. He certainly lays great emphasis on ethics and on liberation from the slavery
of the passions. But it is obvious that in his view man's highest
perfection is to be found at the highest level of knowledge. He
speaks indeed of the intellectual love of God; but it is the *intellectual* love of God to which he refers. Man is perfected insofar as he
has adequate ideas and insofar as his conduct is ruled by such
ideas. We can indeed say that for Spinoza the goal of the human
mind is the intuitive vision of all things in God. But of intuitive
knowledge he says explicitly that "this kind of knowing proceeds
from an adequate idea of the formal essence of certain attributes of
God to the adequate knowledge of the essence of things."[10]
Knowledge of God involves an understanding of the divine nature
and of God's self-expression in the world. And an adequate understanding of God as immanent cause of all things involves a
process of deductive reasoning.

Some writers have regarded Spinoza as a mystic. For example,
Bertrand Russell seems to class Spinoza with the mystics on the
ground that his theory of sin as existing only from the human point
of view and not in relation to Reality as a whole is a mystical doc-

trine.[11] This way of speaking may pass muster if the term 'mysticism' is used in a wide sense, so as to cover the thought of all those who write in such a way as to imply that God is the one reality.[12] At the same time it seems to the present writer that however un-Aristotelian Spinoza may be in some respects, he has more affinity with Aristotle's intellectualist view of human perfection than with Plotinus's sublime concept of "the flight of the alone to the Alone."[13] Even if Spinoza asserts that the mind's intellectual love for God is the love with which God loves himself,[14] knowledge of God does not seem to mean for him a state of ecstatic union in which the subject-object distinction is transcended. His ideal is doubtless that the mind should rise through the second degree or level of knowledge to grasp the whole intelligible system of Nature in a comprehensive act of mental vision. But this is not quite the same thing as the exceptional mystical state which Plotinus is said (by Porphyry) to have attained on several occasions. There may be mystical overtones, so to speak, in Spinoza's thought. To describe him as a 'rationalist', given the customary modern use of the term, can be misleading. But it seems to me to be none the less apt. He desires indeed the elevation of the reason to the highest level attainable; but though arguments can be adduced in support of a different view, I doubt very much whether he envisages a transcending of rational knowledge in some ecstatic union with the One. The highest virtue of the mind is to know God.[15] But it does not necessarily follow that 'knowledge' has to be understood in the sense of ecstasy or rapture.

III

Even if, it may be said, Spinoza's philosophy is not geared to the attainment of mystical states such as we find mentioned by writers such as St. John of the Cross, it is still a mistake to emphasize his idea of arriving at truth about the universe by a deductive or quasi-mathematical process of reasoning. For the more we emphasize this aspect of Spinoza's thought, the more do we tend to obscure the fact that the whole process of reasoning presupposes a personal vision of the universe. After all, we can hardly imagine that Spinoza reached his general vision of the universe simply as the result of a quasi-mathematical process of deduction. The vision clearly preceded the construction of the system. Indeed, it is presupposed by the very premises of the deductive process. The great metaphysicians have had an intuitive understanding of possible ways of seeing the universe or Reality. Such visions are presupposed by the apparatus of argument and proof, the arguments being persuasive devices or instruments to commend the initial visions. Provided that we do not mean by 'visionary' an unbalanced person or one whose ideas are so patently at variance with the facts that they have to be discounted without more ado, we can describe Spinoza as one of the great visionaries in the history of philosophical thought. It is important to bring out and emphasize this basic element of vision. The deductive process of reasoning is of secondary importance, even if it is not an unfortunate excrescence. To lay emphasis on the 'rationalism' of Spinoza and on his employment of a mathematical model of reasoning is to misrepresent him. Indeed, it exhibits a misunderstanding of the real nature of original metaphysics.

We have to proceed carefully here. It can be admitted of course that when Spinoza came to express his philosophy in a systematic manner, he already had certain beliefs about the universe. Indeed, it is worth while emphasizing this point. For example, it helps to dispose of the notion that Spinoza was a Cartesian or that his philosophy was simply a logical development of that of Descartes. It is true that "the stupid Cartesians", as Spinoza described them in a letter to Oldenburg,[16] would hardly have been so eager to dissociate themselves and their master from Spinozism, had they not believed that there was at any rate a plausible case for arguing that the philosophy of Spinoza was a logical development of certain aspects of Cartesianism. It is an obvious fact, for instance, that Descartes' definition of substance, if taken literally, would apply to God alone.[17] And there are clearly other ideas expounded by Descartes which Spinoza can be represented as having exploited. At the same time it is absurd to suppose that Spinoza arrived at his theory of the one substance simply by taking over a definition from Descartes and interpreting it literally. Even if Spinoza, without ever having been a Cartesian, made some use of Descartes' thought, the vision of the universe expressed in the statement that "outside God there is nothing at all, and that he is an immanent cause"[18] was certainly not arrived at as the result of a deduction based on Cartesian premises, nor indeed of Spinoza's own deductive reasoning as expressed in the *Ethics*. It preceded the construction of the system.

It by no means follows however that Spinoza's arguments stand in a purely external relation to his basic vision of the Universe. The policy of representing them in this way is doubtless attractive to those who believe that the only way of obtaining what can properly be described as knowledge of the world is through the particular sciences but who at the same time share Friedrich Waismann's conviction that "to say that metaphysics is nonsense *is* nonsense."[19] For if a sharp distinction is made between the basic vision on the one hand and the apparatus of argument and proof on the other, one is enabled to discount the arguments or to interpret them as persuasive devices to commend a preexisting vision and yet at the same time to ascribe value to the vision as a possible way of seeing the universe or as having a psychological connection with a certain way of life or type of conduct.[20] Though however it is understandable if some admirers of the outstanding metaphysicians insist that it is the vision which counts and is of primary importance, it must be remembered that unless the so-called vision is taken to be simply a matter of feeling or of emotive attitude, it has an intellectual content which acquires definite shape and features only insofar as it is expressed and rendered explicit. We can, I suppose, envisage the possibility of a philosopher taking over a world view ready-made from some source and then looking around, as it were, for arguments to support its validity and commend it to others. But in the case of an original philosopher such as Spinoza it seems clear that the system *is* the vision as given definite form and as communicated. It is the explicitation of the vision.

It is doubtless true that too much emphasis can be placed on the quasi-geometrical trappings of the *Ethics*. Attention has often been drawn to the fact that Spinoza expounded part of Descartes' philosophy *more geometrico* when he was not, even at that time, an adherent of Cartesianism.[21] Moreover, Spinoza's universe is far from being a purely geometrical universe. Substance is for him essentially active, and so are finite things. Indeed, the more active something is, the more reality it possesses and the more perfect it is.[22] At the same time it is questionable whether the formal structure given by Spinoza to his system can be explained simply in terms of the influence of a mathematical model or paradigm of reasoning suggested by the scientific development of the seventeenth century. It is doubtless true that in forming his ideal of deductive reasoning Spinoza was in fact influenced by a mathematical model.[23] But it also seems clear enough that his ideal of reasoning is dictated by his concept of reason and by his general vision of Reality. In a letter to Oldenburg[24] he criticizes Bacon for thinking that the human intellect is fallible by nature. In Spinoza's opinion, if the human intellect starts from definitions which express clear and distinct ideas and axioms which express self-evident or eternal truths and proceeds deductively, it cannot err, except of course by making mistakes analogous to those which the mathematician can make. Further, as he sees the universe as rational through and through, metaphysical deduction will give us knowledge of reality and not simply of the implications of ideas understood in a purely subjective sense. As for Spinoza God is the immanent active cause of all things, he concludes that the proper order of philosophical argument is to start with the concept of the one infinite substance and to deduce the essential properties of God or Nature. It does not follow that the existence of a finite thing can be deduced from its definition. As we have seen, Spinoza denies that this can be done. But the proper order of philosophical reasoning must be deductive. Those philosophers who have taken the objects of sense perception as their point of departure and have placed consideration of the divine nature at the end of their process of reflection "have not observed the order of philosophical argument."[25] In a properly philosophical process of reasoning we should start with that which is first in the order of nature or Reality.

In some respects the situation in regard to Spinoza seems to be analogous to that which obtains in the case of Hegel. It has been remarked often enough that Hegel himself rarely speaks in terms of the triadic concept of thesis, antithesis and synthesis, and that it is a mistake to try to force his thought into this mould or to blame him when this cannot be done. Though however the triadic notion can be overemphasized, the fact remains that Hegel's use of dialectical logic is determined by his general vision of Reality as a teleological process. The life of absolute Spirit cannot, he is convinced, be reconstructed for reflection or consciousness in terms of a logic which freezes antithetical concepts in permanent opposition. A logic of movement, dialectical logic, is required. Though therefore

Hegel's dialectic should not be forced into a rigid triadic mould, it is by no means a superfluous or dispensable element of his thought.

In Spinoza's case use of formulas such as Q. E. D., as found in the *Ethics*, is obviously an inessential feature of his thought. Choice of a deductive method however seems to be governed or implied by the philosopher's general view of the necessary order of Nature and by his idea of the relation between thought and its object. To be sure, the content of the *Ethics* cannot be regarded as a continuous process of deduction simply from the definitions and axioms placed at the beginning of the first part. Nor did Spinoza himself so regard it. He was not ignorant of the fact that at the beginning of other parts he had introduced additional definitions and axioms or postulates, as the subject matter might require. But the overall form of reasoning is deductive. And though Spinoza's philosophy can doubtless be presented in other ways than that in which it is presented in the *Ethics*, he seems to say clearly enough in the treatise on *The Improvement of the Understanding* that it is only through following a deductive procedure that the mind can reflect the order of Nature.

To insist at length on the influence exercised by Spinoza's vision of the universe on his choice of method may seem to be a case of labouring the obvious. Perhaps it is. But the point seems to be of some importance. It is natural for us to think that if we start with a set of definitions and a set of axioms and then develop a process of deductive reasoning, there is no guarantee at all that the conclusions which we draw will do anything more than exhibit the implications of the premises. There is no guarantee that they will reveal to us the necessary structure of Reality. To use the language which is fashionable among some modern Thomists, our philosophy will be 'essentialist', confined within the realm of essence or ideas or, if preferred, abstract possibility. For anyone however who believes that the structure of the universe is necessary, indeed that the whole series of things and events is necessary and cannot be otherwise than it is, and that "the order and connection of ideas is the same as the order and connection of things,"[26] the situation is different, provided, that is to say, that he can find the right starting point. In the order of things the point of departure is the infinite substance. This must therefore be the point of departure in the order of ideas too. It is therefore essential for Spinoza to hold, however implausibly, that he has as clear an idea of God as he has of a triangle.[27] It is only on this assumption that he can deduce the essential properties (or some of them) of *Deus seu Natura*.

Spinoza's basic vision of the universe finds initial expression, as far as the *Ethics* is concerned, in his premises. And the deductive method is required for its explicitation. Of course, given Spinoza's view of the attributes of substance and of the relation between the order of ideas and the order of things, we may think it misleading to speak of his vision of the universe as determining his choice of method. For the concept of the right method might be said to belong to the vision itself. So it does in a sense. But it can hardly be the right method unless the universe is 'rational'. That this is the case seems to be presupposed. And the presupposition governs the choice of method.

How is this presupposition justified? We may be inclined to think that no other justification is possible except the power of the system to give a coherent explanatory account of the essential structure of reality. In other words, the criterion of truth is coherence. The system or the vision rendered explicit is its own justification, the only one which can possibly be given. It might be objected however that a coherent deductive exhibition of the universe as a rational system would not show that the universe *is* rational but only that it *might* be rational. Perhaps therefore Spinoza was wise to maintain that he started with ideas which were true because they were clear and distinct and with self-evidently true metaphysical propositions. This claim may itself involve presuppositions. But what system does not do so? Some philosophers, including Spinoza, have of course tried to establish a philosophy in which there is no legitimately deniable presupposition.[28] In Spinoza's case however it seems pretty clear that an initial world vision was presupposed, even if he believed that the developed system exhibited its validity.

IV

In this essay it has been maintained that Spinoza's vision of the universe is rendered explicit in the deductive system. To put the matter in another way, we are not justified in making a dichotomy between the deductive system and the real mind of

Spinoza. The philosopher's mind is expressed in his writings. At the same time we have made another obvious point, that an explicitation must be an explicitation of something. But what is this something? Presumably it is the basic belief in one infinite necessarily existing substance which expresses itself by a necessity of nature in the world of finite things. The system purports to exhibit systematically the nature of the one substance insofar as we can know it,[29] its self-expression in the series of modes or finite things[30] and the way in which the human mind can rise above the point of view of the worm living in the bloodstream to an understanding of its own relation and that of other things to the divine totality.[31] The system, in other words, expresses the vision of *Deus seu Natura*.

'God or Nature'. The phrase sounds like an attempt to redefine the word 'God', to change the actual use of language, if, that is to say, we take as our standard the way in which Jews and Christians ordinarily conceive and speak about God. Obviously, a philosopher cannot be prohibited from recommending such changes, though we can demand of him that he should not try to conceal what he is doing and that he should be prepared to offer reasons for his procedure.

It is very natural that this line of thought should occur to the reader of Spinoza's writings. For when Christians and Jews (and Moslems too of course) speak about God, they do not ordinarily regard themselves as referring to Nature. It is natural therefore that when they come across a philosopher who uses 'God' and 'Nature' as synonymous terms, they should conclude that he does not really believe in God at all but that he attaches some value to religious emotion (a 'Cosmic emotion' perhaps) or to some religious attitudes and, by his redefinition of the term 'God', is trying to detach this emotion or attitude from God, as they understand the term and reattach it to Nature. Though however this is a natural reaction to Spinoza's identification of God and Nature, such readers might ask themselves whether the philosopher means by 'Nature' precisely what they mean and what are his reasons for the identification.

Anyone who knows a little about Spinoza is aware that he was brought up in the Jewish religion and tradition, that he found himself unable to accept orthodox Judaism and that he was expelled from the synagogue at the age of twenty-four. He came to the

conclusion that the Scriptural picture of God as thinking this or
that, as deciding this or that, as judging, as intervening miraculous-
ly in the natural course of events and so on was thoroughly
anthropomorphic and rationally untenable. It by no means follows
however that he ceased to believe in God. To what extent he was influenced in the development of his thought about God by the
Jewish philosophers of the Middle Ages and by the Cabalistic
writings is a disputed question and one to which no assured answer
can be given. In the *Tractatus Theologico-Politicus*[32] he makes it
clear that in his view the Cabalistic writings contain childish ideas
rather than divine secrets. And in the same work[33] he refers to the
famous philosopher Maimonides only to criticize him, though in a
letter[34] he mentions Chasdai Crescas with some approval. Even if
however there can be prolonged and inconclusive discussion about
particular influences on Spinoza's thought, it seems clear that his
idea of God as the one infinite and necessarily existing substance,
the immanent cause of all things, was formed under the influence of
his philosophical reading. To say this is not of course to suggest that
Spinoza simply took over his idea of God from one of his
predecessors. He could at any rate have found in the writings of
Jewish philosophers the concept of God as a necessarily existing
substance, the idea that the perfections of creatures must somehow
preexist in God, the possibility of the series of finite things being infinite and the notion of the compatibility between acting freely and
acting by a necessity of nature.[35] But the equation of God and
Nature was not derived from Jewish philosophy. As for the Biblical
picture of God, Spinoza did not assert that it was false so much as
that it was adapted to promote piety and obedience among people
at large, and that it should not be taken as the source of
philosophical truth, which must be either self-evident to reason or
demonstrated. To picture a God 'out there', a transcendent creator
endowed with human or quasi-human qualities, is all very well for
the purpose of popular religion. But we cannot speak of God *and*
Nature, if God is conceived as infinite.

Spinoza has no intention however of asserting that the existence of finite things is illusory. It has sometimes been argued that
on his premises he ought to have held that the phenomenal world
was illusion or mere appearance. But in point of fact he does not say
this. True, for him there is only one substance. But substance is so

defined that to say of something that it is a mode of substance is not to say that it lacks all reality. At the same time Spinoza obviously does not interpret the term 'God' as a class name for the plurality of finite things. 'God' is not the name of a collection or of the members of a class taken collectively. He is therefore faced with the task of combining the concept of God as the one all-inclusive substance with admission of the reality of the series of finite things. Here he has an instrument to hand in a distinction already made by Giordano Bruno, the distinction between *Natura naturans* and *Natura naturata*. So far as the present writer is aware, there is no cogent evidence to show that Spinoza took the distinction from Bruno. But it is unlikely that he had no acquaintance with the Renaissance philosophy of Nature in which Nature (in the sense of the spatio-temporal world) was represented as the 'explication' or self-manifestation of the infinite in itself. In any case the distinction enables Spinoza to reconcile, to his own satisfaction at least, the statements that God in himself is eternal[36] and immutable[37] with the evident fact of the successive existence of finite things.

What we have been saying is not of course in any way new. In view however of the emphasis placed by some writers on Spinoza's naturalism and in view of certain attempts by Marxists to represent him as a materialist it is perhaps worth drawing attention once again to his endeavour to develop a view of God and of the relation between God and the world which would be, in his opinion, philosophically justified. The working out of this view is found indeed in the system. But behind this system lies Spinoza's rejection of the traditional beliefs instilled into him in childhood, coupled with his lasting conviction that the word 'God' is not devoid of reference. Whatever other people may have done, Spinoza certainly did not regard himself as an atheist. Obviously, if theism is understood as implying an idea of God rejected by Spinoza, he can quite properly be described as an atheist. It is a question of accurate description, not of emotive reaction. Given the ordinary use of language, it is certainly misleading to describe him as a theist. But he was clearly no deist. And there is no good reason for thinking that his talk about 'God' was insincere. He indignantly rejected the accusation that his aim was to "teach atheism by hidden and disguised arguments."[38] He regarded himself as explaining the 'real' meaning (reference) of the word 'God'.

V

It can indeed be objected that what really counts is where Spinoza ends, not where he begins. We can argue, if we like, that he sought for a philosophically tenable concept of God. But the search ends in sheer naturalism. What Spinoza actually does is to present a certain view of the world or the universe. To call the world 'God' is an idiosyncracy on his part. It does not alter the plain fact that the world is the world and not at all what is commonly understood by the term 'God'. What Spinoza actually does is to present a philosophical system which has to be interpreted with reference to seventeenth-century science. He is of course primarily a philosopher, not a scientist. His correspondence shows indeed an interest in particular scientific questions, such as Boyle's experiments with nitre. And Spinoza himself conducts some experiments. But he is thoroughly dissatisfied with what he regards as the excessively empirical approach of Francis Bacon and with the way in which a scientist such as Boyle tries to combine experimental science with traditional religious ideas. Spinoza goes behind phenomena to their basic presuppositions, or what he considers to be such, and looks for their ultimate causes. In this sense he is a metaphysical philosopher. But transcendence, as understood in a religious context, disappears. The divine mind appears to be identical with the fundamental laws of Nature. And when Spinoza says that the existence of a finite thing cannot be deduced from God considered simply in himself but that the series of modes has to be taken into account, he is really saying that the existence of a finite thing cannot be deduced from any law under which its behaviour can be subsumed but that reference must also be made to empirical causes or antecedent conditions. Talk about 'God' really confuses the issue. For it obscures the fact that Spinoza is thinking in purely naturalistic terms. In ordinary language 'God' signifies a supernatural being. In Spinoza's philosophy the supernatural is conspicuous by its absence. Whatever therefore he himself may have thought, with his religious upbringing and living, as he did, at a time when theological themes were still living issues, his system really demands that the word 'God' should be eliminated from it. The situation would then be clarified instead of obfuscated.

That Spinoza was interested, as far as time allowed, in scientific matters is obvious enough. And he was not such a recluse as to be immune from the influence of the climate of thought of seventeenth-century science. But there seems to be little evidence that he set out to supply a philosophical background for the science of his time, even if he thought that his philosophy did in fact provide such a background. Interpretations of Spinoza which translate his theological language into talk about laws of Nature and the general features of the world tend to give the impression of attempts to state what, in the opinion of the writer, Spinoza ought to have said (or what he 'really' meant) rather than what he did say. Such interpretations express no doubt the laudable intention of making Spinoza intelligible and the desire to show that the eminent philosopher who has sometimes been taken as the 'model' metaphysician[39] possessed a better understanding of the presuppositions of seventeenth-century physics than some of the leading scientists themselves. But such interpretations generally have to be qualified by the admission that Spinoza did not think in such terms or that he would not have agreed with the interpretation given. For example, in a recently published work on Spinoza the author connects the philosopher's theory of the unknowable attributes of God with the idea of "the possibility of alternative scientific accounts of the same phenomena,"[40] remarking that this possibility was a living question for Spinoza and his contemporaries. He then adds however that "the mature Spinoza would not accept this,"[41] namely a view which would make the unknowable attributes knowable in principle. In other words, there is an element of transcendence (in regard to human thought, not of course in regard to the universe itself) which Spinoza did not eliminate but which ought to be eliminated if the 'real' direction of his line of thought is to be clearly exhibited.

These remarks should not be understood as condemning or rejecting all purely naturalistic accounts of Spinoza's philosophy and all interpretations of his thought in the light of contemporary science. Provided that we allow for what we might describe as recalcitrant elements, it is certainly arguable that his system is best seen in the light of the philosophy of Descartes[42] and of seventeenth-century science. We can see it, if we like, as a stage on the way to a naturalistic philosophy concerned with the broadest presuppositions of science. Criticism is then likely to turn on the rigidity of Spinoza's philosophy and to refer to the fact, which the late A. N. Whitehead liked to insist on, that twentieth-century scientific theory differs in important ways from that of the seventeenth century, with the result that we can hardly be satisfied with a seventeenth-century philosophical system. To be sure, the historic Spinoza would hardly have looked on things in this way. For he believed that he had exhibited *the* truth about reality. But the attempt to interpret his significance in the light of the general development of scientific and philosophical thought is quite legitimate.

Spinoza's *Deus seu Natura* remains however ambiguous. As in the case of the Stoic philosophy, of which Spinozism often reminds us, we may well ask ourselves whether we are dealing with a naturalizing of *Deus* or a divinization of *Natura*. The situation is ambiguous. On the one hand we can emphasize *Natura*. On the other hand we can emphasize *Deus*. And if we adopt the second procedure, it is arguable that we ought to look forward to the philosophy of Hegel who maintained that Spinoza's substance should be redefined as Spirit (*Geist*). To introduce the name of Hegel is indeed most unfashionable. But if von Tschirnhaus and G. H. Schuller were right in suggesting that in Spinoza's philosophy the attribute of thought came to occupy a central position in reality, it becomes easier to see a connection between Spinozism and absolute idealism.

This line of thought lies open to the objection that Spinoza's philosophy should be considered in itself and in relation to the problems of his time, not as a forerunner of or as looking forward to a later philosophy which was developed in response to other problems. Spinozism is Spinozism, not a stage in the emergence of Hegelianism. It is true that as far as the general task of metaphysics is concerned, both Spinoza and Hegel can be said to have had similar aims, namely the representation in thought of the nature of the ultimate reality. Spinoza exhibits the nature, properties and activity of the one infinite substance; Hegel regards the task of philosophy as the reconstruction for consciousness of the life of the Absolute. Both men call the ultimate reality 'God'. Both men refuse to admit the propriety of speaking of the infinite *and* the finite; but neither is prepared to look on 'God in himself' as identical with the collection or class of finite things. Though however similarities between the two philosophies are visible if we look at them from such a distance that differences become blurred, their problems are different. For example, in the seventeenth century the philosopher had to come to terms with the new scientific developments, not with the romantic movement. Again, insofar as Spinoza's problems were set by another philosopher, they were set by the philosophy of Descartes (possibly in conjunction with Renaissance philosophy of Nature), whereas Hegel was obviously faced with problems arising out of the thought of Kant and his successors. Again, the two men's conceptions of the ultimate reality were different; and the methods which they employed to exhibit its nature were also different. Spinoza may have looked on his system as expressing timeless truth; but Hegel insisted on the close connection between any system and its historical background. And the plain fact of the matter is that the historical backgrounds of Spinozism and Hegelianism differed in important respects. The philosophy of Spinoza therefore should be seen in its historical context and not treated as a stage in the development of a system of thought belonging to a later and very different age.

True enough. But it is not the intention of the present writer to endorse Hegel's view of the history of philosophy as a necessary dialectical process whereby the universal mind or spirit comes to consciousness of itself. I have no intention of suggesting that the philosophy of Spinoza *must* be transformed into Hegelianism. My contention is rather that Spinoza's philosophy is ambiguous, Janus-faced. If one aspect is emphasized, a naturalistic interpretation becomes reasonable. If another aspect is emphasized, we have a pantheism which can reasonably be seen as demanding the transformation of *Natura* into *Geist*. We can of course try to confine ourselves to exegesis of Spinoza's system as it stands in his writings. But in my opinion such exegesis does not reveal the system as viable. Spinozists would obviously disagree.

It may be said that if there are ambiguities in the system of Spinoza's, this is even more true of the philosophy of Hegel. The former has always tended to be a take-it-or-leave-it system, whereas Hegelianism, as we are well aware, gave rise to very different lines of interpretation. But that there should be ambiguities and tensions in any comprehensive metaphysical system is, in my opinion, only to be expected. Nobody swimming in a river can see the whole river. He can indeed enunciate propositions which must be true for it to be proper to speak of there being a river at all.

And Spinoza doubtless thought that he was doing something analogous in regard to the world. But the fact remains that the swimmer's perspective and range of vision are limited. And though the impulse to understand Reality as a whole is natural enough, the notion that this can be achieved once and for all and with mathematical clarity by the historically conditioned mind is a supposition which most of us nowadays find some difficulty in accepting.

FREDERICK C. COPLESTON

HEYTHROP COLLEGE,
UNIVERSITY OF LONDON

NOTES

¹ William of Ockham, *Opera Theologica, I* (St. Bonaventure, N. Y.: St. Bonaventure University Press, 1967), p. 259. And see also the prologue to Ockham's commentary on the ˌ ˌ ˈ ˌ ˈ ˈ ᵏs of Aristotle's *Physics*. Ockham is actually referring to the different views maintained by Avicenna and Averroes about the subject matter of metaphysics.

² For Spinoza's view of the relation between philosophy and theology see the *Tractatus Theologico-Politicus*, Chaps. 14 and 15.

³ *Tractatus Theologica-Politicus*, Chap. 15. By Scripture Spinoza often understands both Testaments. This may seem to be simply a matter of arguing *ad hominem*, as in the correspondence with Van Blyenbergh. But Spinoza obviously writes as one who has broken with orthodox Judaism and for whom all writings which are used as sources for theological thought possess a pragmatic function. If he were writing to a Moslem, he could make similar remarks about the Koran.

⁴ This is stated in, for instance, Letter 23 (to Van Blyenbergh).

⁵ R. B. Braithwaite, "An Empiricist's View of the Nature of Religious Belief" (Cambridge: Cambridge University Press, 1955).

⁶ Spinoza explains this in Letter 4 (to Henry Oldenburg). See also, of course, the treatise on *The Improvement of the Understanding*.

⁷ *Ethics*, II, Prop. 7.

⁸ For example, in Letter 10 (to Simon de Vries) Spinoza asserts that the existence of a mode cannot be deduced from its definition or essence. Again, in Letter 83 (to von Tschirnhaus) he says that it is impossible to prove 'the variety of things' a priori from the concept of extension. Similarly, in the treatise on *The Improvement of the Understanding* he makes it clear that it is not the series of particular and

mutable things which can be deduced but only the series of "fixed and eternal things", by which he may mean the infinite modes of substance. Some writers have understood Spinoza as saying simply that *we* cannot deduce the existence of particular things. Though however some remarks suggest this line of interpretation, Spinoza seems to be asserting that such a deduction is impossible in principle. It is at any rate true in principle that it is only in the case of God that existence can be deduced from essence.

⁹ What we say about this matter depends to a certain extent of course on the meaning which we give to the word 'philosophy'. For Augustine the Christian religion was the true 'philosophy'. Hence he could look on philosophy as a way of life, the saving wisdom of which had fulfilled and taken the place of true wisdom. When however in the course of the Middle Ages philosophy came to be systematically distinguished from revelation and theology, it could no longer be regarded by Christian theologians in precisely the same way in which Augustine had regarded it. The meaning of the word had undergone a change.

¹⁰ *Ethics*, II, Prop. 40, note 2.

¹¹ Bertrand Russell, *History of Western Philosophy* (London: Allen and Unwin, 1946), p. 594.

¹² In point of fact Spinoza does not appear to deny the reality of finite things or to regard them as illusory.

¹³ *Enneads*, 771b.

¹⁴ *Ethics*, V, Prop. 36.

¹⁵ *Ibid.*, IV, Prop. 28.

¹⁶ Letter 68.

¹⁷ Descartes was of course quite aware of this fact. See *Principles of Philosophy*, I, 51, in *Oeuvres de Descartes*, ed. by Charles Adam and Paul Tannery (Paris: Léopold Cerf, 1897-1913), VIII, 24.

¹⁸ *Short Treatise*, I, Chap. 2.

¹⁹ Friedrich Waismann, "How I See Philosophy," in *Contemporary British Philosophy: Personal Statements,* Third Series, ed. by H. D. Lewis (London: Allen and Unwin, 1956), p. 489.

²⁰ In this case the vision will not of course be considered of real value unless the way of life or type of conduct which it is thought of as tending to promote is itself approved and judged desirable.

²¹ See, for example, Letter 13 (to Oldenburg).

²² *Ethics*, V, Prop. 40.

²³ It is obvious in any case that in the *Ethics* Spinoza sometimes abandons or steps outside the quasi-mathematical framework. Further, we may well think that what is supposed to be deduced is by no means always actually deduced. But the deductive ideal remains.

²⁴ Letter 2.

²⁵ *Ethics*, II, Prop. 10, note.

[26] *Ethics*, II, Prop. 7.

[27] Letter 56 (to Hugo Boxel).

[28] Sometimes the attempt has been made to reach, by reductive analysis, a starting point for deduction which cannot indeed be demonstrated (for it would not then be an ultimate starting point) but can be vindicated by showing that its denial implies its affirmation.

[29] This proviso is required in view of Spinoza's statement that God consists of infinite attributes, coupled with his assertion that we know only two of these attributes, thought and extension.

[30] Spinoza denies that the existence of any given finite mode can be deduced simply from the one substance considered in itself. The existence of the cow in the field cannot be adequately explained without reference to the series of finite modes. In this sense God is not the 'adequate cause' of the cow. But though the series of finite things is without temporal beginning, it is none the less ontologically dependent on the one substance. It could not exist unless the one substance existed; and it cannot be understood except in terms of the causal activity of God.

[31] The passage about the parasitic worm occurs in Letter 32 (to Oldenburg). As for the statement above that the mind 'can rise' to adequate ideas, this must be understood in a sense compatible with Spinoza's determinism. Given the antecedent conditions, some minds rise (and therefore can rise) to the highest level of knowledge, while other minds do not so rise (and therefore cannot do so).

[32] Chap. 9.

[33] Chap. 7.

[34] Letter 12 (to Ludovicus Meyer).

[35] Spinoza applied this idea to God, as it is only in the case of God that activity precedes entirely from the essence or nature of the agent, and is dependent on nothing else.

[36] *Ethics*, I, Prop. 19.

[37] *Ibid.*, Prop. 20, Cor. 2.

[38] Letter 43 (to Jacob Ostens).

[39] The word 'model' should not of course be understood as necessarily implying approbation of metaphysics. The reference is to the way in which Spinoza's metaphysics has sometimes been taken as the best and clearest example of the method and aims of metaphysicians. Whether metaphysics is regarded with approval or disapproval is another question.

[40] E. M. Curley, *Spinoza's Metaphysics: An Essay in Interpretation* (Cambridge: Harvard University Press, 1969), p. 151. It ought to be added that Mr. Curley sees Spinoza's problems as set more by the philosophy of Descartes than by seventeenth-century science in a narrow sense of 'science'.

[41] *Ibid.*

[42] The fact that Spinoza was not a Cartesian obviously does not entail the conclusion that reflection on the philosophy of Descartes was not a powerful instrument in determining the nature of Spinoza's problematics.

Ruth Saw

The Task of Metaphysics for Spinoza

Any rational discipline has as its proper and primary task to present itself as an internally interconnected and coherent system. If it is important to human beings that it should be true, its practitioners cannot be content with premises from which it follows as a hypothetical system, but must either show them as indubitable by their own nature or as grounded in fact. If they are grounded in fact then we must continually appeal to experimentally verified hypotheses which will further anchor the science to our actual world. Mathematics is in the peculiar position of having no possible empirical verification of its theorems, but of being continually verified by application. Mathematics 'works' when applied to the building of bridges and skyscrapers, the knitting of pullovers and the designing of engines. It also appeals to rational beings as intellectually satisfying in itself. Metaphysics is like mathematics in presenting itself as intellectually satisfying to those willing to submit themselves to its discipline; it is unlike mathematics in that it has, in the ordinary sense of the word, no application. Nevertheless, Spinoza makes a determined attempt to exhibit metaphysics as satisfying on all counts. It is an internally coherent system, it justifies itself by its effect on its practitioners, and it could not be effective in this way if it were not at the same time true.

To satisfy ourselves that Spinoza's metaphysic is internally coherent we must simply follow through his exposition in the *Ethics*, making our criticisms and reservations at the appropriate points. It is not to my purpose to make this examination here. I have simply to examine his other contentions that his conclusions, being rationally based on indubitable ideas, are necessarily true, and that to pursue this reasoning and to accept its conclusions is to lead the life of blessedness for man. The title of his first considerable work *Tractatus de Intellectus Emendatione* is illuminating here. It opens with a description of his ends. His object is described as 'the acquisition of distinct and clear ideas such as are produced by the pure intellect, and not by chance physical motions'—that is to say, the ideas that the mind forms when it is active, and not those occurring as the inner side of the physical processes of perception and imagination. The treatise then, concerns the *intellectus emendatio*, variously rendered as 'amendment' (Pollock), 'improvement' (Elwes & Roth), and 'purification' or 'purgation' which is preferred by Joachim. This latter seems to me to express most adequately what Spinoza had in mind. To increase in knowledge is to become more clearly aware of our own ideas and of their interconnections, and this is to be brought about not by improving the mind as if it were an instrument, but by removing false and inadequate ideas which cloud the intellect as if it were a mirror, or better, a pane of glass. When we quietly and calmly contemplate the orderly system of ideas arising in a clear intellect, we are making ourselves into a medium through which God's ideas may shine. The conception of all knowledge as an ordered system, taking its rise from the knowledge of God, sketched in the *Tractatus*, is developed in the *Ethics*. In the *Tractatus*, Spinoza describes his object also as 'to discover the life of blessedness for man'. At this point we may merely note that the active contemplation of the true system of ideas, constituting as it does the proper activity of man, is also the life of blessedness.

There is a further point to be made in relation to the usefulness of sciences. Some subject matters seem more to our point than others. The subject matter for mathematics might be thought of as the modifications of space and their interrelationships, the nature of number, classes, sets and so on. It justifies itself practically by its application. The subject matter of geology is the earth, the structure of its crust shaped by internal and external influences, and practically justified in its predictions of earthquakes, the eruptions of all sorts, and implications for mineralogy and meteorology. I do not intend to embark here on the question of whether metaphysics can have a subject matter. It is enough to say that its practitioners reflect upon the universe, its Maker, its aspects, and the nature and possibility of the changes going on within it. If it has a subject matter, it is space, matter, time, eternity, infinity, God and their interrelationships.

Many ordinary people are willing to suppose that such a study must have a calming, and therefore, beneficial effect upon its practitioners. This is not what Spinoza has in mind. The search for the life of blessedness for man involves the discovery of the ways in which men may be enabled to act more effectively. To find these ways it is necessary to determine the nature of man, and of his environment, including his fellows. Since men are embodied minds or ensouled bodies, their complete description needs the whole set of systematic accounts of the physical world, human communities, and a rational psychology. Since all true statements must be well founded, an account of men and their environment will lead naturally to the basic premisses about space, time, God and the Universe, luminously shown as yielding our more limited conclusions. These premisses, the 'common notions', have a double importance for truth. They constitute the original furniture of the mind, to be seen when we think clearly and well, unhindered by inappropriate emotion. They display themselves ever more clearly, not only as adequate in themselves, but as containing the possibility of rational development. They are the grounds both for truth and coherence. These ideas finally show themselves as related coherently to the one true idea of the Perfect Being, as One, necessarily existing and the ground for everything that is. What is uncovered in the development of this idea is a Being having some of the marks of the God of Moses and the Christian religion, but lacking many others. The virtues which we attribute to men when we praise them are entirely inappropriate in our description of the Perfect Being. The very notion of perfection takes on a new connotation—that of complete reality and activity, together with the notion of rejoicing as the proper accompaniment of complete activity.

At this point we must notice that in the ordinary sense of the word, the pursuit of knowledge may uncover truths which are encouraging, pleasant to contemplate, and therefore easy for men to accept. On the other hand, the truths uncovered may be distasteful in the extreme. It is Spinoza's view that human blessedness consists in the discovering, acceptance and active contemplation of what is disclosed in thinking, no matter what it may be. But is this because what is uncovered by the activity of human reasoning must be 'pleasant' to rational men simply because it is the outcome of reason, or has Spinoza a private guarantee that it will be 'pleasant' because of its content? Suppose we were to think, and reach the conclusion that we were being deceived by a supremely wicked being who wished to enjoy the dismay of the good man when he found that the record of his attempts to be good aroused cosmic laughter. Would human blessedness still consist in knowledge and the contemplation of truth? It might be answered that even then it would be the best that could be achieved by human beings, but it is difficult to avoid the conclusion that Spinoza 'knows' before he begins, that the truth will be satisfying to rational men in all senses. This is not too hard to accept; it fits in with the view that whatever is to be known is already in a sense 'there', and we may delight in foreshadowings of the truth both because it is the truth and because what is foreshadowed is satisfying in itself. More prosaically, we may recall Spinoza's upbringing, and his possession of the fundamental ideas of metaphysics long before he could have understood them. (In justice to Spinoza we must recall that he has removed what many would call 'the consolations of religion'—the belief for example, that the victims of injustice will be compensated in a later life, that a heavenly Father sees and sympathises with our sufferings, and that at some point we shall be reunited with friends who have died before us.)

Even so, there are various 'pleasant' metaphysical systems, and we might go on to ask whether *any* metaphysic would do, or must it be Spinoza's? It might be thought that the taking up of a certain attitude and pursuing a line of argument disinterestedly would satisfy Spinoza's specifications for the life of blessedness. It might then be asked why Leibniz, peacefully and with great acuteness setting out his *Monadology*, did not qualify for achieving human blessedness. The answer for Spinoza, is quite simply that we cannot think about the first things adequately without reaching his conclusions. Furthermore, it is not merely that we must reach Spinoza's conclusions, but that we must also share his starting point. The common ideas are possessed by every rational being, and these ideas will automatically develop themselves into the proper metaphysical system, i.e. Spinoza's. Just as it would be impossible to begin with Euclid's theorems and axioms, think clearly and reach non-Euclidian conclusions, so it would be impossible to allow our common notions to develop themselves into non-Spinozistic conclusions.

How then, is it possible to fail in a rational enterprise? For Spinoza it is not possible to fail in reasoning, but only to allow our reasoning to be clouded by emotion. We may ask for instance, how Leibniz has failed. (We may notice Leibniz's remark that 'If it were not for the Monads Spinoza would be right'!) It is not an accident that the only extended example of error which Spinoza gives us is our mistaken notion that we are free. Men think themselves free because no one can ever see the complete causal sequences leading to any 'action'. Sometimes we know that we have missed an important factor, but sometimes we think that we know it all, granted the unexpected, the unknowable, 'the free choice'. This mistake leads to a whole network of mistaken ideas—human responsibility, the suitability of praising and blaming, resentment, hatred, misplaced and misbegotten love, leading to interference with the lives of others. The next step is to use 'freedom' as a term of praise. To describe someone as a free man is to estimate him highly. Freedom therefore must not be denied to God, and so arises the mistaken view of God as choosing to act in certain ways and standing to us in the relationship of a father to his children or a prince to his subjects. I think that for Spinoza, this is the centre of Leibniz's 'false metaphysic', but how has this happened to such an acute thinker? If metaphysics is, like mathematics, a purifying of the intellect so that the truth can shine through, how can Leibniz have made such a mistake? It can be understood only in the terms of his inappropriate emotion of love of God, not as Spinoza sees it, a rational delight, but as a passive disinclination to withhold any tribute from God.

We may now express some final doubts. What we need is some kind of explanation, not exactly of our interest in men, nor even of our view of their importance. It is natural to us as humans to find ourselves and our companions interesting and important, and yet not expect them to be of cosmic importance. It seems to me however, that at least some notice should be taken of the extraordinary fact that we alone make elaborate systems of mathematics and metaphysics, that we alone concern ourselves with the question whether or not God loves us. Furthermore, we badly need an account of what it means to be a person, for we are certainly persons to one another, even if not to God. All we are given is a minute account of the modal system under the attribute of extension, and of the human body as an instance of a complex body, and an assurance that the system of bodily changes is closely patterned by a system of mental changes. Like any other, the human body is to be thought of as a complex of complexes of simpler and simpler bodies, coming finally to the 'simplest bodies'. Considered as bodies, men are to be described most truly in scientific terms which allow for the complete understanding of their manner of functioning. At the basic level these descriptions are appropriate to inanimate as well as to organic bodies. Spinoza's treatment of these descriptions appears in a number of axioms and lemmas in the *Ethics*, Part II, Proposition 13. Here he distinguishes between 'simplest bodies', i.e. bodies distinguishable from one another in respect of motion and rest, speed and slowness alone, individuals composed of these simplest bodies and distinguishable from one another by their hardness and softness, these qualities arising from the manner of compounding the simplest bodies. Finally, we come to composite individuals composed of bodies of the second order. These are distinguishable from one another by the complexity of the ways in which the second-order individuals are combined, and by the efficiency with which they maintain their unity along with the varying degrees of their internal change. There is no reason why we should not conceive of this process of compounding individuals, producing more and more complex bodies, until we arrived at the notion of the whole of nature as an individual with an infinite number of changes in its parts, yet itself unchanging. The essence of individuals is said to be their conatus, the endeavour with which each persists in its own being. It is one of the paradoxes of Spinoza's position that conatus can belong only to the derived, dissoluble, and in a sense, illusory individuals, and not to the only true individual, God or Substance, nor to the next in metaphysical order, the simplest bodies. The essence of God involves existence, and he could not possibly *not* persist in his own being. As for the simplest bodies, they do not endure, so that they could neither persist nor not persist in their own being.

Having been given this very complete account of the way in which the description of men as physical beings may be reached from the basic level, we suddenly come upon Book II, Axiom 2, 'Man thinks'. This is the first appearance of the whole concept though we have been given, so to speak, all the ingredients of men as bodies. If we are to accept 'man thinks' as axiomatic, we should have been given grounds for his unity as a thinking being. What we have been given is infinite substance, infinitely modified under its known attributes of extension and thought, an account of the unity of a man as a bodily being, and nothing whatever of his unity as a thinking being. More importantly, not only have we been given no comparable account of the terms in which the thinking must be described at the basic level, but it is difficult to see how we could even begin to work out such a description. In later books of the *Ethics* there are descriptions of mental events, but then, as is suitable, the descriptions are in terms of association, of coincidence of ideas and feelings with the consequent building up of more complex states of mind.

We have then, a paradoxical situation in that the only way in which a man, say Peter, can achieve human blessedness is by the adequate knowledge and understanding of his own nature, and of his place in the universe. When he achieves this however he will see that he is not 'Peter' in any important sense but only a complex system of modifications of substance under the attributes of extension and thought. When I say 'in any important sense' I mean that his unity, continuity and consequently his individuality is shifting and unstable and not of such a kind as to make it sensible to speak of him as an important member of the beings in the universe, and certainly not to speak of his future existence. To put it in general terms, to achieve 'our' blessedness we must recognise that 'we' do not exist in any important sense. Why then bother about 'our' blessedness? At this point we must notice, what is to me a strong temptation, and to most people a commonsense course to pursue. It may be said that if we allow Spinoza to speak of persons, to use the pronouns 'we' and 'I' without discussion, and to say of 'us' that 'we feel and know ourselves to be eternal', even though it is in opposition to everything that follows from his own basic principles, we are merely allowing him a way of speaking that is useful in bringing it about that people act in a way that is conducive to happiness. The first answer to this objection is that Spinoza insists on knowledge as the most important element in the life of blessedness, and conse-

quently on the importance of the truths of our beliefs. He nowhere
considers the usefulness of the belief in contrast to its truth, though
we must not forget his reply to his landlady when she asked him
whether she might be saved in her religion. He replied that her
religion was a 'good one'. It might be that Spinoza found himself led
to accept the unsuitability of some truths for some minds, and had
to concede that the sternest truths must be kept for the strongest
thinkers.

The second reply is that if it were really the case that Spinoza
was concerned with the usefulness of the belief in our individuality,
we should expect him to demonstrate this usefulness. He shows the
harmfulness of accepting some of our beliefs, e.g. the illusion of free
will, but though he does not speak of the usefulness in the good life
of assuming our separate and personal identities, neither does he
speak of its harmfulness. We might connect such an illusion with
our mistaken belief that God loves each one of us, but Spinoza does
not make this connection.

My criticism of Spinoza's connection of metaphysics with
human blessedness is that he seems to be dealing in two systems,
one of wise sayings about conduct and its connection with happiness, but appealing to us as would any other system of
morals—Judaic, Christian, Moslem, etc. The second system is a
metaphysic presented in mathematical form but touching the first
system at no point. It is true that the maxims for rational conduct
are exhibited as rational, granted the nature of men, but it is
granted the nature of *men* and not of finite modal systems. This
leads on to a different line of criticism. For Spinoza the point of con-
tact is the connection between clear thinking, i.e. the truth of adequacy, and truth about. Even if Spinoza has established *this* connection, it is not the connection he needs. The connection he needs
is that between our ways of speaking at various levels. In conversation, in moral and political discourse, the suitable terms in which to
speak are the names of the objects of everyday life, men and institutions, tables and chairs, animals and trees, gold and silver. In
mathematics the appropriate terms are points, straight lines and
curves, and figures constructed out of points and lines. In physics
we speak in terms of energy and electrons, in botany plants, roots,
petals, sepals and so on. Now what we need to have shown is not
always a connection between these various ways of speaking,

though some branches of botany use the connection between mathematical figures and plant growth for example. What we need from Spinoza is a demonstration of the connection between mathematical statements and statements belonging to conversation between human beings and moral and political discourse. What he has done is to exhibit the physical universe as an interconnected and mutually determining system of motion/rest, and demonstrated the impossibility of a thinking substance outside the system of extension with all that follows from this as to the place of smaller systems of thinking within the whole, and told us *that* the contemplation of this system will have specific beneficial effects on human happiness.

RUTH SAW

CARSHALTON, SURREY

Errol E. Harris

Spinoza's Theory of Human Immortality

I

There is, perhaps, no great philosopher who presents us, with so much confidence and assurance as Spinoza does, with such stark contradictions so rigorously deduced from indubitable first principles. Our first reaction is the conviction that something must have gone wrong with the reasoning at some obscure point; but more careful examination of his system and his explicit statements reveal that there is no actual inconsistency and that the conflicts in his doctrines are only apparent. Let us first notice briefly what they are.

Spinoza rejects in no uncertain terms the existence of a god conceived, as he traditionally is in the major religions, as an almighty, all-wise, compassionate ruler and judge.[1] Small wonder that, in his day, Spinoza was deemed an atheist.[2] But, on the other hand, he asserts, as indubitable and self-evident, the existence of an infinite, eternal God, in whom all things exist and have their being, and without whom nothing can either be or be understood; God, who is the universal, immanent cause of all things, whether infinite and complete in their kind, or finite and derivative. Small wonder, again, that later commentators called Spinoza a 'God-intoxicated man'.

In Spinoza's God there is nothing contingent.[3] He is a necessary cause of all things and nothing that He does could He have left undone—though this is no limitation upon His power, rather the contrary. Everything that is and occurs is therefore necessarily and inevitably produced by God. We are left in no doubt that Spinoza is a determinist. Free will, he says, is an illusion entertained by men because they are aware of their desires but unaware of the causes of their desires. Yet, on the other hand, Spinoza devotes a fifth part of his greatest work to the subject of human freedom and ends his *Korte Verhandeling* with a chapter on '*De Waare Vryheid*'.

The mind or soul of man, he tells us, is a mode (or idea) in the Attribute of Thought (God's attribute), of which the object is a mode of Extension (another of God's attributes) and nothing else.[4] The soul is the idea of the body, and as the body is altered so is the mind affected. If the body is destroyed the mind is likewise.[5] Nevertheless, the mind can be united not only with its body, but also, through its adequate ideas, with the infinite essence of God; and, through the third kind of knowledge, *Scientia Intuitiva*, with its corollary, the intellectual love of God, the mind of man may be united with God Himself and His infinite intellect, thus it may become immortal (*Onsterfelijk*) and eternal (*aeterna*).

These apparent conflicts in Spinoza's philosophy are well known and there can be no dispute about the statements which seem to involve them. What is less apparent and more disputable is whether they can be resolved in the terms Spinoza offers, and, if so, how. My purpose in this paper is not to discuss all of them in detail, but to consider only the last; to ask whether Spinoza's account of the relation between body and mind is, or can be so understood as to be, compatible with any notion of immortality for the soul; to consider his view of the body-mind relation in particular; to examine Spinoza's conception of immortality, and to decide in what sense, if any, this notion of immortality is acceptable.

II

There have been, in the past, two predominant ways of conceiving human immortality. The first is to regard human personality as consisting of two separable parts, each in some sense complete in itself, a material body and an immaterial soul. On the death of the body, the soul is then thought of as being released, as continuing to live for an indefinitely long time, as it had in the past, but in a disembodied state. The second way of regarding immortality is that adopted in the Christian creeds, which envisage a soul separable from the body, but consider the resurrection of the body essential for the preservation in an after-life of the individuality of each particular person. The soul here does not die, as the body does, but presumably remains after bodily death in some state of suspended existence until such time as it can be reunited with the resurrected body, now somehow rendered indestructible so that the person can live on forever.

Spinoza's theory, at least prima facie, seems incompatible with both of these conceptions. He maintains first that the soul is the idea (which constitutes the human mind) of which the object "is a body, or a certain mode of extension actually existing, and nothing else" (*Ethics*, II, Prop. XIII). If and when the body ceases to exist, therefore, it should follow that its idea ceases to exist likewise—except in the rather special sense that every mode of Extension and of Thought exists eternally in God. This latter existence, however, cannot be equated with human immortality in particular, because it applies to all finite entities without exception, whether they are modes of Extension or of Thought. The eternal existence of the modes in God's eternal and infinite attributes pertains to God. It is not the *continued* existence in time of any one of them beyond its allotted span, and thus by no means is it the continued existence of a human person enjoying successive experiences after the death of his body. It seems to follow, further from the Scholium to Proposition XIII, that body and mind are inseparable and co-terminous. There Spinoza asserts that the relation between them is no different from that between any other *idea* and its *ideatum*: "For of everything there must necessarily be given an idea in God, of which God is the cause, in the same manner as there is an idea of the human body." The only difference between man's mind and the ideas in God of other things is what follows from the difference between the human body and other bodies, the former being, for the most part, more complex. As the human body is more apt than others for doing and suffering many things at the same time, so the human mind is more apt to perceive many things at the same time.

Similarly, we are told in the *Short Treatise* that as the body suffers changes caused by other bodies, so these changes are felt by the soul as sensations (Part II, Introductory footnote) and also that the soul, being an idea of the existence of some thing (*Zaak*) in Nature, endures and changes according as that thing endures and changes (Part II, Chapter XXIII). But in both of these contexts Spinoza qualifies his statement in a way which he then uses to

prove human immortality. To this qualification I shall return
presently. What is to be noted here is that the doctrine of body-
mind relationship is so conceived that the mind (the idea of the
body) cannot be separated from the body and can exist only if and
when the body exists.

It should follow that the immortality of the soul, if it is to be affirmed at all, cannot be conceived, as it was by Plato in the *Phaedo*,
as the continued existence of a disembodied soul after the death
and dissolution of the body.

Nor is the notion of a resurrection of the body anywhere
suggested by Spinoza and it would seem impossible in his system.
For the existence of each finite thing (according to him) is
necessarily caused in the succession of finite causes which flow
endlessly from God's infinite being; and no cause is mentioned, or
seems to be contemplated, which could reconstitute exactly so complex a body as the human organism, once its dissolution has been
brought about by other necessary causes. That such reconstitutive
causes might be included in God's infinite reality is conceivable,
but Spinoza never considers the possibility, nor is there anything in
the nature of things as we experience them that requires us to
assume the actuality of such causes. However that may be,
Spinoza's account of human immortality does not include or require the resurrection of the body as a particular mode of extended
Substance, though it does, as we shall see, require a special interpretation of the nature and status of individual bodies and a
transformed idea of them.

So far, however, we can say that Spinoza's theory of body-mind
relationship is in conflict with both the most usual traditional forms
of the notion of immortality, and would seem to exclude the
possibility of any kind of 'life after death'. Yet Spinoza, in the
Scholium to Proposition XX of *Ethics*, V, says: "And with these
[demonstrations] I have dealt with everything that concerns this
present life. . . .It is, therefore, time now that I should pass to those
matters which pertain to the duration of the mind without relation
to the body." And in Proposition XXIII he declares: "It is not possible for the human mind to be absolutely destroyed with the body,
but something of it remains which is eternal." The first statement is
significant, not simply because no existence of the mind without
relation to the body should be possible consistently with what we

have been told earlier, but also because reference is made to it specifically as 'duration'. It would, however, be quite consistent with this statement subsequently to deny that the mind endures at all without relation to the body; and this is precisely what Spinoza does say in the Scholium to Proposition XXIII: "Our mind . . . can be said to endure, and its existence can be defined by a certain time, only so far as it involves the actual existence of the body." Nevertheless, he maintains in the same place that "we feel and know (*experimur*) ourselves to be eternal." How is all this to be understood so that it is self-consistent?

III

Most commentators resolve the difficulties first by contending that the reference to 'this present life' in the Scholium to Proposition XX, in Part V of the *Ethics*, is a concession to ordinary parlance or a 'momentary slip',[6] and to the mind's duration without relation to the body as a use of 'duration' different from that in which he distinguished it from 'eternity'. Joachim explains[7] that Spinoza is not quite consistent in his use of this word. While, as a rule, he refuses to predicate duration of what is eternal and identifies the former with persistence in time, he also regards duration as that of which time is the measure. Time results from the subdivision of duration into periods. But this subdivision is the work of *Imaginatio*, for strictly duration is indivisible (like Extension generally);[8] and when adequately conceived all its 'parts' are seen as coeval. It then becomes identical with eternity, or, as Joachim puts it, is "the general term of which eternal existence and temporal existence are forms."[9]

Spinoza's otherwise clear distinction between duration and eternity can then be taken seriously, and his attribution of 'immortality' (a term he uses himself only once in the *Ethics*) to the human mind is explained as the identity of its adequate ideas with the eternal and infinite intellect of God. The adequate ideas in human knowledge are thus eternal. In *Scientia Intuitiva* man achieves an adequate knowledge of the essence of things through an adequate idea of the formal essence of certain of God's attributes,[10] and such adequate ideas as constitute this third kind of knowledge (as well as such adequate ideas as constitute the second, scientific kind—*Ratio*) are eternal and timeless. "In eternity there is no *when, before* nor *after*." (*Ethics*, I, Prop. XXXIII, Sch. 2). And as the ideas in which these forms of knowledge consist are part of the complex idea which is the human mind, there must be some part of it 'that remains eternal' when the human body dies and passes away. The use of the word 'remains' here is again regarded as a slip or a concession to ordinary language. It is repeated by Spinoza in subsequent propositions, but there is no need to understand it otherwise than as meaning that there is something eternal in the human mind besides what ceases to 'endure' when its body dies (as we say in arithmetic: $15 \div 6 = 2$, remainder 3). The eternity of the 'immortal' part of the human mind or soul is thus not a continued duration after the death of the body, but a quality of being.

What corresponds in extension to the eternal part of the human mind is then not the human body as a finite mode merely, or as imagined in the first kind of knowledge (*Imaginatio*), but the human body as adequately understood in the second and third kinds of knowledge. As so understood it is an eternal consequence of God's infinite, immanent causality, and must be conceived in its proper place in the total scheme of things, through an adequate idea of the formal essence of (presumably) the attribute of Extension. Inasmuch as adequate ideas are identical with God's, their counterpart in extension will not be any merely finite mode but the whole extended world—*facies totius universi*, for all modes of Extension are mutually connected in the infinite series of causes which flow of necessity from God's nature; and Spinoza explains at some length how simple bodies become included in more complex bodies in a hierarchy that eventually includes the whole of nature.[11]

This interpretation of Spinoza's doctrine, or something very similar to it, is accepted by all the best known commentators. Joachim expounds it with admirable clarity; Leon Roth and Ruth Saw do not depart from it; Stuart Hampshire adheres to it; and much the same view, with minor variations, is taken by John Caird and A. E. Taylor.[12] Indeed, there is a great deal in the Spinoza text to support it. However, I shall not discuss the views of these commentators individually here, nor shall I consider at this point the implications for morality and religion of the conception of human immortality involved. It would be better first to discuss the conception itself, for it leaves difficulties unresolved and significant implications in Spinoza's theory undeveloped.

IV

In the first place, with all due respect to Joachim, as one of the most accurate and careful scholars who has commented on the *Ethics*, it is not wholly correct to attribute the idea of the human body as a finite mode of Extension in interaction with other finite modes, merely to the confusion of *Imaginatio*. "The modes are not 'parts' of Substance," writes Joachim. "The oneness of the modes in God is more intimate than the oneness of parts in a whole. It is the separation of the modes from God (as if they were 'parts' of a whole) which causes the inadequate understanding of the imaginative consciousness, for which Reality becomes a world of finite things."[13] Joachim is certainly right to insist that for Spinoza the finite modes are not separable from God, as material 'parts' may be imagined as separable from a material whole—that conception of whole and parts is certainly inadequate to Spinoza's Substance. And Joachim, too, is fully aware that the unity of the modes in Substance does not preclude or cancel out their multiplicity.[14] But if it is an imaginative error to think of the modes as separable parts, it is not simply an error to think of them as finite and as distinguishable within the unity of Substance. (Joachim, of course, is not suggesting that it is—but *we* should not fall into the error of thinking it so.) And though it may well be only for imaginative consciousness that Reality is *merely* a world of finite things, there really is in a legitimate sense a world of finite things contained in the infinite reality of Substance.

The finite modes really are finite insofar as they are determined by other finite modes and in whatever other ways they may be determined (e.g. by their specific attribute). And these determinations follow necessarily from God's essence and are produced, as are all changes and events in time, by His immanent causation. It follows that the finiteness of man's body is not a figment of the imagination or simply a misconception, nor are the facts of its coming into existence at his birth and passing away at his death. The same applies to his mind as the idea of his (finite) body. It is really finite and its limitations follow necessarily from the nature of things. His finiteness is no misconception, though we can (if only for that reason) entertain misconceptions about it. We cannot, therefore, simply dismiss the notion of the body as a finite mode, nor of the mind as dependent on, or correlative to, it, as inadequate ideas typical of *Imaginatio*. The finite body and the idea of it, which according to Spinoza constitutes the human mind, are actual factors in the nature of Substance. They are parts of Nature, and, even though their essence cannot be adequately understood in isolation from the rest of Nature, and can be adequately understood only in their essential and inseparable relation to the other parts and to Nature as a whole, yet they cannot be dissolved away into Substance as a single, seamless, undifferentiated unity excluding finiteness and temporal change. The character of the finite, as finite, remains in contrast and in opposition to the eternal and infinite, and the problem of reconciling them in the divine nature cannot be sidestepped.

Secondly, it does not help us to understand what Spinoza means by human immortality to assert that the idea of the finite human body exists eternally in God and follows necessarily from His essence, just as the existence of the body itself as a finite mode of Extension follows necessarily from God's infinite essence. For this is true of all finite bodies and all the ideas of them. They are all eternally in God's infinite understanding. If this sort of eternal being is all that is involved in man's immortality he is no more immortal than a fish and rather less so than a piece of granite.

Similarly, it does not help to insist that an adequate idea of the body involves its relations to all other bodies and so involves an adequate idea of the whole of Nature; and that such an adequate idea of Nature would be itself an infinite and eternal idea. Because such an infinite and eternal idea would be the intellect of God and not of man, which, for all his accomplishments, remains finite. True, Spinoza does assert, and with reason on his principles, that insofar as man achieves adequate knowledge his mind becomes united with that of God; but this is surely only to a limited extent, and it is not easy to understand how one can enjoy immortality only to a limited extent, or be eternal only in a limited sense. This surely would involve us in flat self-contradiction. Yet, as Spinoza's very philosophy exemplifies, according to its own principles, man does frame more or less adequate ideas of Nature and of the essence of God. Again we are faced with the problem: How are we to reconcile the finite with the infinite?—and Spinoza's doctrine of human immortality is very largely his answer to the question.

An objector may point out that the difficulty I have raised is spurious, for Spinoza repeatedly asserts that things vary in degree according to the amount of reality their essence includes, and the essence of the human mind is intelligence, and it embraces more of reality the more it conceives things *sub specie aeternitatis*. It could therefore be eternal in a degree, or to the extent to which its ideas were adequate, and to that extent it would be immortal. In short, as Plato and Aristotle alleged, not the whole human soul, but only its thinking part is immortal—in Spinoza's terminology the part that consists of adequate ideas.

But now we are involved in another difficulty (or perhaps the same one over again, seen from a new angle). The personality of man is a single whole and does not consist of separable parts, even though it includes many distinguishable functions and traits. The category of whole and part is inappropriate to the mind, just as Joachim explained it to be inadequate to express the nature of Spinoza's Substance. We cannot, therefore, intelligibly maintain that the human soul is immortal only in bits and pieces, and that other parts die with the body. If it lives at all it must live as a whole. Thus though it is legitimate to hold that we can attain to the truth or to goodness in varying degrees, it hardly seems proper to maintain that we can, *qua* individuals, enjoy eternal life only in some degree of eternity inferior to the eternity of Substance, or only in certain parts of our conscious being.

V

How far is it possible to extract from Spinoza's writings a solution to this problem? The first clue to follow is the one suggested in the previous paragraph. Spinoza has told us that the human mind is the idea of the body; and in Epistle XXXII he says that "The human body is a part of Nature" and "the human mind . . . also is a part of Nature: since I maintain that there exists in Nature an infinite power of thinking, which, so far as it is infinite contains in itself objectively the whole of Nature and whose thoughts proceed in the same way as Nature which, to be sure, is its *ideatum*." This power of thinking is undoubtedly the intellect of God—a system of ideal modes, or ideas, corresponding to the extended modes, or bodies, which constitute the physical world. None of these is a mere collection or congeries of separate or separable items (though, the modes in each attribute are distinguishable and ordered as a system of interrelated terms). The world of extended things, we learn from this letter, as from the *Korte Verhandeling* (and elsewhere), is an indivisible whole, and the order and connection of things is the same as the order and connection of ideas.

In the same letter that I have quoted above Spinoza goes on to say "the human mind is the same power [of thinking] not insofar as it is infinite and perceives the whole of Nature, but insofar as it is finite and perceives only the human body, and in this way I declare that the human mind is part of a certain infinite intellect." But the contents of the divine intellect, as follows both from what Spinoza says in this epistle and from his general position stated repeatedly in various works, is an indivisible and systematic whole; and from what he says further about ideas it becomes apparent that any adequate idea belonging to this system will, in a significant sense, comprehend the whole of it.

For ideas are not static pictures or replicas, in some different medium, of the extended things; they are their 'minds' or consciousness, just as the idea of the human body is its mind and consciousness. But the idea of a relatively simple body, like a stone or a coprolite, taken simply in and by itself, is so rudimentary and inadequate that it hardly merits the name 'mind' at all, though Spinoza is prepared to concede it in some degree.[15] The human body, however, is far more complex and is "apt to do and suffer many things," hence its mind (or idea) is equally complex and is highly developed.

Sir Frederick Pollock complains that Spinoza uses the word 'idea' ambiguously[16] to mean both concept (our more usual sense of the word) and also the counterpart of a physical thing or physiological process (its '*ideatum*'), and that he fails to distinguish between them. But I believe Spinoza did this deliberately and committed no inadvertent confusion. An idea in the sense of 'concept' is abstract, and can be entertained only by a developed mind such as man's. It is one of the complex products (or 'parts') of the 'idea' (in the other sense) of a complex body such as the human organism. And Spinoza did not hold that abstract and general ideas corresponded to anything actually existent. He was no 'realist' (like Plato), in the Mediaeval sense of that word, but was nominalist in his doctrine of general ideas. He regarded them as no more than convenient devices for description and classification—part of a technique or activity of thinking peculiar to men. Such concepts are possible, nevertheless, only for a conscious being, and consciousness is always 'idea' in the other sense—the idea of the body. This we should understand as the direct awareness of the body such as we have in sensation, which is the origin and basis of all 'higher' forms of consciousness. I shall return to this point in a moment; here let us note that concepts and general 'ideas' are part of and are derivative from this more basic consciousness, a fact which Spinoza never forgets. This is why he refuses to distinguish between the two senses of 'idea' and treats one simply as a special form or elaboration of the other.

We must not, however, as I said above, think of ideas or minds as mere reproductions, in the attribute of Thought, of the essences of their corresponding bodies. They are awarenesses, self-conscious and self-illuminating. Every idea implies an *idea ideae*; every knowing a knowledge that one knows, and though each such *idea* is, according to Spinoza, formally distinct from every other (as an act of consciousness), the *idea* and the *idea ideae* are 'objectively' identical and are both substantially one and the same with their (physical) *ideatum*.[17] Each is a mode under a different attribute of the same identical substance. The nature of this dual unity we shall consider more closely below, but first I wish to draw attention to the fact that consciousness, the basic sense of Spinoza's *idea*, even at its most primitive level, is never, *qua* consciousness, confined or limitable to a bare particular of any sort. Its most elementary object is and must be at least a particular distinguished from a background, or set in a context. An entity's idea or consciousness of itself must and can only be its awareness of itself in distinction from something else, and so must any awareness of anything whatsoever. Consciousness, therefore, is always not merely self-consciousness (*idea ideae*) but is also self-transcendent, and tends to comprehension of some whole to which its object belongs. Spinoza never makes this point explicitly but I am sure he was fully aware of it, and if it is taken along with what I have cited above about the wholeness and indivisibility in essence of Nature, of Extension, of the intellect of God, and with what follows from that, very significant consequences ensue for the human mind which will illuminate Spinoza's doctrine of its capacity for eternity. Let us now return to the detail of his view of the relation of body and mind.

First, our ideas are the awareness of our bodies and nothing else. We feel and are conscious of the activities, passivities, and functionings of our bodies, and of other bodies only as and through our own (*Ethics*, II, Props. XIX-XXVI). In becoming conscious of external things we are commonly unaware (because we suppress the awareness) of the mediation of our own sense organs ("the eye sees not itself"), but that mediation is nonetheless an essential condition—as it were, the matrix—of such awareness. Our awareness of the world is thus at the same time our awareness of the body, and it is only by making distinctions, in an appropriate and systematic way, within this total self-awareness, that we distinguish what belongs to our own bodies from what pertains to others. According to Spinoza, we make these distinctions well or ill according as we think adequately or inadequately; and we do the former insofar as we are active (and vice versa), and the latter so far as we are passive—so far as our body suffers effects from interaction with other bodies. Though Spinoza writes as if action depended only on adequate ideas, and as if inadequate ideas resulted only from bodily passivity, to understand him aright we must realize that activity and passivity are each one and the same in both body and mind.

Next we must notice that the body is strictly and in fact related in some way to everything else in the extended world, and all these relations must, therefore, be registered in idea either as passions or otherwise. In *Imaginatio* ideas are confused and *in se* false but they are nevertheless consequences of the impingement of external things upon the body. Thus even so far as its confused ideas are concerned, the mind embraces and reflects the whole of Nature.

But each thing endeavours, so far as it is in itself, to persevere in its own being (*Ethics*, III, Prop. VI), and this *conatus* is the actual essence of the thing itself (*Ibid.*, Prop. VII) and involves not finite but indefinite time (*Ibid.*, Prop. VIII). The mind, both in its confused and in its adequate ideas, is aware of this *conatus* (*Ibid.*, Prop. IX), and the *conatus* is nothing less, in the last resort, than the power of God Himself (cf. *Ethics*, IV, Prop. IV, dem. and I, Prop. XXIV, Cor.). It is by virtue of the *conatus* that the mind advances from *Imaginatio* and confused ideas to *Ratio* and adequate ideas and thence to *Scientia Intuitiva*.

The human mind, therefore, as the idea of the body embraces within its consciousness all the affects of the body and all its relations with the rest of the world, and so is all-inclusive even in its passions and its confused ideas. Its *conatus* is towards action and so impels it to develop (in ways the detail of which we need not here rehearse)[18] towards the perfection of its own being in the intellectual love of God. The result of this development is not just the supplementation of confused ideas by a new set of adequate ideas; it is the transformation of the entire personality on its emotional and practical side, as well as in its theoretical content. Adequate knowledge is not simply part of the mind beside and separable from inadequate ideas still harboured within it. Adequate knowledge is an order of activity, different from the passivity of *Imaginatio*, which annuls all cognate confused ideas, transforms the passions into healthy, positive and beneficient emotions, and divisive and turbulent motives of action into love and compassion. All this, moreover, is the product of the *conatus in suo esse perseverare* of the individual, which is the very power of God (what in Christian doctrine would be called the Holy Spirit) working within him.

This transformation is of mind and body in one. Spinoza quite explicitly says that "he who has a body capable of many things, has a mind of which the greater part is eternal" (*Ethics*, V, Prop. XXXIX), having already stated that the attainment of the third kind of knowledge implies the mind's knowledge of itself and of its body *sub specie aeternitatis* (*Ibid.*, Prop. XXX). This knowledge of the body is surely no mere way of viewing it, as might be some inadequate imagination of it. It must be a conception of the body as it really is in Nature, the more so as the initial feeling of the body in *Imaginatio* was already a confused awareness of the *facies totius universi*, which has become progressively clarified into a true and adequate knowledge of God.

The body is thus revealed as the vehicle of God's own self-revelation in and through the mind of man. The power of God, causing the infinite system of modes which is Nature, and working immanently throughout that system produces man's body, as it produces all others, and *pari passu* produces man's mind, the idea of his body, which it then urges through a process of internal development from *Imaginatio* to *Scientia Intuitiva* and to a revelation of His own infinite and eternal nature, the supreme object of perfect and unadulterable love. It is the love of God Himself, by which in one and the same act He loves Himself and His creation, including man. In short, it is a union or self-identification of man with God.

This knowledge and love of God, the eternal and infinite Substance, transforms all man's emotions and actions, and constitutes the life of blessedness, which is the highest virtue, the final object of rational desire, as well as the completest and most adequate knowledge of Nature. This is man's immortality, and its special character follows from the nature of self-consciousness, which, as was said above, is no inert replica of the extended world, but is an active self-awareness of the body, that embraces in its purview and comprehension all its relations to other bodies and the infinite, eternal character of the essence of Substance to which it belongs.[19] Consciousness is self-transcendent. It cannot exist simply in space and time and at the same time be aware, as it is, of the interrelations of all parts of space and time. It cannot be limited within a restricted space or period, and also know the relations of that restricted space and period to the rest of the extended world. In order to enjoy that knowledge it must somehow be identical with its object(s), as it is impossible for the body as a finite mode of Extension to be identical with its causes and effects. Although the body is related to all other bodies and registers within itself their effects, it can do so only if it is distinguished from them as the mind cannot be distinguished from them if it is to be conscious of them. Spinoza insists that *idea* and *ideatum* are identical, but a finite mode of Extension cannot be similarly identical with other finite extended modes with which it is in spatio-temporal and causal relations. The mind, on the other hand, is knowing these relations and their systematic integration into one individual as the whole of Nature (*totius facies universi*), transcends all spatial and temporal limits and is one with the whole eternal structure.

Time and space, the coming to be and passing away of finite things in the material world, are then seen as partial features or aspects of a single, indivisible, infinite and absolute totality—the eternal being of God or Substance. They are not unreal, for they do proceed necessarily from the divine essence. They are actual elements within the reality of Nature and do constitute a real and necessary attribute of God. Only for the imagination are they merely fleeting episodes of ephemeral significance. Their finiteness is not illusory, for their mutual determinations are essential to the multiplex unity of Substance. But their existence in itself is not of ultimate significance, for it can neither be nor be conceived except through the infinite being of God, in which they all live and move. To understand the world in this way is to conceive things adequately and is the part of *Scientia Intuitiva*; and any mind that has perfected its knowledge to this degree has transcended the finite nature of its body, and the transient existence of things in space and time in a synoptic awareness of "all time and all existence."

It follows, as Spinoza says, that "the human mind cannot be absolutely destroyed with the body, but there is something besides (*aliquid remanent*) which is eternal." It transcends, in its consciousness, the temporal as well as the spatial limits of the body, while yet, paradoxically, being identical in substance with the body, as its idea. It is its ideal, its conscious, character that is transcendent, and this transcendence is typical of all consciousness, even of *Imaginatio*. There is a valid sense, therefore, in which every mind is in some degree eternal. All consciousness is in some degree transcendent of its immediate object in time and space; and to the extent that it is not limited, as its object is limited, it participates (if we may, like Plato, use a term which is not wholly appropriate) in eternity. For to be aware of spatio-temporal relations is, of necessity, not be merely one term in any such relation. To be conscious of space and time is to transcend space and time—to be eternal. To be adequately conscious of the whole structure of Nature as it really is, to know it as God knows it, would be to be united with God and to share (if, again, so inappropriate a word may be permitted) in His eternal being.

Obviously this eternal reality cannot be an extended duration. If this is the nature of man's immortality it cannot possibly be an "after-life" or temporal existence prolonged beyond the temporal existence of the body. For the mind transcends the body just because its consciousness is *not* in time and so far as it does *not* endure. It transcends time and space in the sense that time and space are *for* it and it is not in them. Consciousness embraces time and space as orders or wholes, and so is aware of the place within these orders of the body, of which the human mind is the conscious life. The human mind is thus both finite and potentially infinite, both the idea of a finite mode of Extension (and thus itself a finite mode of Thought) and, nevertheless, in being idea, capable of adequate knowledge of the total scheme of things. It is thereby self-transcendent and eternal.

The objection may be raised that this conception of immortality dissolves away human individuality, which, in accordance with this view, cannot survive the body. What "remains", if we follow

Spinoza, is the impersonal eternal essence of Substance with which the mind in *Scientia Intuitiva* has become identified. This must inevitably be the same for all minds, for there is only one infinite being, as Spinoza spares no effort to demonstrate; and to become identified with it must be to become wholly absorbed into it and as a distinct individual to be obliterated by it.

This objection, however, is misconceived. Immortality, we have seen, is not a matter of the "survival" of his body by any personality. Nothing "remains" in the sense of continuing in time. What remains when we have accounted for the mortal form of experience is an eternal awareness of God's essence and the complex system of the world. It is an awareness enjoyed by each and every individual who attains to adequate knowledge, and it transforms and perfects his personality by developing it to its fullest moral capacity. So far from being lost or swallowed up in the boundless ocean of Substance, the individual personality becomes whole, internally harmonious and perfectly self-determined. The limitations of bodily life are clearly understood in their relation to the rest of Nature—nothing is blurred or obliterated—but these limitations are no restriction to the mind's self-awareness as a necessary and intimate pulse in the total life of the universe. Temporal transience is not felt as an irremediable handicap or an inescapable confine.

All that Spinoza writes in the final propositions of the *Ethics* about human blessedness and the eternal nature of man's mind follows from what has here been set out. "The greatest endeavour of the mind and its greatest virtue is to understand things by the third kind of knowledge." This kind of knowledge gives the greatest satisfaction. It is the highest good and to enjoy it (blessedness) is its own reward. It would be ridiculous to imagine that any gratification of the appetites or indulgence of lesser desires, for however long a period, could be more satisfactory and could thus serve as a reward of virtue. Equally absurd is the assumption that men can become truly virtuous through fear of eternal punishment. Nothing is more ludicrous than to speak as if virtue were a hardship to be endured for the sake of carnal pleasures promised later, or to escape greater pains threatened in an everlasting after-life.

Further, a mind that understands the eternal nature of things and its own place in the total scheme, which thus enjoys God's knowledge of Himself and is eternal in the knowledge of His eternal essence, will be unconcerned about the temporal limits of the body.

Its concern for the life of the body will be to understand its place in nature adequately and truly, and to act accordingly. Its longevity or otherwise will therefore become of minor importance. The actual time and eventuality of its death will have little significance, once the third kind of knowledge and the intellectual love of God have been attained. "So far as human bodies are capable of many [acts], there is no doubt but that their natures can be referred to minds which have a great awareness (*cognitio*) of themselves and of God, and of which the greater part and the most important (*praecipua*) is eternal, and that therefore they should scarcely fear death." (*Ethics*, V, Prop. XXXIX, Sch.) For death will have been transcended in the sublime contemplation of the totality of being—the infinite and eternal reality of God.

This interpretation of Spinoza's theory does not equate human immortality with the idea, eternal in God's intellect, of the finite mode of Extension which is the human body. Nor does it identify, as the 'body' of that part of the human mind which is eternal, the whole face of nature conceived *sub specie aeternitatis*. This indeed is the *ideatum* of the eternal idea—or, at least, the *ideatum* is nothing less than this. But for man it is so only through the registration in the finite human body of the effects and relations to that body of the rest of Nature. Immortality, then, while being no extended duration beyond the temporal life of the body, consists in the mind's transcendence of the body's finite limits, because of the inherently transcendent character of consciousness—a transcendence characteristic of idea, as such. The accepted interpretation of Spinoza seems to me to overlook, or to fail to stress sufficiently, this element of transcendence in the nature of consciousness. Thus it fails to draw out its implications, and so leaves unresolved the difficulties which I outlined in Section IV.

ERROL E. HARRIS

NORTHWESTERN UNIVERSITY

NOTES

[1] Cf. *Korte Verhandeling van God, de Mensch, en deszelfs Welstand, Deel* I, Chap. VII. Hereinafter cited as *KV*.

[2] Cf. Hume, *A Treatise of Human Nature*, I, Part IV, Sec. 5.

[3] Cf. KV, *Deel* I, Chap. IV.

[4] Cf. *Ethics*, II, Prop. XIII.

[5] Cf. KV, II, *Voorreeden*, footnote; *Ethics*, II, Prop. XIV, *et seq.*

[6] Cf. H. H. Joachim, *A Study of the Ethics of Spinoza* (Oxford: Oxford University Press, 1901), p. 296. Joachim, nevertheless, points out that for Spinoza 'this present life' would naturally mean 'our life so far as we are imaginative', i.e. the life of *Imaginatio*, associative thinking, passion and illusion.

[7] *Op. cit.*, pp. 294 ff.

[8] Cf. KV, I, Chap. II.

[9] *Loc. cit.*

[10] *Ethics*, II, Prop. XL, Sch. 2.

[11] Cf. *Ethics*, II, Lem. VII, Sch.: "*Et si sic porro in infinitum pergamus, facile concipiemus, totam Naturam unum esse Individuum, cujus partes, hoc est omnia corpora, infinitis modis variant, absque ulla totius individui mutatione.*" "And if we proceed still further to infinity, we can easily conceive that the whole of nature is one individual whose parts, that is, all bodies, vary in infinite ways without any change of the individual as a whole."

[12] Cf. H. H. Joachim, *op. cit.*, Book III, Chap. IV; Leon Roth, *Spinoza* (London, 1945), pp. 140-63; Ruth Saw, *The Vindication of Metaphysics* (London, 1951), pp. 128-36; Stuart Hampshire, *Spinoza* (London, 1946), pp. 126-32; John Caird, *Spinoza* (London, 1910), Chap. XVI; A. E. Taylor, "Spinoza's Conception of Immortality," *Mind*, 5, No. 18, New Series.

[13] *Op. cit.*, p. 299.

[14] *Op. cit.*, p. 300.

[15] *Ethics*, II, Prop. XIII, Sch.: "Individual things . . . are all, though in varying degrees, beminded (*animata*). For of each thing there is of necessity an idea in God . . ."

[16] Cf. *Spinoza, His Life and Philosophy* (London, 1912), Chaps. VI and IX.

[17] *Ethics*, II, Prop. VII, Sch., Prop. XXI, Sch., and Prop. XLIII.

[18] See *Ethics*, V, Props. I-XVII and XXVIII.

[19] "Proceeds from an adequate idea of the formal essence of certain attributes of God to the adequate knowledge of the essence of things." *Ethics*, II, Prop. XL, Sch. 2.

Bibliography
(Compiled by E. M. Curley)

CONTENTS

Introductory Note
I. Works
    1. Complete Works   267
    2. Selected Works   268
    3. Single Works   268
        a. *Compendium Grammatices*   268
        b. *Epistolae*   269
        c. *Ethica*   269
            1. Commentaries   270
        d. *Renati des Cartes Principia* and
            Cogitata Metaphysica   270
        e. *Stelkonstige Reeckening*   271
        f. *Tractatus de Deo et Homine*   271
        g. *Tractatus de Intellectus Emendatione*
            et de Via   271
        h. *Tractatus Politicus*   272
        i. *Tractatus Theologico-Politicus*   272
            1. Commentaries   273
    4. Selections   273
II. Bibliographies, Indexes, Catalogues   273
III. Monographs   274
IV. General Works with Sections on Spinoza   286
V. Special Collections on Spinoza   290
VI. Articles and Essays on Specific Topics   291

Introductory Note

1.   The aim of this bibliography is to give, as a supplement to the existing works of Oko and Wetlesen, as comprehensive as possible a listing of the Spinoza literature published for the first time during the period January, 1960, to December, 1972, in the major European languages. Also included are revised and successive editions, reprints of important first editions, and collections of articles and essays originally published before 1960.

2.   We have done our best to give complete and accurate bibliographical details for each entry. A number of items were verified from the originals. When the item could not be inspected, the best available bibliographical sources were followed (see below). In a few cases an asterisk (*) against an entry indicates that it could not be verified in a reliable source.

3.   The major bibliographical tools consulted were:
Bibliographie de la Philosophie
Bulletin Signalétique
Essay and General Literature Index
Internationale Bibliographie der Zeitschriftenliteratur
The Philosopher's Index
Répertoire Bibliographique de la Philosophie
Monographic publications were verified in the various national Bibliographies and Book Indexes (e.g. British National Bibliography and Library of Congress).

4.   For each monograph all the reviews that could be located have been listed, including discussions in books and periodical

articles as well as book reviews proper. If the review was substantial enough it was listed separately in Section VI under the author of the review.

5.   The six sections are each arranged alphabetically by main entry. For the convenience of the user, some items were indexed in more than one section. For example, *Martial Gueroult. Études sur Descartes, Spinoza. . .* 1970, is listed as a general work in Section IV, whereas Gueroult's articles relevant to this bibliography and contained within the above mentioned title, are individually indexed in the Section on Specific Topics.

6.   In accordance with normal library practice, the German vowels, ä, ö, ü are used alphabetically in the forms ae, oe and ue; (e.g. Härting, Halbfass, Hall, *not* Halbfass, Hall, Härting).

The work on this bibliography was done in the Department of Philosophy, Research School of Social Sciences, at the Australian National University. The final result is the work of four research assistants, Mrs. Jocelyn Harding, Mr. David Kipp, Mrs. Jan Murray and Mrs. Jean Norman, under the supervision of E. M. Curley.

I. WORKS

1. *Complete Works*

Spinoza, Benedictus de. *Oeuvres, I: Court traité.* Traité de la réforme de l'entendement. Principes de la philosophie de Descartes. Pensées métaphysiques. Traduction et notes, par Charles Appuhn. Paris: Garnier-Flammarion, 1964. 445p. (Garnier-Flammarion. Texte intégral, 34.)

———.*Oeuvres, II: Traité théologico-politique.* Traduction, notice et notes de Charles Appuhn. Paris: Garnier-Flammarion, 1965. 384p. (Garnier-Flammarion. Texte intégral, 50.)

———.*Oeuvres, III: Éthique démontrée suivant l'ordre géométrique et divisée en cinq parties.* Traduction et notes par Charles Appuhn. Paris: Garnier-Flammarion, 1965. 381p. (Garnier-Flammarion. Texte intégral, 57.)

———.*Oeuvres, IV: Traité politique.* Lettres. Traduction et notes par Charles Appuhn. Paris: Garnier-Flammarion, 1964. 382p. (Garnier-Flammarion. Texte intégral, 108.)

———.*Opera-Werke.* Lateinisch und Deutsch, hrsg. von K. Blumenstock, Vol. 1. Darmstadt: Wissenschaftliche Buchgesellschaft, 1967. Contents: 2 Bd. Tractatus de intellectus emendatione. Ethica. Latein und Deutsch. Darmstadt, 1967. vi, 565p.

2. Selected Works

Spinoza, Benedictus de. *Chief Works.* Translated from the Latin
with introduction by R. H. M. Elwes. Vol. I: Theologico-
political treatise, political treatise. Vol. II: Ethics, On the improvement of the understanding, Selected letters. Gloucester,
Mass.: Peter Smith, 1962. [First published in 1883.] 387p,
420p.

_____.*Emendazione dell'intelletto-Principi della filosofia
cartesiana-Pensieri metafisici.* Introduzione, traduzione e note
di Enrico de Angelis. Torino: Boringhieri, 1962. 311p.

_____.*Etica e Trattato teologico-politico.* A cura di Remo Cantoni e
Franco Fergnani. Torino: Unione tipografico-editrice torinese,
1972, 747p. (Classici della filosofia, 10.)

_____.*Opera scelte.* Traduzione, introduzione e note a cura di Arturo
Deregibus. Milano: Principato, 1970, 210p. (Collana filosofica
principato.)

_____.*Textes traduits, choisis et présentés par Louis Millet.* Paris:
Bordas, 1970, 128p. (Sélections philosophiques Bordas.)

3. Single Works

a. Compendium Grammatices

Spinoza, Benedictus de. *Abrégé de grammaire hébraique* [Compen-
dium grammatices linguae hébraeae]. Introduction et traduction française et notes par Joël Askenazi et Jocelyne Askenazi-
Gerson. Paris: J. Vrin, 1968. 242p. (Bibliothèque des textes
philosophiques.)

_____.*Hebrew Grammar* [Compendium grammatices linguae
Hebraeae]. Edited and translated with introduction by M. J.
Bloom. London: Vision, 1963.

b. *Epistolae*

Spinoza, Benedictus de. *The Correspondence of Spinoza.* Translated with introduction and notes by A. Wolf. London: Frank Cass; New York: Russell & Russell, 1966. 502p.

_____ .*Letters to Friend and Foe.* Edited with a preface by Dagobert D. Runes. New York: Philosophical Library, 1966. 110p.

c. *Ethica*

Spinoza, Benedictus de. *Ethica.* [Voorafgegaan door] *Het vertoog over de zuivering des verstands.* Uit het Latijn vertaald, ingeleid en toegelicht door Nico van Suchtelen. Amsterdam: Wereld-Bibliotheek, 1969. 301p. (W.-B. paperback.)

_____ .*The Ethics.* Translated by R. H. Elwes. In *The Rationalists* [Selections from Descartes, Spinoza and Leibniz]. New York: Doubleday, 1962. 471p.

_____ .*L'Éthique.* Paris: Gallimard, 1964. 384p. (Coll. "Idées".)

_____ .*Éthique.* Textes choisis et présentés par Ferdinand Alquié. Paris: Presses Universitaires de France, 1961. viii, 152p. (Coll. "Les grands textes".)

_____ .*Éthique.* Traduction nouvelle avec notes par Louis Millet. Paris: Bordas, 1970. 255p. (Coll. Textes Philosophiques.) Review: Dumas, Jean-Louis. *Les études philosophiques,* **3** (1971), 399-401.

_____ .*Die Ethik.* Schriften und Briefe. Hrsg. von Friedrich Bülow. Stuttgart: Kröner, 1966. xxxii, 337p. (Kröners Taschenausgabe, 24.)

_____ .*Ethica* [testo latino tradotto da Gaetano Durante. Noti di Giovanni Gentile rivedute e ampliate da Giorgio Radetti]. Florence: Sansoni, 1963. xxviii, 856p. (Classici della filosofia, X.) Text in Italian and Latin; introductory matter and notes in Italian.

_____ .*Ethica ordine geometrico demonstrata.* Testo latino tradotto da Gaetano Durante. Firenze: G. C. Sansoni, 1960. 169p (Classici della filosofia, X).

_____.*Etica* [Da: Ethica more geometrico demonstrata]. Traduzione, introduzione e commento di Raffaele Mango. Napoli: L. Loffredo, 1969. 110p.

_____.*Etica* [Ethica more geometrico demonstrata]. A cura di Piero Martinetti. Bologna: Edizioni scolastiche Patron, 1969. 210p.

_____.*Ethik.* Translated by J. Stern, edited and introduction by H. Seidel. Leipzig: Reclam, 1972. 427p.

c. *Ethica*

1. Commentaries

Gueroult, Martial. *Spinoza.* Tome I: Dieu (Ethique I). Paris: Editions Montaigne, 1968. 623p. (Coll. analyse et raisons, 12.)

Joachim, Harold Henry. *A Study of the Ethics of Spinoza* (Ethica ordine geometrico demonstrata). New York: Russell & Russell, 1964. 316p. Reprint of 1901 edition.

Zarrillo, Amelia. *L'etica di Benedetto Spinoza.* Marcianise: Ediz. La diana, 1963. 47p.

d. *Renati Des Cartes Principia* and *Cogitata Metaphysica*

Spinoza, Benedictus de. *Earlier Philosophical Writings: The Cartesian Principles and Thoughts on Metaphysics.* Translated by F. A. Hayes with introduction by D. Bidney. Indianapolis: Bobbs-Merrill, 1963. xxxvi, 161p. (The Library of Liberal Arts, 163.)

_____ .*I principi di filosofia di Cartesio e l'Appendice.* A cura di Bruno Widmar. Lecce: Edizioni Milella, 1970. (Collana di Studi e Testi, 13.)

_____ .*Principles of Cartesian Philosophy.* Translated by Harry E. Wedeck with introduction by Dagobert Runes. New York: Philosophical Library, 1961. 192p.

_____ .*The Principles of Descartes' Philosophy.* Translated from the Latin with an introduction by Halbert Hains Britan. La Salle, Ill.: Open Court, 1961. lxxxi, 177p. (Open Court Classics.)

_____ .*Pensieri di metafisica.* Traduzione e commento di Angelo Scivoletto. Firenze: F. Le Monnier, 1966. xvi, 82p. (Coll. di filosofia e pedagogia ad uso delle scuole.)

   e. *Stelkonstige Reeckening*

Spinoza, Benedictus de. *Algebraic Calculations of the Rainbow*, 1687. [Facsimile of the original Dutch text]. Introduction by G. ten Doesschate. Nieuwkoop: B. de Graaf, 1963. xxvi, 24p. (Dutch Classics on History of Science, 5.)

   f. *Tractatus de Deo et Homine*

Spinoza, Benedictus de. *The Nature of God.* In *Classics in Philosophy and Ethics.* A course of selected reading by authorities; particular attention is directed to the introductory reading guide by C. E. M. Joad. New York: Philosophical Library, 1960.

_____ .*Kurze Abhandlung von Gott, dem Menschen und seinem Glück*, hrsg. von. C. Gebhardt. 4. Aufl. Hamburg: F. Meiner, 1965. (Philosophische Bibliothek Bd. 91.) Reprint of 1922 edition.

_____ .*Dio, natura, uomo* (Pagine scelte dalle opere). Introduzione, traduzione e note di Giovanni Casertano. Napoli: Il Tripode, 1969. 139p. (Classici di filosofia e pedagogia.)

   g. *Tractatus de Intellectus Emendatione et de Via*

Spinoza, Benedictus de. *How to Improve Your Mind.* With biographical notes by Dagobert Runes. New York: Philosophical Library, 1960; New York: Citadel Press, 1963. 90p.

_____ .*Tractatus de intellectus emendatione; et de via, qua optime in veram rerum cognitionem dirigitur.* Translated from [his] Latin by W. Hale White; translation revised by Amelia

Hutchinson Stirling. Freeport, N. Y.: Books for Libraries, 1969. xxx, 62p.

———— .*Traité de la réforme de l'entendement et de la meilleure voie à suivre pour parvenir à la vraie connaissance des choses.* Texte, traduction et notes par Alexandre Koyré. 3ᵉéd. Paris: J. Vrin, 1964. xxii, 115. (Bibliothèque des textes philosophiques.) 4ᵉéd. Paris: J. Vrin, 1969.

———— .*L'emendazione dell'intelletto.* Traduzione, introduzione, commento di Marco Berte. Padova: Liviana, 1966. vii, 175p. (Studium sapientiae, 4.)
Review: Reale, M. A. D. *Filosofia,* **19** (1968), 315-20.

———— .*De intellectus emendatione.* A cura di Lino Rossi. Padova: R. A. D. A. R., 1969. 113p. (Classici della filosofia.)

————.*Abhandlung über die Läuterung des Verstandes.* Nachwort Professor Dr. Hans Kelm. 2 Aufl. Leipzig: Reclam, 1960. 83p.

h. *Tractatus Politicus*

Spinoza, Benedictus de. *Philosophie et politique. Textes choisis par Louis Guillermit.* Paris: Presses Universitaires de France, 1967. 142p. (Les grands textes.)

———— .*Traité politique.* Texte, traduction, introduction et notes par Sylvain Zac. Paris: J. Vrin, 1968. 272p. (Bibliothèque des textes philosophiques.)

i. *Tractatus Theologico-Politicus*

Spinoza, Benedictus de. *Theologisch-politischer Traktat.* Uebertr. u. eingel, nebst. Anm. u. Reg. von Carl Gebhardt. Hamburg: Meiner, 1965. xxxvii, 423p. (Philosophische Bibliothek, 93.)

———— .*Lo stato e la libertà.* A cura di Bruno Widmar. Galatina: Stablimenti tipografica della Editrice salentina (1971?).

———— .*Trattato teologico-politico.* Presentazione, traduzione e note di Sante Casellato. Firenze: La Nuova Italia, 1972. 364p. (Classici della filosofia, 8.)

———.*Trattato teologico-politico.* Introduction by E. Giancotti Boscherini. Torino: NUE, 1972.

i. *Tractatus Theologico-Politicus*

1. Commentaries

Malet, André. *Le traité théologico-politique de Spinoza et la pensée biblique.* Paris: Société d'Éditions Les Belles Lettres, 1966. 320p. (Dijon. Université. Publications 35.)

Strauss, Leo. *Spinoza's Critique of Religion.* Translated by E. M. Sinclair. New York: Schocken Books, 1965. 351p.

Zac, Sylvain. *Spinoza et l'interprétation de l'Écriture.* Paris: Presses Universitaires de France, 1965.

4. *Selections*

Spinoza, Benedictus de. *On Freedom of Thought.* Selections from *Tractatus Theologico-Politicus* and *Tractatus Politicus.* Edited and translated by J. E. Jessop. Montreal: Mario Casalini, 1962. xxxvi, 132p. (International Institute of Philosophy. "Philosophy and World Community.")

———.*Reflexions and Maxims.* Edited by Dagobert D. Runes. [Abbreviated edition of the *Spinoza Dictionary*, published by Philosophical Library in 1951]. New York: Philosophical Library, 1965. 92p.

II. BIBLIOGRAPHIES, INDEXES, CATALOGUES

Altwicker, Norbert. *Bibliographie* [on Spinoza], *1924-1968.* In his *Texte zur Geschichte des Spinozismus*, pp. 393-410. Darmstadt, 1971.

Bamberger, Fritz. *The Early Editions of Spinoza's* Tractatus Theologico-Politicus. Studies in Bibliography and Booklore, Vol. 5, pp. 9-33. 1961.

Giancotti Boscherini, Emilia, comp. *Lexicon Spinozanum.* 2 vols.
La Haye: M. Nijhoff, 1970. Vol. 1, xi, 629p.; Vol. 2, ix, 744p.
(International Archives of the History of Ideas, 28.)
Index to the works of Spinoza.
Review: Röd, W. *Philosophischer Literaturanzeiger,* **25** (1972),
170-75.

Offenberg, Adri K. "Spinoza's Library, the Story of a Reconstruction." *Quaerendo,* **3** (1973), 309-21.

Oko, Adolph S., comp. *The Spinoza Bibliography.* Boston: Hall,
1964. 700p. Comprehensive list covering the period up to 1942.

Spinoza-Bibliographie. *Börsenblatt für den Deutschen Buchhandel,* **18** (1926), 739-40.

Van der Linde, A., ed. *Benedictus Spinoza, Bibliographie.*
Nieuwkoop: B. de Graaf, 1961. 121p. Unchanged reprint of the
Hague, 1871 edition.

Vereniging Het Spinozahuis, Rijnsburg. Catalogus van de
bibliotheek der Vereniging Het Spinozahuis te Rijnsburg.
Leiden: E. J. Brill, 1965. 59p.

Wetlesen, Jon. *A Spinoza Bibliography.* Particularly on the period
1940-1967. Oslo: Universitetsforlaget, 1968. 88p.

_____ .*A Spinoza Bibliography 1940-1970.* 2d rev. ed. Arranged as a
supplementary volume to A. S. Oko's *Spinoza Bibliography.*
Oslo: Universitetsforlaget, 1971. 47p.

III. MONOGRAPHS

Alain [pseud.]. See Chartier, Emile.

Balet, Leo. *Rembrandt and Spinoza.* New York: Philosophical
Library, 1962. 222p.
Review: Long, W. *Personalist,* **44** (1963), 392.

Banfi, Antonio. *Spinoza e il suo tempo.* Lezioni e scritti vari a cura
di L. Schirollo. Fierenze: Vallecchi, 1969. 332p. (Socrates, 6.)

Barwirsch, Josef Franz. *Spinoza—nach dreihundert Jahren.* Vaduz: Fido Anstalt, Abteilung Verlagsrechte, 1971. Review: Röd, Wolfgang. *Philosophischer Literaturanzeiger,* **26** (1973), 65-67.

Belaief, Gail. *Spinoza's Philosophy of Law.* The Hague and Paris: Mouton, 1971. 151p. (Studies in Philosophy, 24.)

Bidney, David. *The Psychology and Ethics of Spinoza.* A study in the history and logic of ideas. 2d ed. New York: Russell & Russell, 1962. 454p.

Boasson, J. J. *Ratio en beatitudo in Spinoza's wijsbegeerte.* Leiden: E. J. Brill, 1963. 24p. (Mededelingen vanwege het Spinozahuis, 19.)

Bollacher, Martin. *Der junge Goethe und Spinoza.* Tübingen: Neimeyer, 1969. 253p. (Studien zur deutschen Literatur, 18.) Review: Barwirsch, Josef. *Philosophischer Literaturanzeiger,* **24** (1971), 143-46.

Borgia, Salvatore. *Spinoza. La Libertà e lo Stato.* Lecce: L'orsa maggiore, 1968. 118p.

Brijkman, G. *La judéité de Spinoza.* Paris: Vrin, 1972. 136p.

Caird, John. *Spinoza.* Freeport, N. Y.: Books for Libraries, 1971. (Reprint of 1888 edition.)

Calvetti, Carla Gallicet. *Spinoza, I presupposti teoretici dell'irenismo etico.* Milano: Società Editrice Vita e Pensiero, 1968. 257p. (Pubblicazioni dell' Università Cattolica del Sacro Cuore, Scienze Filosofiche, 12.) Review: Muratore, U. *Rivista rosminiana di filosofia e di cultura,* **63** (1969), 306-7.

Chartier, Émile. *Spinoza* [par] Alain. Paris: Gallimard, 1965. 191p. (Idées. 82.) First published in 1949.

Chiereghin, Franco. *L'influenza dello spinozismo nella formazione della filosofia hegeliana.* Padova: Cedam, 1961. 192p. (Università di Padova. Pubblicazioni della Facoltà di Lettere e Filosofia, 36.)

Review: Di Vona, P. *Rivista critica di storia della filosofia,* **16** (1961), 229-32.

Plebe, A. *Giornale critico della filosofia italiana,* **41** (1962), 134-35.

Bortot, R. *Filosofia,* **13** (1962), 685-86.

Pozzo, G. M. *Giornale di metafisica,* **17** (1962), 557-59.

Schirollo, L *Pensiero,* **7** (1962), 294-96.

Contri, S. *Rivista rosminiana di filosofia e di cultura,* **57** (1963), 149-52.

Cramer, Wolfgang. *Die absolute Reflexion.* Band 1: *Spinozas Philosophie des Absoluten.* Frankfurt/Main: Klostermann, 1966. 119p.
Review: Barwirsch, Josef. *Philosophischer Literaturanzeiger,* **22** (1969), 200-1.

Crapulli, Giovanni, and Giancotti Boscherini, Emilia. *Ricerche lessicali su opere di Descartes e Spinoza.* Roma: Ed. dell' Ateneo, 1969. 186p. (Lessico intellettuale europeo, 3.)

Cresson, Andre. *Spinoza. Sa vie, son oeuvre, sa philosophie.* Nouv. édit. Paris: Presses Universitaires de France, 1960. (Coll. "Philosophes.")

Crippa, Romeo. *Studi sulla coscienza etica e religiosa del Seicento. Le passioni in Spinoza.* Milano: Marzorati, 1965. 127p. (Pubbl. dell'Istituto di Filosofia dell'Università di Genova.)
Review: Di Vona, P. *Rivista critica di storia della filosofia,* **23** (1968), 108-9.
C. A. F. S. *Salesianum,* **29** (1967), 249-50.
Deregibus, A. *Giornale di metafisica,* **23** (1968), 361-63.

Curley, E. M. *Spinoza's Metaphysics: An Essay in Interpretation.* Cambridge: Harvard University Press, 1969. 174p.
Review: De Dijn, H. *Tijdschrift voor filosofie,* **32** (1970), 335-38.
Parkinson, G. H. R. *Philosophy,* **45** (1970), 342-43.
Seligman, Paul. *Journal of the History of Philosophy,* **10,** No. 1 (1972), 91-95.
von Leyden, W. *Philosophical Quarterly,* **21** (1971), 264-65.
Kashap, P. *Man and World,* **4** (1971), 100-113.

de Deugd, Cornelius. *The Significance of Spinoza's First Kind of Knowledge.* Assen: van Gorcum, 1966. 284p. (Wijsgerige

Teksten en Studies, 15.)
Review: de Dijn, H. *Tijdschrift voor filosofie,* **29** (1967), 176-79.
Di Vona, P. *Rivista critica di storia della filosofia,* **23** (1968), 461-63.
Kneale, M. *Philosophy,* **43** (1968), 293-94.
Robbers, H. "De betekenis van de eerste soort van kennen in Spinoza's Denken." *Wijsgerig perspectief op maatschappij en wetenschap,* **8** (1967-68), 107-11. On *de Deugd. The Significance of Spinoza's First Kind of Knowledge.*
Wernham, A. G. *The Philosophical Quarterly,* **18** (1968), 366-67.

_____.*Wordsworth en Spinoza.* Leiden: E. J. Brill, 1969. 19p. (Mededelingen vanwege het Spinozahuis, 25.)

Delbos, Victor. *Le Spinozisme.* Cours professé à la Sorbonne en 1912-1913. 4ᵉ éd. Paris: J. Vrin, 1964. 216p. (Bibliothèque d'histoire de la philosophie.) First edition 1916.

Deleuze, Gilles. *Spinoza.* Paris: Presses Universitaires de France, 1970. 126p.
Review: De Dijn, H. *Tijdschrift voor filosofie,* **32** (1970), 122-23.

_____.*Spinoza et le problème de l'expression.* Paris: Éditions de Minuit, 1968. 332p. (Arguments, 37.)
Review: de Dijn, H. *Tijdschrift voor filosofie,* **31** (1969), 572-82.
Declève, H. *Dialogue,* **10** (1971), 164-67.

den Tex, Jan. *Spinoza over tolerantie.* Leiden: E. J. Brill, 1967. 24p. (Mededelingen vanwege het Spinozahuis, 23.)

Deregibus, Arturo. *La filosofia etico-politica di Spinoza.* Torino: Editore G. Giappichelli, 1963. xvi, 320p. (Università di Torino. Pubblicazioni della Facoltà di Magistero, 25.)
Review: Reymond, M. *Studia philosophica,* **23** (1963), 234.
Brunello, B. *Rivista rosminiana di filosofia e di cultura,* **58** (1964), 145-47.
De George, R. T. *Philosophical Studies,* **14** (1965), 267-68.
Di Vona, P. *Rivista critica di storia della filosofia,* **19** (1964), 236-37.
Graneris, G. *Filosofia e vita,* **5** (1964), 109-10.

de Vries, Theun. *Baruch de Spinoza in Selbstzeugnissen und Bilddokumenten.* Dargestellt. Aus. d. Niederländ. [Ms.] übertr.

von Elizabeth Meter-Plaut. Den dokumentar. u. bibliograph.
Anh. besorgte d. Autor. Reinbek b. Hamburg: Rowohlt, 1970.
190p. (Rowohlts Monographien, 171.)

_____.*Spinoza als staatkundig denker* [Rede uitgesproken te
Rijnsburg op 18 Mei 1963]. Leiden: E. J. Brill, 1963. 24p.
(Mededelingen vanwege het Spinozahuis, 20.)

Di Vona, Piero. *Studi sull'ontologia di Spinoza*. Parte I. L'or-
dinamento delle scienze filosofiche. La "ratio." Il concetto di
ente. Firenze: La Nuova Italia, 1960. viii, 276p. (Pubblicazioni
dell'Istituto di Storia della Filosofia dell'Università degli Studi
di Milano, 4.)
Review: Arata, C. *Rivista di filosofia neo-scolastica*, **54** (1962),
114-15.
Fanizza, Fr. *Il Pensiero*, **6** (1961), 220-23.
Gasperini, G. *Giornale di metafisica*, **18** (1963), 527-29.
Montull, T. *Estudios filosóficos*, **12** (1963), 561-62.

_____.*Studi sull'ontologia di Spinoza*. Parte II: La necessità—Le
divisioni dell'essere. Firenze: La Nuova Italia, 1969. xv, 336p.
(Pubblicazioni della Facoltà di Lettere e Filosofia dell'Univer-
sità di Milano. Sezione a cura dell'Istituto di Storia della
Filosofia, 15.)
Review: Reale, M. A. D. *Filosofia*, **22** (1971), 234-40.

Duff, R. A. *Spinoza's Political and Ethical Philosophy*. New York:
Kelley, 1970.S-75

Dujovne, León. *Baruj Spinoza*. Buenos Aires: Biblioteca Popular
Judía, 1969. 32p.

*Ehrlich, Robert S. *Monarch Literature Notes on the Philosophy of
Baruch Spinoza*. New York: Monarch, 1965.

Feuer, Lewis Samuel. *Spinoza and the Rise of Liberalism*. London:
Mayflower, 1960. 323p.
Review: Kline, G. L. *The Journal of Philosophy*, **58** (1961), 350-
52.
Deleuze, G. *Erasmus*, **14** (1961), 390-91.

Frank, Dimitri Frenkel. *Spinoza*. Amsterdam: De Bezige Bij, 1964.
111p. (Literaire reuzenpockets, 105.)

Frenkel, H. S. *De noodwendigheid van het Spinozisme.* Leiden: E. J. Brill, 1965. 16p. (Mededelingen vanwege het Spinozahuis, 22.)

Friedmann, Georges. *Leibniz et Spinoza.* Édition revue et augmentée. Paris: Gallimard, 1962. 352p. (Bibliothèque des idées.)
Review: P.-M. S. *Revue philosophique de la France et de l'étranger,* **91** (1966), 259.

Frigo, Gianfranco. *Matematismo e spinozismo nel primo Schelling.* Padova: Cedam, 1969, 102p. (Pubblicazioni della Scuola di Perfezionamento in Filosofia del'Università di Padova. Quaderni di Storia della Filosofia, 3.)

Gallicet Calvetti, Carla. See Calvetti, Carla Gallicet.

Giancotti Boscherini, E. *Spinoza.* Edizioni Astrolabio, 1972.

Goossens, J. *Bayle en Spinoza.* Leiden: E. J. Brill, 1961. 19p. (Mededelingen vanwege het Spinozahuis, 17.)

Groen, J. J. *Ethica en Ethologie: Spinoza's leer der affecten en de moderne psychobiologie.* Leiden: E. J. Brill, 1972. (Mededelingen vanwege het Spinozahuis, 29.)

Gueroult, Martial. *Spinoza.* Tome I: Dieu (Éthique, I). Paris: Éditions Montaigne, 1968. 623p. (Coll. analyse et raisons, 12.) [Tome II: L'âme (Ethique, 2) will be an analysis of Spinoza's physics and his theory of cognition. Tome III: will be an analysis of Parts 3-5 of the Ethics.]
Review: Brodeur, J.-P. *Dialogue,* **10** (1971), 162-64.
Bruch, J.-L. *Revue Philosophique de la France et de l'étranger,* **95** (1970), 207-25.
De Dijn, H. *Tijdschrift voor filosofie,* **32** (1970), 332-35.
Deschepper, Jean-Pierre. "Les yeux de l'âme: le Spinoza de M. Gueroult." *Revue philosophique de Louvain,* **69** (1971), 465-94.
Dufour-Kowalska, G. *Revue de théologie et de philosophie,* No. 4 (1970), 283-84.
Agaesse, P. *Archives de philosophie,* **32** (1969), 288-96.
Deleuze, G. *Revue de métaphysique et de morale,* **74** (1969), 426-37.
Dreyfus, G. *L'âge de la science,* No. 3 (1969), 240-75.

Matheron, A. *Revue internationale de philosophie,* **26** (1972), 199-203.

Reale, M. A. D. *Filosofia,* **23** (1972), 175-87.

Zac, Sylvain. "Le Spinoza de Martial Gueroult." *Revue de synthese,* **92** (1971), 251-79. On *Gueroult, Spinoza, Tome I.*

Guzzo, Augusto. *Il pensiero di Spinoza.* 2ª ed. Torino: Edizioni di "Filosofia," 1964. 302p.
  Review: Semerai, G. *Giornale critico della filosofia italiana.* **43** (1964), 441-44.
  Battaglia, F. *Rivista internazionale di filosofia del diritto,* **41** (1964), 453-54.
  Bortot, R. *Giornale di metafisica,* **21** (1966), 125-26.

Gysens-Gosselin, M. *Hegel en Spinoza.* Leiden: E. J. Brill, 1971. 11p. (Mededelingen vanwege het Spinozahius, 27.)

Hallett, H. F. *Creation, Emanation and Salvation: A Spinozistic Study.* The Hague: M. Nijhoff, 1962. xi, 234p.
  Review: Deledalle, G. *Les études philosophiques,* **18** (1963), 220.
  Wernham, A. G. *The Philosophical Quarterly,* **13** (1963), 263-65.
  Houde, R. *Dialogue,* **3** (1964), 106-7.

Hampshire, Stuart. *Spinoza.* New York: Barnes & Noble, 1961. 176p.

Hansen, Oskar. *Spinoza.* Aarhus, Denmark, 1965.

Harris, E. *Salvation From Despair.* The Hague: M. Nijhoff, 1973. xix, 270p.

Hebeisen, Alfred. *Friedrich Heinrich Jacobi.Seine Auseinandersetzung mit Spinoza.* Bern: Paul Haupt, 1960. 71p. (Sprache und Dichtung. Neue Folge, Bd. 5.)
  Review: Tilliette, X. *Archives de philosophie,* **25** (1962), 306.
  Verra, V. *Filosofia,* **12** (1961), 583-85.

Horn, J. E. *Spinoza Staatslehre.* Neudr. d.2 Ausg. Dresden, 1863. Aalen. Scientia Verl., 1964. xii, 201p.

Hoyack, Louis. *Spinoza als uitgangspunt.* Deventer: N. Kluwer, 1965. 214p. (Mens en kosmos.)

Hubbeling, H. G. *Spinoza*. Baarn: Het Wereldvenster, 1966. 130p.
(Wijsgerige monografieën.)
Review: Robbers, H. *Bijdragen*, 28 (1967), 103.
De Dijn, H. *Tijdschrift voor filosofie*, 28 (1966), 739-41.

_____.*Spinoza's Methodology*. Assen: Royal Van Gorcum, 1964.
158p. (Philosophia religionis, XI.) 2d. ed., Assen: Royal Van
Gorcum, 1967. 158p. (Philosophia religionis, XI.)
Review: 1964 ed. Collins, J. *The Modern Schoolman*, 42 (1964-
1965), 429.
MacGregor, G. *Personalist*, 46 (1965), 390-91.
Robbers, H. *Bijdragen*, 27 (1966), 332.
De Dijn, H. *Revue philosophique de Louvain*, 64 (1966), 642-44.
Di Vona, P. *Rivista critica di storia della filosofia*, 21 (1966),
436-39.
van der Bend, J. G. *Algemeen Nederlands tijdschrift voor
wijsbegeerte en psychologie*, 58 (1966), 107-8.
De Dijn, H. *Tijdschrift voor filosofie*, 29 (1967), 786-89.
Obertello, L. *Giornale di metafisica*, 22 (1967), 96-98.

_____.*Logica en ervaring in Spinoza's en Ruusbroecs mystiek*.
Leiden: E. J. Brill, n. d.

Jacobi, Friedrich Heinrich. *La dottrina di Spinoza*. Lettere al
signor Moses Mendelssohn [ueber die Lehre des Spinoza].
Trad. F. Capra. 2ª ed. riveduta da V. Verra. Bari: Laterza,
1969. 240p. (Classici della filosofia moderna.)

Jaffé, H. L. C. *Spinoza en het beeldend denken*. Leiden: E. J. Brill,
1965. 17p. (Mededelingen vanwege het Spinozahuis, 21.)

Joachim, Harold Henry. *A Study of the Ethics of Spinoza* (Ethica
ordine geometrico demonstrata). New York: Russell and
Russell, 1964. 316p. Reprint of Oxford: Clarendon Press, 1901
edition.

Kayser, Rudolph. *Spinoza: Portrait of a Spiritual Hero*. Introduc-
tion by Albert Einstein. Translated by Amy Allen and Maxim
Newmark. New York: Greenwood, 1968. Reprint of New York:
Philosophical Library, 1946 edition.

Lacroix, Jean. *Spinoza et le problème du salut*. Paris: Presses
Universitaires de France, 1970. 128p. (Initiation philosophique,

91.)
Review: Bancal, J. *Giornale di metafisica*, **25** (1970), 702-6.
Moreau, J. *Les études philosophiques*, No. 4 (1970), 552.

Levin, D. *Spinoza, the Young Thinker Who Destroyed the Past.*
New York: Weybright & Talley, 1970.

Lindner, Herbert. *Das Problem des Spinozismus im Schaffen
Goethes und Herders.* Weimar: Arion-Verlag, 1969. 206p.
(Beiträge zur Deutschen Klassik, Bd. 11.)
Review: Träger, C. *Deutsche Literaturzeitung*, **83** (1962), 103-6.

McShea, Robert J. *The Political Philosophy of Spinoza.* New York:
Columbia University Press, 1968. 214p.
Review: Ross, R. *Journal of the History of Philosophy*, 8 (1970),
215-17.
Wernham, A. G. *The Philosophical Quarterly*, **20** (1970), 272.

Malet, André. *Le traité théologico-politique de Spinoza et la pensée
biblique.* Paris: Société d'Éditions Les Belles Lettres, 1966.
320p. (Dijon. Université. Publications 35.)
Review: Antoine, P. *Archives de philosophie*, **31** (1968), 318-20.
Payot, Chr. *Revue de théologie et de philosophie*, **101** (1968),
119-20.
Zac, S. *Les études philosophiques*, **22** (1967), 229-30.
Halbfass, W. *Erasmus*, **20** (1968), 4-6.

Mark, T. C. *Spinoza's Theory of Truth.* New York: Columbia
University Press, 1972.

Martineau, James. *A Study of Spinoza*, 3d ed. Freeport, N. Y.:
Books for Libraries, 1971. Reprint of 1895 edition.

Matheron, Alexandre. *Individu et communauté chez Spinoza.*
Paris: Éd. de Minuit, 1969. 648p.
Review: Moreau, J. *Les études philosophiques*, **25** (1970), 405-
7.

――――.*Le Christ et le salut des ignorants chez Spinoza.* Paris:
Aubier-Montaigne, 1971. 280p.
Review: Zac, S. *Les études philosophiques*, No. 1 (1972), 99-
100.

Meerloo, J. A. M. *Spinoza en het probleem der communicatie.* Leiden: E. J. Brill, 1972. 16p. (Mededelingen vanwege het Spinozahuis, 28.)

Millet, Louis. *Pour connaître la pensée de Spinoza.* Paris: Bordas, 1971. 144p.
Review: Dumas, Jean-Louis. *Les études philosophiques,* No. 3 (1971), 399-401.

Mini, F. Slavio. *Richard Simon e il metodo storico-critico di B. Spinoza: Storia di un libro e di una polemica sullo sfondo delle lotte politico-religiose della Francia di Luigi XIV.* Firenze: Felice Le Monnier, 1972. xvi, 129p.

Misrahi, Robert. *Spinoza.* Paris: Seghers, 1964. 220p. (Coll. "Philosophes de tous les temps.") 2ᵉéd., 1966.
Review: 1964 éd. Coelho, A. *Rivista portuguesa de filosofia,* **21** (1965), 93.
Montull, T. *Estudios filosóficos,* **14** (1965), 401-2.
Crippa, R. *Giornale di metafisica,* **21** (1966), 666-68.
Mesnard, P. *Revue d'histoire et de philosophie religieuse,* **45** (1965), 375-82.

———.*Spinoza: La vita, il pensiero e testi esemplari.* Traduzione di Marina Caccio. Milano: Accademia; Firenze: Sansoni, 1970. (I Memorabili, 5.)

Moreau, Joseph. *Spinoza et le spinozisme.* Paris: Presses Universitaires de France, 1971. 126p.

Oudin, Charles. *Le spinozisme de Montesquieu.* Genève: Slatkine Reprints, 1971. Reprint of 1st edition, 1911.

Pérez-Espejo, Sergio. *Formallogische und dialektische Identität bei Spinoza.* Frankfurt/Main: Michler, 1964. 71p. [Dissertation, Frankfurt/Main: Teildruck.]

Préposiet, Jean. *Spinoza et la liberté des hommes.* Paris: Gallimard, 1967. 320p.

Révah, Israël-S. *Spinoza et Juan de Prado.* Paris: Mouton, 1960, 164p. (Coll. "Études juives.")
Review: Cantera, F. *Sefarad,* **20** (1960), 197-98.

de Angelis, E. *Filosofia*, **13**, Suppl. (1962), 663-70.

Röd, Wolfgang. *Spinozas Lehre von der Societas*. Torino: Edizione di Filosofia, 1969. 62p. Reprinted from *Filosofia*, **18** (1967), 777-806; **19** (1968), 671-98.
Review: Barwirsch, Josef. *Philosophischer Literaturanzeiger*, **22**, No. 5 (1969), 317-18.

Röhrich, Wilfried. *Staat der Freiheit*. Zur politischen Philosophie Spinozas. Darmstadt: Melzer, 1969. 108p.

Rottner, Eli (Edward Rudnicki). *Aus Spinozas Heimat*. Dortmund, 1972. 136p.

Rousset, Bernard. *La perspective finale de l'*Éthique *et le problème de la cohérence du spinozisme*. L'autonomie comme salut. Paris: J. Vrin, 1968. 246p. (Bibliothèque d'histoire de la philosophie.)
Review: Zac, S. *Les études philosophiques*, No. 1 (1970), 108.

Sassen, Ferdinand. *Kerngedachten van Spinoza*. Roermond: J. J. Romen & Zonen, 1967. 230p.
Review: L. F. *Dialoog*, **7** (1966-1967), 267.

*Scoleri, Domenico. *La filosofia del diritto di B. Spinoza*. Negli oppunti per il corso universitario 1958-1959. Pref. di D. A. Cardone. Reggio Calabria: Stab. tip. La voce di Calabria, 1965. 103p.

Segal, Q. *Scripta Hierosolymitana*. Jerusalem: The Magnes Press, 1968. 253p. (Further Studies in Philosophy, 20.)
Review: Wagner, H. *Archiv für Geschichte der Philosophie*, **51**, No. 3 (1969), 305-11.

Sen, Sanat Kumar. *A Study of the Metaphysics of Spinoza*. Santiniketan (India), Visvabharati: Centre of Advanced Study in Philosophy, 1966. 227p.

Steffen, Hermann. *Recht und Staat im System Spinozas*. Bonn: Bouvier, 1968. 147p. (Schriften zur Rechtslehre und Politik, 56.)

Strauss, Leo. *Spinoza's Critique of Religion*. Translated by E. M. Sinclair. New York: Schocken Books, 1965. 351p.

van der Bend, J. G. *Dr. J. D. Bierens de Haan en Spinoza.* Leiden: E. J. Brill, 1968. 16p. (Mededelingen vanwege het Spinozahuis, 24.)

———.*Het Spinozisme van Dr. J. D. Bierens de Haan.* Mit einer ausführlichen Zusammenfassung in deutscher Sprache. Groningen: Wolters, Noordhoff, 1970. 177p.
Review: de Dijn, H. *Tijdschrift voor filosofie,* **33** (1971), 790-95.
Sassen, F. *Algemeen Nederlands tijdschrift voor wijsbegeerte en psychologie,* **63** (1971), 281-82.

van der Hoeven, P. *De cartesianische fysica in het denken van Spinoza.* Leiden: E. J. Brill, 1973. (Mededelingen vanwege het Spinozahuis, 30.)

van der Tak. W. G. *B. de Spinoza.* 's-Gravenhage: Kruseman, 1961. 184p. (Helden van de geest, 6.)

van Niftrik, G. C. *Spinoza en de sectariërs van zijn tijd.* Leiden: E. J. Brill, 1962. 15p. (Mededelingen vanwege het Spinozahuis, 18.)

Vleeschauwer, Herman Jean de. *More seu ordine geometrico demonstratum.* Pretoria: University of South Africa, 1961. 87p. (South Africa University. Mededelings Communications C.27.) In French.
Review: Mancini, I. *Rivista di filosofia neo-scolastica,* **54** (1962), 395-96.

von Schmid, J. J. *Spinoza's staatkundige verhandeling in de ontwikkeling van de staatsleer.* Leiden: E. J. Brill, 1970. (Mededelingen vanwege het Spinozahuis, 26.)

Vries, Theun de. *Spinoza, beeldenstormer en Wereldbouwer.* Amsterdam: Becht. 240p.

Wolfson, Abraham. *Spinoza: A Life of Reason.* 2d. enl. ed. New York: Philosophical Library, 1969. 347p.
Review: Bolthrunis, J. B. *Thomist,* **34** (1970), 711-12.
Rice, L. C. *The Modern Schoolman,* **48** (1970-1971), 187-89.

Wolfson, Harry Austryn. *The Philosophy of Spinoza.* 2 vols. New York: Schocken, 1969. Reprint from 1934 edition.
Review: de Lucca, J. *Dialogue,* **6** (1967), 89-102.

Zac, Sylvain. *L'idée de vie dans la philosophie de Spinoza*. Paris: Presses Universitaires de France, 1963. 284p. (Bibliothéque de philosophie contemporaine.)
Review: Valcke, L. *Dialogue*, **3** (1964), 104-6.
Wahl, J. *Revue de métaphysique et de morale*, **69** (1964), 95-100.
Israël, G. *Les nouveaux cahiers*, **2** (1966), 27-28.
Brunner, F. *Revue de théologie et de philosophie*, **98** (1965), 327-28.

_____.*La morale de Spinoza*. 2ᵉ édit. revue et augmentée. Paris: Presses Universitaires de France, 1966. 119p. (Initiation philosophique, 39.)

_____.*Spinoza et l'interprétation de l'Ecriture*. Paris: Presses Universitaires de France, 1965. 243p.
Review: Israël, G. *Revue philosophique de la France et de l'étranger*, **160**, No. 2 (1970), 191-205.
Lévinas, E. *Les nouveaux cahiers*, **2** (1966), 22-26.
Decloux, S. *Nouvelle revue théologique*, **88** (1966), 322-23.
Dubarle, A-M. *Revue des sciences philosophiques et théologiques*, **50** (1966), 469-70.
Jacob, A. *Les études philosophiques*, **21** (1966), 441-42.
Antoine, P. *Archives de philosophie*, **31** (1968), 157-60.

Zarrillo, Amelia. *L'etica di Benedetto Spinoza*. Marcianise: Ediz. La diana, 1963. 47p.

Zweig, Arnold. *Baruch Spinoza*. Porträt eines freien Geistes, 1632-1677. Leipsig: Inselverlag, 1961; Darmstadt: Melzer, 1968. 61p.

IV. GENERAL WORKS WITH SECTIONS ON SPINOZA

Blondel, Maurice. *Dialogues avec les philosophes*. Descartes-Spinoza-Malebranche-Pascal-Saint Augustin. Paris: Éditions Aubier Montaigne, 1966.

Bréhier, Émile. "Spinoza." In his *The Seventeenth Century*, pp. 155-96. Translated by Wade Baskin. Chicago: University of Chicago Press, 1966. (The History of Philosophy.)

Chevalier, Jacques. *Histoire de la pensée.* T. 3, *La pensée moderne, de Descartes a Kant.* Paris: Flammarion, 1961. Pp. 270-321 devoted to Spinoza.

Chichkine, A. *Ethique de Spinoza* (in his *Ethique*), pp. 113-57. Moscou: Ed. en langues étrangères.

Collins, James Daniel. *The Continental Rationalists. Descartes, Spinoza, Leibniz.* Milwaukee: Bruce, 1967. 177p.

Copleston, Frederick Charles. "Spinoza." In his *A History of Philosophy*, Vol. 4: *Descartes to Leibniz*, pp. 205-63. London: Burns and Oates, 1960.

de Lacharrière, René. *Études sur la théorie démocratique, Spinoza, Rousseau, Hegel, Marx.* Paris: Payot, 1963. 218p. (Bibliothèque politique et économique.)

Faggiotto, Pietro. *Il problema della metafisica nel pensiero moderno.* Parte I: Bacone, Galilei, Cartesio, Hobbes, Spinoza, Locke. Padova: Cedam, 1969. 244p.
Review: Pieretti, A. *Rivista di filosofia neo-scolastica,* **61** (1969), 788-89.

Feuerbach, Ludwig. *Gesammelte Werke.* Hrsg. von Werner Schuffenhauer. Bd. II: Geschichte der neueren Philosophie von Bacon von Verulam bis Benedikt Spinoza. Bearb: Wolfgang Harich. Berlin: Akademie-Verlag, 1969. 522p.

Flew, Anthony, ed. *Body, Mind and Death.* From Hippocrates to G. Ryle on the question "What is consciousness?" New York: Macmillan, 1964.

Gabaude, Jean-Marc. *Liberté et raison.* La liberté cartésienne et sa réfraction chez Spinoza et chez Leibniz. Toulouse: Association des Publications de l'Université de Toulouse, 1970-. (Publications de la Faculté des lettres et sciences humaines de Toulouse. Série A, 13.) Tome I: Philosophie refléxive de la volonté. Toulouse, 1970. xii, 434p. Tome II: Philosophie compréhensive de la nécessitation libératrice. Toulouse, forthcoming. 340p.

Gilson, Étienne Henri, and Langan, Thomas. "Benedictus Spinoza." In their *Modern Philosophy: Descartes to Kant,* pp. 127-44. New York: Random House, 1963.

Gueroult, Martial. *Études sur Descartes, Spinoza, Malebranche et Leibniz*. Hildesheim: G. Olms, 1970. 289p.

Heimsoeth, Heinz. *Atom, Seele, Monade, Historische Ursprünge und Hintergründe von Kants Antinomie der Teilung*. Mainz: Verlag der Akademie der Wissenschaften und der Literatur, Wiesbaden, 1960. 142p. (Akademie der Wissenschaften und der Literatur, Mainz. Geistes und Sozialwissenschaftliche Klasse, Abhandlungen, 1960, Vol. 3.)
Review: Wagner, H. *Kantstudien,* **53** (1961-1962), 246-54.
Kahl-Furthmann, G. *Philosophischer Literaturanzeiger,* **15** (1962), 11-18.
Kaulback, F. *Zeitshrift für philosophische Forschung,* **17** (1963), 3-41.

Henrich, Dieter. *Der ontologische Gottesbeweis Sein Problem und seine Geschichte in der Neuzeit*. Tübingen: J. C. B. Mohr, 1960. xii, 275p.
Review: Gómez Caffarena, J. *International Philosophical Quarterly,* **3** (1963), 617-24.
Kern, W. *Scholastik,* **39** (1964), 87-107.
Möller, J. *Hegel-Studien,* **2** (1963), 329-34.

Jaspers, Karl. *Aus dem Ursprung denkende Metaphysiker*. Anaximander, Heraklit, Parmenides, Plotin, Anselm, Spinoza, Laotse, Nagarjuna. München: Piper, 1966. 350p. (Piperpaperback.)

Jocobs, L. "Spinoza." In *Jewish Philosophy and Philosophers*. Edited by Raymond Goldwater. London: Hillel Foundation, 1962.

Lo Guidice, Francesco. *Il problema morale nella filosofia di Cartesio, Spinoza e Croce*. Cosenza: MIT, 1970.

*Melchiorre, Virgilio. "Sartre, Spinoza, S. Agostino" (Tre vie alla libertà). In *Libertà e responsabilità*, pp. 14-28. A cura del Centro di Studi Filosofici di Gallarate. Padova: Ed. Gregoriana, 1967. (Collana di Studi Filosofia, 13.)

Namer, Émile. *Machiavel*. Paris: Presses Universitaires de France, 1961. 256p. ("Les grands penseurs.")

Review: Decerf, P. *Revue philosophique de Louvain,* **63** (1965), 144-45.
Annales de l'Université de Paris, **32** (1962), 591-92.

Romback, Heinrich. *Substanz, System, Struktur.* Die Ontologie des Funktionalismus und der philosophische Hintergründ der modernen Wissenschaft. Bd. II. Freiburg: Karl Alber, 1966. 527p.
Review: Weymann-Weyhe, W. *Philosophisches Jahrbuch,* **74** (1966-1967), 407-11.
Wahl, J. *Revue de métaphysique et de morale,* **73** (1968), 128-29.

Roth, Leon. *Spinoza, Descartes and Maimonides.* New York: Russell and Russell, 1963. 148p.

Swabey, William Curtis. "Spinoza." In his *Ethical Theory from Hobbes to Kant,* pp. 15-25. New York: Philosophical Library, 1961.

Thomas, George Finger. *Religious Philosophies of the West.* New York: Scribner's, 1965.

Vaughan, Charles Edwyn. *Studies in the History of Political Philosophy before and after Rousseau,* Vol. 1. Edited by A. S. Little. New York: Russell & Russell, 1960.

Vorländer, Karl. *Geschichte der Philosophie* (Gekürzte Ausg.). IV: Philosophie der Neuzeit. Bearb von Heinrich Knittermeyer. Mit Quellentexten, darunter d. ungekürzte Wiedergabe von Spinozas "uber die Verbesserung des Verstandes" u. bibliograph. Erg. vers. von Eckhard Kessler. Reinbek b. Hamburg: Rowohlt, 1966. 241p. (Rowohlts deutsche Enzyklopädie 261/62: Sachgebiet Philosophie.)
Review: Del Negro, W. von. *Zeitschrift für philosophische Forschung,* **22** (1968), 163-64.

Walther, M. *Metaphysik als anti-Theologie: die Philosophie Spinozas im Zusammenhang der religionsphilosophischen Problematik.* Hamburg: Meiner. viii, 176p. (c. 1971.)

Whittaker, Thomas. *Reason.* A philosophical essay with historical illustrations (Comte and Mill, Schopenhauer, Vico, Spinoza).

New York: Greenwood Press, 1968. 217p. [Copyright 1934.]

V. SPECIAL COLLECTIONS ON SPINOZA

Altwicker, Norbert, comp. *Texte zur Geschichte des Spinozismus.* Darmstadt: Wissenschaftliche Buchgesellschaft, 1971. 415p.

*de Angelis, Enrico, ed. *Schriften zur Philosophie Spinozas.* Hildesheim: Georg Olms, 1971(?). (Olms Studien, Bd. 15.)

Grene, M., ed. *Spinoza: A Collection of Critical Essays.* Garden City, N. Y.: Anchor Press/Doubleday, 1973. xviii, 390p. Reprints (Wolfson, Hallett, Hampshire, et al.), translations (Gueroult, Kolakowski) and original articles (Curley, Donagan, et al.).

Hessing, Sigfried, ed. *Spinoza: dreihundert Jahre Ewigkeit, Spinoza-Festschrift 1632-1932.* 2. verm. Aufl. Den Haag: M. Nijhoff, 1962. xlii, 205p.
Review: Kunz, H. *Studia philosophica,* **23** (1963), 234-35.

Inquiry, **12**, No. 1 (1969), 1-144. Oslo, Universitetsforlaget. Entire issue devoted to Spinoza.

Kashap, Paul, ed. *Studies in Spinoza, Critical and Interpretive Essays.* Berkeley: University of California Press, 1972. Essays by S. Alexander, A. E. Taylor, Ruth Saw, Stuart Hampshire, G. Parkinson, et al.

Les études philosophiques, No. 3, juillet-septembre, 1972. Devoted to Spinoza with articles by Caillois, Matheron, Moreau, Zac, et al.

The Monist, **55**, No. 4 (Oct., 1971), 527-685. La Salle, Illinois, Open Court. Entire issue devoted to Spinoza.

Vereniging Het Spinozahuis, Rijnsburg. *Mededelingen vanwege het Spinozahuis.* No. 1- (1934-). Leiden: E. J. Brill. Indexed in Brinkmans and Répertoire Bibliographique de la Philosophie.

Wijsgerig perspectief, **8**, No. 2 (1967). Devoted to Spinoza with articles by Hubbeling, de Deugd, et al.

VI. ARTICLES AND ESSAYS ON SPECIFIC TOPICS

Agaesse, P. "Le Spinoza de M. Gueroult." *Archives de philosophie*, **32** (1969), 288-96. A critical study of *Gueroult, M., Spinoza*. Tome I. Paris, 1968.

Agrawal, Brahma Swamp. "Absolutism and Pantheism." *Darshana International*, **7** (April, 1967), 23-27.

Akselrod, L. I. "Spinoza und der Materialismus." In *Texte zur Geschichte des Spinozismus*, compiled by Norbert Altwicker, pp. 142-71. Darmstadt, 1971.
Also published in *Spinoza in Soviet Philosophy*, edited by G. L. Kline, pp. 61-89. New York: Humanities Press, 1952.

Alderisio, Felice, ed. Un articolo inedito de B. Spaventa circa l'unità organica della filosofia di Bruno e circa l'attinenza di questa con la filosofia di Spinoza. *Giornale critico della filosofia italiana*, **45** (1966), 218-25.

Altmann, Alexander. "Moses Mendelssohn on Leibniz and Spinoza." In *Studies in Rationalism, Judaism, and Universalism*, edited by Raphael Loewe, pp. 13-45. London: Routledge and Kegan Paul, 1966. In memory of Leon Roth.
Also published in Altmann, A. *Studies in Religious Philosophy and Mysticism*, pp. 246-74. Ithaca: Cornell University Press, 1969.

Altwicker, Norbert. "Spinoza." Tendenzen der Spinoza-Rezeption und Kritik. In his *Texte zur Geschichte des Spinozismus*, pp. 1-58. Darmstadt, 1971.

Arnold, Matthew. "The Bishop and the Philosopher." In his *Essays, Letters, and Reviews*, collected and edited by Fraser Neiman, pp. 43-68. Cambridge: Harvard University Press, 1960.

Aron, W. "Baruch Spinoza et la médicine." *Revue d'histoire de la medécine hébraïque*, **18**, No. 65 (1965), 61-78; No. 69 (1965), 113-211.

_____ ."Freud et Spinoza." *Revue d'histoire de la médecine hébraïque*, **19**, No. 3 (1966), 101-16; **20** (1967), 53-70, 123-30, 149-60.

Astrada, Carlos. "Goethe y el pantéismo spinociano." In his *Ensayos filosoficos*, pp. 85-104. Bahia Blanca: Universidad Nacional del Sur, 1963.

Auvray, P. "Richard Simon et Spinoza." In *Religion, érudition et critique à la fin du XVIIe siècle et au début de XVIIIe* [par Baudouin de Gaiffier et al.], pp. 201-14. Paris: Presses Universitaires de France, 1968. (Université de Strasbourg. Bibliothèque des centres d'études supérieures spécialisés.)

Bachem, R. "Rediscovery of Spinoza by Schleiermacher, Arnold and Renan." *Revue de littérature comparée*, 41, No. 4 (1967), 581-83.

Baensch, Otto. "Die Entwicklung des Seelenbegriffs bei Spinoza als Grundlage für das Verständnis seiner Lehre vom Parallelismus der Attribute." In *Texte zur Geschichte des Spinozismus*, compiled by Norbert Altwicker, pp. 232-77. Darmstadt, 1971.
Also published in *Archiv für Geschichte der Philosophie*, 20, No. 3/4 (1907), 332-44, 456-94.

Barnard, Frederick. "Spinozism." In *The Encyclopedia of Philosophy*, edited by Paul Edwards, Vol. 7, pp. 541-44. New York: Macmillan Co. and Free Press, 1967.

Beck, Lewis White. "Spinoza." In his *Six Secular Philosophers*. Religious themes in the thought of Spinoza, Hume, Kant, Nietzsche, William James, Santayana, pp. 27-41. New York: Harper and Row, 1960.

Belaief, Gail. "The Relation Between Civil Law and a Higher Law: A Study of Spinoza's Legal Philosophy." *Monist*, 49 (1965), 504-18.

Ben Gurion, David. "Lasset uns gutmachen das Unrecht." In *Spinoza: dreihundert Jahre Ewigkeit, Spinoza-Festschrift 1632-1932*, edited by Siegfried Hessing, pp. 1-9. Den Haag, 1962.

Bennett, Jonathan. "A Note on Descartes and Spinoza." *Philosophical Review*, 74 (1965), 379-80.
Reply: Donagan, A. *Philosophical Review*, 75 (1966), 380-82.

Ben-Shlomo, Joseph. "Shmuel Hugo Bergman's 'The History of Philosophy from Nicholaus Cusanus to the Age of Enlightenment' " (in Hebrew). *Iyyun,* **22** (1971), 54-66.

Bergman, S. H. "Les dialogues philosophiques de Moses Mendelssohn" (in Hebrew). *Iyyun,* **20,** Nos. 1-4 (1969), English summary, 306-8.

Bertman, Martin A. "Rational Pursuit in Spinoza's *Tractatus de Intellectus Emendatione.*" *New Scholasticism,* **44** (1970), 236-48.

Birnbaum, Ruth. "Baruch Spinoza-Martin Buber, Dialectic and Dialogue." *Personalist,* **48** (1967), 119-28.

Blair, R. G. "Imagination and Freedom in Spinoza and Sartre." *Journal of the British Society for Phenomenology,* **1** (1970), 13-16.

Blondel, Maurice. "Une des sources de la pensée moderne." L'évolution du spinozisme. In his *Dialogues avec les philosophes* (Descartes-Spinoza-Malebranche-Pascal-Saint Augustin), pp. 11-40. Paris: Editions Aubier Montaigne, 1966.

_____."Un interprète de Spinoza, Victor Delbos 1862-1916." In his *Dialogues avec les philosophes,* pp. 271-80. Paris: Editions Aubier Montaigne, 1966.

Blüh, Otto. "Newton and Spinoza." In *Proceedings of the International Congress on the History of Sciences, 10th, Ithaca, 1962,* pp. 701-3. 2 vols. Actes du dixième Congrès international d'histoire des sciences. Paris: Hermann, 1964. (Actualités scientifiques et industrielles, 1307.)

Boasson, J. J. "L'interét actuel de Spinoza." *Miscelânea de estudos a Joaquim de Carvalho,* No. 8 (1962), 795-815.

Boehm, Rudolf. 'Dieses war die Ethic und zwar Niederländisch, wie sie Spinoza anfangs verferttiget. Spinozas "Korte Verhandeling" eine übersetzung aus einen lateinischen Urtext?' *Studia philosophica Gandensia,* **5** (1967), 175-206.

_____."Spinoza und die Metaphysik der Subjektivität." *Zeitschrift fur philosophische Forschung,* **22** (1968), 165-86.

Borne, Étienne. "Le panthéisme, est-il un athéisme?" *Les études philosophiques*, **21** (1966), 341-55.

Bossart, William H. "Is Philosophy Transcendental?" *Monist*, **55** (1971), 293-311.

Bowman, Carroll R. "Spinoza's Doctrine of Attributes." *Southern Journal of Philosophy*, **5** (1967), 59-71.

———."Spinoza's Idea of the Body." *Idealistic Studies*, **1** (1971), 258-68.

Brann, Henry Walter. "Schopenhauer und Spinoza." *Schopenhauer-Jahrbuch*, **51** (1970), 138-52.

———."Schopenhauer and Spinoza." *Journal of the History of Philosophy*, **10** (1972), 181-96.

———."Spinoza and the Kabbalah." *Hartwick Review*, **3** (1967), 61-66.

Brinker, M. "L'être déterminé et sa relation à l'éternité et au temps selon Spinoza" (in Hebrew). *Iyyun*, **17**, No. 4 (1966), 193-211; English summary, 279-80.

Brucar, I. "Spinoza und die Ewigkeit der Seele." In *Spinoza: dreihundert Jahre Ewigkeit, Spinoza-Festschrift 1632-1932*, edited by Siegfried Hessing, pp. 10-14. Den Haag, 1962.

Bruch, Jean-Louis. "La doctrine spinoziste du 'De Deo'." *Revue philosophique de la France et l'étranger*, **160** (1970), 207-25.

Brunner, Constantin. "Das Lamm Benedikt Spinoza." In *Spinoza: dreihundert Jahre Ewigkeit, Spinoza-Festschrift 1632-1932*, edited by Siegfried Hessing, pp. 15-23. Den Haag, 1962.

Calvetti, Carla Gallicet. "I diritti della persona umana nel *Tractatus theologico-politicus* di Spinoza." In *Studi di filosofia e di storia della filosofia in onore di Francesco Olgiati*, pp. 321-44. Milano: Società Editrice Vita e Pensiero, 1962. (Pubbl. dell' Università cattolica del Sacro Cuore. Serie terza. Scienze filosofiche, 6.)

———."I presupposti teoretici della tolleranza in Spinoza." *Rivista di filosofia neo-scolastica*, **57,** No. 4 (1965), 420-47; No. 5 (1965), 623-49.

_____ ."Il 'calvinismo' di Spinoza." *Rivista di filosofia neo-scholastica,* **60,** Nos. 4-5 (1968), 377-409.

_____ ."Il pensiero di Spinoza." *Rivista di filosofia neo-scolastica,* **56** (1964), 202-8.

_____ ."Il problema della persona in Spinoza." *Rivista di filosofia neo-scolastica,* **54** (1962), 289-317.

_____ ."Spinoza e il *De Providentia* di Zwingli." *Rivista di filosofia neo-scolastica,* **61** (1969), 387-424.

Carnois, Bernard. "Peut-on et doit-on fonder la morale?" *Dialogue,* **8** (1970), 612-34.

Casertano, Giovanni. Introduzione. In *Spinoza, Benedictus de,* pp. i-xxxv. Dio, naturo, uomo (pagine scelte dalle opere). Introduzione, traduzione e note di G. Casertano. Napoli-Firenze: Il Tripode, 1969.

Cassirer, Ernst. "Spinoza." In *Texte zur Geschichte des Spinozismus,* compiled by Norbert Altwicker, pp. 172-215. Darmstadt, 1971.
Also published in Cassirer, Ernst. *Das Erkenntnisproblem in der Philosophie und Wissenschaft der neueren Zeit,* pp. 73-125. Bd. II. Berlin, 1922.

*Christian, William A. "Spinoza on Theology and Truth." In *The Heritage of Christian Thought: Essays in Honor of Robert Lowry Calhoun,* edited by R. E. Cushman and E. Grislis, pp. 89-107. New York: Harper and Row, 1965.

Chubb, J. N. "Spinoza's Arguments for the Existence of God." *Indian Journal of Theology,* **17,** No. 3 (1968), 116-25.

Clarke, W. Norris. "A Curious Blindspot in the Anglo-American Tradition of Anti-Theistic Argument." *Monist,* **54** (1970), 181-200.

Coelho, Antonio. "O problema da liberdade em Espinosa." *Rivista portuguesa de filosofia,* **20** (1964), 293-313.

Colie, R. L. "Spinoza in England, 1665-1730." *Proceedings of the American Philosophical Society,* **107** (1963), 183-219.

Corsano, Antonio. "Il Magalotti e l'ateismo." *Giornale critico della filosofia italiana,* **53** (1972), 241-62.

Cottier, G. M. M. "Idolâtres ou athées? La courbe d'une problématique." *Nova et Vetera, Suisse,* **44**, No. 1 (1969), 66-74. Author discusses Spinoza, Pierre Bayle and Voltaire.

——."Signification de la dialectique chez Hegel." *Revue Thomiste,* **69** (1969), 378-411.

De Angelis, Enrico. "Il metodo geometrico da Cartesio a Spinoza." *Giornale critico della filosofia italiana,* **43** (1964), 393-427.

Deborin, Alexander. "Die Weltanschauung Spinozas." In *Texte zur Geschichte des Spinozismus,* compiled by Norbert Altwicker, pp. 110-41. Darmstadt, 1971.
Also published in *Marxistische Bibliothek,* Bd. XIII, pp. 40-74. Berlin: Verlag für Literatur und Politik, 1928.

de Deugd, Cornelius. "Old Wine in New Bottles? Tillich and Spinoza." In *Royal Institute of Philosophy Lectures,* Vol. 2, pp. 133-51. Talk of God. New York: St. Martin's Press, 1969.

——."Over de termen rationeel en rationalistisch." *Levende talen,* **210** (1961), 329-38.

——."Spinoza's kennisleer." *Wijsgerig perspectief op maatschappij en wetenschap,* **8** (1967-68), 92-106.

de Dijn, H. "Ervaring en theorie in de Staatkunde, een analyse van Spinozas *Tractatus Politicus.*" *Tijdschrift voor filosofie,* **32** (1970), 30-70. "Summary: Experience and theory in politics. An analysis of Spinoza's *Tractatus Politicus,*" pp. 70-71.

——."Over de interpretatie (van de Schrift) volgens Spinoza." *Tijdschrift voor filosofie,* **29** (1967), 666-704.

——."Spinoza en het expressie-probleem." *Tijdschrift voor filosofie,* **31** (1969), 572-82. Analysis and critical study of *Deleuze, G., Spinoza et le problème de l'expression.* Paris, 1968.

——."Kroniek van de Spinoza-literatuur 1960-1970." *Tidjschrift voor filosofie,* **34** (1972), 130-39.

Deleuze, Gilles. "Spinoza et la méthode générale de M. Gueroult."

Revue de métaphysique et de morale, **74** (1969), 426-37. Critical study of *Gueroult, M., Spinoza*. Tome I. Paris, 1968.

de Lucca, John. "Wolfson on Spinoza's Use of the *More Geometrico.*" *Dialogue*, **6** (1967), 89-102. Discussion of *Wolfson, H. A., The Philosophy of Spinoza*. New York, 1934. Reprint, 1960, 1969.

De Rosa, Guiseppe. "La religione nella vita e nel pensiero di Spinoza." *Divus Thomas*, **64** (1961), 241-65.

de Vries, Theun. "Spinoza als politischer Denker." *Deutsche Zeitschrift für Philosophie*, **12** (1964), 1312-27.

d'Hautefeuille, François. "Bergson et Spinoza." *Revue de métaphysique et de morale*, **65** (1960), 463-74.

Diliberto Reale, Maria Adonella. See Reale, Maria Adonella Diliberto.

Di Vona, Piero. "L'analogia del concetto di 'res' in Spinoza." *Rivista critica di storia della filosofia*, **16** (1961), 48-78.

_____."Il concetto di filosofia nel *Tractatus de intellectus emendatione* di Spinoza." *Rivista critica di storia della filosofia*, **15** (1960), 376-403.

_____."Contrasti di idee sull'essere nel pensiero di Spinoza." *Acme*, **16** (1963), 217-91.

_____."Logica e metafisica in Spinoza e nel suo tempo." *Rassegna di Scienze filosofiche*," **22** (1969), 321-33. Napoli.

Donagan, Alan. "A Note on Spinoza, *Ethics, I, 10.*" *Philosophical Review*, **75** (1966), 380-82.
Reply to: Bennett, J. "A Note on Descartes and Spinoza." *Philosophical Review*, **74** (1965), 379-80.

Doney, Willis. "Spinoza on Philosophical Skepticism." *Monist*, **55** (1971), 617-35.

Dreyfus, Ginette. "La méthode structurale et le Spinoza de Martial Gueroult." *L'âge de la science*, No. 3 (1969), 240-75. Critical study of *Gueroult, M., Spinoza*. Tome I. Paris, 1968.

E.M. Curley

Droop, Fritz. "Fünf Szenen aus dem Leben Spinozas." In *Spinoza: dreihundert Jahre Ewigkeit, Spinoza-Festschrift 1632-1932*, edited by Siegfried Hessing, pp. 24-39. Den Haag, 1962.

Dubiez, F. J. "Baruch de Spinoza, 1632-1677." In *Ons Amsterdam*, **21**, No. 1 (January, 1969), 2-12.

Dubnow, Simon. "Die Gestalt." In *Spinoza: dreihundert Jahre Ewigkeit, Spinoza-Festschrift 1632-1932*, edited by Siegfried Hessing, pp. 40-42. Den Haag, 1962.

Dufrenne, Mikel. "La connaissance de Dieu dans la philosophie spinoziste" (Étude parue dans *Revue philosophique de la France et de l'étranger*, octobre-décembre 1949). In his *Jalons*, pp. 112-26. La Haye: M. Nijhoff, 1966. (Phaenomenologica. Collection publiée sous le patronage des centres d'Archives Husserl, 20.)

———."Dieu et l'homme dans la philosophie de Spinoza" (Étude parue dans *L'Homme, métaphysique et conscience de soi*). In his *Jalons*, pp. 28-69. La Haye: M. Nijhoff, 1966. (Phaenomenologica. Collection publiée sous le patronage des centres d'Archives Husserl, 20.)

Dunin-Borkowski, Stanislaus. "Spinoza nach dreihundert Jahren." In *Texte zur Geschichte des Spinozismus*, compiled by Norbert Altwicker, pp. 59-74. Darmstadt, 1971.
Also published in Dunin-Borkowski, Stanislaus. *Spinoza nach 300 Jahren*, pp. 64-92. Berlin, 1932.

Ebbinghaus, Julius. "Über den Grund der Beschränkung unserer Erkenntnis auf die Attribute des Denkens und der Ausdehnung bei Spinoza." In his *Gesammelte Aufsätze*, pp. 194-210. Vorträge und Reden. Hildesheim: Georg Olms. 1968. 340p.

Eckstein, Walter. "Zur Lehre vom Staatsvertrag bei Spinoza." In *Texte zur Geschichte des Spinozismus*, compiled by Norbert Altwicker, pp. 362-76. Darmstadt, 1971.
Also published in *Zeitschrift für öffentliches Recht*, **13**, No. 3 (1933), 356-68.

Eisenberg, Paul. "How to Understand *De Intellectus Emendatione*." *Journal of the History of Philosophy*, **9** (1971), 171-91.

Epstein, Fanny. "On the Definition of Moral Goodness." *Iyyun,* **19** (1968), 153-69.

Esposito, Joseph L. "God and the Possibility of Philosophy." *International Journal for Philosophy of Religion,* **3** (1972), 103-15.

Evans, J. L. "Error and the Will." *Philosophy,* **38** (1963), 136-48. Reply: O'Hear, Anthony. "Belief and the Will." *Philosophy,* **47** (1972), 95-112.

Fabro, C. "La dissolution de l'Homme-Dieu dans le rationalisme spinozien." *La table ronde,* No. 250 (1968), 46-57.

Falgueras Salinas, Ignacio. "El establecimiento de la existencia de Dios en el *Tractatus* de Espinosa." *Anuario Filosófico,* **5** (1972), 99-151.

Fleischmann, Eugène J. "Die Wirklichkeit in Hegels Logik. Ideengeschichtliche Beziehungen zu Spinoza." *Zeitschrift für philosophische Forschung,* **18** (1964), 3-29.

Floistad, Guttorm. "The Knower and the Known." *Man and World,* **3** (1970), 3-25.

———."Spinoza's Theory of Knowledge Applied to the *Ethics*." *Inquiry,* **12** (1969), 41-65.

Foss, Laurence. "Hegel, Spinoza and a Theory of Experience as Closed." *Thomist,* **35** (1971), 435-46.

Furlán, Augusto. "Idea y concepto en Spinoza y Santo Tomás." *Sapientia,* **24** (1969), 23-48.

Gabaude, Jean-Marc. "Ambiguïté spinozienne." *Revue de l'enseignement philosophique,* **21**, No. 6 (1971), 1-7.

Gagnebin, Samuel. "Essai d'interprétation de l'idée de joie dans la philosophie de Spinoza." *Studia philosophica,* **21** (1961), 16-50.

Galichet, F. "Le problème de l'illusion chez Spinoza." *Revue de métaphysique et de morale,* **77** (1972), 1-19.

Garulli, Enrico. "Antonio Labriola lettore di Spinoza." *Giornale critico della filosofia italiana,* **41** (1962), 251-57.

———."L'idea spinoziana della filosofia in alcuni recenti studi." *Il pensiero,* **10** (1965), 224-38.

Geach, P. T. "Spinoza and the Divine Attributes." In *Reason and Reality,* edited by G.N.A. Vesey, pp. 15-27. London: Macmillan, 1972. (Royal Institute of Philosophy Lectures, Vol. 5.)

Gebhardt, Carl. "Der gotische Jude." In *Spinoza: dreihundert Jahre Ewigkeit, Spinoza-Festschrift 1632-1932,* edited by Siegfried Hessing, pp. 43-47. Den Haag, 1962.

Gherasim, Vasile. "Die Bedeutung der Affectenlehre Spinozas." In *Spinoza: dreihundert Jahre Ewigheit, Spinoza-Festschrift 1632-1932,* edited by Siegfried Hessing, pp. 48-59. Den Haag, 1962.

Giaconi, Carlo. "La scolastica della controriforma e il pensiero laico di Spinoza." *La civiltà cattolica,* a.120, **2,** No. 3 (1969), 239-48.

Giancotti Boscherini, Emilia. "Nota sulla diffusione della filosofia di Spinoza in Italia." *Giornale critico della filosofia italiana,* **42** (1963), 339-62.

Giuletti, Giovani. "Recenti studi spinoziani (continua)." *Revista rosminiana di filosofia e di cultura,* **66** (1972), 179-97.

Goossens, Jean. "Spinoza en de tijd." *Dialoog,* 1 (1960-1961), 61-80.

Gram, Moltke S. "Spinoza, Substance, and Predication." *Theoria,* **34** (1968), 222-44.

Grunwald, Max. "Der Lebensphilosoph Spinoza." In *Spinoza: dreihundert Jahre Ewigkeit, Spinoza-Festschrift 1632-1932,* edited by Siegfried Hessing, pp. 60-67. Den Haag, 1962.

Gueroult, Martial. "La lettre de Spinoza sur l'infini." (Lettre XII à Louis Meyer.) (Étude extraite de l'ouvrage de M. Gueroult sur Spinoza.) *Revue de métaphysique et de morale,* **71** (1966), 385-411.

_____ ."Le cogito et l'ordre des axiomes métaphysiques dans les *Principia philosophiae cartesianae* de Spinoza." *Archives de philosophie,* **23** (1960), 171-85.
Also published in his *Études sur Descartes, Spinoza, Malebranche et Leibniz,* pp. 64-78. Hildesheim: Georg Olms, 1970. (Studien und Materialien zur Geschichte der Philosophie, Bd.5.)

_____."La définition de la vérite" (Descartes et Spinoza). In *Congrès des societes de philosophie de langue française, 12th, Brussels & Louvain, 1964,* pp. 43-51. La vérité: Actes. Vol. 2, Séances plénières. Louvain: Éditions Nauwelaerts, 1965. Also published in his *Études sur Descartes, Spinoza, Malebranche et Leibniz,* pp. 55-63. Hildesheim: Georg Olms, 1970. (Studien und Materialien zur Geschichte der Philosophie, Bd.5.)

_____."La preuve de 'simple vue' chez Spinoza et chez Malebranche." In *L'homme devant Dieu,* pp. 303-8. Mélanges offerts au Père Henri de Lubac. Tome II: *Du moyen âge au siècle des lumières.* Paris: Aubier-Montaigne, 1964. Also published in his *Études sur Descartes, Spinoza, Malebranche et Leibniz,* pp. 79-84. Hildesheim: George Olms, 1970. (Studien und Materialien zur Geschichte der Philosophie, Bd.5.)

Härting, Thomas. "Hegel und die spinozistische Substanz." Zur Kritik einer theologischen Präokkupation. *Philosophisches Jahrbuch,* **75** (1967-1968), 416-19.

Hall, A. Rupert, and Hall, Marie Boas. "Philosophy and Natural Philosophy. Boyle and Spinoza." In *Mélanges Alexandre Koyré, publiés à l'occasion de son 70ᵉ anniversaire,* pp. 241-56. T.II: *l'aventure de l'esprit.* Paris: Hermann, 1964. (Coll. 'Histoire de la pensée', 13.)

Hallett, H. F. "Über das vermeintlich Unmoralische von Spinozas politischer Theorie." In *Spinoza: dreihundert Jahre Ewigheit, Spinoza-Festschrift 1632-1932,* edited by Siegfried Hessing, pp. 68-72. Den Haag, 1962.

Hammacher, Klaus. "Spinozas Gedanke der Identität und die Begründung im menschlichen Verhalten." *Zeitschrift für philosophische Forschung,* **23** (1969), 24-35.

Hampshire, Stuart. "Spinoza: Excerpt." In *The Proper Study: Essays on Western Classics,* edited by Quentin Anderson and Joseph Anthony Mazzeo, pp. 427-48. New York: St. Martin's Press, 1962.

_____."Spinoza and the Idea of Freedom." *Proceedings of the*

British Academy, **46** (1960), 195-215.
Reprint. London: Oxford University Press, 1961. 21p. (Dawes Hicks Philosophical Lecture. Proceedings of the British Academy.)
Also reprinted in *Studies in the Philosophy of Thought and Action,* pp. 48-70. British Academy Lectures. Selected and introduced by P. F. Strawson. London: Oxford University Press, 1968. (Oxford paperbacks, 155.)

——."Spinoza's Theory of Human Freedom." *Monist,* **55** (1971), 554-66.

——."A Kind of Materialism." Presidential address in *Proceedings and Addresses of the American Philosophical Association, 1969-1970,* **63** (September, 1970), pp. 5-23.

Harris, Errol E. "Spinoza's Theory of Human Immortality." *Monist,* **55** (1971), 668-85.

Henle, Mary. "Psychological Concept of Freedom: Footnotes to Spinoza." *Social Research,* **27** (1960), 359-74.

Hessing, Siegfried. "Die Glückseligkeit des freien Menschen." In his *Spinoza: dreihundert Jahre Ewigkeit, Spinoza-Festschrift 1632-1932,* pp. 73-100. Den Haag, 1962.

——."Salve Spinoza!" In his *Spinoza: dreihundert Jahre Ewigkeit, Spinoza-Festschrift 1632-1932,* pp. xxxv-xlii. Den Haag, 1962.

*Hoede, Karl. "Spinoza." *Die Bruderschaft,* **5** (1963), 14-15.

Hönigswald, Richard. "Spinoza." In *Texte zur Geschichte des Spinozismus,* compiled by Norbert Altwicker, pp. 75-109. Darmstadt, 1971.
Also published in *Deutsche Vierteljahrsschrift für Literaturwissenschaft und Geisteswissenschaft,* **6** (1928), 447-85.

Hubbeling, H. G. "Spinoza's metafysica in verband met zijn methode." *Wijsgerig perspectief op maatschappij en wetenschap,* **8** (1967-68), 77-91.

Humber, James M. "Spinoza's Proof of God's Necessary Existence." *The Modern Schoolman,* **49** (1972), 221-33. (March, 1972; volume named as 1971.)

Hyman, Arthur. "Spinoza's Dogmas of Universal Faith in the Light of Their Medieval Jewish Background." In *Biblical and Other Studies,* edited by Alexander Altmann, pp. 183-95. Cambridge: Harvard University Press, 1963. (Philip W. Lown Institute of Advanced Judaic Studies. Ser., No. 1.)

———."Spinoza's Dogmas of Universal Faith in the Light of their Medieval Background." In *Congrès international de philosophie médiévale, 2d Cologne, 1961,* pp. 731-36. Die Metaphysik im Mittelalter, ihr. Ursprung und ihre Bedeutung: Vorträge des II. . . Im. Auftrage der Société internationale pour l'étude de la philosophie médiévale, hrsg. von Paul Wilpert. Berlin: W. de Gruyter, 1963. (Miscellanea mediaevalia, Bd. 2.) Expanded version of this article in *Biblical and Other Studies.* See previous entry.

Janke, Wolfgang. "Tugend und Freiheit. Spinozas kontemplative Begründung der Ethik." (Eth. V. Prop. 21-36.) In *Sein und Ethos,* hrsg. von Paulus M. Engelhardt, pp. 329-49. Untersuchungen z. Grundlegung d. Ethik. Mainz: Matthias-Grünewald, 1963. (Walberberger Studien der Albertus-Magnus-Akademie. Philosophische Reihe, 1.)

Jaspers, Karl. "Spinoza." In his *The Great Philosophers,* Vol. 2, pp. 273-387. The Original Thinkers, ed. by Hannah Arendt. New York: Harcourt, Brace and World, 1966.

Jonas, Hans. "Spinoza and the Theory of Organism." *Journal of the History of Philosophy,* **3** (1965), 43-57.

Kaplan, F. "Le salut par l'obéissance et la necessité de la révélation chez Spinoza." *Revue de métaphysique et de morale,* **78** (1973), 1-17.

Kauz, Frank. *Substanz und Welt bei Spinoza und Leibniz.* Freiburg: Alber, 1972. 232p.

Kessler, Warren. "A Note on Spinoza's Concept of Attribute." *Monist,* **55** (1971), 636-39.

Klatzkin, Jakob. "Der Missverstandene." In *Spinoza: dreihundert*

Jahre Ewigkeit, Spinoza-Festschrift 1632-1932, edited by Siegfried Hessing, pp. 101-8. Den Haag, 1962.

Klausner, Joseph. "Der jüdische charakter der Lehre Spinozas." In *Spinoza: dreihundert Jahre Ewigkeit, Spinoza-Festschrift 1632-1932*, edited by Siegfried Hessing, pp. 109-33. Den Haag, 1962.

Kline, George L. "Spinoza East and West: Six Recent Studies in Spinozist Philosophy." *Journal of Philosophy*, **58** (1961), 346-55.

Knecht, Yvonne. "Temps et modes chez Spinoza." *Dialectica*, **22** (1968), 214-37.

Kouznetsov, Boris. "Spinoza et Epstein." *Revue de synthèse*, **88** (1967), 31-52.

Kupisch, Karl. [Spinoza und Christus.] In *Der Ungekündigte Bund*, hrsg. von Dietrich Goldschmidt und Hans J. Kraus, pp. 116-17. Neue Begegnung von Juden und Christlicher Gemeinde. Stuttgart: Kreuz-Verlag, 1962.

Lacroix, Jean. "Le salut par la foi selon Spinoza." *Giornale di Metafisica*, **25** (1970), 65-73.

Lewinter, R. "Georg Groddeck, ou la psychanalyse selon Spinoza." *Les temps modernes*, **24**, No. 273 (1969), 1665-90.

Liaci, Maria Teresa. "Precedenti medievali nella metafisica di Spinoza." In *Congrès international de philosophie médiévale, 2d, Cologne, 1961*, pp. 724-30. Die Metaphysik im Mittelalter, ihr. Ursprung und ihre Bedeutung: Vortràge des II. . . Im. Auftrage der Societe internationale pour l'etude de la philosophie médiévale, hrsg. von Paul Wilpert. Berlin: W. de Gruyter, 1963. (Miscellanea mediaevalia, Bd.2.)

Liebeschütz, H. "Hermann Cohen und Spinoza." *Bulletin für die Mitglieder der Gesellschaft der Freunde des Leo Breck Institute* (Tel-Aviv), No. 12 (1960), 225-38.

Loda, Franceso. "Aspetti del positivismo giuridico di Benedetto Spinoza." *Studi parmensi*, **11** (1962), 125-216.

_____ ."Politicità e giuridicità nell'itinerario pedagagico di Spinoza." *Rivista internazionale di filosofia del diritto,* **41** (1964), 563-608.

Löwith, Karl. "Spinoza. Deus sive natura." In *Gott, Mensch und Welt in der Metaphysik von Descartes bis zu Nietzsche,* pp. 197-252. Göttingen: Vandenhoeck & Ruprecht, 1967.

Macintosh, J. J. "Spinoza's Epistemological Views." In *Reason and Reality,* edited by G. N. A. Vesey, pp. 28-48. London: Macmillan, 1972. xix, 243p. (Royal Institute of Philosophy Lectures, Vol. 5.)

MacIntyre, Alasdair. "Spinoza, Benedict (Baruch)." In *The Encyclopedia of Philosophy,* edited by Paul Edwards, Vol. 7, pp. 530-41. New York: Macmillan Co. and Free Press, 1967.

McKeon, Richard. "Spinoza on the Rainbow and on Probability." In *Wolfson, Harry Austryn. Jubilee Volume on the Occasion of His Seventy-Fifth Birthday,* pp. 533-59. 3 vols. [Vols. I-II: English section; Vol. III: Hebrew section]. Jerusalem: American Academy for Jewish Research, Saul Lieberman, 1965.

McMinn, J.B. "A Critique on Hegel's Criticism of Spinoza's God." *Kantstudien,* **51** (1959-1960), 294-314.

McNeill, John J. "The Relation Between Philosophy and Religion in Blondel's Philosophy of Action." *Proceedings of the American Catholic Philosophical Association,* **44** (1970), 220-31.

McShea, Robert. "Spinoza: Human Nature and History." *Monist,* **55** (1971), 602-16.

_____ ."Spinoza on Power." *Inquiry,* **12** (1969), 133-43.

Marcianu, Marc. "Ein Bekenntnis." In *Spinoza: dreihundert Jahre Ewigkeit, Spinoza-Festschrift 1632-1932,* edited by Siegfried Hessing, pp. 134-40. Den Haag, 1962.

Marcus, John T. "East and West: Phenomenologies of the Self and the Existential Bases of Knowledge." *International Philosophical Quarterly,* **11** (1971), 5-48.

Martelli, Maria Caterina. "Aristocrazia di pensiero in Spinoza." *Sophia,* **40** (1972), 354-56.

Martins, Mario. "Camilo Castelo Branco e Bento de Espinosa." *Revista portuguesa de filosofia,* **27** (1971), 113-24.

Maspétiol, R. "L'état et le droit selon Spinoza." In *La théologie chrètienne et le droit,* pp. 157-76. Paris: Sirey, 1960. (Archives de philosophie du droit, 5.)

Matera, Rocco. "J. G. Fichte dal rifiuto del deismo alla conquista della liberta" (aforismi sulla religione e il deismo). *Annali della Facoltà di lettere e filosofia università di Napoli,* **13** (1968), 175-206.

Matson, Wallace I. "Spinoza's Theory of Mind." *Monist,* **55** (1971), 567-78.

Mazzantini, Carlo. " 'Laetitia' e 'beatitudo' in alcuni testi, apparentemente contradittori, dell'"Ethica' di Spinoza." *Atti della Accademia delle scienze di Torino* (Classe di scienze morali, storiche, e filologiche), **95** (1960-1961), 99-121.

———."Ragioni per un rinnovato dialogo con B. Spinoza." In his *Filosofia e storia della filosofia* (1933-1959), pp. 267-99. Torino: Bottega d'Erasmo, 1960.

Meerloo, Joost A. M. "Spinoza: A Look at His Psychological Concepts." *American Journal of Psychiatry,* **121** (1965), 890-94.

Mesnard, Pierre. "Un nouveau visage de Spinoza." *Revue d'histoire et de philosophie religieuse,* **45** (1965), 375-82.

Metzger, L., ed. "Coleridge's Vindication of Spinoza: An Unpublished Note." *Journal of the History of Ideas,* **21** (1960), 279-93.

Mijnskovic, Ben. "Spinoza's Ontological Proof." *Sophia,* **12** (1973), 17-24.

Mondolfo, Rodolfo. "Il contribuo di Spinoza alla concezione storistica." In *Studi in onore di Antonio Corsano* (Università degli studi di Bari, Facoltà di lettere e filosofia). Manduria: Lacaita, 1970.

Moreau, Joseph. "La conversion spirituelle et le spinozisme." In *Hommage à Georges Bastide*, pp. 137-278. Paris: Press Universitaires de France, 1970. Also published in *Les études philosophiques*, No. 2 (1970), 179-90.

Morris, Clarence. "Sur la théorie politique de Spinoza." In *Mélanges en l'honneur de Jean Dabin*, pp. 171-78. T.I: *Théorie générale du droit*. Paris: Ed. Sirey, 1963.

Mugnier-Pollet, Lucien. "Expression et altérité. Remarques sur la portée de la politique selon Spinoza." In *Annales de la Faculté des Lettres et Sciences humaines de Nice*, 1 (1967), 73-83.

Myslicki, Ignacy. "Spinoza und das Ideal des Menschen." In *Spinoza: dreihundert Jahre Ewigkeit, Spinoza-Festschrift 1632-1932*, edited by Siegfried Hessing, pp. 141-48. Den Haag, 1962.

Nádor, Georg. "Leges et regulae. Bemerkungen zu Spinozas Gesetzesbegriff." *Studium generale*, 19 (1966), 696-98.

Naess, Arne. "Freedom, Emotion, and Self-subsistence: The Structure of a Small, Central Part of Spinoza's *Ethics*." *Inquiry*, 12 (1969), 66-104.

Natanson, Harvey B. "Spinoza's God: Some Special Aspects." *Man and World*, 3 (1970), 200-223.

Naulin, Paul. "La connaissance du bien et du mal selon Spinoza." *Les études philosophiques*, 24, No. 3 (1969), 359-70; 25, No. 1, 13-24.

*Nicolai, Heinz. "Goethe-Spinoza-Jacobi. Zu Weltbild und Naturanschauung." In *Gratulatio Festschrift für Christian Wegner zum 70 Geburtstag am 9.9.1963*, pp. 40-62. Hamburg, 1963.

Nidditch, P. H. "Spinoza." In *A Critical History of Western Philosophy*, edited by D. J. O'Connor, pp. 187-203. New York: Free Press of Glencoe; London: Collier-Macmillan, 1964. (Free Press Textbooks in Philosophy.)

Niemirower, I. "Spinozaverehrung eines Nichtspinozisten." In

Spinoza: dreihundert Jahre Ewigkeit, Spinoza-Festschrift 1632-1932, edited by Siegfried Hessing, pp. 149-50. Den Haag, 1962.

Noone, John B. "Spinoza's World-View." *Southern Journal of Philosophy*, **7** (1969), 161-69.

Odegard, Douglas. "The Body Identical with the Human Mind: A Problem in Spinoza's Philosophy." *Monist*, **55** (1971), 579-601.

Ohana, J. "Le sophisme de l'évidence *ex terminis*. A propos de l'opposition Descartes-Spinoza au sujet de la liberté." *Revue philosophique de la France et de l'étranger*, **90** (1965), 151-68.

Parkinson, G. H. R. "Language and Knowledge in Spinoza." *Inquiry*, **12** (1969), 15-40.

_____."Spinoza on the Power and Freedom of Man." *Monist*, **55** (1971), 527-53.

Petrovici, Ion. "Eine Spinozahuldigung." In *Spinoza: dreihundert Jahre Ewigkeit, Spinoza-Festschrift 1632-1932*, edited by Siegfried Hessing, pp. 151-55. Den Haag, 1962.

Pflaum, Heinz. "Rationalismus und Mystik in der Philosophie Spinozas." In *Texte zur Geschichte des Spinozismus*, compiled by Norbert Altwicker, pp. 216-31. Darmstadt, 1971.
Also published in *Deutsche Vierteljahrsschrift für Literaturwissenschaft und Geistesgeschichte*, **4** (1926), 127-43.

Pignoloni, E. "Gioberti e il pensiero moderno." *Rivista rosminiana di filosofia e di cultura*, **64**, No. 3 (1970), 155-75; No. 4 (1970), 231-47. Analyse de la critique serree du spinozisme (et notamment de son aspect panthéiste) par Gioberti.

Pines, Shlomo. "Spinoza's *Tractatus theologico-politicus*, Maimonides and Kant." In *Further Studies in Philosophy*, edited by O. Segal, pp. 3-54. Jerusalem: Magnes Press, 1968. (Scripta Hierosolymitana, 20.)

Pinto Ferreira, J. A. "Uriel da Costa." *Revista portuguesa de filosofia*, **25** (1969), 329-43.

Pupi, Angelo. "Spinoza alla soglia dell'età romantica." *Rivista di filosofia neo-scolastica*, **52** (1960), 523-57.

Radner, Daisie. "Spinoza's Theory of Ideas." *Philosophical Review*, **80** (1971), 338-59.

Raphael, D. D. "Spinoza." In *Jewish Philosophy and Philosophers*, edited by Raymond Goldwater. London: Hillel Foundation, 1962. 200p.

Razumovski, I. P. "Spinoza und der Staat." In *Texte zur Geschichte des Spinozismus*, compiled by Norbert Altwicker, pp. 377-92. Darmstadt, 1971.
Also published in *Spinoza in Soviet Philosophy*, edited by G. L. Kline, pp. 149-61. New York: Humanities Press, 1952.

Reale, Maria Adonella Diliberto. "L'errore come fatto teoretico nella filosofia di Spinoza." *Filosofia*, **18** (1967), 265-94.
Reprint. Torino: Edizioni di Filosofia. [1967?] 30p. (Studi e ricerche di storia della filosofia, 80.)

——."Rassegna Spinoziana." *Filosofia*, **21** (1970), 411-32.

——.*Sul De intellectus emendatione di Benedetto Spinoza*. Torino: Ed. di Filosofia, 1968. 8p. (Studi e ricerche di storia della filosofia. 91.)

Rennes, J. "Spinoza." *Cahiers rationalistes*, No. 222 (1964), 186-208.

Rensch, Bernhard. "Spinoza's Identity Theory and Modern Biophilosophy." *The Philosophical Forum* (Boston), **3** (1972), 193-206.

Révah, Israel-S. "Aux origines de la rupture spinozienne: Nouveaux documents sur l'incroyance dans la communauté judéo-chrétienne d'Amsterdam à l'époque de l'excommunication de Spinoza." *Revue des études juives*, **3** (123), Nos. 3-4 (1964), 359-431.

Rice, Lee C. "The Continuity of 'Mens' in Spinoza." *New Scholasticism*, **43** (1969), 75-103.

——."Spinoza on Individuation." *Monist*, **55** (1971), 640-59.

Ricuperati, G. "Libertinismo e deismo a Vienna. Spinoza, Toland e il Triregno." *Rivista storica italiana*, Napoli, **79** (1967), 628-95.

Riley, Isaac Woodbridge. "The Enlightenment: Benedict de Spinoza (1632-1677)." In his *Men and Morals: The Story of Ethics*, pp. 219-29. New York: Frederick Ungar, 1960.

Röd, Wolfgang. "Spinozas Lehre von der societas." *Filosofia*, **18** (1967), 777-806; **19** (1968), 671-98.
Reprint. Torino: Ed. di Filosofia, 1969. 62p.

_____ ."Van den Hoves 'Politische Waage' und die Modifikation der Hobbesschen Staatsphilosophie bei Spinoza." *Journal of the History of Philosophy*, **8** (1970), 29-48.

Rolland, Romain. "Der Lichtstrahl Spinozas." In *Spinoza: dreihundert Jahre Ewigkeit, Spinoza-Festschrift 1632-1932*, edited by Siegfried Hessing, pp. 156-63. Den Haag, 1962.

Rotenstreich, Nathan. "Freedom, Reflection and Finitude." *Philosophy and Phenomenological Research*, **33** (1972), 163-73.

Sass, Karl. "Spinozas Bibelkritik und Gottesbegriff." In *Spinoza: dreihundert Jahre Ewigkeit, Spinoza-Festschrift 1632-1932*, edited by Siegfried Hessing, pp. 164-70. Den Haag, 1962.

Sassen, Ferdinand. "De betekenis van Spinoza." *Wijsgerig perspectief op maatschappij en wetenschap*, **8** (1967-68), 65-67.

Saw, Ruth L. "Personal Identity in Spinoza." *Inquiry*, **12** (1969), 1-14.

_____ ."The Task of Metaphysics for Spinoza." *Monist*, **55** (1971), 660-67.

Schaub, Marianne. "Spinoza ou une philosophie politique galiléenne." In *Historie de la philosophie*, T. III, *La Philosophie du monde nouveau* (XVIe et XVIIIe siécles). Sous la direction de François Châtelet. Paris: Hachette, 1972.

Schneider, Herbert W. " 'Chevalier' Ramsay's Critique of Spinoza." *Journal of the History of Philosophy*, **3** (1965), 91-96.

Schüling, H. "Die konstruktive Psychologie Spinozas." *Philosophia naturalis*, **9** (1965), 230-45.

Schuhmann, Karl. "Le concept de réflexion dans *l'Éthique* de Spinoza." *Revue philosophique de Louvain*, **65** (1967), 449-66.

Schwarzschild, Steven S. "Do Noachites Have to Believe in Revelation? [A passage in dispute between Maimonides, Spinoza, Mendelssohn and H. Cohen.] A Contribution to a Jewish View of Natural Law." *Jewish Quarterly Review,* **52** (1961-1962), 297-308; **53** (1962-1963), 30-65.

Sciaky, I. "La ragion di Stato in Spinoza." *Accademia nazionale dei Lincei (Rome), Rendiconti della Classe di Scienze morali,* Atti. 8ᵃser., **16** (1961), 8-18.

Seligman, Paul. "Some Aspects of Spinozism." *Proceedings of the Aristotelian Society,* **61** (1960-1961), 109-28.

Semerari, Guiseppe. "L'ambiguità di Spinoza." *Giornale critico della filosofia italiana,* **43** (1964), 428-38.

——— ."La teoria spinoziana della immaginazione." In *Studi in onore di Antonio Corsano* (Università degli studi di Bari, Facoltà di lettere e filosofia). Manduria: Lacaita, 1970, pp. 747-64.

Shmueli, Efraim. "Hegel's Interpretation of Spinoza's Concept of Substance." *International Journal for Philosophy of Religion,* **1** (1970), 176-91.

——— ."Some Similarities between Spinoza and Hegel on Substance." *The Thomist,* **36** (1972), 645-57.

Siegel, Carl. "Vom grundlegenden Dualismus in Spinozas System." In *Spinoza: dreihundert Jahre Ewigkeit, Spinoza-Festschrift 1632-1932,* edited by Siegfried Hessing, pp. 171-81. Den Haag, 1962.

Sigad, R. "La logique de Spinoza" (in Hebrew). *Iyyun,* **17**, No. 4 (1966), 212-39; English summary, pp. 277-79.

Simon, Ernst. "Zu Hermann Cohens Spinoza-Auffassung." In *Wissenschaft des Judentums im deutschen Sprachbereich,* hrsg. von K. Wilhelm, Bd. II, pp. 539-50. Tübingen: Mohr, 1967.

Sokolov, V. V. "On the Evolution of Spinoza's Political and Philosophical Ideas." *Soviet Studies in Philosophy,* **2** (1963-1964), 57-62. New York.

Sokolow, Nahum. "Der Jude Spinoza." In *Spinoza: dreihundert Jahre Ewigkeit, Spinoza-Festschrift 1632-1932*, edited by Siegfried Hessing, pp. 182-92. Den Haag, 1962.

*Sol, J.-P. "Commentaire sur un thème spinoziste." Homo IV. *Annales de la Faculté des Lettres*, 1 (1965), 139-45. Toulouse.

Spinka, Matthew. "Baruch Spinoza's Deterministic Pantheism." In his *Christian Thought, from Erasmus to Berdyaev*, pp. 34-39. Englewood Cliffs, N. J.: Prentice-Hall, 1962.

Stahovski, N. "Les origines du concept d'essence humaine en philosophie moderne. Les contributions de Hobbes et de Spinoza" (En roumain). *Revista de filozofie*, 15, No. 2 (1968), 233-42. Suite de: Cercetari filozofice. Bucuresti.

Strauss, Leo. "Anleitung zum Studium von Spinozas theologisch-politischem Traktat." In *Texte zur Geschichte des Spinozismus*, complied by Norbert Altwicker, pp. 300-361. Darmstadt, 1971.
Also published in Strauss, Leo. "How to Study Spinoza's Theological-Political Treatise." In his *Persecution and the Art of Writing*, pp. 142-201. New York: Free Press, 1952.

———.Preface to *Spinoza's Critique of Religion*. In his *Liberalism, Ancient and Modern*, pp. 224-59. New York: Basic Books, 1968.

———."Zur Bibelwissenschaft Spinozas und seiner Vörlaufer." In *Wissenschaft des Judentums im deutschen Sprachbereich*, hrsg. von K. Wilhelm, Bd. I, pp. 115-37. Tübingen: Mohr, 1967.

Strauss, M. "L'universel et l'individuel dans l'ontologie de Spinoza" (in Hebrew). *Iyyun*, 11, No. 4 (1960), 188-204; English summary, pp. 237-38.

Strich, Fritz. "Goethe und Spinoza." In his *Kunst und Leben; Vorträge und Abhandlungen zur deutschen Literatur*, pp. 90-100, 242. Bern: Franke Verlag, 1960.

Sullivan, Celestine J. "Spinoza and Hume on Causation." In *Proceedings of the International Congress of Philosophy, 12th, Venice and Padua, 1958*, Vol. 12. History of modern and contemporary philosophy. Firenze: Sansoni, 1961.

Teo, Wesley K. H. "The Relation of Substance to Attributes in

Spinoza." *Kinesis,* **1** (1968), 15-21.

Ternois, R. "Saint-Evremond et Spinoza." *Revue d'histoire littéraire de la France,* **65** (1965), 1-14.

Thomas, George Finger. "Pantheism: Spinoza." In his *Religious Philosophies of the West,* pp. 170-96. New York: Scribner's, 1965.

Thomas, Henry. "Baruch Spinoza (1632-1677)." In his *Understanding the Great Philosophers,* pp. 207-17. New York: Doubleday and Co., 1962.

Van der Bend, J. G. "Het probleem subject-object in de Wijsbegeerte van Spinoza." *Tijdschrift voor filosofie,* **31** (1969), 327-62.

_____ ."Schleiermachers *Reden über die Religion* en Spinoza." *Algemeen Nederlands tijdschrift voor wijsbegeerte en psychologie,* **61** (1969), 93-106.

van der Hoeven, P. "Over Spinoza's interpretatie van de cartesianische fysica en de betekenis daarvan voor het systeem der ethica." *Tijdschrift voor filosofie,* **35** (1973), 27-86.

Vanni-Rovighi, Sofia. "L'ontologia spinoziana nel *Cogitata metaphysica.*" *Rivista di filosofia neo-scolastica,* **52** (1960), 399-412.

Van Riet, Georges. "Actualité de Spinoza." *Revue philosophique de Louvain,* **66** (1968), 36-84.

_____ ."Actualité de Spinoza." In his *Philosophie et religion,* pp. 125-73. Louvain: Nauwelaerts, 1970. (Bibliothèque philosophique de Louvain, 23.)

Vaughan, Charles Edwyn. "The Social Contract: Spinoza." In his *Studies in the History of Political Philosophy before and after Rousseau,* edited by A. S. Little, Vol. 1, pp. 62-129. 2 vols. New York: Russell and Russell, 1960. Reprint of Manchester: Manchester University Press, 1925 edition.

Verra, Valerio. "F. H. Jacobi: lo spinozismo di Lessing." *Filosofia,* **13** (1962), 249-75.

_____ ."F. H. Jacobi: Spinozismo e ateismo." *Filosofia,* **13** (1962),

453-84.

Vita, Luis Washington. [Prólogo] "Ao Tractatus de intellectus emendatione de Espinosa." In his *Monólogos y diálogos*, pp. 91-102. São Paulo: Conselho Estadual de Cultura, Comissao de Literatura, 1964.

Von Königsberg nach Haifa. *Börsenblatt für den Deutschen Buchhandel*, **18** (1962), 1124.

Vygotskij, L. S. "Spinoza et sa conception de l'émotion, à la lumière de la psychoneurologie moderne" (en russe). *Voprosy filosofii, S. S. S. R.*, No. 6 (1970), 119-30.

―――."Spinoza's Theory of the Emotions in Light of Contemporary Psycho-neurology." *Soviet Studies in Philosophy*, **10** (1972), 362-82.

Wahl, Jean. "L'idée de vie dans la philosophie de Spinoza." *Revue de métaphysique et de morale*, **69** (1964), 95-100.

Watt, A. J. "The Causality of God in Spinoza's Philosophy." *Canadian Journal of Philosophy*, **2** (1972), 171-89.
Reply: E. Harris, ibid., 191-97.
Reply by Watt to Harris, **2** (1973), 541-44.

―――."Spinoza's Use of Religious Language." *New Scholasticism*, **46** (1972), 286-307.

Wetlesen, Jon. "A Reconstruction of Basic Concepts in Spinoza's Social Psychology." *Inquiry*, **12** (1969), 105-32.

Wienpahl, Paul. "Ch'an Buddhism, Western Thought, and the Concept of Substance." *Inquiry*, **14** (1971), 84-101. Related via the philosophy of Spinoza.

―――."Spinoza and Mental Health." *Inquiry*, **15** (1972), 64-94.

―――."Spinoza and Wang Yang-Ming." *Religious Studies*, **5,** No. 1 (1969), 19-27.

Williamson, R. K. "On Curley's Interpretation of Spinoza." *Australasian Journal of Philosophy*, **51** (1973), 157-61.
Reply by Curley, ibid., 162-64.

Wolfson, Harry Austryn. "The Philonic God of Revelation and His Latter-Day Deniers." *Harvard Theological Review,* **53** (1960), 101-24.

_____."Spinoza and the Religion of the Past." In his *Religious Philosophy: A Group of Essays,* pp. 246-69. Cambridge: Harvard University Press, 1961.
Also published in *Texte zur Geschichte des Spinozismus,* compiled by Norbert Altwicker, pp. 278-99. Darmstadt, 1971. (Article in German.)

_____."Spinoza und die Religion der Vergangenheit." In *Texte zur Geschichte des Spinozismus,* compiled by Norbert Altwicker, pp. 278-99. Darmstadt, 1971.
Also published in Wolfson, H. A. *Religious Philosophy,* pp. 246-69. Cambridge: Harvard University Press, 1961. (Article in English.)

Wren, Thomas E. "Is Hope a Necessary Evil—Some Misgivings about Spinoza's Metaphysical Psychology." *Journal of Thought,* **7** (1972), 67-76.

Wunderli, Jürg. "Über Spinozas Beitrag zur Leib-Seele-Problematik unter Berücksichtigung der Relation zur modernen Psychosomatik." *Gesnerus,* **25** (1968), 101-11.

Würzner, M. H. "Bernard Nieuhoff en zijn beoordeling van het spinozisme." *Tijdschrift voor filosofie,* **24** (1962), 53-80.

Yovel, Y. "La critique de la religion et l'interprétation de l'Écriture chez Spinoza et chez Kant" (in Hebrew). *Iyyun,* **17**, No. 4 (1966), 240-69; English summary, pp. 274-77.

Zac, Sylvain. "Les avatars de l'interpretation de l'Écriture chez Spinoza." *Revue d'histoire et de philosophie religieuse,* **42** (1962), 17-37.

_____."État et nature chez Spinoza." *Revue de métaphysique et de morale,* **69** (1964), 14-40.

_____."Rapports de la religion et de la politique chez Spinoza et J.-J. Rousseau." *Revue d'histoire et de philosophie religieuse,* **50**, No. 1 (1970), 1-22.

———."Les thèmes spinozistes dans la philosophie de Bergson." In *Les études bergsoniennes*, Tome VIII, pp. 121-58. Henri Bergson. Paris: Presses Universitaires de France, 1968.

Zweig, Arnold. "Der Schriftsteller Spinoza." In *Spinoza: dreihundert Jahre Ewigkeit, Spinoza-Festschrift 1632-1932*, edited by Siegfried Hessing, pp. 193-95. Den Haag, 1962.

Index of Authors

(By William Sacksteder)

References to entries in the notes include both the page number and the footnote number or numbers, thus, 137n5, or 137nn5,7.

Anscombe, G. E. M., 85
Aristotle, 198-99, 219, 253
Arnauld, A., 167
Armstrong, D. M., 83n9
Augustine, St., 217
Ayers, M. R., 8, 27-30, 33n26

Bacon, F., 222
Bagehot, W., 188n43
Beck, L. W., 3, 6n1
Bennett, J., 82n2, 161, 185n13
Boyle, R., 200-1
Braithwaite, R. B., 216, 232n5
Bruno, G., 227
Burke, E., 102-5

Caird, J., 250, 262n12
Clifford, W. K., 159-63, 162, 180-82, 184n2, 189n54
Cohen, M. R., 137n1
Cumming, R. D., 113n1
Curley, E. M., 3, 210, 214n46, 234n40

Descartes, R., 139-45, 148, 153, 155-56nn1-7, 157n19, 163-69, 184n5, 185nn16-23, 186nn25&27-30, 187nn36-42, 193, 194n11, 196, 198, 200-1, 231, 234nn40&42

Frankena, W. K., 99nn11&21

Geach, P., 177, 188n47
Gewirth, A., 170, 187n36

Hampshire, S., 151-52, 156nn17 &18, 179, 189n51, 198, 213n12, 250, 262n12
Hare, R. M., 88, 92, 99n6, 100n22
Haserot, F. F., 191, 194nn1&2
Hegel, G. W. F., 222, 230-31
Hicks, G. D., 200, 213n19
Hobbes, T., 53, 102-4, 114n4, 117, 137-38n5
Höffding, H., 33n15
Hubbeling, H. G., 157nn19&20
Hume, D., 62, 92-93, 160, 166-67, 184n4, 196, 209, 261n2

Huxley, T. H., 160, 167, 179-80, 184n3, 189n52

James, W., 160-1, 167, 182-83, 184n10, 188n43, 189n55
Joachim, H. H., 83n7, 149-51, 156nn12-14, 198-99, 207-8, 213n9, 214n41, 236, 249-51, 253, 262nn6,7,9&12-14
John of The Cross, St., 219

Leibniz, G. W., 71, 73, 189n54, 208-9, 238-39
Locke, J., 137-38n5, 166, 178, 185n24, 180, 188n49, 189n53
Lucian, 163

Machiavelli, N., 110
Madison, J., et al., *Federalist Papers*, 137-38n5
Matheron, A., 201, 213nn27-29
Matson, W. I., 43
Melden, A. I., 25-26, 33n25
Moore, G. E., 92-93, 95, 99n14

Nakhnikian, G., 161, 185n11
Newman, Cardinal J. H., 159, 166-67, 186n26
Newton, I., 199

Ockham, William of, 215, 232n1
Oko, A. S., 3, 6n2

Oldenburg, H., 205-6

Parkinson, G. H. R., 38, 62-65, 71-72
Pepper, S., 90-99, 99nn8&9
Plato, 248, 253, 259
Plotinus, 219, 233n13
Pollock, F., 254, 262n16
Price, H. H., 160, 184n7, 188n49

Rivaud, A., 207, 214n40
Roth, L., 83n12, 250, 262n12
Russell, B., 83n8, 218-19, 233n11

Saw, R., 196, 198, 208-9, 212n2, 211, 214nn42-44, 250, 262n12
Schliermacher, F., 3, 6n4
Schopenhauer, A., 58
Sextus Empiricus, 156n7, 163, 176
Sidgwick, H., 92-93, 97, 99n11
Strachey, L., 159, 184n1
Strawson, P. F., 96-97, 99n17
Stout, A. K., 156n8

Taylor, A. E., 4, 6n5, 250, 262n12

Waissman, F., 221, 233n19
Wetlesen, J., 3, 6n3
Whitehead, A. N., 229
Williams, B., 188n44
Wolfson, H. A., 192, 194nn3&4, 198, 213nn10&17

Index of Topics

(By William Sacksteder)

In view of the interlocking and ubiquitous nature of Spinoza's vocabulary, we do not cite each mention or use of his terms, but only extended discussions which are definitive, problematic, or comparative.

Action, 14, 32n9, 208-9; human, 24-25, 35; and passion, 111-13, 120; voluntary, 182-83

Activity, 42-43, 237-39

Affection, 58-59

Affirmation and negation, 168-70

Agnosticism, 159, 179-80

American Constitution, 137n5

Antinaturalism, ethical, 92-93

Appetite, 16, 18, 35-36, 58

Argument, philosophical, 222-24

Aristocracy, 125, 128-33

Association of ideas, 42

Atheism, 227, 245

Atoms, 200-1

Attributes, 51, 55-56, 59, 61-68, 191-94, 199; extension, 250; infinite, 193; objectivist and subjectivist interpretations, 191-94

Axioms, 216, 222-24; ethical, 87-94

Beatitudo, see Blessedness

Belief, 175-84, 189n51; degrees of, 166; (Descartes), 164; ethics of, 159-63, 166, 178-84; and forced option, 160; on insufficient evidence, 160; usefulness of, 242; as voluntary action, 162-63, 177-84, 189n51

Body, composite, 201-12; external, 70, 76-79; human, 11-12, 15-16, 61-82, 202-4, 206-12, 240, 246-61; and mind, see Mind and body; parts of, 69-78; resurrection of, 246-48; simple, 197-202; simple and composite, 11-12, 240

Brain, 69, 78, 80-81

Cabalistic writing, 226

Cause, 8-31, 41-42; double, 18-19, 25-26; efficient and final, 9-10, 17-19; external and internal, 19-21; of self, 19

Cells of the body, 71-73

Christian doctrine, 257

Circumstances, extrinsic and intrinsic, 27-30

Cogito (Descartes), 141-42, 145, 148

Common notions, 237-39
Conatus, 10-19, 21-26, 31n2, 32nn7, 11&13, 35-36, 74, 94-96, 240, 256-57
Condition, necessary, 29
Consciousness, 43-44, 51-52, 54, 58, 60, 254-61
Consequences, 160-62, 181-82
Consolations of religion, 238
Conversation, ordinary human, 242-43

Death, 246-47
Definition, 216, 222-24; descriptive (Pepper), 90; ethical, 87-94; persuasive (Stevenson), 90; rational, 90-93
Democracy, 117-18, 125, 129-37
Desire, 16, 32n12
Detachment, 45-47
Determinism, 41, 44-46, 88, 245
Deus seu Natura, 217, 230
Dominion, 118, 125-27, 134-37; best form, 135-36
Doubt, 139-55, 159, 167, 175-76; genuine and verbal, 139, 143-49; reason for, 144-49, 155; verbal, 143, 152-55
Duration, 249-51, 261; of mind, 248

Egoism, ethical, 94, 96-97
Emendatio, 236
Emotion, 74-75, 120, 239; active, 44
Emotivism, ethical, 92, 94
Endeavor, *see Conatus*
Energy, 198-99, 202, 205, 208
Entity, of reason and real, 13
Error (Descartes), 164-65
Essence, 12-15, 32n7, 58, 192-93
Eternity, 249-53, 255-61
Ethics, and politics, 120-23; of virtue and of duty, 85-87, 94-98
Evidence, insufficient, 182

Exhortation, *see* Philosophy, utility of
Explanation, causal, 8, 35, 46

Facies totius universi, see Nature, whole of
Feeling, nontactual, 72-75, 79-80, 83nn16&17
Finite and infinite, 251-53
Form, 12
Formaliter and *objectiva,* 255
Freedom, 7-8, 20-31, 35-42, 109-13, 121, 124, 165-66, 208, 239, 245-46; of mind, 44-46
Free will, 54

God, 216, 222, 234nn30&35, 245-46; as deceiving (Descartes), 140-42, 145-49; expression of, 32n11; infinite essence of, 251-52, 256-61; intellect of, 253; knowledge of, 236-38, 259-61; love of, 219, 239, 246, 256-61; power of, 256-57
God's knowledge, 72-73
Good, 95; and evil, 120
Government, *see* Dominion

History, 101-13
Holy Spirit, 257
Human nature, 101-13, 119-21

Idea, 156n10, 168-78, 192, 210, 254-61, 262n15; adequate and inadequate, 236, 256-58; of body, 49, 57-65, 253-61; of body in God, 63-64; clear and distinct, 139-52, 155, 165-66, 177, 216, 222-24; complex, 82n6; (Descartes), 164-67, 187nn40-41; doubtful, 139-40, 150-53; general, 254; *ideae,* 255-61; and *ideatum,* 247, 254-55, 258, 261; and image, 52, 57, 173; and image (Descartes), 163,

187nn39-40; object of, 69-77; as proposition, 210; simple and complex, 172-74; true, 149-52

Idealism, 53, 65

Ideatum, 253

Identity, 203-4; as matter of degree, 210-11; personal, 209-12

Imagination, 172-76, 249-53, 256-61, 262n6

Immortality, 46, 246-61

Importance, human, 239-43

Impression, 76-77

Individual, 11-12, 35-37, 102, 119-20, 202-8, 240-42, 253, 262n15

Individualism, 105-9, 112-13

Individuality, 259-60

Individuation, 195-212

In itself, 11, 31n3

Intellect, 53; infinite, 246, 254-61; and will, 167-69, 174

Interaction, with external things, 11, 35

Intuitionism, ethical, 88-89, 93

Judgment, 174; (Descartes), 144, 164-67, 186nn25&30; (Geach), 176-77; suspension of, 167, 174-76

Justice, 125

Knowledge, 217-19, 236-43; adequate, 260; first kind, *see* Imagination; intuitive, *see* Knowledge, third kind; second kind, 219, 249-52; third kind, 218, 246, 249-53, 256-61; three kinds, 249-50, 256-61

Law, natural (physical), 27-28

Laws of nature, 119, 123-27

Liberty, *see* Freedom

Life after death, 259-60

Logic, dialectical, 222-23

Love of God, 121

Man, 49-51, 54-55, 58; natural, 112, 235-43

Martyr, 17

Materialism, 53-54, 65-68; central state, 66-68

Mathematics, 235-37, 239

Meaning, 56

Medicine, 36-38

Metaphysics, 4-5, 67, 215-17; descriptive (Strawson), 212; usefulness, 235-43

Method, 112, 219-24; deductive, *see* Reasoning, mathematical; mathematical, 233n23, 242-43

Mind, 49-60, 67; active and passive, 256-61; activities (operations), 50-51; collection of mental states (Hume), 62-65; as complex idea, 62-65; human, 15-16, 35-38, 61-82, 246-61; as idea of the body, 246-48, 251-53, 256-61; power of, 46-47; temporal continuity, 81; thinking part, 253

Mind and body, 4, 43-45, 49-60, 120, 246-61; double-aspect theory, 56, 60; dualism, 62, 195, 200; identity of, 61-82; interactionism, 54, 60, 62, 76; neutral monism, 66; occasionalism, 62; parallelism, 55-56, 60, 204, 210; pre-established harmony, 62; reductionism (epiphenomenalism), 53-54, 60, 62, 65-66

Modes, 10-14, 55, 61-68, 225-27, 232-33n8; finite, 234n30, 247-61; finite and infinite, 251-52; infinite, 232-33n8

Monad (Leibniz), 239

Monarchy, 125, 128-30, 132-33

Morality, and ethics, 94-98; new, 85-87, 94-98; related to Metaphysical, Epistemological and Psychological principles

(MEP), 87-98, 118-20

Motion, 51-53; and rest, 9-12, 31nn4&6, 81, 197-200, 205, 208

Multitude (political), 125-37

Mysticism, 218-19

Natura naturans and *Natura naturata* (Bruno), 227

Naturalism, 228-31

Natural right, 123-27

Nature, 119, 225-31; whole of, 204-5, 250-53, 256-61, 262n1

Necessary Being, 21

Necessity, logical, 10, 12; logical and causal, 20-21

Nervous system, 66, 77

Nominalism, 254

Order, 201; causal, 75; of Nature (common), 45-46; rational, 45-46

Pain, 74-75

Pantheism, 231

Participation (Plato), 259

Particular things, 107, *also see* Modes

Passion, 16, 33n23; liberation from, *see* Freedom of mind

Peace and security, 127, 135-36

Perception, 52-53, 70-78, 192; unconscious, 72, 74

Perfection, human, 217-19, 237, 256-61

Personality, 260

Person, identity of, 195-212

Perspective, 79

Petites Perceptions (Leibniz), 71

Philosophy of mind, *see all entries under* Mind

Philosophy, utility of, 36-42, 44-47; as way of life, 232n9

Physics, 9-11, 19, 197-204

Pineal gland (Descartes), 54

Pleasure, 74-75

Political theory, 101-13, 118-23

Possibility, 27-30

Power, 8, 10-31, 32n7, 124; absolute political, 132-33; active, 74-75; human, 38-40; of the mind, 44-47; of thing and person, 27-31

Predicates, corporeal and mental, 62-68

Principles (Cartesian), 87-88

Privacy, 51

Proposition (Descartes), 170-73

Punishment, 260

Qualities, occult, 15

Realism (Platonic), 89, 254

Reality, degrees of, 252-53

Reason, 22, 24, 110-13; dictates of, 36-38, 121-22, 125-27, 135

Reasoning, mathematical, 219-24; philosophical, 215-17

Reflection, 31-42, 45-47, 183

Religion and politics, 122-23

Rights, common, 124-25; fundamental, 127-31

Saying (Geach), 177

Scientia intuitiva, see Knowledge, third kind

Self-awareness, *see* Self-consciousness

Self-consciousness, 255-61

Self-transcendence, 255-61

Sensation, 72

Skepticism, 139-55, 157n19, 176

Sleep-walking, 54, 70-71

Society, 101-10; (Burke), 102-5; (Hobbes), 102-3

Solipsism, 57

Soul, 49-50, 55, 246-49, *also see* Idea of body; disembodied, 246-48; unity with substance, 101-2

Space, 258-61
State, 125-27; of Nature, 134
Subject, 62-69
Substance, 50, 55-56, 65, 221-27, 234n30, 251-53
Suicide, 17
Supreme Authorities, 125-26
System, 235-36, 243

Terms (Descartes), 172-73
Theism, 227
Theology, 215-17, 232n2
Thought, 59, 241; (Descartes), 163-64

Time, 249-50, 258-61
Toleration, 163
Truth, as coherence, 224

Understanding, 51
Unity of soul and substance, 101-2

Virtue, 22-23, 95-96, 257-61
Vision, 220-24
Volition, .26; (Descartes), 164-65

Whole and part, 251-53
Will, 16, 58; (Descartes), 164-66
Words, 176-77